Upper Darby Public Libraries

<u>Sellers/Main</u>
610-789-4440
76 S. State RD

<u>Municipal Branch</u>
610-734-7649
501 Bywood Ave.

<u>Primos Branch</u>
610-622-8091
409 Ashland Ave.

Online renewals:

www.udlibraries.org
my account

Connecting you to literacy,
entertainment, and life-long learning.

THOMAS HARDY: HIS LIFE AND FRIENDS

Thomas Hardy: His Life and Friends

F. B. PINION

St. Martin's Press　　New York

B

Hardy

© F. B. Pinion 1992

First published in the United States of America in 1992

Printed in Hong Kong

ISBN 0–312–07570–7

Library of Congress Cataloging-in-Publication Data
Pinion, F. B.
      Thomas Hardy: his life and friends / F. B. Pinion.
            p.   cm.
      Includes bibliographical references (p.   ) and indexes.
      ISBN 0–312–07570–7
      1. Hardy, Thomas, 1840–1928—Biography.   2. Hardy, Thomas,
   1840–1928—Friends and associates.   3. Authors, English—19th
   century—Biography.   4. Authors, English—20th century—Biography.
   I. Title.
      PR4753.P56   1992
823'.8—dc20
[B]   91–38715
                                                                    CIP

Contents

205989

Contents

List of Illustrations

Preface and Acknowledgements

An important part of the basic research for this book was made more than twenty years ago, when, after examining all the Hardy correspondence and material that was accessible in England and Scotland, I was aided by a grant from the University of Sheffield, and made copious notes on all that was relevant at Colby College, Yale University, the New York Public Library, Princeton, the Library of Congress, and the University of Texas, Austin. My aim then was to write a biography of Hardy at some appropriate time during my retirement.

As soon as this began I undertook the editorship of *The Thomas Hardy Society Review*. For some years much time was devoted to completing the editorial work on Hardy's letters to Mrs Henniker which had been initiated by Miss Evelyn Hardy, to the editing of several of his novels and all his short stories, and to a commentary on his poems, followed by essays on his art and thought. Before the end of this period, when it was learned that Robert Gittings intended to complete his biography of Hardy, and Michael Millgate was commissioned to write another, my project was abandoned.

Not until recently, when I wrote essays on fictional autobiography in Hardy and on his friendship with Mrs Henniker, did the case for a biography with emphasis on Hardy's friendships occur to me. This was strengthened after turning again to biographies of Leslie Stephen and Edmund Gosse, and reading later ones on both, particularly in the attempt to evaluate why Hardy felt certain in retrospect that Stephen was 'the man whose philosophy was to influence his own for many years, indeed, more than that of any other contemporary'. Stephen's essays and autobiographical work led me to conclude that the powerful impact of his personality and unremitting intellectual integrity, quite at odds with his ultra-cautious conservative policy as editor of *The Cornhill*, gave Hardy the courage he needed to challenge conventional beliefs much more seriously and dynamically than he had ever dared to do in his early works after the failure of *The Poor Man and the Lady*.

Although continuity has been broken for brief intervals to indicate how much Hardy's principal friendships meant to him, the design of this biography has been to keep as closely in contact with him and his work as possible. In consequence many of his friendships have been restricted to incidental roles, although some, notably that with T. E. Lawrence, have assumed unanticipated importance. Hardy and Emma became acquainted with many members of the upper classes, and to see his life in due proportion greater attention to them needs to be paid than will be found in his *Life*, as a result of excisions advocated by Sir James Barrie and others. More importantly but for the same reason, efforts have been made to ensure that nothing significant has been omitted from the account of Hardy's early formative years. How easily proportion may be lost can be seen from the seven volumes of his collected letters. With the exception of half-a-dozen to his sister Mary at the outset, only one non-business letter has survived up to the time of his marriage at the age of 34 (all the letters of their courtship being destroyed many years later by Emma), and less than half of one volume represents the first half of his life.

The overriding aim has been to avoid fictional assertion, and to present facts as far as they are ascertainable, even at the cost of including frequent modifiers such as 'perhaps', 'probably', 'possibly' and 'it seems'. Much is known about Emma and Hardy, but the whole truth about them, Emma especially, can never be known. The contemporary evidence which is adduced must be subjective to varying degrees, and Hardy's poems, which have great biographical value, are sometimes misleadingly mood-dictated. Where such uncertainty is inherent, informed readers will prefer their own surmises and judge for themselves.

Most of my sources will be found in the Bibliography and References. I have drawn from many unpublished letters, particularly those of Emma and Florence Hardy, but my recent indebtedness is mainly to the editing and indexing of Hardy's letters by R. L. Purdy and Michael Millgate, and to the latter's widely researched Hardy biography, which draws from previously inaccessible sources. In addition I owe much to the scholarly detail of the former's bibliographical study of Hardy; I am indebted also to Robert Gitting's researches.

It has been a great advantage to become familiar with some of Hardy's homes, and I am especially grateful to Mr Linee for his expert conclusions on structural alterations at the birthplace, even more on its extension; to Mr and Mrs Jesty for their kind invitations to Max Gate, and their readiness to answer questions on many occasions; also to Mrs Marjorie Bruce of Sturminster Newton and her son, for allowing me to see the interior of Riverside Villa, and for explaining the changes that have taken place, particularly in the surroundings, since the Hardys lived there.

For their assistance on several occasions over a long period, I am most grateful to Mrs Gertrude Bugler, R. N. R. Peers of the Dorset County Museum, Michael Millgate, and John Antell (on Puddletown, the Sparks family, and other relatives). For help at various points in the preparation of this book, I wish to thank the Revd Professor C. F. D. Moule, the Revd George Moule, the Wiltshire Record Office at Trowbridge, T. R. W. Moore of the National Trust, Professor Dale Kramer (for copies of Florence Hardy's letters to H. G. Wells), Roger Evans and Paul Reynolds (for respectively supplying and reading sections of the 1912 Bradshaw), Major J. T. Morton of Edinburgh Castle (for information on the Scots Greys), James Goldie (on Lanhydrock House), Malcolm Wynn (on Launceston), Mr and Mrs L. C. Hayward (on Forde Abbey), Angela Allott and Edwin Fleming (on Elizabeth of Austria).

For copying photographs from which to make a selection of illustrations I am grateful to Mr Roy Wilson of Sheffield University Library. Mrs Bugler has most generously provided two (7b, 8b), the copyright of which is hers. Copyright acknowledgements are made to Cassell & Co. (3a), Cambridge University Press (4a), and to Hollis & Carter (8a). The Chancellor photograph of Mrs Henniker (4b) belongs to the author, and the copyright is his. Other illustrations are taken from *The Early Life of Thomas Hardy*, *The Latter Years of Thomas Hardy*, Handley Moule's *Memories of a Vicarage* (1b), F. W. Maitland's *The Life and Letters of Leslie Stephen* (3b), Lady St Helier's *Memories of Fifty Years* (6a), H. J. Moule's *Dorchester Antiquities* (6b), Edward Clodd's *Memories* (6c), Viola Meynell (ed.), *Friends of a Lifetime* (7a), and William Bellows' *Edmund Gosse: Some Memories* (8c).

I am especially grateful to my wife for her patience in giving critical attention to the text at successive stages in its composition, and for her assistance in proof-reading. Finally I wish to thank Margaret Cannon and Valery Rose for their valuable co-operation on behalf of the publishers.

1

Ancestry and Birth

Tradition, family and local, is often invoked to support the unverifiable, and it pleased Thomas Hardy in his later years to think that the descent of the Dorset Hardys from Clement le Hardy, Baily of Jersey, whose son John probably landed at Wareham, then a port, and settled at Weymouth in the fifteenth century, was confirmed by oral tradition. Descendants included Admiral Hardy, captain of Nelson's flagship in the battle of Trafalgar, the Elizabethan Thomas Hardye of Frampton who endowed Dorchester Grammar School, and others who had been landed proprietors of standing in the Weymouth area and in or near the Frome valley from Woolcombe, Toller Whelme, Frome St Quintin, and Up Sydling down to Dorchester and on to Wareham. Hardy was reminded of all this on 30 September 1888, when he walked from the railway station at Evershot past the site of Woolcombe House to Bubb Down, whence he gazed over Blackmoor, 'the Vale of the Little Dairies', with his own family decline and the genealogical 'down, down, down' theme of *Tess of the d'Urbervilles* very much in mind.

In his letter of 18 April 1881 to Kegan Paul he writes with less assurance of his Jersey ancestry, but thinks it is confirmed by strong physical resemblances between his family and the other Dorset Hardys. Of his direct progenitors he says that 'from time immemorial' they have all been 'master-masons, with a set of journeymen masons under them'; he has 'certain knowledge of four generations'. There must be a considerable element of exaggeration in this status claim. An entry in one of his notebooks reveals his discovery in 1908 that John Hardy, a widower, lived alone in Back Street, Puddletown, early in the eighteenth century. The marriage in 1777 of Hardy's great-grandfather, another John Hardy of Puddletown, to Jane Knight of Woodsford in the Frome valley explains why Hardy took pleasure in tracing many of his Knight relatives of the past in the register he borrowed from the vicar of Stinsford in 1921. John Hardy had two sons, the elder of whom, Thomas, married Mary Head in December 1799, and it was for this couple that he built, two and a half miles away, the

1

thatched cottage on the western fringe of Puddletown Heath where the author, the third successive Thomas Hardy, was born. The land on which it stood had been leased on a lifehold basis from the lord of the manor, one of the Pitt family of Kingston Maurward House, not far from Stinsford church.

Baptized on 30 October 1772, Mary Head was five if not six years older than her husband. No evidence has been discovered to explain why and when she came to Puddletown. After being orphaned, she had spent several years at Fawley in Berkshire (her birthplace, the Marygreen of *Jude the Obscure*), and then a period at Reading. Her memories of Fawley were 'so poignant that she never cared to return to the place after she had left it as a young girl', Hardy wrote. Whether she was the person to whom his cousin Theresa darkly alluded when she told Hermann Lea that the fate of Tess had been suffered by 'a relative of theirs' remains conjectural, although an illegitimate child was born to a Mary Head in 1796 and christened Georgiana Reed at Reading in 1803.

The house to which Thomas Hardy moved from Puddletown with his wife and baby daughter Martha, when it was ready for habitation in 1801, was the only one in that outlying part of Stinsford parish. Behind it, on the northern side of the Frome valley, stretched the wild uneven heath, an extensive upland bright with gorse in spring, and with heather in summer, the sombre wintry tones of its foreground eventually supplying the Egdon Heath overture to *The Return of the Native*. At first heath-cropping ponies were their only friends, Mary Hardy told her grandson Thomas. Adders and lizards were common in summer, and bats flew alarmingly about the bedrooms in the evenings. A path flanked by tall bracken in the summer led westward down to a dip and continued for a short distance up to the road which gave Bockhampton, further south, access to the Puddletown or London road from Dorchester, which ran almost immediately to the north. Several tracks had been worn by vehicles over the neighbouring heathland. So isolated was the Hardy cottage that until about 1805 it was used as a dumping-station by smugglers from the south coast. At one time up to 80 tubs, each holding about four gallons of spirits, were hidden in the closet under the staircase. They were brought at night, either in carts or by men on horseback, and deposited outside; a whiplash across a windowpane summoned Thomas at two or three o'clock in the morning to stow away the contraband, which was collected after dusk the next evening, when 'groups of dark long-bearded fellows' arrived to transport the tubs, slung in twos or fours over the shoulders, for local deliveries. Sometimes they were hidden not far off, in one of those almost cone-shaped pits, a feature of the heath, from which chalk had been quarried over the centuries for building purposes. When, some time after 1805, a second house, which became the tranter's, was built about a hundred yards below, discretion gained the upper hand, allaying Mary Hardy's fears. Her husband could not afford to lose his reputation; he had already undertaken the revival of church music at Stinsford, and his building business depended largely on the goodwill of both the steward and the owner of the Kingston Maurward estate. In course of time a lane leading up to the Hardy cottage developed; along this more houses were built, and the hamlet was called Higher Bockhampton.

In May 1803, when it had become alarmingly obvious that Napoleon was using the period of peace, initiated by the Treaty of Amiens in 1802, for the strategic furtherance of vast imperial aims, war was renewed between England and France. Hundreds of large, flat-bottomed boats were built to transport the French invasion army across the Channel from Boulogne, and defensive preparations were hurriedly made along the south coast of England from Kent to Dorset and beyond. The troops, which included Hanoverians in George III's German Legion, were reinforced by the militia, enlisted soldiers who trained full-time periodically and were subject to military service whenever required. In addition there were volunteers throughout the country, who regularly gave up much of their spare time to train for local emergencies. Hardy's grandfather became one in 1803, when his wife was expecting her second child. Mary Hardy told her grandson how anxious she was at the time, and he remembered it in 'The Alarm', where he heightened the tension by making it coincide with the false alarm that was given on 1 May 1804, when the alert was spread by flaring beacons on heights which included Rainbarrow, the highest of three adjacent tumuli half a mile from her home.

From 1805, the year which saw Napoleon's invasion plans shattered at Trafalgar, to 1815, the year of his final defeat at Waterloo, Mary Hardy bore five more children. It can be assumed that family sustenance depended much on home production. There were outbuildings for storage, and probably for a horse, a cow, and a pig or two; a space may have been enclosed for the protection of poultry against nocturnal marauders such as foxes and poachers.

Thomas Hardy's building business must have prospered, for by 1829 he was the leaseholder of almost two acres along the upper part of Higher Bockhampton lane, at least one half of it being meadowland below the front garden and orchard. The younger children learnt from their elder brothers and sisters, but their general education owed much to their parents. At a relatively early age the girls assisted their mother in and around the house; the boys were trained by their father to help in building, gardening, and other outside activities. What formal education, if any, they received elsewhere remains unknown. It must have been a very busy and crowded household. Thomas's musical prowess and his wife's keen interest in the dances of the period (clear evidence of which is found in her grandson's poem 'One We Knew') suggest that the Christmas-party tradition of *Under the Greenwood Tree* had, for one of its main sources, entertainment before a log-fire on the wide, open hearth below the central chimney-breast at the south end of the living-room that almost monopolized the ground floor of the original Hardy home at Higher Bockhampton.

However limited their educational opportunities, the Church undoubtedly contributed significantly to the cultural as well as the spiritual life of the Hardys. Where and when their interest in church music originated is uncertain; the writer Thomas Hardy thought there could be an early trace of this inheritance in his discovery that a namesake of his, living in Dorchester in 1724, subscribed to 'Thirty Select Anthems in Score' by Dr Croft, organist of the Chapel Royal and Westminster Abbey. His grandfather as a young man had been one of the instrumentalists for the choir which sang in the large, impressive Jacobean gallery of Puddletown church, though it is not clear from Hardy's references whether he played a violoncello or bass-viol. At Stinsford he found the singing, led by an old oboist, woefully inadequate. Such was his zeal that, with the vicar's ready agreement, he soon discovered string-players ready to perform with him twice each Sunday with a select group of adult and junior choristers in the small western gallery which overlooked the nave and chancel of St Michael's. Twenty years later Mr Murray, a new vicar, arrived, and chose to live by the church, at Stinsford House, property of the Earl of Ilchester, to whom he was related. He was an ardent musician and violinist; young James and Thomas Hardy would practise with him two or three times a week, and their father joined them occasionally. The playing of the latter at Stinsford and elsewhere was to make him famous locally, Hardy recalling him in William Dewy and, with some humorous exaggeration, in the account of Mr Yeobright's playing at 'Kingsbere'. The Stinsford string-choir probably reached its peak when the instrumentalists, never more than four, were all Hardy players from Higher Bockhampton, where they could practise frequently. Their leader had been joined by James and Thomas (Hardy's father), and by their brother-in-law James Dart, a neighbour. In 1892 Hardy wrote down his mother's recollections of 'the three Hardys as they used to appear passing over the brow of the hill to Stinsford church on a Sunday morning':

> They were always hurrying, being rather late, their fiddles and violoncello in green-baize bags under their left arms. They wore top hats, stick-up shirt collars, dark blue coats with great collars and gilt buttons, deep cuffs and black silk 'stocks' or neckerchiefs. Had curly hair, and carried their heads to one side as they walked. My grandfather wore drab cloth breeches and buckled shoes, but his sons wore trousers and Wellington boots.

Most of Hardy's knowledge of the choir and its carol-singing on parish rounds (which continued after its disbandment in 1843) came from his father.

In church the instrumentalists were not content with playing well-known tunes such as the 'Old Hundredth', 'New Sabbath', 'Devizes', 'Wilton', 'Lydia', and 'Cambridge New' to the Tate and Brady metrical psalms which were regularly sung as hymns; they attempted (with what real success the author Thomas Hardy often wondered), 'to their own great satisfaction and the hearty approval of the musical vicar', elaborate settings for canticles and anthems. The morning and evening hymns of Bishop Ken, played respectively to Barthélémon and Tallis throughout the year, were a much more reliable stimulus to confident congregational participation in the singing. All this music was familiar later to Hardy in his boyhood. When Arthur Shirley succeeded 'the musical vicar' Mr Murray in December 1837 changes in the church service were inevitable. Of distinguished lineage, and unwaveringly influenced at Oxford by the Tractarian movement, he worked devotedly at Stinsford, instituting daily matins and more than trebling the number of communion services. Gradually a situation developed which contributed to the genesis of *Under the Greenwood Tree*. Shirley chose to live in the Georgian vicarage near the church, and the choir lost favour in his sight. Perhaps it declined after the death of Hardy's grandfather; perhaps the players needed the enthusiastic leadership and responsiveness they had enjoyed with Mr Murray; the new High Church fervour, which was quite exceptional in the region, may not have won their full approval. Whatever the reason, they had to retire when a barrel-organ was installed; it was turned by James Hardy and later played by his daughter Theresa.

With the passing of time the renewal of the Hardy lifehold tenure had become more urgent; family eviction for the advantage of a lord of the manor, on the death of a lifeholder, continued to be a source of distress and instability in Dorset, as Hardy's novels illustrate. Usually such a tenure was held on three lives. In 1835 his grandfather's tenure was renewed by William Morton Pitt of Kingston Maurward, the lifehold extending to the younger sons, James, born in 1805, and Thomas, born in 1811. Still unmarried, unlike his brothers and sisters, the latter lived at home with his parents. James was employed by his father, and lived just below, on the other side of the lane. The eldest brother John, who had married one of the Dart family, worked independently, and lived at Fordington on the south-east outskirts of Dorchester. Of the three sisters, Martha the eldest and Jane the youngest (named after a sister who had died in infancy) were married to brothers, and lived at Upwey near Weymouth.

Hardy's grandfather died suddenly in 1837; he was playing in church one Sunday and brought in for burial the next. As the remaining instrumentalists were among the chief mourners, 'there could be no such quiring over his grave as he had performed over the graves of so many', Hardy writes; his poem 'The Choirmaster's Burial' indicates that the churchyard rites may have been curtailed because of adverse wintry weather. Perhaps it was his mother who led him to believe that his grandfather's devotion to church music at Stinsford, 'to no worldly profit', had taken up time which might often have been spent for the benefit of his family. The presentation of *The Book of Common Prayer* to his son Thomas on 2 July 1823, when Mrs Morton Pitt laid the foundation stone of the bridge over the Frome at Lower Bockhampton, suggests that his father constructed it and was a reputable builder. His most historic feat in the romantic eyes of his youthful grandson Thomas was the building of a vault under the chancel of Stinsford church for the interment of Lady Susan, daughter of Stephen Fox, first Earl of Ilchester, and her husband William O'Brien, the 'handsome Irish comedian' whom she had met during private theatricals at Holland House, and whom she married secretly in 1764, creating scandal in aristocratic circles that she had 'stooped' to an actor; 'even a footman were preferable', Horace Walpole wrote. After her father's death, her brother gave Stinsford House to the O'Briens, and helped to secure William's appointment as Receiver General for Dorset. He died in 1815, but Lady Susan lived on until 1827, and Hardy's father when he was a chorister in the church gallery used to see her in a red cloak, as she walked old and lonely in her neighbouring garden. She had known his father well, and he (Hardy writes) 'carefully heeded her tearful instructions to build the vault for her husband and later herself, "just large enough for us two"'.

After his death James and Thomas maintained the building business in their mother's name, and, effectively, under her management. She was far from domineering, but she kept the accounts, and advised when critical decisions had to be made. Her evident partiality for Thomas, her youngest son, who remained at home and did much to help her after his marriage just before Christmas 1839, was pronounced in the will she made in January 1841, long before her death, bequeathing him all her property in consideration of his 'kindness and affection' towards her. He was an attractive young man, whose courtesy and amiable disposition won many friends. Some years later James decided that he and his family could do better if he set up his own business; the 1851 census describes him as a mason (bricklayer) 'employing two labourers'.

Tradition of the kind which is often started locally with mischievous intent, or based long afterwards on some writer's irresponsible surmise, holds that Thomas was a womanizer. How and when Jemima Hand and he became acquainted can be imagined. She had been in the service of the Revd Charles Redlynch Fox-Strangways, of the Ilchester family, when he was rector of Maiden Newton, seven miles north-west of Dorchester, and had accompanied his family on their seasonal visits to London and to Weymouth, a fashionable seaside resort ever since it had been honoured by the frequent summer visits of George III and Queen Charlotte. After the rector's death, towards the end of 1836, she was appointed cook at Stinsford House while it was still the home of the vicar Mr Murray. She must have been attracted by Thomas Hardy very early, probably during one of those evening services

which took place in the afternoon during winter, when she turned
to watch as he played the violin against the dimming light of the
west gallery window. How her son, the writer, imagined the scene
is commemorated in his poem 'A Church Romance'. He knew that
'to her more travelled glance' his young handsome father had
appeared 'rather amusingly old-fashioned' in his blue swallow-
tailed coat with gilt embossed buttons, 'red and black flowered
waistcoat, Wellington boots, and French-blue trousers'. Jemima
had excellent practical skills, and her ambition was to be a cook in a
London 'club-house', taking her brothers and sisters with her, a
plan brought to nought by her marriage but put to good use by her
son in *The Hand of Ethelberta*.

Hardy loved to trace her descent from the Swetman and Childs
families of north-west Dorset. His short story 'The Duke's Reappearance' is based on an improbable tradition that the rebellious
Duke of Monmouth, after his defeat at Sedgemoor in 1685, took
refuge in the home of one of the Swetmans at Townsend, part of
the village of Melbury Osmond near the northern or back entrance
to the park of Melbury House, which subsequently became the
home of the Ilchesters; the story fictionalizes the more credible
family tradition that his two daughters narrowly escaped being
raped by some of the victorious soldiers. Jemima's mother Elizabeth suffered degradation as a result of her marriage at Melbury
Osmond to George Hand, a country labourer who proved to be a
violent and unfaithful drunkard. When he refused to have his
children baptized at church, she baptized them at home; when he
died of consumption in 1822, she had him buried by the grave of
his mistress, as Hardy records dramatically in 'Her Late Husband'.
Disinherited by her father, the unusually well-read Betty Hand
was compelled to seek poor relief during her widowhood. Maria,
the eldest of her seven children, was brought up by her paternal
grandparents at Puddletown, a village which, with its crafts and
small industries, in addition to farming and woodland employment, was uncommonly self-supporting. Here in 1828 she married
James Sparks, a cabinet-maker. It can be assumed that, eight to
eleven years later, her sister Jemima Hand visited her from Stinsford, calling in her courtship days on Thomas Hardy and his
widowed mother at Higher Bockhampton. Finding herself pregnant late in 1839, she returned to Melbury Osmond. Accompanied
by James Sparks, Thomas Hardy walked there on the eve of his
wedding (which took place on Sunday, 22 December), having to

guess their later route as it grew darker and one of them climbed a handpost only to find, on lighting a match, that the direction letters had been eroded (an event recalled near the opening of Hardy's story 'Interlopers at the Knap'). A Sparks family tradition, stressing the role of James in ensuring that Hardy duly wedded his sister-in-law, is based on a descendant's account of the above events, which, bordering at times on malice, suggests that the source of its high-spirited humour was tainted to some extent by familial envy of the fame which Jemima's son acquired.

By Christmas Day the married couple were probably at home, where celebrations which began in the cider country were no doubt continued. In his youth Thomas Hardy was expert in the performance of jigs, hornpipes, and other folk-dances, with (his son writes) 'all the old movements of leg-crossing and hop'); and it is hard to believe that time was not found at Higher Bockhampton for festivities, both congratulatory and seasonal, lasting into the New Year. Thomas was 28, his wife 26; and it can be assumed that his mother, now 67, welcomed the advent of a cheerful, intelligent young woman who was practical, industrious, and well qualified to assume domestic responsibilities. Mary Hardy may privately have regarded the circumstances of her favourite son's marriage as unfortunate, but she had good cause to be sympathetic. Premarital pregnancies were too common to be considered a disgrace in the community at large; she remembered her own, almost exactly 40 years earlier.

The author Thomas Hardy was born at about eight o'clock on the morning of Tuesday, 2 June 1840, a few months after the marriage of Queen Victoria and Prince Albert. The labour had been distressingly long, and the delivery critically difficult, for he was a frail baby with a large head. Until the monthly nurse, who lived near, observed him move, and exclaimed to the surgeon, 'Stop a minute: he's alive enough, sure!' it was thought he was dead. There were times of depression in his life when he wished he had not been 'rescued' in this way. He soon made good progress, and was taken to Stinsford church for his christening on 5 July. The Hardy bias prevailed over any inclination to call him Christopher after some of Jemima's ancestors, including members of the Childs families. It was a name which appealed to Hardy later, and he gave it to a character after his own heart, a musician in *The Hand of Ethelberta*.

Nothing further is known of his infancy 'save the curious fact that on his mother's returning from out-of-doors one hot afternoon, to him asleep in his cradle, she found a large snake curled up on his breast, comfortably asleep like himself. It had crept into the house from the heath hard by, where there were many.'

The Main Hardy Genealogy

John Hardy (1755–1821) m. 1777 Jane Knight (1757–1825);
　　　　4 children: Thomas (below), Mary (died in infancy), Mary (also died in infancy), John

Thomas Hardy (1778–1837) m. 1799 Mary Head (1772–1857);
　　　　7 children: Martha, John, James, Mary, Jane (died in infancy), Thomas (below), Jane

Thomas Hardy (1811–92) m. 1839 Jemima Hand (1813–1904);
　　　　4 children: Thomas (below), Mary (1841–1915), Henry (1851–1928), Katharine (1856–1940)

THOMAS HARDY (1840–1928) m. (1) 1874 Emma Lavinia Gifford (1840–1912); (2) 1914 Florence Emily Dugdale (1879–1937)

2

School and Manor

The impression given by Hardy that his father was easy-going and not very businesslike probably arose less from his equable temperament than from those anxieties which made his mother continually wonder whether their assets would be adequate for her children's needs. With her wider experience and intelligent observation, she realized the importance of giving them the most suitable education possible. There were times when building activities slowed down; payment for work on the Kingston Maurward estate was often delayed or overlooked, and it was difficult or unwise to remonstrate with employers who could place large contracts elsewhere. Like his brother James, Thomas could not afford to slacken; there was much to be done, apart from building. Livestock had to be tended. Business in Dorchester and further afield necessitated a pony and light 'springcart'; in his early years he probably undertook the haulage of all his building material; later, as work expanded, this was done for him by the tranter. The provision for cooking over the open hearth, and for warmth in winter, required regular attention. Loads of peat and logs had to be fetched and stacked. This supply of fuel could be augmented by dead branches which had been brought down and lay at hand in Thorncombe Wood, ready for removal when time could be found for an evening or weekend foray. For 'quick ignition' (as Hardy wrote in *The Dynasts*) heather and furze were cut on the heath, then bundled, and kept in dry storage near the house. Thomas probably continued much in the way to which he had been accustomed in his father's time. He may have undertaken new ventures; he kept bees, and loved cider-making. Jemima and his mother did what they could in the gardens, but the harder tasks of digging, vegetable-production, fruit-picking and pruning in the orchard, hedging, and general maintenance depended on her husband's labour and enterprise.

One of the major tasks that confronted him, with James as his chief assistant, was the expansion of his home, to provide greater privacy and more adequate accommodation for both his mother

11

and his own family. When the work was completed is not known, but it would be irrational to assume that it was delayed for years, until Mary Hardy was less capable of looking after herself. Most of the building could have taken place in the spring and summer of 1840, if not earlier. Bricks of the kind used for the original cottage were obtained, probably from a demolition in the neighbourhood, and two adjacent cottages were formed, the new one for Hardy's grandmother at the southern or Thorncombe Wood end, with a continuation of the thatched roof at a slightly lower level, a separate entrance, and a winding staircase constructed to give a sense of security to one in her declining years. (The lean-to outhouse which was erected about this time on the south side of the extension was replaced by the present one most probably near the end of the last century.) Hardy's father may have earned the gratitude his mother expressed in her will by all the additional indoor work he did for her convenience and comfort as winter approached. Partitioning upstairs in the old home at this stage and later perhaps, as the Hardy children grew up, could have been carried out at any convenient time and without much difficulty. A passage withdrawn from Hardy's first version of his *Life*, to the effect that the house built by his great-grandfather John 'was meant to be enlarged but never was' suggests the oversight of a writer who, when the major structural extension took place, was either unborn or far too young to have any conscious or abiding recollection of it.

Jemima's second child Mary was born on 23 December 1841. A few years later Mary Hand, one of her two younger sisters, came to nurse her after a serious miscarriage, to manage the household, and especially to care for the elder child, whose frailty was again a source of perturbation. She stayed for a long period, and Thomas Hardy, who owed so much to her in his very early years, always remembered her with affection. Elizabeth Downton, the monthly nurse who was present at his birth, and gave his mother the preference in 'clashing cases', told Jemima the story of a woman who consulted her because she had been troubled for years by the ghost of a wife whose widower was courting her. Betty's reply, 'Oh, that were no ghost. Now if she'd only been dead a month or two . . . there might have been something in your story. But Lord, much can she care about him after years and years in better company!', must have inspired Hardy, after hearing the story in 1897, to write 'Friends Beyond' and 'Jubilate', in both of which poems he thinks of dead worthies in Stinsford or 'Mellstock' churchyard, rejoicing to be free from 'old terrestrial stress'. The former includes Lady Susan as well as his grandfather ('William Dewy').

The third of Hardy's 'In Tenebris' poems recalls how, on a wild winter night, the smallest and feeblest of his company, weak from his 'baptism of pain', he drowsed by the chimney-nook corner, waking fitfully but with never a wish to resume his activities in the world around him. The epigraph from the Vulgate expresses his regret that his life had been prolonged. The two adjoined recollections are, nevertheless, more hopeful, though they are of times when he might easily have passed away before learning that 'the world was a welter of futile doing'. They form a striking visual contrast. The first tells how in the broken sunshine that heralded spring he cleared a crocus border of snow, happy in the thought that he 'quickened the year' by turning over and tidying the soil to make it look as if summer had come. He must have remembered the second in creating the dark nocturnal heath storm that was fatal to Eustacia Vye, when Thomasin Yeobright lifts her baby as high as her head to save it from the drenching fronds of the tall bracken. His mother and he were benighted in the middle of Puddletown Heath (part of 'Egdon') on the 'loneliest of eves', but, as she held him up ('upheld' him) to protect him from the long straggling heather which blackened beneath him, he had no fear, 'deeming her matchless in might and with measureless scope endued'. They had a remarkable affinity, and, as he told Edward Clodd when she died at the age of 90, she always regarded him as 'her rather delicate "boy"'.

The enthusiasm of Hardy's father for music and dancing had not diminished. Jemima was rather relieved when his instrumental services were no longer required at church, but carol-singing round the parish on Christmas Eve continued, as in his father's time (and in *Under the Greenwood Tree*), players and singers being rewarded at the end with plentiful refreshments at the Hardys', where celebrations ended promptly in traditional style when Christmas Day began at midnight. Thomas and his brother James enjoyed playing at New Year parties and wedding festivities.

Hardy remembered his father in the late 1840s: 'about five feet nine in height, of good figure, with dark Vandyke-brown hair, and a beard which he wore cut back all in the custom of his date; with teeth that were white and regular to nearly the last days of his life, and blue eyes that never faded grey; a quick step, and a habit of bearing his head a little to one side as he walked'. Jemima was rather short, and her Roman nose and large countenance would have better befitted a taller woman, Hardy thought. She had chestnut hair, grey eyes, and 'a trim and upright figure', which she carried so buoyantly in walking that strangers, about to overtake her, even when she was nearly 70, thought she was young, he added.

She was a great reader all her life; by following stories with her, he was able to read at the age of three. He loved to hear her sing, and as late as 1919 was delighted to receive a copy of Thomas Haynes Bayly's poems because it included popular songs which she sang when he was a child. One of her regrets was that she could not play the old piano on which her children practised. The tunes Hardy's father played on his violin – jigs, hornpipes, reels, waltzes, and country-dances – were soon familiar to him. He was excited to see him dance, and eager to imitate. Such ecstasy was roused in him as he performed to his father's music that he could hardly hide his tears. He was just as keen to play; when he was four his father gave him a small accordion, and he was 'of quite tender years' when he learned to tune a violin.

It is not surprising that a frail and precocious boy, nursed with tender care, fondly protected during his infancy, and encouraged to develop enjoyable activities, formed attachments to his home and parents, particularly his mother, which were far too strong for time to erode. As a young writer he was happiest in his native place. During his marriage years, especially after coming to live in Dorchester, it drew him like a magnet. Success and fame did not weaken his allegiance; it was strengthened during his later years. Such heartfelt loyalty to his family characterized a man whose usual self raised him above pretentiousness.

One bitterly cold day he was in the garden with his father, who, noticing a half-frozen fieldfare, idly tossed a stone at it. By chance it struck the bird, which fell dead. Tommy picked it up, and found it 'light as a feather, all skin and bone, practically starved'. He could never forget how it felt in his hand. So at an early age, sensitively alive to joy and pain, he began to glimpse the Darwinian cruelty of natural law. He was an oddly imaginative boy. One day, while crossing 'the eweleaze' (his father's possibly, below the garden), he went down on his hands and knees, pretending to eat grass in order to see what the sheep would do. When he looked up they were gathered closely round him, gazing in astonishment, as well they might. Such was his happiness in those early years he had no wish to grow up. The realization of this occurred to him in circumstances he could remember for the rest of his life more distinctly than any other of his childhood experiences. He lay on his back in the sun, with his straw hat over his face, thinking how useless he was; as the sun's rays shone through the interstices of the straw, he thought of other boys' ambitions; 'he did not want at all to be a man, or to possess things, but to remain as he was, in the same spot, and to know no more people than he already knew (about half a dozen)'. When he told his mother his views, thinking she would be sympathetic, she was shocked and hurt; he was sorry she remembered what he told her. The recollection was transferred to the youthful hero of *Jude the Obscure* with modifications in accordance with one feature of its theme. Late in life, again with change of setting, he returned to it in the poem 'Childhood among the Ferns'.

Outings to Dorchester with one or both of his parents were undoubtedly a source of excitement. In April 1925, when conversing with Colonel T. E. Lawrence, he recalled entering a public-house with his father and seeing a number of redcoats. His memory tricked by the long interval of time, he imagined the soldiers were members of the Scots Greys regiment, stationed in Dorchester at a later period. He was only six, he said, telling how he was overcome by the fumes of the strong ale they were drinking. More often he was taken to Stinsford church, where the services created a dramatic early impression on him. On wet Sunday mornings, when he was kept at home, he would stand on a chair, a white tablecloth round him serving as a surplice, and read from Morning Prayer, his cousin (James's son Augustus) playing the clerk with loud 'Amens' while their grandmother sat by, representing the congregation. He would then deliver a sermon composed largely of phrases dear to the Stinsford vicar. Another of his habits was to recite fervently 'And now another day is gone' from Dr Watts's hymns, when the setting sun intensified the Venetian red of the back wall by the staircase on which he sat in the living-room. The repeated observation that Tommy would have to be a parson, since he had no bent for practical pursuits, cost his mother many misgivings.

During the agitation for the repeal of the Corn Laws, which continued to protect wealthy farmers and landowners, making flour and bread very costly for the poorer classes, the young Hardy must have overheard more than one argument on the subject. The little actor's passions were stimulated, and he made his protest by taking the small wooden sword which his father had made for him, dipping it in the blood of a pig which had just been killed, and brandishing it as he paraded round the garden crying out 'Free trade or blood!' The free trade which followed repeal in 1846 made little difference to the cost of bread for a number of reasons, not least the American Civil War, and it was not until about 1870, when railways opened up the central wheat belt in the USA, that prices fell as a result of importing large quantities of corn. Farmers had taken advantage of poor-law relief and kept wages low; in Dorset they were often no more than seven shillings a week. Unemployment was common; outbreaks of violence and arson, such as occurred soon after the end of the Napoleonic war, led to hangings; poaching, often to transportation. Many workers left country areas to seek higher wages in towns and industrial centres, or to emigrate. Reminders of emigration occur in Hardy's fiction, most distressingly in 'Interlopers at the Knap', a story which emphasizes the shocking contrast between rural poverty and the affluence of farming landowners. The Corn Law question is an important social factor in *The Mayor of Casterbridge*.

The Hardys often met relatives at Puddletown, sometimes walking there with their children across the heath. They were most closely in touch with some of Mrs Hardy's, who increased in number during Hardy's boyhood. Her mother Betsy lived there for a brief period before her death in 1847; in November of the same year his aunt Mary, who had helped to nurse him, was married from Higher Bockhampton to the Puddletown shoemaker and cobbler John Antell. Two (possibly all three) of her brothers came to live there as bricklayers; the name Henery, as Henry Hand's was usually pronounced and sometimes spelt, is preserved in *Far from the Madding Crowd*, which has Puddletown as its main setting. Jemima often walked with her son on the heath; in one poem he recalls walking with her along the Roman road, the old Icening Way which ran from Norfolk to the south-west of England via Sarum (old Salisbury) and Dorchester, and could at that time be traced in its straight course past Rushy Pond, not far south from their home. Once they diverted themselves by crossing the heath disguised in cabbage-nets, to find what the effect would be when they called on one of Jemima's sisters, Maria Sparks or Mary Antell. Hardy's mother did not lose her sense of humour.

The Kingston Maurward estate was sold to Francis Pitney Brouncker Martin, an amateur meteorologist, in 1844, and by the next year he and his wife, Julia Augusta, were in residence. The house, between Stinsford church and Lower Bockhampton on the northern side of the Frome valley, stood above a lake and well-designed gardens, below which a path from the church accompanied one of the waterways of the divided river as far as the bridge at Lower Bockhampton. The tradition that one of the Pitts faced the mansion with stone in 1794 at great expense, after George III had expressed reservations about its being built in brick, was transferred by Hardy to 'Enckworth Court' in *The Hand of Ethelberta*. The main entrance of the house overlooked Kingston Park, which stretched down to a road running east in general, first uphill along the Icening Way route, then turning for Bockhampton Cross and on below the western extremity of 'Egdon Heath' and on to Tincleton, then across more heath to Wareham. A path not far from the Stinsford end of this road crossed the remainder of the park (which extended north to the Dorchester–Puddletown road) and led to Higher Bockhampton. It was often used by the Hardys on their way to and from Stinsford church and Dorchester. To reach the former they passed the lodge by the entrance to the avenue leading up to Kingston Maurward House, and took the next turning left past the Hardings' farm. To the east of Kingston Maurward House stood the old manor, once the home of the Grey family, dating back to Elizabethan times. Near it were the main farm buildings, including a long, large barn. Beyond were the walled fruit and vegetable gardens, below which the farm road had access to Lower Bockhampton.

Francis Martin decided not to let his farm; eventually he found he was running it at a loss. Hardy's father did construction work and renovations for him, sometimes driving there with Tommy. They met Mrs Martin, who persuaded Mr Hardy to leave him with her whenever time permitted. Childless herself, she found him a delightful companion and most interesting conversationalist. He was like a son to her; she would take him in her lap and fondle him until he was quite a big boy. He loved her in return, painted watercolours of animals and sang to please her, one of his songs being 'I've journeyed over many lands, I've sailed on every sea'. It was she who taught him the rudiments of writing. She walked round the house and gardens with him, revealing a style of life beyond his experience or dreams. Years later he remembered 'the thrilling "frou-frou" of her four grey silk flounces' as they brushed against the font when she entered church on Sundays, even more when she bent over to greet him and caused him to throb with 'tender feeling' before she reached her seat. He sat with other members of his family. The mural monument in the aisle on his left, to some of the Greys who were related to the Pitts, often held his gaze. Among its striking sculptured features was a gruesome skull which both horrified and fascinated him. It haunted his memory and, as the poetry of his early and later years continually shows, may be said never to have been far from his vision of life, whatever his moods.

So delicate was Hardy during his early boyhood that he received no regular education until the new Church of England school was opened at Lower Bockhampton in the late summer of 1848, on the side road leading to the old manor farm at Kingston Maurward. Small as it was, it had been splendidly built in stone at the Martins' expense, with a house attached for the head teacher. The Martins continued to defray the greater part of the expenses. From the first they were given unstinted administrative support by Arthur Shirley, the vicar, who remained actively interested in the welfare of the school for many years. Hardy was the first pupil to enter the schoolroom, and he waited there in lonely apprehension until the other pupils were ushered in by the schoolmaster and his wife, his assistant teacher, two by two from the premises they had temporarily occupied. Hardy soon discovered that his writing had to conform to copybook style. He was more proficient in geography and arithmetic, delighting particularly in solving the rule-of-three problems in Francis Walkingame's primer. Usually the children played on the greensward across the road. Hardy and Fanny Hurden, another delicate child from Higher Bockhampton, were two of those who, whenever the weather was inclement, were allowed to stay in the schoolroom during the lunch-hour; in winter they sat by the stove. One day he pushed past her, causing her to collide against it and burn her hands badly. He could never forgive himself for his thoughtlessness, as he told Walter de la Mare when they visited her grave at Stinsford in 1921; she had died young sixty years earlier, and he remembered her in 'Voices from Things Growing in a Churchyard'.

The railway link connecting Dorchester with London was completed in 1847. Towards the end of 1849 – the year in which Albert, the Prince Consort, made his memorable visit to Dorchester while

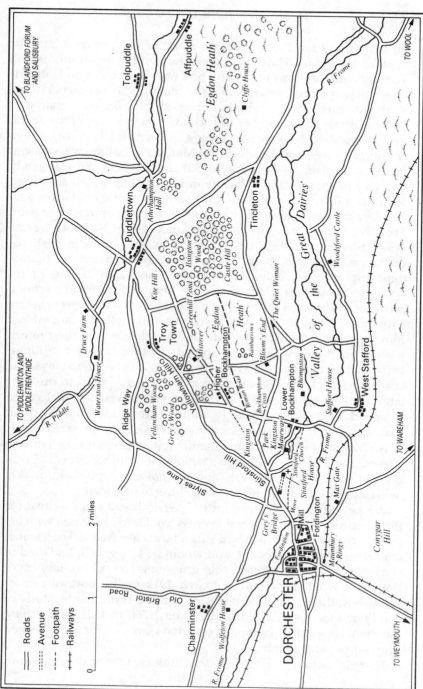

Bockhampton and the Surrounding Area

on his way to lay the foundation stone of the Portland harbour breakwater – Mrs Hardy travelled to London by train, taking Tommy with her 'for protection'. She was on her way to Hatfield, which they reached by coach, to act as nurse and housekeeper to her youngest sister Martha, who had married John Brereton Sharpe in 1841, and was expecting her fifth child. After serving in the army, her husband had taken up farming in Hertfordshire, his native county, and was now bailiff on the Marquis of Salisbury's estate at Hatfield. Stylish, well educated, but improvident, he was ready and racy in speech, with a facility in story-telling which combined with his military past to make him seem romantic to Hardy, who had him in mind when he drew the more unscrupulous Sergeant Troy; his handsome aunt was the prototype for Bathsheba Everdene. Sharpe's restless temperament made him relinquish his managerial post and, after finding it impossible to secure a permanent appointment, leave England for Canada in 1851 with his growing family. At Hatfield Hardy attended a private school, rather of the Squeers kind, he later thought, for a few weeks before Christmas; his ability in geography and arithmetic did not endear him to bigger boys, who bullied him 'mercilessly'. On their return journey in the New Year, he and his mother stayed one night, before catching a train at Waterloo station, at the Cross Keys, the coaching-inn at Clerkenwell where, he was delighted to discover later, Shelley, his favourite poet ('our most marvellous lyrist') used to spend weekends with Mary Godwin. It pleased him to think that, for economical reasons, both parties slept in the same room. This short stay left him a few memorable impressions of London streets, the Pantheon ('then a fashionable pantechnicon'), Cumberland Gate into Hyde Park, and the noise of Smithfield market 'with its mud, curses, and cries of ill-treated animals'.

The period of 'the hungry forties', when bread was too dear for the labouring classes, was not over. When Hardy returned with his mother from Hatfield he heard that a boy who used to keep watch over sheep near their home, and whom he knew well, had died of starvation. He remembered this gruesome fact all his life, mentioning it when he wrote in March 1912 to the portrait-painter William Rothenstein, who had sent him the Hammonds' study of conditions for the village labourer from 1760 to 1832, and calling attention especially to chapters on what Hardy in his reply termed 'the last peasant revolt'.

There is nothing in Hardy's *Life* to indicate that he did not return to his school at Lower Bockhampton, nor is it likely that his mother would keep him at home for months unnecessarily, however much she may have disapproved of the schoolmaster, whose drunken habits had become the talk of the neighbourhood. The relevant evidence is slight, but it suggests that he did return. His mother's intention had been to send him there until he was 'sturdy enough to go further'. After describing his London impressions, Hardy writes that 'by another year he was judged to be strong enough to walk further than to the village school, and after some postponements he was sent to a Dorchester day-school' where the master was 'an exceptionally able man, and a good teacher of Latin'. He did not attend his new school until the end of September 1850. It was Nonconformist, and at first he could not understand why no time was spent on the repetition and testing of the Church Catechism, to which he had been boringly accustomed at his previous school, only on the Ten Commandments, which were revised once a week. Whichever route he took there, it constituted a walk of little under three miles. Often, particularly at first, he must have arrived home tired out, and the practice of 'early to bed and early to rise' was an inevitable consequence during the school week.

Julia Augusta Martin was proud of her school, and took an active interest in it. When she discovered that her favourite pupil had been removed, to be sent to a Nonconformist school, she was hurt. In consequence relations between the Martins and the Hardys soon cooled. About this time (whether for the same reason is not clear from Hardy's version of events) his father lost his building work on their estate. His business may not have suffered seriously; he had an engaging personality, and a good reputation, and soon obtained contracts further afield. He would have moved had he not held his 'rambling dwelling, field, and sandpits attached' for life.

Hardy's next meeting with Mrs Martin took place in most memorable circumstances. He had not visited her for a long time, and welcomed the opportunity of seeing her which suddenly occurred when a local farmer's daughter called in the afternoon to take him to the harvest-supper which was to be held in the barn at Kingston Maurward. She must have been well-known to the Hardys, for, finding his mother away from home, she left word, probably with his grandmother, where they were going. Perhaps, as his mother had done, she thought Tommy would serve as a protection, in addition to being a useful dancing-partner when eligible young men were not to be had. When they arrived the 'supper' was over, and tea was being taken. Non-commissioned officers, invited by Francis Martin from the Scots Greys at Dorchester barracks, joined the company, but the entertainment to which Hardy's escort looked forward did not begin until the Martins and their house-party arrived, to lead off the opening dances. The red uniforms of the soldiers lent a distinctive colouring to the scene.

Astonished to see him there, his idol Mrs Martin came over to him as soon as propriety allowed, exclaiming (reproachfully, he thought), 'O Tommy, how is this? I thought you had deserted me!' He assured her he had not, and never would desert her. Finding him eager to dance, she introduced him to a niece of about his age who was staying with her. If Hardy enjoyed the dancing, his ecstasy was short-lived, for the Martins and their house-party soon left. Afraid to make his way home alone, he waited until he was famished and tired out, not having eaten or drunk since his one o'clock meal. Not until three in the morning did his 'strapping young woman' companion choose to depart. The singing of old traditional ballads – soon to pass out of fashion and recollection, as railways brought the latest songs from London – by young women from the village, as they leaned against each other on a bench by a corner wall, had helped to hold his attention. Years later, in his poem 'The Harvest-Supper', he recalled one of the ballads sung that night, with its story of false Sir John, the parrot, and the cage of glittering gold; he had met it under varying titles, one being 'May Colvine'. He conjectured that the festive event took place about 1850; if, as there is every reason to believe, officers of the Scots Greys were present, it was almost certainly in 1852. What his parents felt as they waited more and more anxiously for his return can be imagined; all we are told is that a 'reproof' from both of them ended 'the day's adventure'. It was the only harvest-supper and dance he ever saw 'save one that he dropped into by chance years later'. Francis Martin the meteorologist, whose farming had been 'much to his pecuniary loss', sold his estate, and left with his wife for London, in 1853. Years were to pass before Hardy met her again.

3

Further Education

By this time Hardy's grandmother had seen many changes at Higher Bockhampton. The path leading down towards Cuckoo Lane had become a narrow road along which houses had been built and attractive gardens developed. A tranter named Keats (or Keates) had lived in a house below her field, and she remembered how, sitting at home in the stillness of the night, she could hear him beating out the tune with his feet as he danced at a party in his house a hundred or more yards off. After his death (by 1835) his business, which included small-scale farming since he held land on both sides of the lane amounting to more than four acres, was conducted by his two sons, William, who lived almost opposite the Hardys and next door to James, and his younger brother Charles, who remained at home with his mother. Hardy remembered her in *Under the Greenwood Tree*, where Mrs Dewy, as the choir assembles before carol-singing round the parish, tells Susan to 'run down to Grammer Kaytes's' to see if she can borrow some larger candles; and again in *A Pair of Blue Eyes*, where the reference to 'poor deaf Grammer Bates' (originally Cates) by the pig-killer Robert Lickpan suggests that Hardy had seen or heard pig-killing at the tranter's as well as at home. In 'The House of Hospitalities' he recalls Christmas parties which he and his parents had attended there. The communal well was sunk just outside its entrance gateway.

In Hardy's youth the lane with its 'few scattered dwellings' was known as Cherry Alley from its avenue of flowering trees. Previously it had been dubbed 'Veterans' Valley', because men from the forces, including two army officers, had successively retired there. It was a peaceful spot, with an attractive entourage, and a good carrier-service to and from the market town of Dorchester. Two of the inhabitants who must have had a special interest for the boy Hardy were a militiaman, husband of the nurse who attended his birth, and a retired naval officer, Thomas Drane, who took part in the battle of Trafalgar before he was made a lieutenant, and lived opposite the communal well. Masts rose above the trees in his garden; and his house and outbuildings, which stood back

23

from the lane, sported weather-cocks. He undoubtedly furnished hints for the old sea-captain, Eustacia's father, and the white mast outside his home on Mistover Knap; the original name 'Drew' reinforces this surmise. The veterans set standards which were emulated by their neighbours, the general effect being one of quaint and colourful fastidiousness among wilder and more natural surroundings. Features which caught the eye included green shutters, brass-knockered doors, neatly trimmed hedges, well-kept gardens and orchards, some with box-edged gravel paths, and some with green door entrances, their posts crowned spherically in white. Trees flanked the holdings on either hand, much more densely and deeply to the south, where Thorncombe Wood overshadowed the small pastoral slopes which included Mrs Hardy's field, with its stabling, sandpits, and other utilities. In the upper part of the 'valley', where it was most picturesque, all the dwellings except the Hardys' at the very top were on the opposite of the lane. With the passing of time lifeholds 'fell into hand', and some of the old houses were replaced by more common labourers' cottages and buildings. The dilapidation and change which Hardy saw years later are described at the opening of 'Enter a Dragoon', where, some years before its demolition, a doomed thatched cottage, imagined opposite the common well, has been divided into two tenements for labouring-class families.

Approximately half a century before he wrote this story Hardy had discovered his grandfather's periodical copies of C. H. Gifford's *History of the Wars of the French Revolution*. Its torn pages and fascinatingly 'melodramatic prints of serried ranks, crossed bayonets, huge knapsacks, and dead bodies' sowed the seeds which eventually produced *The Trumpet-Major* and, much later, his major work *The Dynasts*. He may, so specific is the detail, have attempted like the boy Clym Yeobright, a picture of the battle of Waterloo, 'with tiger-lily pollen and black-currant juice, in the absence of water-colours'. He referred many questions to his grandmother, from whom he heard the story of the false invasion alarm and the flaming beacon on Rainbarrow, where he was shown the remains of the brick chimney around which the sheltering hut of turf walls had been occupied by the keepers John Whiting and James P— (as he remembered in *The Dynasts*). Her memory was still remarkable. One hot thundery summer's day during his childhood he heard her say, 'It was like this in the French Revolution.' She told his mother that she was ironing her best muslin gown when the news

came that the Queen of France, Marie Antoinette, had been guillo-
tined; she could still see the pattern of her dress, as it was when
she put down her iron and stood still, shocked by the event. The
poem 'One We Knew' indicates that in her later years she tended
to entertain memories rather than live in the present. She would sit
'with cap-framed face' gazing at the embers in the hearth as she
dipped into the past, holding her grandchildren Thomas and Mary
spellbound at her knees. She told them about the execution of
Louis XVI and the Reign of Terror; the ambition and arrogance of
Napoleon; and the fear his invasion preparations excited in Dorset.
Often she talked excitedly about the dancing that was fashionable
during the Napoleonic period, when French tunes became as
popular as British. She recalled 'the wild "poussetting" and "alle-
manding"' in mansions, ordinary homes, and outdoors; she described in detail how the dancers lined up, and the figures the
couples trod, in country dances. She talked about her youthful
terror whenever she passed the gibbet (which found its place in
Jude the Obscure) on the road from Fawley to Wantage; she could
still see it as it creaked and swayed 'in the lightning flash'. There
can be little doubt that Wantage was 'the neighbouring town'
where she heard the shrieks of a small child as it was lashed 'at the
cart-tail'.

Mary and Tom must have spent much time with her in her
sitting-room and garden. She showed them where the decorated
maypole used to be hoisted annually, and described the 'garland'
at the top, consisting of two intersected hoops of flowers, and how
the band played as couples whirled round, hoping to find partners
for life. Her description of the scene appealed to Hardy's visual
imagination; later he thought it redolent of pagan England, and
revived it with added detail at the end of *The Return of the Native*. A
heavy snowfall reminded his grandmother of one extremely severe
winter when the snow was so deep that she found, on her way to
Stinsford church, she could make better progress by walking along
the tops of frozen snow-capped hedges. The extent to which he
portrayed her in Mrs Martin, grandmother of the handsome young
astronomer Swithin St Cleeve in *Two on a Tower*, is a matter of
conjecture, though there can be no mistaking her appearance in
the 'woman of eighty, in a large mob cap, under which she wore a
little cap to keep the other clean', who sits by the wood fire, gazing
at the flames. During her nap she had gone 'straight back' to her
'old county again, as usual', and found it just as it was 'three-score

years ago'; yet, she supposes, if she went there hardly anyone would be left alive to say 'dog how art!'. The whole context suggests that this expression, found nowhere else in Hardy's fiction, was one to which his grandmother had been habituated in her Berkshire days, as was the word 'harlican', a term of reprobation used by old Drusilla Fawley to her great-nephew Jude when he is late bringing water from the well at Marygreen. It was probably in her company that Hardy became familiar with the use of tinder-boxes and candle-snuffers.

There was one story which must have appealed strongly to the imagination of the Hardy children. Their grandfather left Puddletown very late one night when he was a young man, to cross the heath on his way home. He had noticed two men watching him in the village, and felt certain they were intent on attacking and robbing him. The first part of his journey took him through a green field called 'Coomb', where he picked up several shining glowworms and placed them on the brim of his hat. On the heath, near Greenhill Pond, as the men were overtaking him, he decided to work on their 'superstitious feelings'. 'He accordingly rolled a furze faggot into the path, and, sitting down upon it, took off his hat, placed it on his knees, stuck two fern-fronds on his head to represent horns, and, pulling out from his pocket a letter he chanced to have with him, began reading it by the light of the glow-worms.' The men approached, stopped short suddenly, and then bolted off at full speed. Within a few days the rumour spread that the Devil had been seen at midnight by Greenhill Pond, studying the list of his victims by glow-worm light.

A writer's imaginative, moral, and spiritual growth usually depends for its early development on factors outside schools; and church and home were to contribute signally to Hardy's particular gifts. Features of many of his stories came from his parents, whose recollections often evoked nothing but wonder, sometimes horror and a sense of human injustice which later quickened his awareness of tragic chance, and awakened the humanitarian zeal of his most powerful novels. Frequently his mother was reminded of superstitions, superstitious practices, and even stories bordering on the preternatural, which had become familiar to her during her girlhood at Melbury Osmond. Several of them are to be found in Hardy's poems and short stories; others enter *The Woodlanders*. The story she told of a girl who committed suicide, and whose body was cast uncoffined into a grave at crossroads on Hendford Hill near Yeovil (all in accordance with ancient practice) must have been the crucial source for Hardy's late prose narrative 'The Grave by the Handpost'. Her accounts of incubus effects on a woman and of conjurors or witch-doctors combined with the gruesome hanging of an innocent youth to furnish the main suggestions for 'The Withered Arm'. How the youth came to be hanged, almost certainly at Dorchester, was told by Hardy's father; it made the son realize the tragedy of life more than anything he had heard. During the period which followed the Napoleonic war, when revolts by ill-paid agricultural labourers were common, the youth had been present by chance when a rick was fired; he was arrested and hanged as an example to the guilty. So slim and light was he that he had to be placed in the heaviest fetters procurable, too weighty almost for him to drag along, in order to ensure that his neck was mercifully broken at the first 'drop'. (The last details Hardy reserved for another story, 'The Winters and the Palmleys'.) In his letter to William Rothenstein of March 1912, he recalled a story told by his father of a man he knew who was hanged at this time, simply for observing that it would be a 'light night' to a farmer whose ricks were fired before morning broke.

Hardy and his sister Mary found each other's company so congenial that they frequently read and played together indoors and out. A heavy-fruiting apple tree in the garden had a fork so low that, with little difficulty, they could soon climb up among the branches. In 'Logs on the Hearth' he remembers how they stood together on a bending bough as she laughed and waved her hand. The neighbouring heath afforded an ample playground; they knew some of its deep conical pits, and which of them provided the best holly for Christmas decorations. They were familiar with Rushy Pond, said to have been scooped out by fairy shovels; with Rainbarrows, named after the ravens which had haunted them in the remote past; and, down below, by the Tincleton road, with Heedless William's Pond, named, according to a local tradition (which is changed in setting and circumstances at the end of Hardy's story 'A Tragedy of Two Ambitions'), from the carter whose whip handle grew into a willow tree after he had been drowned there. Nearer home they ventured into Thorncombe Wood and, on the other side, by Snail's Creep, through a narrow strip of thorn and woodland, to Grey's Wood; in both woods they went nutting together. In winter they learned how poaching continued locally after nightfall. Sometimes foxes had been heard barking in the woods during the night, and deer from the heath seen against the snow in front of the house. Christmas Eve recalled the traditional superstition they had been told, that oxen knelt down at midnight; it made them think of the cows in the barton near the bottom of their lane.

When Hardy began school in Dorchester he knew the ways to Stinsford so well that, if it were not too muddy, he would save time by heading for the path so many of his ancestors and relatives had followed across the fields of Kingston Park to the lane from Bockhampton Cross and on to the Dorchester road, where the stone pillar on the hill (commemorated in *The Mayor of Casterbridge*) indicated the mile or more he had to walk. The memorial tower to Admiral Hardy on Blackdown which he often noticed in the distance when he set off may have raised wishful thoughts of distant kinship, and have acted as a spur to his own ambition. Although he had lunch at the home of his uncle James Sparks's two spinster sisters near Hardye's school in South Street, he found time to discover much of interest in Dorchester; even so, he may not have ventured as far as Maumbury Rings, the Roman amphi-theatre or 'Coliseum' just outside the town, near the Weymouth road, before he was taken there by his father to a 'No Popery' demonstration.

Anti-Catholic feeling had been roused in the country by Cardinal Wiseman when he returned from Rome in 1850 as Archbishop of Westminster. Effigies of the Pope and the Cardinal were carried in procession from Fordington Hill round Dorchester, followed by a long train of people posturing as priests, monks, and nuns, and preceded by a young man discharging Roman candles, until the amphitheatre was reached. In the centre a huge rick of furze, with a gallows above, had been prepared. The effigies were 'slung up, and the fire blazed till they were blown to pieces by fireworks contained within them'. If the report is true that one of his father's workmen was revealed when the wind blew aside a monk's hood, Hardy must have found this display, which excited a tumultuous blend of fierce and jocular feeling, even more extraordinarily memorable.

He would have learned that the county town of Dorchester had been a large Roman encampment, protected on the north-east side by the Frome river, and elsewhere by walls running in straight lines approximately north–south and east–west. Avenues of trees, planted in the early part of the eighteenth century, overarched the streets which followed this ancient enclosure, and others marked the approaches to the town from the south, east, and west, the last two leading to High Street, which, from the east, climbs steadily to 'Top o' Town', and is divided into High West Street and High East Street above and below St Peter's Church, almost opposite which Corn Street leads to South Street and the Weymouth road. From the bottom of High Street Hardy had most probably walked by the river below the large prison which stood on the site of the old castle, in order to see the hangman's cottage; he would pass trees on his left which had been climbed by men and boys intent on watching when executions took place over the main entrance to the gaol. To the right stretched open country, with low-lying meadowland and waterways in the foreground. He would know where Judge Jeffreys had lodged in High West Street during one of his 'bloody assizes', and he may have discovered Gallows Hill, at the south-east corner of the town, where many of Monmouth's supporters had been hanged. Years later he heard that Jeffreys' notorious executioner Jack Ketch had lashed his bare-backed victims with his knotted whipcord cat-o'-nine-tails by the town pump in Corn Street, before they were escorted, bleeding, back to prison by the constables.

The school which Hardy attended had been established by the British and Foreign School Society to provide an education without denominational bias, unlike the 'National' schools, which were pledged to Church of England religious teaching. Its premises stood in a yard off South Street which had led to the old Grey-hound Inn (where Bob Loveday in *The Trumpet-Major* stables his horse), very near Cornhill or Corn Street. Isaac Last, the master in charge, was an able teacher who could be severe when necessary. Hardy, bookish and proficient, gave no trouble; he found the work easy, and, being ready to help them, became popular with fellow-pupils. He did not begin Latin until 1852.

He was small for his age, and still far from sturdy. Often he could not have looked forward to his long walk home. After leaving school through the arched passage into South Street, he turned right past Durngate Street into the broadening Cornhill, with the Antelope Hotel on the other side and, in the middle, near the junction with High Street, the town pump encased within the lower part of a tall stone obelisk, which had been erected in 1784 on the site of the Cupola or market-house. Ahead of him, immediately next to the Bow, a pavement which curved by the east end of

St Peter's, was a short street leading to North Square. On the corner below this stood the new Town Hall building, with a large ground-floor hall which served as the Corn Exchange. Hardy could have had no more than a hazy recollection of the town Hall which stood there until 1847 (or 1848), almost rubbing shoulders with St Peter's chancel, its balcony stretching over a high and broad arched passage which gave access to North Square or the Bull Ring. Here at the crossroads, the *carrefour* of *The Mayor of Caster-bridge*, the weekly market was held. On such days streets and pavements, Cornhill especially, would be thronged with stalls, containers, agricultural implements, and people. Carrier vans from villages far and near lined each side of the High Street; doorsteps, bow-windows, shopkeepers' wares, trestle-tables, boxes, pur-chasers, and sellers made it difficult for pedestrians to make progress along the pavements; only a narrow tortuous passage was left for through-traffic in the street. In places horses for sale were tied in rows, their forelegs on the pavement; commodious recesses in front of houses might be used to pen pigs for sale.

As he turned down High East Street, Hardy would notice on the left two prominent bow-windows, one above the other, over the pillared entrance to the King's Arms Hotel. Here and at the Antelope rich farmers wined and dined at all seasons of the year. Further down, on the same side, stood the Three Mariners' Inn (which he was to sketch from memory, for its architectural interest) and, at the bottom, the White Hart, an inn which had space, in front and to the rear, for several carrier-vans and vehicles. The first stream of the divided Frome flowed past it under Swan Bridge, built with dull red brick. Opposite the White Hart, a road curved into Fordington High Street, a short way along which stood a less distinguished-looking inn called Noah's Ark, with a back entrance by the river path. Crossing Swan Bridge, Hardy would enter the avenue of trees pointing straight ahead to Stinsford Hill. To the right, on a hill overlooking the Frome valley, the tower of St George's, the parish church of Fordington, formed a prominent landmark. After a few hundred yards, he crossed the main river at Grey's Bridge, an impressive stone structure which had been commissioned by Lora Grey, the last of the Grey family who had owned the Kingston Maurward estate for centuries; she had mar-ried George Pitt, who had built the new manor house early in the eighteenth century. Further on, a kissing-gate showed where a path began its way across meadows by the river, and continued

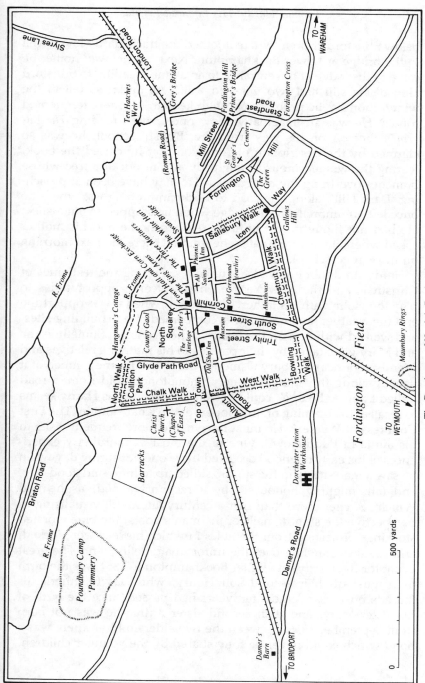

The Dorchester of Hardy's Boyhood

Slyres Lane
London Road
Ten Hatches Weir
Grey's Bridge
(Roman Road)
Fordington Mill
Prince's Bridge
Standfast Road
Fordington Cross
TO WAREHAM
Mill Street
Cemetery
St George's
Fordington
The Green
Hill
Way
Gallows Hill
Salisbury Walk
Icen
R. Frome
The White Hart
Swan Bridge
The Three Mariners
Town Hall and Corn Exchange
Hangman's Cottage
The King's Arms
Phoenix Inn
All Saints
Old Greyhound (earlier)
Chestnut Walk
R. Frome
County Gaol
Almshouse
Cornhill
St Peter's
North Square
The Antelope
Museum
South Street
Old Ship Inn
Trinity Street
Glyde Path Road
North Walk
Colliton Park
Chalk Walk
West Walk
Bowling Walk
Top o' Town
Albert Road
Fordington Field
TO WEYMOUTH
Maumbury Rings
Christ Church
(Chapel of Ease)
Barracks
Dorchester Union Workhouse
Bristol Road
R. Frome
Poundbury Camp 'Pummery'
Damer's Road
Damer's Barn
TO BRIDPORT

0   500 yards

below Stinsford church, where it joined the track Hardy knew well
to the bridge at Lower Bockhampton. Next, on his way home, he
came to the lodge at the entrance to an avenue leading to Stinsford
House. He still had two miles to walk. As darkness fell in the
winter months, he probably chose to keep to the more frequented
routes. He was an imaginative boy; once, when reading *The Pil-
grim's Progress* on his way from the 'British' school, he was so
alarmed by the description of Apollyon that he closed the book,
fearing the winged monster might fly at him out of a tree whose
branches overhung the road ahead. He may have been approaching 'Dark Hill', along the road to Bockhampton Cross, where he
once left an umbrella in the hedge when he stopped to cut a stick.
He had not thought of it until he reached home and his mother
asked where it was; fortunately he found it there the next morning
on his way to school.

Hardy no doubt enjoyed his holidays. During the festivities of
Christmas and the New Year he had welcome opportunities to
play the violin with his father. In summer, when it was opportune
and the weather favourable, he accompanied him to building-sites,
and walked with him on the heath in the evenings. Sometimes he
and Mary were taken by their parents to his mother's relatives and
friends at or near Melbury Osmond; the return journey, much of it
usually along the straight, lonely, monotonous old Roman road
'called Long-Ash Lane', could be very wearisome, as Hardy seems
to recall at the opening of 'Interlopers at the Knap' and in 'The First
Countess of Wessex'. He must have made more frequent visits to
his aunts in Puddletown. One of the most extraordinary experiences of his early boyhood occurred there one hot sunny day when
he saw a man sitting in the stocks, sidled up to him, said good-day,
and felt 'mightily honoured' by a responsive nod, as he told
William Archer more than half a century later, still visualizing in
perspective the shining nails of the man's boots, the blue worsted
stockings projecting from the holes in which his legs were locked,
and the flies crawling over the unfortunate delinquent. The great
event for the Hardys at Higher Bockhampton in 1851 was the birth
in August of their second son Henry, who was to inherit his
father's business. Almost ten years had passed since the birth of
his sister Mary, and their second sister Katharine was not born
until September 1856. Between the two elder children there was a
bond which could never be fully shared by the younger children,

who, if one can judge by their temperaments in later life, seem to have grown up in easier circumstances at home.

Hardy began Latin under Mr Last in the autumn of 1852, using the old Eton grammar *An Introduction to the Latin Tongue* and soon graduating, it seems, to readings in Eutropius and Caesar. During the Christmas holidays he broke new ground by accompanying his father on the violin at parties, partly because his mother felt that he would benefit from seeing more of life. His father objected, fearing that he might hear and see too much. Subsequently, at the same season, and at weekends, and in the summer, he played at village weddings and at parties in farmhouses, sometimes remote as in the story of 'The Three Strangers', where the picture of the boy about twelve 'who had a wonderful dexterity in jigs and reels, though his fingers were so small and short as to necessitate a constant shifting for the high notes, from which he scrambled back to the first position with sounds not of unmixed purity of tone', is based on recollections of his own difficulties on such occasions. Once, a year or two later, his hostess was so concerned for him, after he had played 'The New-Rigged Ship' continuously for three quarters of an hour to 'twelve tireless couples', that she clutched his bow-arm and stopped him, fearing he would 'burst a blood-vessel'. One winter about this time, when the sparkling snow was encrusted by a severe frost, and he and his father were returning home about three o'clock in the morning, the moonlight revealed the astounding sight of 'a white human figure without a head' against a hedgerow. Hardy, being thoroughly tired after a night of fiddling, would have hastened past, but his father, realizing the gravity of the situation, went to the rescue, lest the man were frozen to death. Very tall and thin, and in a long white smock, he leant against the bank in drunken stupor, his head hanging so low as to be invisible at a distance. They supported him home, and pushed him through the door, hearing as they left a stream of abuse from his wife, which she then turned on her husband, whom she promptly knocked down. It might have been kinder to leave him where they found him, Hardy's father wryly remarked.

The Scots Greys, who were stationed at the cavalry barracks to the north-west of the town before leaving for the Crimean War of 1853–6, brought music of another kind to Dorchester when they arrived in 1852. They had a splendid band, and frequently gave concerts in the town. Their playing of the 'Dead March' in *Saul* at the funeral of a 'comrade' created a 'profound sensation', and was long remembered in the neighbourhood. If Hardy did not hear any of the solemn strains (and he may have done, even had he been indoors at school), he certainly heard comments on this stirring event both in Dorchester and at home. Though the period of the novel is earlier, Mr Penny in *Under the Greenwood Tree* is 'moved in soul' by the recollection of it; at the end of the century Hardy was reminded of it in 'Enter a Dragoon', where it is played by the Scots Greys during their 'slow and dramatic march through the town' at the funeral of John Clark, who had recently returned from service and sickness in the Crimea. The barracks were situated in Fordington parish, which spread extensively to the south and even to the west side of Dorchester; the story makes it clear that the interment took place in the churchyard at Fordington on the opposite side of the town.

If Hardy's parents ever felt any qualms about sending him to a Nonconformist school they thought his regular attendance at Stinsford church services a prophylactic. By this time he was the choir-boy recalled in his poem 'Apostrophe to an Old Psalm Tune'; an early passage in *A Laodicean* indicates that this tune, remembered as late as 1916, was 'New Sabbath' and perhaps 'his once favourite air'. Soon, as he says in his *Life*, he knew the morning and evening services, including the rubrics, by heart, as well as large portions of the new version of the psalms, which were introduced when the old Tate and Brady metrical psalms were still being sung as hymns. Later there was no resistance to the suggestion that he, in company with the two sons of the vicar, Mr Shirley, should become a Sunday School teacher. In this way he came to know a dairymaid four years older than himself, a 'pink and plump damsel' whom he presented as Marian in *Tess of the d'Urbervilles*; this good-looking girl, 'by no means a model of virtue in her love-affairs', had an amazingly retentive verbal memory, and insisted on reciting in class 'the long gospels before Easter'. Unfortunately for him, an unwilling listener, she never missed a word. About this time or earlier, probably at weekends, he penned the love-letters which a few of the village girls sent to sweethearts on service in India; he was chosen to act as an amanuensis, and to read the replies, because he was judged to be of 'tender years', unable to understand the full implications of what he wrote and read.

Education for most young people ending at about the age of

twelve, Hardy was privileged in having parents who appreciated the importance of scholarship, and who could afford private schooling for their children. As the old grammar school (Hardye's), in its ancient buildings below the equally ancient 'Napper's Mite' (Napier's Almhouse) in South Street, did not enjoy a high reputation at the time, it was fortunate that Isaac Last, with the encouragement of Congregationalists in and around Dorchester, set up a private academy, which was opened in 1853. Continuing his studies under this 'accomplished schoolmaster', Hardy took, in addition to Latin and elementary drawing, advanced courses in arithmetic, algebra, and geometry. His mathematical work had a distinctly practical or technical bias, including business or commercial studies and the whole of Tate's *Mechanics* and Nesbitt's *Mensuration*. The following year he began French with one of the teachers who taught at Miss Harvey's school, which his sister Mary attended, at South Grove Cottage. Hardy must have been a pleasing and apt pupil, for his headmaster awarded him prizes, first at the end of 1854, then in the summer of 1855, when he received Theodore Beza's *Novum Testamentum* for progress in Latin. His mother, it seems, bought him the first two volumes of *The Popular Educator* for Christmas; he received the third the following Whitsuntide, and continued buying this valuable periodical (published by 'that genius in home-education, John Cassell') 'whenever he had any pocket-money'. Before leaving school, this publication had enabled him to make progress in the study of German at home.

By this time he may have found more use for the copy of Dryden's *Virgil* which his mother had given him about 1848, with Samuel Johnson's *Rasselas* and a translation of Bernardin de Saint-Pierre's *Paul et Virginie*. Whether he had returned to these two novels or not, he preferred James Grant's *The Scottish Cavalier* and romances by G. P. R. James and the elder Dumas. Cheap paperback editions made Bulwer-Lytton's novels popular, and Hardy 'wept over his heroines'. He read Shakespeare's tragedies 'for the plots only, not thinking much of *Hamlet* because the ghost did not play his part up to the end as he ought to have done'. His interest in Harrison Ainsworth's novels seems to have developed rather later.

There had been a serious outbreak of cholera at Fordington in 1849; a worse began in August 1854, particularly by the river below Swan Bridge, in the slum area which contained the 'Mixen Lane' of *The Mayor of Casterbridge*, where poverty-stricken people and ne'er-do-wells had tended to dwell in their later years. Hardy's parents had most probably made him feel it was a place to be shunned, and he must have hurried past with misgivings when the plague was at its worst, and smoke from the burnt bedding and clothes of the dead could be smelt, day after day, over the low-lying pastures below the church.

One day, when Hardy was fourteen, a pretty girl who had passed him on horseback near the South Walk, just after he had come out of school, turned and smiled at him; the next day he saw her again with an old gentleman, perhaps her father. She was a complete stranger, but he fell madly in love with her, and wandered about day after day, in the hope of seeing her again. Some of Mr Last's boarders were sympathetic, and looked out for her, but she never appeared, and it took him a week to recover. His recurrent propensity to imagine himself in love was to be the subject of mockery in *The Well-Beloved*, where this 'desperate attachment', with slight modifications, is one of the earliest to be recalled by the hero, Jocelyn Pierston. A year or more later Hardy lost his heart to a girl who had come to Dorchester from Windsor, but he was soon disillusioned on finding that she was not in the least interested in Herne the Hunter or Anne Boleyn, whom he had been reading about in Ainsworth's *Windsor Castle*.

Though the seamier side of life increasingly emerged, with stories of past and present, and common gossip and comment on drunkenness, and on domestic quarrels and violence, sometimes with reference to relatives of his at Puddletown, Hardy remembered almost idyllic scenes: wheat-weeding, meetings at the Higher Bockhampton well, cider-making, and harvesting in the second of three fields on the eastern side of the road from Bockhampton Cross to Lower Bockhampton. In the poem 'At Middle-Field Gate in February' he recalls the young women of about twenty he saw working there in his boyhood, including Ann West, whose marriage on a frosty day in February 1855 he remembered more than twenty years later when he read about 'the beautiful phenomenon called "the silver frost"' in Canada:

> How dry it was on a far-back day
>   When straws hung the hedge and around,
> When amid the sheaves in amorous play
> In curtained bonnets and light array
>   Bloomed a bevy now underground!

It was from a very different kind of experience, when he was fifteen and saw the candle-lit vault under Stinsford chancel, that he created a vivid scene in *A Pair of Blue Eyes*.

Hardy's claim that 'the first effusion of his to see the light of print was an anonymous skit in a Dorchester paper on the disappearance of the Alms-House clock' has proved difficult to substantiate. This may have been the brief humorous letter which appeared in the *Dorset County Chronicle* in January 1856 on the irregularity of Dorchester clocks, and especially on the waywardness of the clock outside Napper's Mite, though it is not 'a plaintive letter from the ghost of the clock' which had disappeared (as Hardy remembered it). Perhaps that is how he planned his skit in the first place.

The Crimean War, which had been fought with heavy losses, ended in March 1856, but celebrations of the peace treaty were deferred in Dorchester until 30 June, to commemorate also the anniversary of Queen Victoria's coronation. Competitive sports were organized within the prehistoric earthworks of Poundbury ('Pummery'), 'an elevated green spot' beyond the cavalry barracks, with the Frome river on its northern flank. Tea was served in the West Walks, where, in the evening, the green trees, the flags, banners, and illuminated Chinese lanterns suspended from them, and the crowds of 'gaily dressed' people wandering up and down, created an unusually colourful and animated scene. As it was a public holiday, and the details, especially of the events organized at Poundbury, are faithfully reproduced in *The Mayor of Casterbridge* (in circumstances devised to suit the plot), it could be assumed that Hardy saw all these things. There is no certainty that he did; perhaps his father was unable to take him, and his cautious mother did not encourage him to go as an independent spectator; perhaps they and their children went to see relatives and celebrations at Puddletown. The details he gives are brief, such as might have been taken from a programme of events; he could easily have acquired them, as he did many others for his novel, from old newspapers and records in the County Museum library.

There is no doubt that he attended Cooke's Circus when it came to Dorchester less than two weeks later. It presented the battle of Alma and other scenes from the recent war, in addition to the usual equestrian feats. Chief among these was the play of 'Turpin's Ride and the Death of Black Bess', which Hardy remembered with dramatic clarity for the return of Sergeant Troy in *Far from the*

Madding Crowd. He did not see it at 'Greenhill' Fair (on Woodbury Hill, east of Bere Regis), he told Rebekah Owen in 1893, but at Cooke's Circus, where 'Black Bess was carried out on a board'. The novel gives more satisfying detail, 'the gallant and faithful Bess' being carried out on a shutter by 'twelve volunteers from among the spectators'. Hardy watched this exciting finale a few weeks after his sixteenth birthday; he had just left school, and was about to begin an architectural career.

4

Hicks, Barnes, and Bastow

The builder Thomas Hardy had done important work for the architect Benjamin Ferrey when the west front of Stafford House, to the south of Lower Bockhampton, was built. Here, below the plank crossing of a Frome rivulet on the north side of the western garden area, the boy Hardy had discovered the weir which was to become the focal point in both the narrative and time-theme of 'The Waiting Supper'. About this time, from the same place, he may have wandered down the valley to the nine-hatched weir, and watched the body of a drowned boy being hauled to land from the pool. At first he had thought by 'some curious trick of light' that it was a girl, and it was the memory of this which suggested the fatal climax of *The Return of the Native*, where the heroine is drowned in the pool below Shadwater Weir. It is possible that he witnessed the recovery of the body when his father and another builder were employed very near, by the architect John Hicks, on restoration work at Woodsford Castle, a manor farmhouse which had been built as a castle in the fourteenth century. Late in his life Hardy could not remember whether it was there or elsewhere that Hicks, finding he had no definite career in mind, 'tested him by inviting him to assist at a survey'. Indirectly Hardy had received some excellent training for this at school, and John Hicks was so impressed that he offered to take him into his office as an apprentice. On 11 July 1856, not many days after leaving school, he was articled for three years to receive instruction in surveying and architectural drawing, the premium (usually £100) to be paid midway through his training-period. Her husband being a 'ready-money man', Mrs Hardy suggested a substantial reduction for immediate payment, which was settled at £40.

Hardy's second wife Florence reported that, soon after he began his architectural apprenticeship, he and his mother had to listen to a sermon from Mr Shirley at Stinsford on the presumption shown by members of the lower classes in seeking professional status. This, assuming its complete authenticity, may have been no more than coincidental; it would be rash to infer any animus against the

Hardys. It could place the Revd Arthur Shirley in the Establishment tradition which assumed that class distinctions existed by the will of God: 'The rich man in his castle, The poor man at his gate, God made them, high or lowly, And order'd their estate.' He was, after all, a contemporary of the society lady Miss Rigby (afterwards Lady Eastlake), who had condemned *Jane Eyre* for its immorality, and asserted that it was 'a murmuring against God's appointment' to present a governess ready to marry her master, and proclaim that they were equal in the sight of God. How Lady Eastlake would have reacted to the subversiveness of Hardy's first novel, *The Poor Man and the Lady*, had it been published, is easy to guess; it is not surprising that Alexander Macmillan had to reject it.

John Hicks's office was on the ground floor of 39 South Street, almost opposite Napper's Mite and Hardye's Grammar School. When Hardy arrived he found two other apprentices, Herbert Fippard, a young man of 21 who was on the point of finishing his articles and leaving, and Henry Bastow of Bridport, in his first year and a year or so older than Hardy. Bastow and he grew very friendly, and often gave time to books when they ought to have been drawing. Hicks did not seem to mind; he was a good-natured, almost jovial man, son of a Gloucestershire rector who had been a good classical scholar. He knew some Hebrew, had ability in Greek, but was 'less at home', it proved, in Latin. He specialized in Gothic architecture and in the renovation of neglected churches. After practising in Bristol, he had come to Dorchester about 1850, one of his first Dorset assignments being the restoration of his brother's church of Piddletrenthide by 1852. Just before Hardy entered his office he had rebuilt the east end of St Peter's, Dorchester, in perpendicular style. In connection with minor alterations, completed in 1857, Hardy produced a ground plan of the church on 4 August 1856; it is a model of fine draughtsmanship.

On Saturday, five days later, he must have reached Hicks's office in a perturbed state; he had just come from witnessing the execution of Martha Browne for the murder of her unfaithful husband at Birdsmoorgate near Broadwindsor in west Dorset. He had arrived early at the gateway of the county gaol, and, being short of stature, had been allowed a place near the front of a mass of spectators who waited in the drizzling rain to watch the whole drama of the last rites and preparations, the drop, and the sight of the suspended body, over the main entrance of the prison. Hardy was much impressed by the calm bearing of this handsome woman, and it was not until he heard the thud of the drop that he was roused to a shocked sense of reality. The steady rain had made the white cap cling to her face; he remembered its features, and described to Lady Pinney in January 1926, when she was collecting evidence on the case, 'what a fine figure' the body of Martha Browne presented 'against the sky as she hung in the misty rain, and how the tight black silk gown set off her shape as she wheeled half-round and back'. Later that year he recalled seeing the execution 'without much emotion'; because boys are like that, he supposed. Some people are less sensitive than Hardy; Byron, after watching from a front seat and through an opera-glass, three robbers beheaded in Rome, opined that everything was worth seeing *once*.

About this time, and later, a number of Stinsford girls, usually older than himself, attracted his attention. In 1888 he remembered four of these 'village beauties': 'Alice P— and her mass of flaxen curls'; Emily Dart 'and her mere prettiness'; Rachel Hurst 'and her rich colour, and vanity, and frailty, and clever artificial dimple-making' (probably, he later thought, the original to some extent of Arabella in *Jude the Obscure*); and Elizabeth Bishop, a gamekeeper's red-haired daughter who despised him and married early. Her smiles, her singing, and her beautiful outdoor complexion enchanted him, and his fascination shines in 'To Lizbie Browne', the lyric in which he later 'celebrated her'. Deeper and more enduring was his attachment to a girl younger than himself, Louisa Harding, daughter of the farmer who lived near Stinsford church. She was sent to a boarding-school at Weymouth, and he went there on Sundays until he discovered the church she and her fellow-pupils attended; she ventured 'a shy smile' of recognition, and this was the sole reward for these time-consuming lovelorn efforts.

One of the seasonal festivities which marked the end of 1856 took place on Christmas Day, when the Hardy players assisted in celebrating the marriage of one of William Keats's daughters. The happiness which had been brought by the birth of Hardy's sister Kate in September, however, was offset in January, when his 'gentle, kindly grandmother' died in her eighty-fifth year. Her decease led to important structural changes in the Hardy abode. The stairway at the north end of the original cottage had probably been restructured in reverse earlier, perhaps at the time when a partition was built to create an office at that end of the living-room for Thomas Hardy the builder. Upstairs access to her bedroom may have been provided for emergencies during her final decline. After her death the two cottages became one with a new porched entrance, windows on brick bases replacing the two former front doors and frames. Hardy's recollection of the old entrance to his boyhood home provides the opening verse of 'The Self-Unseeing', which he wrote after his father's death:

> Here is the ancient floor,
> Footworn and hollowed and thin,
> Here was the former door
> Where the dead feet walked in.

Other changes included the transfer of some of the more domestic chores to the house which was taken over. In the old living-room the open fire-place, at the south end, had been flanked by a large brick oven on the left and a copper for washing on the right (a front corner of the room). The copper had to be removed to provide new access; the hearth was reduced; and the door of the oven was removed to the wall by the fireplace in granny's old room, where baking now took place and meals were usually served.

Hardy benefited most by inheriting her bedroom, which became his study. He could rise as early as he wished. In the poem 'Four in the Morning' he recalls getting up as daylight dawns, and hearing a mower's 'wheezed whettings' of his scythe down in the valley. The flight of whistling birds from the poet's window-ledge to a safe distance in the apple trees is the subject of 'A Bird-Scene at a Rural Dwelling'. As Hardy, short of stature, stooped to descend by 'the crooked stair', he felt he was living in a room 'not much higher than the between-decks of a frigate'. He remembered such details when he wrote about Blooms-End in the final book of *The Return of the Native*. Eventually a steep step-ladder was substituted for his grandmother's stairway to create more room for storage upstairs and down.

After reading several books of the *Aeneid*, and some Horace and Ovid, mainly before breakfasting at eight o'clock, he acquired a facility in Latin which enabled him, on his way to and from Dorchester, 'to beguile his lonely walks by imaginary conversations therein', as Jude did at about the same age. He may, like Jude, have been consciously aiming to qualify for university entrance and a career in the Church. If he had difficulties in construing, and he and Henry Bastow were unable to agree on translations, Hardy would seek grammatical enlightenment from William Barnes, who lived next door to Hicks's office and taught in his 'Classical and Mathematical School' behind his home. Finding that his own interpretation was usually correct, Hardy was encouraged to revisit this mentor, who was already a philologist in several languages, and whose poetry and scholarship he grew to admire.

Born in 1801 in the Vale of Blackmoor near Sturminster Newton, where he attended school and was selected to work in a solicitor's office, Barnes had continued this kind of employment at Top o' Town, Dorchester. His artistic skills showed in woodcuts, engravings, and verse. After being in charge of a school at Mere in Wiltshire, north of his native vale, he returned to Dorchester, where he opened a successful school in Durngate Street. Two years later, in 1837, it was transferred to more commodious quarters next to Napper's Mite almshouses. He was a keen antiquary, and wrote an account of Maumbury Rings which appeared in the May 1839 number of the *Gentleman's Magazine*, to which he had contributed since 1830. Barnes's enthusiasm for local antiquities led to practical work in the vicinity with his pupils which broadened their interests, and helped to produce some outstanding scientists and mathematicians. In his spare time he continued to write poetry, which came to him with comparative ease. His aim was to be ordained, and with this in view he registered as early as 1837 at St John's College, Cambridge, for a ten-year period, at the end of which he was required to be in residence and to study for three terms (not necessarily consecutive) before he could sit for his degree. His disappointment in 1846 at not being made head of Hardye's Grammar School because he was not in Holy Orders was great. As soon as he was eligible for ordination the next year he was given the curacy of Whitcombe, three miles south-east of Dorchester. Later that year he bought the house on the opposite side of South Street where he was living when Hardy made his acquaintance.

After the death of his wife Julia, whom he fell in love with soon after his first arrival in Dorchester, his school declined and his fame grew. His first volume of dialect poems had appeared in 1844; his second appeared in 1859, and a third in 1862. They were collected and published years later as *Poems of Rural Life in the Dorset Dialect*, and include some of the very best English pastoral and lyrical verse. Like Tennyson, Barnes had a keen ear for the musical effects attainable through variation and discreet repetition of vowel sounds. He had read French and Italian from his youth onwards, and spent much time in the study of Welsh, Russian, Hebrew, Persian, and Hindustani. Philology remained his greatest pursuit. His linguistic coinages, in support of his obsessive campaign for the use of Anglo-Saxon words and derivatives, did nothing to stem the cultivated development of our more Latinized tongue, but they had effects on Hardy's poetry which were not always beneficial. In 1860 he received a pension of £70 from the Civil List. With this and £200 a year from the living of Winterborne Came, which he received from Captain Damer in 1862, Barnes was happy to relinquish his school and devote himself to his two churches and scattered parishioners. In this work he was assisted by two of his daughters. Many distinguished people, including Americans and the poets Coventry Patmore, Allingham, and Tennyson, came to visit him at his rectory, an idyllic-looking thatched cottage in a beautiful garden on the Wareham road about half a mile beyond where Hardy was to live from 1885, not long before Barnes's death, for the remainder of his equally long life. The outlook of these two poets was very different; nothing could destroy the faith of Barnes in the goodness of God, which he saw in the beauty of nature and in the derivative beauty of art.

On 10 August 1858, two years and a day after seeing the execution of Martha Browne at close range, Hardy was about to sit down for breakfast when he remembered that a man was to be hanged at Dorchester at eight o'clock. Taking the large brass telescope which had been a family heirloom, he hurried uphill to a point on the heath (Rainbarrow, he said in his old age) whence he could see the front of the gaol, its stone entrance shining white in the sunlight, the gallows upon it, the murderer James Seale in white fustian, and the executioner and other officials in dark clothing. He had scarcely focused all this when the white figure dropped; so unexpectedly sudden was the motion that the glass almost fell out of his hands. 'He seemed alone on the heath with the hanged man, and crept homeward wishing he had not been so curious.'

By this time Hardy had probably begun to learn Greek without the aid of a tutor. His copy of the *Iliad* is dated 1858, and a note in the volume proves that by 1860 he had made a study of those Homeric books and passages which Jude had read when, contemplating the learned achievements which make him euphorically certain that he will become a Doctor of Divinity, he is rudely awakened by the missile which heralds the tragic mischance of his life.

Meanwhile serious doctrinal argumentation had sprung up between Hardy and Bastow, who had chosen to be baptized by immersion, and was so convinced of the rightness of this, the New Testament form of adult baptism, and so earnest in presenting the case for it, that his junior colleague was almost persuaded to follow suit, despite his High Church upbringing. When he turned to his vicar for advice, he was lent a copy of Hooker's *Laws of Ecclesiastical Polity*, from which he derived little help; the curate of another parish had nothing to offer except a most elementary handbook on the sacraments. Hardy procured elsewhere what books and information he could on paedobaptism, and the debate between him and Bastow in the office became so heated at times that Mrs Hicks in her drawing-room above sent messages requesting them to make less noise.

Hardy's position *vis-à-vis* Bastow worsened when two of the latter's friends, sons of the Revd Frederick Perkins, the Baptist minister, joined in the controversy. They were both competent classical scholars 'fresh from Aberdeen University', and their frequent references to passages in the original New Testament, the Greek version, made it expedient for Hardy, after working hard at night on his old one, to obtain the German scholar Griesbach's text, which he had seen advertised as the most correct; he purchased his Bohn Library edition on 7 February 1860. How seriously he took the issue may be seen from the fact that, after promising to attend a prayer-meeting with Bastow and the minister's sons in the vestry of the chapel, across the road from the White Hart, he kept the appointment punctually, when he would have preferred watching Cooke's popular circus enter the town, only to find, when the brothers arrived late, that they had given priority to this spectacle. Most of the arguments Hardy assembled for paedobaptism from the New Testament and the Christian Fathers are adduced by the hero of *A Laodicean* when he takes up the cudgels on the heroine's behalf against the Baptist minister Mr Woodwell, 'a recognizable drawing of Perkins the father', Hardy admitted. Nevertheless, it was these Scots, the Perkins, who first impressed on him the necessity of 'plain living and high thinking', a characteristic he was to share with Clym Yeobright. When the great argument subsided, Hardy and Bastow would take their copies of the Greek New Testament into the fields, reading from them, sometimes on the gate of the eweleaze enclosure below Kingston Maurward House. Such readings ended when Henry Bastow's term of four years with John Hicks expired, and he joined an architect's office in London, shortly before leaving in 1860 to set up his own practice in Tasmania.

Hardy's life was not all earnestness. He looked back on this period as one of contrasts. Working in Dorchester, which was very evidently an agricultural centre, he was in touch not only with professional life but with improvements which were unknown in the 'world of shepherds and ploughmen' where he lived. To such people, as it is to the rustics who assemble at Warren's malthouse, the uprooting of an apple tree that used to produce two hogsheads of cider a year, or the fixing of an iron pump and stone trough over an old well (as could have happened at Higher Bockhampton by the time *Far from the Madding Crowd* was being written), was an exciting event. Added to such environmental changes in Hardy's life from day to day there were those of his 'inner life'. He would be up studying Greek or Latin from six to eight o'clock, before breakfast and his long walk to the office in South Street, where usually he would be engaged on Gothic architecture all day, except when he was working on building sites. Then, often in the evenings, he would 'rush off with his fiddle under his arm, sometimes in the company of his father as first violin and uncle as 'cellist, to play country-dances, reels, and hornpipes at an agriculturalist's wedding, christening, or Christmas party', occasionally in 'a remote dwelling among the fallow fields'. There was no shortage of such engagements for the Hardys, as it was their 'firm principle' not to charge for their services, almost all their hosts being friendly acquaintances. Sometimes, rather than disappoint young couples whose zest for dancing seemed inexhaustible, they stayed on until they were tired out, and did not reach home until nearly dawn. Hardy was much stronger than he had been; otherwise he would not have been able, 'like a conjuror at a fair, to keep in the air the three balls of architecture, scholarship, and dance-fiddling, without ill effects'.

Illness delayed Mary Hardy's admission to the ladies' teacher-training college of Sarum St Michael, at a corner of the Close in front of Salisbury Cathedral. The course began in January, but she was not able to take her place until 3 April 1860; she had been recommended by Mr Shirley. Unlike many trainees, she had no teaching experience, but her private-school qualifications, including French, were good, and she showed distinct ability in painting and music. She was to become a church organist in villages where she taught before becoming headmistress of a school in Dorchester; at home she had practised on her mother's old table-piano, which Hardy had tuned at various times. He may not have found time to keep pace with her in the art of painting, though his watercolour of Athelhampton Hall (largely Tudor, said to occupy the site of King Athelstan's old palace), near Puddletown, is dated 1859. In her later years Mary became a talented portrait-painter. Hardy informed his friend Sir Henry Newbolt in June 1920 that he first visited Salisbury Cathedral as an architect's pupil in 1860; his *Book of Common Prayer* shows that the visit coincided with the singing of the *In quo corriget* section of Psalm CXIX ('Wherewithal shall a young man cleanse his way?') which he remembered in *Jude the Obscure*.

As John Hicks's senior apprentice, after Bastow's departure, he visited several Dorset churches, making preliminary surveys, measurements, and sketches for restoration work; in this way, as he writes in his *Life*, he was 'passively instrumental in destroying or in altering beyond identification' beautifully carved work in stone and wood from the Gothic period to the Jacobean and Georgian. Accounts of church restoration carried out by Hicks which Hardy prepared for the grateful reporter of the *Dorset County Chronicle* suggest that he visited churches where the preparatory work had been done by Bastow, including Rampisham, Powerstock, and St Mary's, Bridport. It is reasonable to suppose that he noticed the name Swithin Cleeves, that of the seventeenth-century rector of the first of these parishes, which, slightly modified, he gave much later to the hero of *Two on a Tower*. He made drawings for Hicks of Athelhampton church, and was present at its consecration on 31 December 1861. His pencil drawing of a font in Coombe Keynes church, dated 8 April 1861, seems to denote his involvement in renovations there; and sketches in a similar style suggest his association with restoration further south at East Lulworth and, in west Dorset, at North Poorton near Beaminster. Hicks had work in hand further west, at Hawkchurch (now in Devon) and Bettiscombe, near the Devon border. Whether or not Hardy's work took him to either place, his various missions during this early phase of his architectural career acquainted him at a most impressionable age with parts of his fictional Wessex for the first time. Sketches made in 1861 of Glastonbury Abbey ruins and of pillars and capitals in Stinsford church, before alterations were carried out that year, testify to the keen interest he took in furthering his architectural knowledge in his spare time.

Other important results followed Bastow's departure. Hardy, 'like St Augustine, lapsed from the Greek New Testament back again' to 'pagan' or classical writers, especially Homer. He was able to attend more of Barnes's public readings of his poems, which he recalled when he wrote his obituary in 1886:

> The poet's own mild smile at the boisterous merriment provoked by his droll delivery of such pieces as 'The Shy Man', 'A Bit o' Sly Coorten', and 'Dick and I' returns upon the memory as one of the most characteristic aspects of a man who was nothing if not genial; albeit that, while the tyranny of his audience demanded these broadly humorous productions, his own preferences were for the finer and more pathetic poems, such as 'Wife a-Lost', 'Woak Hill', and 'Jaäy a-past'.

Hardy found time also for a broader self-education, studying the contemporary world through the *Saturday Review*, and not missing controversial books. He was, he says, among the earliest acclaimers of *The Origin of Species*, which had been published in November 1859. So familiar was he from his country environment with the struggle for existence between the species, or the 'nature red in tooth and claw' of Tennyson's *In Memoriam*, that he accepted most of Darwin's evidence readily, though it seems fair to assume that he could not share his sense of grandeur in contemplating 'the production of the higher animals' from 'the war of nature'. Hardy had not lost his Christian faith; he could accept a universe of 'general laws' without fully realizing, or confronting, their opposition to a belief in Providence. Another consequence of Bastow's absence was that Hardy had more time to spend with other friends.

5

The Moules of Fordington

Chief among Hardy's friends at this time were some of the sons of the Revd Henry Moule, vicar of St George's, Fordington, and one of the most zealous, enterprising, intelligent, and able Churchmen of his time. Centred on the south-east side of Dorchester, his parish included a large agricultural region south of the town, extending beyond the Weymouth road north of the huge pre-historic earthworks of Maiden Castle, and still further north on the western side of Dorchester. Here, between the cavalry barracks and the north-west corner of the town, less than a mile directly from St George's Church, a growing number of his parishioners lived; and it was mainly as a result of his determination and drive that a new church or chapel-of-ease was built for their convenience and benefit in 1847.

Son of a solicitor and banker at Melksham, Wiltshire, Henry Moule had been educated at Marlborough Grammar School. As a result of winning a scholarship at St John's College, Cambridge, he underwent the most critical influence on his life. Like Patrick Brontë, he became a disciple of the zealous Evangelical reformer Charles Simeon of King's College. After taking his degree in 1821, he accepted a travelling tutorship with Admiral Hotham's family which took him to France and Switzerland. His second curacy was at Gillingham in north Dorset, where he had sole charge of a parish which brought him many troubles. They were not nearly as intract-able as those which he soon found confronting him after his appointment to Fordington in 1829. With its low-lying congeries of crowded, unhygienic cottages, where filth, drunkenness, vice, misery, disaffection, and crime were all too common, it was mani-fest that his pastoral labours would be herculean and lengthy. His task was aggravated in 1831, when political agitation led to local rioting, violence, and rick-burning, and he not only organized security patrols but served on them himself. His predecessor had not faced up to his more normal ministerial responsibilities. Henry Moule told Francis Kilvert in 1874 that when he came to Fording-ton no man had ever received Holy Communion except the parson, the clerk, and the sexton; women communicants ceased to come when he refused to pay them for their attendance. When he asked why there was no water in the font for christening, the clerk exclaimed, 'Water, sir! The last person never used no water. He spit into his hand.'

Moule's denunciatory sermons and criticism of the choir quickly made him unpopular; after losing half his congregation, he led the singing himself for several years. Local young men jeered at his sons, and periodically tore up his vicarage railings and garden plants. He was dubbed a Methodist. Hostility against him increased when he brought local race-meetings to an end; convinced that they encouraged intemperance and immorality, he had worked on key patrons until he succeeded. For five years, in Kilvert's words, 'none of his family or flock could go into Dorchester without being insulted and baa-d after like sheep'. He provided two school-houses for daily attendance, the first being built thirty years before W. E. Forster's Act of 1870 made elementary education compulsory for all. Sunday schools were organized, Mrs Moule taking charge of the girls'; she supported her husband most conscientiously, and knew every house in the parish. Weekday services were held, and 'cottage lectures' were given to small adult groups. Henry Moule's 'good fight' continued unabated for a quarter of a century until recognition of his worth gained ground with remarkable rapidity. This was due almost entirely to his brave example and strenuous efforts (which Hardy made central to the fictional narrative of 'A Changed Man' in 1900) in stemming the spread of cholera during its worst outbreak at Fordington, in 1854. Thereafter the work of this Evangelical was more rewarding and agreeable, but it was just as purposive. Nobody did more to raise moral and social standards in this parish, and Hardy had him personally in mind to some extent when he drew Angel Clare's father in *Tess of the d'Urbervilles*. His vicarage became the centre for meetings of regional Evangelical Church of England clergymen, among whom were men of distinction as well as of high endeavour. 1859 was revival year, and St George's was thronged to overflowing.

As Fordington belonged to the Duchy of Cornwall, and Prince Albert was the President of the Council, Moule had addressed the first of a series of letters to him when cholera struck his parish for the second or third time. In this communication of 12 September 1854 he describes the conditions responsible for the spread of the epidemic. Eleven hundred people, more than a third of the population, were crowded in cottages by the river. Its mill-pond, from which they drew water for their washing 'and sometimes even for culinary purposes', received half their filth, in addition to that from the county gaol and from elsewhere. He had little doubt about the origin of the disease. About the middle of August, when cholera in London had penetrated the Millbank Penitentiary, 700 of the convicts imprisoned there had been transferred to the Dorchester cavalry barracks, which remained unoccupied after the departure of the Scots Greys for the Crimea. Henry Moule had discovered that the 'body-linen' of the prisoners, and their bedding and blankets, had not been replaced when they left London, as the public had been informed. Despite his protests, their clothing had been washed by two Fordington women who lived in the Holloway Road above the river, and since then 26 of his parishioners had died of cholera. Warders had frequented some of the houses where deaths had subsequently occurred, one such visit being made as late as Thursday, 31 August. Moule's appeal in his later correspondence for housing amelioration stirred no effective response from the Duchy.

Hardy's mother was one of his admirers. She attended a number of his services at Fordington, and recalled how, when she visited her brother in Dorchester about 1830, she had first seen him preach in the riding-school of the barracks, before taking up the guinea that had lain on the drumhead throughout the service, and hastening away for matins at Fordington church. He was 'a fine, noble-looking young man', she thought, as 'he preached at the drumhead, the congregation of soldiers standing in the saw-dust'. He must have been known to Hardy when, after almost breaking down with stress, he deputized as chaplain at the execution of Martha Browne. His interests and activities in pursuit of public welfare can be gauged from his publications, which include: 'Barrack Sermons, Preached in the Riding School of the Cavalry Barracks at Dorchester' (c.1845), 'Eight Letters to His Royal Highness Prince Albert as President of the Council of the Duchy of Cornwall' (1855), 'Sixty Original Hymns' (c.1856), 'My Kitchen Garden' (1860), 'Manure for the Million. A Letter to the Cottage Gardeners of England' (1861), 'The Impossibility Overcome, or The Inoffensive, Safe, and Economical Disposal of the Refuse of Towns and Villages' (1870), 'The Advantages of the Dry Earth System in the Removal of Sewage and Excreta' (1870), 'On the Warming of

Churches' (1870), 'National Educational Expenses: How to a Large Extent These May be Met. A Letter to the Hon. W. E. Forster' (1871, after the passing of the Elementary Education Act), 'A Manual of Moule's Dry Earth System' (1877) (he had designed and patented earth-closets since 1860), and 'Harvest Hymns' (1877). In 1879, the year before his death, Moule sent a scheme for the drainage of Dorchester to its mayor and council. He was a man for whom godliness extended to all 'walks of life'. He believed in education for all, one of his most interesting proposals being 'Boarding schools for children of the operative classes' in 1856; and he set an example in using scientific knowledge for the betterment of mankind, his own most useful endeavours being directed towards sanitation, soil-improvement, and horticultural food-production. The improvements he recommended for the cholera-stricken area of Fordington included new housing with adequate space for gardening, a provision calculated to reduce drunkenness and benefit family life and health. Just after his death in February 1880, Matthew Arnold discussed him with Hardy, who emphasized the changes he had made in Fordington during the previous fifty years. Henry Moule's achievements reminded Hardy of Arnold's words 'Energy is genius'.

Mrs Moule has been described as 'a fine and saintly woman', and Hardy probably had her in mind in his presentation of Mrs Clare more than he assumed very late in life, when he said that whatever resemblances existed were accidental. She and Henry were married in 1824, and, one child having died in infancy, were left with seven sons, 'the seven brethren' as Hardy referred to them when Charles, the last of them, died in 1921. Benefiting from excellent early education at home, all were scholarly. The high esteem in which they came to be held for their personal qualities, example, and participation in Fordington life and welfare, is illustrated by the return of George from China in 1867, when parishioners met him and his wife and three children at the station, removed the horses from the hired carriage which had been sent to meet them, and drew them all the way to the vicarage steps. He was the elder of the two brothers who were missionaries in mid-China, of which he was consecrated Bishop at St Paul's Cathedral in 1880. The eldest of the family, Henry Joseph, a gifted landscape-painter, spent much time travelling in Europe as secretary and tutor in one noble family after another; then, after becoming an estate-manager is Scotland and elsewhere, returned to Dorchester, where he settled as curator of the Dorset County Museum for the remainder of his life. Charles was an eminent classical scholar, and Hardy was at Fordington vicarage at the beginning of November 1857 when the news arrived of his election to a fellowship at his college, Corpus Christi, Cambridge, where, after teaching at Marlborough College (as did his brothers Horace and Handley), he became successively tutor and librarian, then President until his death in 1913. Handley, the youngest (born like Mary Hardy on 23 December 1841), had a most distinguished career. He was a student and fellow of Trinity College, Cambridge, before teaching at Marlborough College. When his doubts were resolved, he was ordained at Ely and assisted as curate at Fordington during most of the last eight years of his father's life. Then followed a long period at Cambridge. He was the first principal of Ridley Hall, a theological college for graduate ordinands which was founded by members of the Evangelical party in the Church of England and opened in January 1881. After holding this position for nineteen years, he was appointed Norrisian Professor of Divinity at the University. Shortly afterwards he became Bishop of Durham.

One of his early friends remembered him as a happy and charming boy; he and Hardy must have become acquainted when the latter was at Mr Last's academy. Soon after the Crimean War began, it seems, his father bought him a telescope through which he invited his friends, including Hardy, to observe stellar space; he was on the roof of a friend's house with this telescope when news came of the capture of Sebastopol. Whether it was ever mounted on the tower of St George's Church (as has been claimed) is very uncertain; the discussion of such a possibility may have lingered in Hardy's mind when he planned his novel *Two on a Tower*. Handley's larger three-inch achromatic telescope was erected on the roof of the vicarage. How it stimulated the astronomical interest already fostered in Hardy by Cassell's *Popular Educator* is vividly illustrated in Gabriel Oak's observations from Norcombe Hill in *Far from the Madding Crowd*. Star-gazing was still a hobby to Handley when he was Bishop of Durham. Only the evening before he received a letter from him congratulating him on his birthday in 1919, Hardy had been listening to the reading of the fourteenth chapter of the Book of Job. When he heard the words 'all the days of my appointed time will I wait, till my change come', he interrupted and said, 'That was the text of the vicar of Fordington one Sunday evening about 1860.' A later reading of his reply to Handley on this, and on the vicar's heroic work during the cholera years (it is included in his *Life*), must have prompted Hardy to write the poem 'Waiting Both'.

Hardy's friendship with the Moules was strengthened when Handley's eldest brother became interested in him. Henry J. Moule may have visited Higher Bockhampton first when his father thought of renting land from Hardy's father 'for experiments in his well-known hobby of spade husbandry' during the second half of the 1850s. When he died in 1904, Hardy had known him forty-seven years. He remembered him first as he stood by, freely but helpfully criticizing the watercolour he was sketching. 'H. J. M.' was about fifteen years his senior, but such was his enthusiasm for watercolouring that he frequently called at the Hardys', interested perhaps as much in Mary's performance as in Thomas's. They may have encouraged him to talk about his travels in Europe. When Hardy returned home in poor health, after working in London from 1862 to 1867, Henry wrote, advising him to take up a fresh-air career in estate-management. He spent a day or two with Hardy and his wife at Wimborne, and they conversed long into the night, one subject being Emma Hardy's proposal that they should produce a book on Dorset, the text by her husband, the landscape and architectural illustrations by Moule. Correspondence on the subject followed, 'but nothing came of it, there being doubts "if Dorset pure and simple would pay"'. On New Year's Eve 1883 Henry was inspired to write verses on barrows and flint arrow-heads, a copy of which he sent to Hardy, who had touched on the subject in *The Return of the Native*. When, soon after this, both went to live in or near Dorchester, their correspondence declined but their friendship remained steadfast. A man of firm orthodox faith, he and Hardy respected each other too highly to argue controversial differences, and found plenty of common interest in books, antiquities, local history especially, and painting. One of the stories he told Hardy became 'Old Mrs Chundle', and he is remembered in the watercolourist at the opening, though the locality of the fictional setting may not indicate where the tale originated.

It was Horatio Mosley, the fourth of the Moule brothers, however, who had the greatest influence on Hardy in his early years. Handsome and dark-bearded, Horace, as he was known, was about eight years older; he was friendly, popular, scholarly, and a splendid teacher. His father ran a small school for fee-paying pupils at the vicarage, and Horace assisted in their education. He was 'rich in manifold gifts', his brother Handley wrote, played the piano, and had often acted as organist at his father's services from the age of twelve. Why, in 1854, he had moved without a degree from the University of Oxford to Cambridge has never been completely explained, though it seems that his failure to obtain a degree at the second university for several years was due to mathematical shortcomings. It was not until 1867 that he obtained his first degree there; his MA followed in 1873. Pre-eminently he was a classical scholar. At Cambridge his long dissertation *Christian Oratory: An Inquiry into its History during the First Five Centuries* won him the Hulsean Prize in 1858; his work on 'salient points' in the history of the Roman Republic was published two years later as an aid to examination candidates. Handley, who benefited from his tuition in the classics, remembered appreciatively 'his subtle faculty for imparting, along with all due care for grammatical precision, a living interest in the subject-matter, and for shedding an indefinable glamour of the ideal over all we read'. Horace wrote verse, and at the time was already providing reviews and occasional essays for London periodicals. It was owing to his leadership that a group of his father's pupils and his brothers met weekly to discuss literary subjects, and to write prose and verse, from which a selection was published in 1859.

Just how Horace Moule discovered Hardy's educational aspirations and offered to assist him remains uncertain; he was 'always ready to act the tutor in any classical difficulty', Hardy writes with reference to a period when he wished to extend his knowledge of Greek literature. It was his advice probably that led Hardy to begin reading the *Saturday Review* in 1857; he must have found it difficult at first, and far too informatively diversified for regular or exhaustive reading. Founded in November 1855, and written by men of distinction, it supplied surveys of current affairs at home and abroad, with literary reviews, and articles, often vigorously critical and of a sceptical cast, on contemporary thought and tendencies. In 1857 Moule gave Hardy an elementary textbook on experimental science and natural philosophy; the next year, one on the wonders of geology. In the summer, with another friend, they had found time for long walks and talks on books and kindred subjects. It seems likely therefore that Hardy would be conversant with the leading thought of the lecture 'Oxford and the Middle-Class Examinations' which Horace gave in the Town Hall, Dorchester, on 15 November 1858 to members of the local Working Men's

Mutual Improvement Society. Its subject, the recent changes at Oxford which made the University more accessible to the middle classes, was obviously one of the utmost importance to Hardy, who still contemplated a career in the Church. Thirty-five years later his main preoccupation was the final planning of a novel which had for one of its major themes, with Oxford as its background, the opening of university doors to deserving members of the 'working class'.

In all, it seems clear that Horace Moule was anxious to help his father's work and follow him in promoting the educational prospects of the less privileged. The outside activities which he assiduously followed may have been directed by determined efforts to cope with temperamental and private problems. Whether his parents sensed them at this stage or not, it seems unlikely that Hardy did. Away from the safeguards of living with his family and of opportunities which he grasped for taking a lead in altruistic causes, Moule lacked the protection he needed. Whatever the temptations (and he seems to have been drawn to his own sex rather than to women), his brooding created depression, which in the end led to excessive drinking. Early in 1860, when he was living in the Close at Salisbury and preparing two students for entrance examinations at Oxford and Cambridge, one of them noted in his diary that Moule was a dipsomaniac who suffered from DT. Whether Hardy, who visited Salisbury the same year, met him there, or knew anything of his addiction at the time, remains very doubtful. At home Horace found it relatively easy to discipline himself by helping his father, as he loved to do, and it is significant that he gave a lecture on temperance at Fordington in 1861, urging complete abstinence for those who found it difficult to drink in moderation. A year later he played the new organ at Christ Church, the chapel-at-ease near the cavalry barracks in West Fordington.

The friend who accompanied Hardy and Moule in their walks and talks was Hooper Tolbort, a brilliant young linguist who had attended William Barnes's school and owed much to his teaching; he was now apprenticed to his uncle, a Dorchester chemist. As there was no scope for his gifts locally, Horace Moule encouraged him to sit for the Oxford Middle-Class Examinations of 1859; he was placed first out of 900 candidates. Among the books Hardy read as a result of discussions with these two friends, he was most impressed by Walter Bagehot's *Estimates* of 1858, a collection of literary studies, and *Essays and Reviews*, published in 1860. These contributions to progressive religious thought registered very mildly some of the effects on honest theological minds of the 'higher criticism' which originated from historical and scientific analyses of the Bible by university professors in Germany. Seen as a threat to the foundations of the Church of England, the scepticism of their authors towards the miraculous was regarded with such alarm by representatives of the diehard majority that they were branded as 'the seven against Christ'. Hardy's interest may have been excited by reports in the *Dorset County Chronicle* of proceedings against one of them, holder of a benefice in the diocese of Salisbury, because he had 'questioned among other things the eternity of Hell'. By this time Tolbort, with Moule's encouragement, had decided to take the competitive examination for admission to the Indian Civil Service. This he did in 1862 with the highest distinction, gaining first place by a large margin, a feat Hardy thought fit to include in the first short story he wrote, 'Destiny and a Blue Cloak', where it is offered as a proof that competitive examinations would 'put good men in good places' and sweep away 'all bureaucratic jobbery'.

Horace Moule must have regarded Hardy's prospects of academic success less optimistically. He did not realize how keen this young man was to live the life of a scholar. Hardy was working with 'translations at his elbow' on either the *Agamemnon* of Aeschylus or the *Oedipus* of Sophocles, and wished to read more Greek plays. As his father had insisted on his making his own way in architecture by 1862, he sought Moule's counsel, hoping he would advise him to continue his Greek. In the circumstances Horace thought the best course was to further his career in architecture as much as he could. The result was that Hardy, except in a fragmentary way in later years, gave up the study of Greek in the original.

His contract with Hicks had been renewed for a year in 1859 because of his immaturity; he was too youthful to leave home, his parents must have thought. From 1860 he was retained as a paid assistant at fifteen shillings a week. His father undoubtedly wished him to aim at bettering his prospects. This does not imply that he could not afford to keep his son *in statu quo*. His business had expanded, and continued to expand; the 1861 census shows that he employed six full-time assistants; the 1871, eight men and a boy. Hardy did not exaggerate when he stated that his father would not have refused to advance him money had he qualified for a university career.

His purchase of John Keble's *The Christian Year*, a book of poems for all Sundays and holy days, in September 1861, shows that his faith was by no means shaken at this stage of his career; and notes in this, and in his prayer-book and Bible, provide precise evidence of his many church attendances from 1861 to 1863. He had become a great lover of church music, as well as of secular, and his sensitiveness to it is reflected in his poetry, more especially of his later years, when he had acquired the technical skill and the confidence to modulate verse in more subtle variations. *The Christian Year* introduced him to more accomplished devotional poetry than the majority of the hymns he knew, but all the literary forms that had stood the test of time in the Church of England – its hymns, common services, biblical readings, and the new version of the psalms – were to influence his style, both in prose and poetry.

Whether he still hoped to be ordained or not, Hardy had taken Horace Moule's advice to heart, deeming it prudent to save for eventualities, and to pursue in the meantime (as he writes in the *Life*) 'the art and science of architecture on more advanced lines'. A passage beginning with almost these very words in the opening chapter of *Desperate Remedies* suggests his realization that work in Hicks's office had not been altogether sufficiently demanding:

Owen's progress in the art and science of architecture had been very insignificant indeed. Though anything but an idle young man, he had hardly reached the age at which industrious men who lack an external whip to send them on in the world, are induced by their own common sense to whip on themselves. Hence his knowledge of plans, elevations, sections, and specifications, was not greater at the end of two years of probation than might easily have been acquired in six months by a youth of average ability – himself, for instance – amid a bustling London practice.

When Hardy left by rail on Thursday, 17 April 1862, to find work with a leading London architect, he was almost 22. He had at last decided that it was time to leave home, and he had made preparations for this, perhaps on his parents' advice, by living for some time, except at weekends, in Dorchester, 'either with Hicks or at lodgings'. Pessimistically provident, he bought a return ticket to ensure his ability to travel back should he reach the end of his financial resources. Finding no use for it within the six months of its validity, he threw it away.

6

Arthur Blomfield and London

'Wait till you have walked the streets a few weeks. . . . Only practical men are wanted here', Hardy was told by a bachelor, who looked him up and down when he inquired for lodgings on the afternoon of his arrival in London. He seems to have found accommodation very quickly, nevertheless: at 3 Clarence Place, Kilburn, to the north-west of Regent's Park, and on the edge of the country. He soon found he liked the High Church services at St Mary's, Kilburn, and he and his room-mate Shaw, a young architect from a socially superior home, became good friends. At Kilburn toll-gate he could catch an omnibus which would take him via the Edgware Road into the city, or to Hyde Park, or for visits to Kensington.

He had at least two introductory letters which he hoped would help him to obtain the kind of work for which he was qualified. The one addressed to Benjamin Ferrey of Trinity Place, Charing Cross, the architect for whom Hardy's father had worked at Stafford House, seemed the more promising. He received Hardy politely, remembered his father, and promised assistance, but there the matter ended. The second recommendation was from John Hicks to his friend John Norton (Ferrey's former pupil) of Old Bond Street; they had known each other in Bristol. Norton behaved with exemplary thoughtfulness and generosity; he had no vacancy but, rather than have such a youthful-looking stranger to London left with time on his hands, he invited him to draw in his office until he found regular employment. When Hardy arrived to begin on Monday, 28 April, Norton informed him that a friend he had met at the Royal Institute of British Architects had told him he needed 'a young Gothic draughtsman who could restore and design churches and rectory-houses'. Having already recommended Hardy, he sent him off at once to St Martin's Place near Trafalgar Square, where Hardy was engaged to start work the following Monday at a salary of £110 a year.

59

His new employer, Arthur William Blomfield, was a man of considerable prowess and distinction. His father, formerly Bishop of Chester and for many years a friend of Wordsworth, had been Bishop of London for nearly thirty years, ill-health causing him to retire in 1856, not long before his death. Arthur, his fourth son, had been educated at Rugby and Trinity College, Cambridge, where he was remembered particularly for his energy and rowing achievements. He was handsome, witty, genial, engaging, and versatile: a good singer, a watercolourist, and a talented actor. At the age of 33, he was now President of the Architectural Association. This position and his Church of England background helped to bring him many valuable commissions, chiefly in the designing and restoration of churches. His personal qualities brought him many social engagements. Frequently out of his office, he required assistants whom he could trust. He would know in a very short time what an able recruit he had in Thomas Hardy, whose architectural work was usually well-finished and very reliable, but he was quick to discover what other interests they had in common, especially in the Church and music. It speaks highly of his personality and understanding that he could create general harmony in his office, and a sense of security in a rather diffident newcomer, conscious of social shortcomings in himself which he could hardly disguise. Hardy was drawn to Blomfield, and their friendship lasted many years, until the latter's death.

Not many weeks passed before Hardy summoned up courage to visit Mrs Martin, the lady of Kingston Maurward House whose petting and vicariously maternal affection had kindled his boyhood love. She and her husband, who had continued his meteorological work and was now a fellow of the Royal Geographical Society, lived at 14 Bruton Street, off Berkeley Square. Hardy's sense of inferiority, which was to grow into his 'poor man and the lady' complex, must have increased uncomfortably as he approached; perhaps he was relieved when the door opened to recognize the butler who had served the same family at Stinsford and looked little different. He was taken aback, however, by the changes which time had wrought in 'the lady of his dreams', remembering them three years later in his poem 'Amabel'. The shock of this experience was unforgettable, and he recalled it imaginatively at the end of *Two on a Tower*. So ill at ease was he during their meeting that, for emotional and social reasons, he did not venture to call again. They corresponded at intervals, and he kept five of her letters. The first seems to have been written after the Martins had left London; they were in England a few months, and she invited him to stay a few days with them at Winchester. In 1872 he sent her a copy of *Under the Greenwood Tree*. Then, after hearing of the success of *Far from the Madding Crowd*, she asked him to send news of himself and his sisters and family. From Lyndhurst, where the Martins finally settled, she wrote in 1887 requesting copies of his novels for a welfare home in which she took an interest. On receiving eight volumes, she asked if he could send, at the lower rate his publishers charged him, copies of all his novels except *Under the Greenwood Tree*, which she had already; this set was intended for the village library. She was obviously rather poor by this time, and her repeated assertion that *Far from the Madding Crowd* was 'the best book of the age' after J. H. Shorthouse's *John Inglesant* testifies to the religious nature which she shared with Lady Constantine in *Two on a Tower*. She invited him to come, meet Miss Braddon, and see the New Forest. Then, as earlier, he did not comply. His early failure to do so may have been to his disadvantage, for the Martins were well connected, and Mrs Martin's cousin Hamilton Aidé, a successful poet and novelist, attracted many famous people to Lyndhurst.

Hardy's move to London was to prove the most important of his career; he made it not just for professional advancement but also for educational and cultural enrichment. In retrospect he thought the timing of his 'migration' had been influenced by exciting prospects of the International Exhibition at South Kensington. It was to last six months, opening on 1 May, when a choir of 4000 sang Tennyson's ode for the occasion to the music of Sterndale Bennett. Lines had been added to the first draft in honour of its patron Prince Albert, who had died the previous December; it was largely owing to his influence that the first of these international exhibitions had taken place at the Crystal Palace in 1851. Their displays of industrial achievement and expertise were important for trade, but their immense appeal came from a wide range of exhibits, from the new photography to ancient jewellery found in an Egyptian tomb. Hardy was drawn again and again to the galleries where excellent selections of English, French, Dutch, Flemish, and German painters were on view, stimulating a life-interest that would have important consequences for his fiction. His first surviving letter, written from Kilburn on 17 August 1862, informs his sister Mary, who was still at her Salisbury training-college, that he usually attended the exhibition two or three evenings a week, before working in the reading-room at Kensington Museum. He had 'found' their cousin Martha Sparks, then employed as a lady's maid in London, and had taken her there one evening. Evidently he was busy, for he had not attended a theatre since Mary was with him in the capital. He admired the beauty of St Thomas's Church, Salisbury, and hopes she will visit it, if she has not already done so, before she leaves college. A postscript indicates that he has had to interrupt his letter to hear and comment on extracts read from Ruskin's *Modern Painters* by his friend Shaw.

With Horace Moule, who had been in London the previous week, he had attended an evening service at a Roman Catholic chapel designed by Pugin, before having supper together at the Old Hummums hotel. A painting by Gérôme which they had seen together at the Exhibition inspired Moule to write the poem 'Ave Caesar', which appeared in *Once a Week* on 6 September. Hardy had found time, no doubt, to visit important buildings in London as soon as he could. He went further afield, making excursions to Windsor Castle, which he sketched on 24 August, his interest heightened by memories of Harrison Ainsworth's novel, and, in September, to Dover, where he sketched a scene for watercolouring. In the autumn he would meet Hooper Tolbort, fresh from his success in the Indian Civil Service examination, either at his lodgings or at the Marylebone Library and Scientific Institution, where his friend busied himself translating 'into and from dead and living languages'.

Attending perhaps with Shaw or with Martha Sparks, Hardy danced at Willis's (or Almack's as it was traditionally known from the eighteenth century) in 1862, when 'the pretty Lancers and Caledonians were still footed there to the original charming tunes . . . and every movement was a correct quadrille step and gesture'. The following year when new types of dancing became the craze, and regular customers objected to 'plebeian' invasions and uproar, balls were discontinued. Fippard's account at Hicks's office of his dancing experiences at the Argyle Rooms near Piccadilly Circus and the Cremorne Gardens near Battersea Bridge made it imperative for Hardy to visit these popular and notorious haunts, which acted as magnets to moneyed prostitute-seeking men. He danced so little at either that, when he wrote his *Life*, he wondered whether he had danced there at all. He had seen for himself, and heard enough from Fippard and London friends, two of whom worked in Benjamin Ferrey's office, to conjure up many years later vivid, exciting scenes at both, together with tone and atmosphere, in the imaginative creation of his poem 'Reminiscences of a Dancing Man'. He could have associated 'the Prince of Sin' with either, but his main subject is dancing to the music of the French composer Jullien, the platform throbbing to wild quadrilles at Cremorne as the gas-jets wink and the lustres clink, and to the thunderous polka tunes in the crowded smoky rooms at the Argyle. In a fit of enthusiasm Hardy bought an old violin, with which he accompanied a pianist at his lodgings in selections from romantic operas at Covent Garden and the Queen's Theatre, Haymarket, which they attended sometimes two or three times a week, so becoming familiar with such great singers as Mario, Tietjens, Nilsson, Patti (then new to the scene), Giuglini, and Parepa. Florence Hardy records that hearing *Il Trovatore* near the end of his life reminded him of his first year in London, when he was strong and active, and enjoyed life immensely.

The fact that Mary Hardy treasured and preserved several of the letters her brother wrote to her during these London years affords striking testimony to the affection that existed between them. They are unusually informative. Writing to her on 3 November 1862, he tells her not to return copies of the *Saturday Review*. In January she would be teaching at Denchworth in Berkshire. If she brought them to Higher Bockhampton, they would be available whenever he wanted them. He expected to be home for a brief period at Christmas, and might bring his friend Shaw for a day or two. Hardy had been given two tickets to attend a *conversazione* in the Architectural Association rooms, one by Blomfield and the other by a committee member; he had invited Shaw, who lent him a dress coat for the occasion. They found themselves among a gathering of three or four hundred, including many ladies 'in full dress'. After 'much speechifying from learned professors', there was music, followed by coffee in cups which seemed unusually small to Hardy. Blomfield proposed his membership, and he was elected later in November. His father and Miss A—— (probably the aunt of Mary's college friend from Dorchester) had come to see him in London, and he had taken them to the opera *Lurline* at Covent Garden. One morning when she was seeking a post, his father started out alone; they were to meet at the Monument.

Finding he had time to spare, he had climbed to the top, before setting off with her to the Thames Tunnel, which he was anxious to examine with a builder's eye.

It is not known how long Hardy stayed at home that Christmas, whether he brought Shaw with him, whether he revived his violin-playing at parties or visited relatives at Puddletown, or whether, as seems unlikely, he saw Louisa Harding. On this shy acquaintanceship the texts of Hardy's *Life* (complicated by post-humous revision made on the advice of J. M. Barrie) are so bewilderingly at variance that the truth can never be known. One tells us that 'he used to meet her down to his twenty-third or twenty-fourth year on his visits to Dorset from London'. Another refers to the poem 'To Louisa in the Lane', written not many years before his death, and to her 'nameless green mound' in 'Mellstock' churchyard which 'was visited more than once by one to whom a boyish dream had never lost its radiance'. The poem, written after her death, shows the nature of the dream; like 'The Passer-By', it reveals his belief that she loved him; additionally it expresses hope in their spiritual reunion on earth after his death. Against this, the *Life* presents the story of their meeting in 'the hollow of the lane', as he was walking from Dorchester towards Bockhampton Cross, and of his being so overcome by bashfulness that he could say no more than 'Good evening' as they passed. The account closes with 'That "Good evening" was the only word that passed between them.'

If Hardy's Christmas stay at home was brief, it was probably because he was anxious to complete an essay for which he had been researching at the South Kensington Museum (then housed in iron sheds nicknamed 'the Brompton Boilers'), hoping to win the silver medal awarded by the Royal Institute of British Architects. Four alternative subjects had been set, and he had chosen 'On the Application of Coloured Bricks and Terra Cotta to Modern Architecture'. Perhaps he thought that his self-extenuating Latin motto (which could never have been submitted in English), '*Tentavi quid in eo genere possem*', would be placatory. In February 1863, while Hardy was anxiously waiting to hear the result, Blomfield moved from St Martin's Place, within earshot of St Martin's bells, to lighter and more commodious first-floor rooms at 8 Adelphi Terrace. 'We can see from our windows right across the Thames, and on a clear day every bridge is visible. Everybody says that we have a beautiful place', Hardy informed his sister. In the same

letter of 19 February he tells Mary that he is very busy designing a
country mansion in another prize competition. He had been giving
thought to this since December, when the plan for its imaginary
site was exhibited at a meeting of the Architectural Association. He
was clearly ambitious to succeed as an architect at this stage.

The prizes which had been offered by William Tite for this
competition were worth three pounds and two pounds, and not
surprisingly there were very few competitors. Hardy won the first,
and received two books at a meeting of the Architectural Association in April, both on early French Gothic, a subject in which his
interest had been roused by Arthur Blomfield; they were William
Nesfield's *Specimens of Mediaeval Architecture* and Norman Shaw's
Sketches from the Continent. Hardy's interest in the first was to
dictate his choice of Henry Knight's itinerary in northern France
after his desertion of the heroine in *A Pair of Blue Eyes*. His success
in the RIBA competition had been announced in March, but he did
not receive his medal until 18 May, when it was presented by the
President, T. L. Donaldson, at a general meeting of the Institute.
He was chagrined to hear that he had not dealt sufficiently with
the subject, and astonished to learn that he had virtually overlooked the use of 'moulded and shaped' bricks. As he had not seen
the second announcement which added this item to the original
subject, Hardy wrote in explanation, hoping he would be allowed
to extend his essay and thereby qualify for the additional cash
prize of ten pounds which had been denied him. He was informed
that the sum had been reserved for a prize on the same subject the
following year, and that he was eligible to submit another essay
then. He had been tricked by chance.

About this time, perhaps, Hardy witnessed an example of how
artistic theory can be based, even by a famous architect, on a
misinterpretation of simple fact; he recorded it with concealed
amusement in 'Memories of Church Restoration' more than forty
years later. George Gilbert Scott was giving a peripatetic lecture to
a group of young architects in Westminster Abbey.

He, at the top of a ladder, was bringing to our notice a feature
which had, he said, perplexed him for a long time, why the
surface of diapered stone before him should suddenly be discontinued at the spot he pointed out, when there was every reason
for carrying it on. Possibly the artist had decided that to break
the surface was a mistake; possibly he had died; possibly any-

thing; but there the mystery was. 'Perhaps it is only plastered over', cried the reedy voice of the youngest pupil in our group. 'Well, that's what I never thought of', replied [Scott], and taking from his pocket a clasp knife which he carried for such purposes, he prodded the plain surface with it. 'Yes, it *is* plastered over, and all my theories are wasted', he continued, descending the ladder not without humility.

Hardy's letter of 19 February 1863 shows that he was sending copies of the *Saturday Review* regularly to his sister at Denchworth. Her playing the organ at church was of special interest to him; she had been very nervous when called on to play a pedalled instrument with two manuals, but she found she could manage with practice, and became the regular organist. Hardy asks if Kate (who was only six) is coming to live with her. Both sisters wanted each other's company, and their mother consented; Mary lived conveniently near her school (and church), and it would be better for Kate to attend with her than to walk in all weathers between Higher and Lower Bockhampton. In London, Hardy told his sister, there were great preparations for the arrival of Princess Alexandra of Denmark, who was to marry Edward, Prince of Wales, at St George's Chapel, Windsor, on 10 March. The royal couple would drive in procession, after travelling by train from Gravesend, over London Bridge, via Fleet Street, the Strand, Charing Cross, Pall Mall, Piccadilly, Hyde Park, and Edgware Road, to Paddington Station for Windsor. That evening people swarmed in the streets and open spaces of London to see the illuminations, Hardy among them. Six people were killed in the crush near the Mansion House after he left that vicinity; in Bond Street his waistcoat buttons were torn off and his ribs 'bent in' before he could escape into a doorway.

The sketch which Hardy made of a crowded beach on Good Friday at Brighton suggests that he spent a few days there at the beginning of April; late in the same month he was at Denchworth, where he sketched the church on the 26th. His watercolour of St James's Park shows that he was back in London two days later. About this time he moved from Kilburn to 16 Westbourne Park Villas, north of Kensington and west of Paddington. In this high, three-storeyed house, he occupied a rear room on the second floor, overlooking gardens and stables and the spire of St Stephen's Church, a view which he sketched in 1866. The reason for the move may have been that he wanted a room where he could study more strenuously; he may have wished to be more conveniently placed for his activities in London or for travel outside. One suggestion is that his cousin Martha Sparks or one of her brothers lived not far away; another, that perhaps he was already friendly with Eliza Nicholls, a lady's maid who lived near until the late summer. Her mistress, wife of the barrister C. R. Hoare, was the daughter of Lieutenant-Colonel John Mansel of Smedmore House near Kimmeridge Bay, Dorset. For several years Eliza had lived by the bay while her father served as a coastguard; late in the 1850s an operation had compelled him to retire, and he had moved to his wife's birthplace at Findon in Sussex. On 3 September Hardy sketched Gad Cliff and Worbarrow Bay, a few miles west of Kimmeridge Bay. It is possible that the Hoares were on holiday at Smedmore House at the time, and had taken Eliza Nicholls with them, and that he had travelled down from London to meet her. His sketch of Dorchester from Stinsford Hill, dated September, suggests that he was on his way home for a holiday.

Whatever the reasons for his removal to Westbourne Park Villas, Hardy began studying in earnest as soon as he settled there. It had been suggested, probably by Horace Moule, 'that he might combine literature with architecture by becoming an art-critic for the press, particularly in the province of architectural art'. On 12 May 1863, with this in distant prospect, he began a groundwork study of the schools of painting, recording facts, often with individual characteristics, very briefly for reference and recall. His interest in pictures, at home and abroad, never failed. When he had given up his plan to be an art critic, he followed for several months a self-imposed course at the National Gallery, devoting twenty minutes after lunch, whenever it was open, to the study of the masters purely for their intrinsic merits, and restricting himself to one each visit. Such a method, he maintained, would furnish greater insight into schools and styles than any guidebook.

Evidence that Hardy intended to devote more time to reading, and to study with writing in view, is not hard to find. He acquired an edition of Shakespeare in ten volumes, worked systematically through much of Samuel Neil's *The Art of Reasoning*, and studied method in effective composition, sending his 'analyses' to Horace Moule, who, on 2 July 1863, complimented him on them, being specially interested in his conclusions on the style of *The Times*. He did not recommend imitation; one should not read for style but for thoughts. In the end an author must write his own style; if he is full of his subject, he had 'only to pay that attention to method and arrangement which is obvious to any mind of vigorous tone, in order to write well'. He counsels him to jot down 'in brief concentrated form' every thought that occurs to him on a particular subject, then, after a day or two, look them over and arrange them 'into heads'. One result of this advice may be found in the frequent notes of a brief sententious kind which Hardy chose to include in his *Life* for the years 1865–7. Writing from Dorchester again in February 1864, Moule discussed the use of the subjunctive with Hardy, and recommended him to become a London correspondent for some country newspaper; his 'chatty description of the Law Courts and their denizens' was '*just* in the style that would go down'. Moule had sent G. Smith's essay on American slavery, thinking his style '*very* good' and his 'vigour in argument first rate', as if after all something could be learned on the art of composition from the works of the best writers.

A curious example of Hardy's studious application in 1863 is afforded by the notes he made on basic psychology in *The Passions of the Human Soul*, a translation of a work by the French social theorist Charles Fourier. They take the form of an analytical summary followed by illustrative diagrams, one showing the intellect and the will serpentining round the trunk of the passions, another presenting the passions at the core of the tree, the intellect and the will being secondary or outer tissues, all three passing from a chaotic stage when they are 'impossible monsters' (coinciding with the 19–40 age-range of the third diagram, it seems) to one of flowering 'moral harmony' from which ramify the 'affectives' of friendship, love, 'familism' (flowering or fructifying), and ambition. With further analyses of physical energy and sensuous awareness, of the emotions, and of intellect and will, the whole may have helped Hardy basically when he studied the working of character in fiction. He absorbed something useful from it, but must, sooner rather than later, have found it too chronologically clear-cut and questionable to remain the guide he seems to have thought it initially when he headed his diagrammatic page 'Human Passion, Mind, and Character'.

As Hardy's letter to Mary just before Christmas discloses, he had been reading some of Thackeray's novels, believing him to be the greatest novelist of the time, on the assumption that the novel ought to be 'a perfect and truthful representation of actual life'. As these novels 'often have anything but an elevating tendency', he thinks they are 'particularly unfitted for young people'. He recommends *Vanity Fair*. (Hardy's judgement seems to have been directed by the traditional axiom that art should instruct as well as please, and it is clear that his view of the novel, apart from any bearing it had on Thackeray, was to change considerably before he could claim in 'The Profitable Reading of Fiction' that in its highest form it is, like other artistic modes, 'more true . . . than history or nature can be'.) He had been working at shorthand, and could now manage 40 words a minute. Whether he was thinking of journalism in his spare time or of making notes from speeches or from books for self-improvement is not clear. He obviously felt that he and his sister needed a holiday; he expected to see her at Higher Bockhampton when he arrived after Christmas, and added: 'We must have a "bit of a lark".'

He had played an important part in designing All Saints', New Windsor. For this reason he was present when the foundation stone was laid on 21 November by the Crown Princess of Germany, formerly Princess Royal of England. Blomfield handed the trowel but, finding her glove smeared with mortar, she soon returned it, hastily whispering 'Take it. Take it!', an incident which Hardy fictionalized in 'An Indiscretion in the Life of an Heiress'. Blomfield's *bonhomie* and personal interest in his assistants and pupils ensured that a genial atmosphere prevailed in his office, but there must still have been times when Hardy felt, or was made to feel, his social inferiority. His ability and the friendly interest his master took in him earned him respect nevertheless, and he was quick to realize the bravado or affected masculinity of juniors, most of them from public schools, who pretended to be *au fait* with 'romantic or risqué details' concerning women of ill-repute. As he could read music, he became a welcome member of Blomfield's office choir, one result of their practices being the occasional singing of glees and catches during their work hours. Such was the master's enthusiasm that, in the absence of a good alto, he sometimes urged Hardy, if he met one in the Strand, to invite him to join them. At his request, Hardy joined him in the choir of his church, St Matthias's, Richmond, for the special service inaugurating the organ, which was played by one of his pupils.

The London Hardy first knew belonged to the age of Dickens and Thackeray. 'Judge and Jury' mock trials supplied entertainment of a vulgar and even blatantly indecent kind at the Coal Hole and the Cider Cellars. Temple Bar still stood. Hungerford market, where he occasionally lunched at a coffee-house, was to become the site of Charing Cross Station; from his room at Adelphi Terrace he could watch the construction of the Hungerford railway bridge and of the Thames Embankment. Sometimes he lunched or dined with his friends from Ferrey's office at Bertolini's, once the home of Sir Isaac Newton, where Tennyson had dined with his friends, and Swinburne with 'The Cannibal Club'. Evans's popular underground supper-rooms, where 'respectable' people were not infrequently seen the worse for drink, still existed in Covent Garden, and Hardy visited them at least once. On his way to Adelphi Terrace he was pleased to catch sight of famous prize-fighters behind their liquor bars in the region of Seven Dials. Charles Kean and his wife still performed Shakespeare at the Princess's Theatre, and the comedian Buckstone, actor-manager since 1853, played the leading part in *The American Cousin* at the Haymarket. Many changes were to take place before Hardy left London, often heightening contrasts between splendid new buildings and much that remained old and squalid. Nothing served to accentuate the gulf between rich and poor more than Hyde Park in summer, when the aristocracy and the *nouveaux riches* flaunted their illusions of grandeur in elegant carriage parades, a colourful and satirical view of which Hardy adapted to *A Pair of Blue Eyes*, after sketching it for his unpublished novel *The Poor Man and the Lady*.

Victorian fiction, such as *Jane Eyre*, had given a semblance of ratification to the fashionable phrenology of Franz Gall, and it was far from discredited when Hardy, on 21 September 1864, submitted his cranial 'bumps' to the inspection of Dr Donovan at 111 Strand. The report he received was neither consistent nor very flattering, though it gave credit for language and tune sense. Even so, brief passages in three of Hardy's novels, including an explicit reference to Gall towards the end of *The Trumpet-Major*, suggest that he did not altogether discount such 'phrenological theory'.

Mary Hardy had written from Denchworth on 19 May, describing a visit she had made to Fawley in Berkshire. She thought it a pretty village, among the finest hills she had ever seen. The people were original and hearty. In her search for relatives of her grandmother, she had found one Head family living there, but no such name in the churchyard. The parish clerk referred to two brothers of that name who had been 'well-to-do' farmers in a neighbouring hamlet. One had left his bride the day after their wedding, and nothing more was heard of him until he returned in his old age. (With this story the first seed of *Jude the Obscure* was sown.) Steps were being taken to demolish the old church and start building the new, Mary added. Hardy was so interested that he went there (from Denchworth, no doubt) and sketched the old church in the autumn. He joined his family for Christmas, but spent the evening of Boxing Day at Puddletown with his cousin Nathaniel Sparks, home from Rode in Somerset, where he worked as a carpenter and repaired violins in his spare time; earlier that day they had walked with friends 'on George Wood's farm', north of his home at Athelhampton Hall. On New Year's Day 1865, Hardy received from Horace Moule a copy of *Thoughts of the Emperor M. Aurelius Antoninus*, inscribed with a maxim of the author which was to solace him in times of stress, 'This is the chief thing: Be not perturbed; for all things are according to the nature of the universal.'

As son of the late Bishop of London, Blomfield was requested by the Church to ensure that, before cuttings were made through city churchyards for railroad construction, human remains were removed and duly interred. *Sed quis custodiet ipsos custodes*? Having reason to fear that this had not happened in one area, he set a clerk-of-works on duty when hundreds of coffins and bones in huge quantities were removed from St Pancras churchyard, and deputed Hardy to check at irregular evening hours, he himself to 'drop in' at any time to ascertain that 'neither his assistant nor the clerk-of-works was a defaulter'. One late autumn, therefore, at nightfall, Hardy watched exhumations by the light of flare-lamps and saw 'mournful processions' of coffined and uncoffined skeletons carried away, among them fragmented assemblages in new coffins. Once when Blomfield was with him a coffin fell apart, disclosing a skeleton and two skulls. Hardy must have remembered such macabre whims of fate when, thinking of restorations of the minster and of the graveyard reburials which followed, he wrote 'The Levelled Churchyard' at Wimborne in 1882.

His master was ready to confide in him. One morning when he arrived he found Blomfield looking fixedly at the drawing of a newly completed church on the opposite wall. 'Hardy', he said, 'that tower has fallen.' It was a serious business, a well-known architect having been imprisoned a few years earlier when one of his buildings fell, killing people nearby. Blomfield's plan was vindicated, for the tower was rebuilt exactly to the original design, and was standing 'without a crack' more than fifty years later when Hardy wrote the early part of his *Life*. Unfortunately it is not known how much original work Hardy was allowed to undertake or, with complete certainty, for what churches. Blomfield's commissions were so numerous that much of Hardy's work must have been too repetitively mechanical to excite more than routine interest in the long run.

By 1865 his zest for architecture had already cooled, and he was devoting more and more time to literary pursuits. At the end of 1864 he had sent his sly and amusing satirical narrative sketch 'How I Built Myself a House' to the editor of *Chambers's Journal*, where it appeared anonymously on 18 March. Horace Moule had given him a copy of Francis Palgrave's *The Golden Treasury* in January 1862, soon after its publication, and the interest this anthology kindled made Hardy buy several volumes of the poets in 1865. The study of language and literature, and the writing of verse were soon to become his prime avocation.

There were two memorable events for Hardy in 1865. The first occurred when he joined the crowd below the hustings near the front of St Paul's in Covent Garden to hear the philosopher John Stuart Mill, whose essay *On Liberty* he greatly admired, addressing a crowd as the Liberal candidate for Westminster at the general election. Mill stood bareheaded and pale, as if perilously exposed and out of place, so dissimilar in style and appearance was he to the usual demagogue. Most of his audience understood little of what he said, but they were not wholly unimpressed by his earnestness and sincerity. In this respect, Hardy, who long remembered the clear cameo relief of his face and large brow against the blue shadow cast by a church 'which, on its transcendental side, his doctrines antagonized', may have associated him with Clym Yeobright and his 'sermons on the mount' at the end of *The Return of the Native*. The second occasion was grander and more solemn, when the famous statesman Lord Palmerston was buried at Westminster Abbey on 27 October. Indirectly through Blomfield, Hardy and two of his office colleagues had obtained tickets which admitted them to the triforium. The next day he wrote to his sister Mary, describing the event in great detail, and supplying architectural sketches to indicate how fortunately placed they had been to see the whole ceremony; he had never been 'so much impressed', and wouldn't have missed it for anything. Knowing how keenly interested as an organist she would be in the music, he mentioned the most memorable items: the singing of the opening sentences to Croft, Beethoven's Funeral March during the procession from the choir to the vault, and the Dead March in *Saul* at the close. As his father had taken to reading newspapers, he had sent him one on Palmerston's life, and was sending him another on the funeral. He had posted her a copy of *Barchester Towers*, which was considered the best of Trollope's novels, and recommended Bulwer-Lytton's *Pelham*.

Hardy agreed with Mill on liberty of thought and expression, but he was cautious, and preferred not to voice emergent beliefs which ran counter to convention and orthodoxy until he had reached conviction. He was still searching for the truth which, in the words of the evangelist St John (one of Hardy's favourite maxims years later), would make him free. He was always to love the Church for the combined aesthetic appeal of its music, words, and architecture, and, it should be stressed, for 'the beauty of holiness' which its hymns, prayers, psalms, and biblical readings continually conveyed. The virtues it preached remained for him the bedrock of western civilization, but its theological dogma had been left in a limbo of inert acceptance and dubiety ever since he had read Darwin, *Essays and Reviews*, and books on new scientific discovery and thought. Before resolving his religious dilemma, he thought it prudent to read John Henry Newman's *Apologia*, fervently wishing to be convinced by him because Horace Moule liked him so much. He found his style charming but his logic unsatisfactory, his thought proceeding too much by way of 'converging probabilities'. As time went on he was to find much surer foundations for his developing beliefs in a philosopher whose leading views J. S. Mill already supported. This was the French sociologist Auguste Comte, who had died in 1857, and whose works were being systematically translated into English. His fundamental argument was that, having no assurance of life after death, we should concentrate our efforts on the amelioration of life here on earth. The volume, *A General View of Positivism*, came out in 1865, and Moule's copy of it afforded Hardy his first glimpses of a 'religion of humanity' which aimed at the zealous promotion of justice, altruism, and the raising of standards for all through education and science.

Edward Beesly, professor of history at University College and one of the translators of Comte's works, was a prominent member of the Reform League which held its meetings on the ground floor below Blomfield's office. The extremism of this radical group led it to invite Swinburne to stand as a parliamentary candidate. Blomfield's pupils, 'Tory and Churchy young men', in Hardy's words, used to indulge their 'satire at the League's expense', in their master's absence, by 'letting down ironical bits of paper on the heads of members' until their resident secretary intervened and the practical jokers had to apologize.

So much did Hardy wish to learn and achieve that it is no wonder he wrote on his twenty-fifth birthday: 'Not very cheerful. Feel as if I had lived a long time and done very little.' By the summer of 1865 he had dedicated himself chiefly to poetry. 'For nearly or quite' the last two years of his stay in London he read no prose except newspapers and weekly reviews. As 'the essence of all imaginative and emotional literature' was to be found in poetry, he decided to read nothing but verse. He 'preferred Scott the poet to Scott the novelist', and thought *Marmion* the most Homeric poem in the English language. He found much to admire in Byron's *Childe Harold* and Tennyson's *In Memoriam*, and read even Wordsworth's *Excursion*. Though he never ceased to marvel at the wealth of Shakespeare's linguistic and imaginative resources, the poet with whom he became most sympathetic was Shelley. When he wrote on 23 August 1865, 'The poetry of a scene varies with the minds of the perceivers. Indeed, it does not lie in the scene at all', he was formulating and unconsciously repeating an old philosophical thought with which Shelley agreed when he concluded, in a passage brought to Hardy's notice by Bagehot's essays, 'that nothing exists but as it is perceived'. Such was Hardy's enthusiasm that he gave talks on poets and poetry to Blomfield's pupils and assistants when time permitted or was made for such occasions. It says much for his intelligent appreciation of poetry, and for his relations with his colleagues, that he could find such a willing audience.

Hardy's contemporary notebooks indicate that he aimed at being a writer. They served to familiarize him with appealing quotations and words from many poets, for several of whom *The Golden Treasury* was his main source. They include sketches and reminders of things seen and heard, outlines of stories, and even suggestions for ballads, with first-draft stanzas. Clearly he is intent on fashioning his own style, both in prose and verse. He notes less common distinctions of meaning produced by adverbial additions to common verbs, initiates word-inventions of analogous types, and pays attention to special word usage in the Old Testa-

ment and the *Book of Common Prayer*. As some of his early poems
confirm, he seems to have decided to draw his poetic language
from the deep well of literary tradition. Yet, however preoccupied
he was in 'the practice and study of English poetry', he worked
assiduously through course-work in French readings and translations for a term or two from October 1865, under the excellent
tuition of a 'most charming' Frenchman, Professor Stièvenard, at
King's College. He was to draw from the French language for his
poetry, and derive pleasure and instruction from the reading of
French works, especially for *The Dynasts*.

He was still friendly with Eliza Nicholls, and spent his 1866
Whitsun holiday with her at Findon, where he sketched the church.
More important, it was there that Hardy saw for himself the
knackery business which provided details for the hauntingly macabre scene in *The Hand of Ethelberta* where the heroine and her sister
discover the source of Neigh's income. Eliza may have inspired the
thought of 'The Musing Maiden', one of several poems Hardy
wrote at Westbourne Park Villas in 1866. On 6 June he visited
Hatfield for the first time since he stayed there with his mother,
and found it much changed; he 'regretted that the beautiful sunset
did not occur in a place of no reminiscences', so that he could have
enjoyed it 'without their tinge'. He was becoming reflective and
sententious. The future novelist is seen in a note which gives
priority to the particular over the general, and in such thoughts as
(on the last day of 1865): 'To insects the twelvemonth has been an
epoch, to leaves a life, to tweeting birds a generation, to man a
year', and (later): 'The defects of a class are more perceptible to the
class immediately below it than to itself.' With this we have the
first hint of one aspect of *The Poor Man and the Lady*.

Hardy's early poetry shows conclusively that by 1866 he had
jettisoned his belief in the Providence of his early Christian faith.
With it he gave up the idea of being ordained, towards which, as
he says, 'he had long had a leaning', and of combining a rural
curacy, like that of Barnes, with the writing of poetry. After
studying *The Students' Guide* to the University of Cambridge (and
information sent with it from Cambridge, at his request, by Horace
Moule), he concluded that he did not wish to wait for at least three
years before being admitted, and that for conscientious reasons he
could no longer think of taking a degree to qualify for the Church.
He could not reconcile the views of the precociously scientific
Shelley in *Queen Mab* and *The Revolt of Islam* with Christian

theology, and his enthusiasm for Swinburne's poetry shattered his respect for narrow Victorian puritanism and the denial of life preached by the Church. His poem 'A Singer Asleep' recalls how he read from the first volume of *Poems and Ballads* as he walked down a terraced street whose pavements reflected the summer sunshine into his eyes; his letter of 1 April 1897 to Swinburne suggests that *Atalanta in Calydon* may have been one of the poet's 'early works' which he read during this 'buoyant' period of impassioned revolt, as he walked 'along the crowded London streets' at the 'imminent risk of being knocked down'.

His interest in the theatre increased. He had seen Samuel Phelps in *Othello* and greatly admired his Falstaff. During the winter of 1866–7 he saw this ageing actor in a series of Shakespeare's plays at Drury Lane, with Helen Faucit (Lady Martin) in *Macbeth* and *Cymbeline*. Often accompanied by one of Blomfield's pupils, he sat in the pit with an edition of the text supported on the barrier in front of the orchestra – a severe test for any actor who noticed them, he thought. Later he said that he studied Shakespeare more closely from the age of 23 to 26 than at any other time; like the architect-poet and hero of *Desperate Remedies* who 'despises the pap-and-daisy school of verse', he became familiar with 'the very dregs of the foot-notes'. The following spring he was so moved by the performance of Mrs Scott-Siddons, a descendant of the famous actress Mrs Siddons, in *As You Like It* that he wrote the sonnet 'To an Impersonator of Rosalind'.

By this time, as may be seen in another sonnet, 'To an Actress', Hardy regarded his architectural duties as mere 'formal journeywork'. He no longer wished to seek advancement in his profession, 'caring for life as an emotion rather than for life as a science of climbing'. In practice this means he preferred a literary career. His new ambition was to write blank-verse plays, and with this in mind he thought of spending six to twelve months as a stage supernumerary. He sought the advice of Mark Lemon, editor of *Punch*, friend of Dickens, and an ardent amateur actor, and of Mr Coe, stage-manager of the Haymarket 'under Buckstone's lesseeship'. The former could not recommend any association with the professional theatre, and Hardy's first sight of stage realities made him abandon his theatrical dream. His uncollected poem 'A Victorian Rehearsal' suggests greater tragedy in the unattractive and tangled life of actors and actresses than in the play they are rehearsing. His only appearance on the stage was in a Covent

Garden programme which began on 26 December 1866, his performance being limited to the part of a 'nondescript' in Gilbert à Beckett's pantomine *Ali Baba and the Forty Thieves*, and in the harlequinade which followed, an Oxford and Cambridge boat-race scene in which young men introduced fashions for 1867 (by Samuel Brothers of Ludgate Hill) as they mingled with ballet ladies in a 'grand University Revel'. This opportunity to observe stage practicalities would not have arisen had not the man who produced iror.-work for Blomfield's churches undertaken to make the 'machinery' for the pantomime.

During the last year or so Hardy's interest in opera and concerts had been maintained. He attended oratorios at Exeter Hall, and a number of Dickens' later readings in the Hanover Square Rooms. From grave to gay, from hymn to dance, in oratorios and operas, music had helped enormously to tune Hardy's ear to poetic flights which were almost wholly beyond his inexpert practice at the time. One of his projects had been to turn the book of Ecclesiastes into verse; he gave it up on discovering that the original was unmatchable. The poems which he had been sending to editors in 1866 were all rejected. So much time had he given to composition, often a most demanding and frustrating task, and to reading, evening after evening 'from six to twelve', that by the spring of 1867 he was exhausted. There were times in the morning when he felt he had hardly enough energy to maintain his hold on pencil and square. As heat and the stench from the muddy banks of the Thames at low water increased in the summer ('the Metropolitan main-drainage system not having yet been constructed') his health declined, until at length Blomfield recommended that he should leave temporarily for the country to regain his strength; his post would be kept open until October. By chance Hardy received a letter from his old employer John Hicks, asking if he could recommend an experienced assistant to help him with his church-restoration work, as he was frequently hampered by gout. Hardy seized this face-saving opportunity of returning home in July, leaving his poems, and most of his books and belongings, at Westbourne Park Villas. He had no determined aim, though he wished to continue writing and felt tempted to remain in the country. The recognition that his farewell might not be temporary seems implicit in his writing the poem 'Heiress and Architect' specially for Arthur Blomfield, and presenting it to him at 8 Adelphi Terrace just before his departure.

7

First Verse and Fiction

The young man who returned home to recover his health in the summer of 1867 was very different from the Hardy who set off to London in April 1862. Then, although ambitious to advance in architecture, he was still inclined to the Church; now he had rejected all thought of a Church career, and preferred to regard architecture as a means to an end, not as an engrossing vocation but as a secondary one. At no other stage of his career did a change of such far-reaching magnitude take place than when he was reading, studying, and learning to think for himself at 16 Westbourne Park Villas. It was his philosophical birthplace. Knowledge which gave direction to his thought had been acquired before he left home for London, but only after a period of perplexity and prolonged reflection did he draw conclusions. They seemed to have crystallized suddenly after long absorption, and they were clear-cut, coherent, and uncompromising. Unlike Wordsworth, who, at almost the same age, had been 'wearied out with contrarieties' and had 'yielded up moral questions in despair' when bewildered by the abstract reasoning of revolutionary philosophers, Hardy had found himself finally in no intellectual quandary. There were, as far as he could find, no tenable arguments against the new philosophy, which was basically scientific and more true to the universe and man's place within it than any previous creed. Only by recognizing it and all its implications could a new religion or philosophy develop which would be adequate to the physical, moral, and spiritual needs of mankind. Hardy accepted it boldly and challengingly, confident that the advancement of civilization depended on its recognition. The best guide to his thought on the subject is provided by several of the poems he wrote in London from 1865 to 1867.

The question of heredity or the lottery of birth seems to have been very much to the fore; his footnote to 'Discouragement' suggests that he attempted to give it expression on and off from 1863 to 1867, though the manuscript sonnet gives the more likely date 1865–7. How can one reconcile belief in Providence with the 'hap' of birth? Hardy is thinking not so much of socio-economic differences and consequent advantages or disadvantages (though they are not precluded) as of physical determinants in sexual attraction, and innate biases of body, mind, and temperament which affect behaviour. To Hardy the full recognition of relative human helplessness in the sway of such hereditary impulses or forces was frightening. His thought was promoted by Hamlet's

> So, oft it chances in particular men
> That, for some vicious mole of nature in them,
> As in their birth, wherein they are not guilty,
> Since nature cannot choose his origin. . . .

The injustice of birth affects the whole of one's life; there is no recompense in heaven; any heaven or happiness is to be found in one's brief existence on earth. Hardy had already taken his first step along the road to his Unfulfilled Intention theory.

The loss of belief in a God of love is the subject of 'Hap'. If Hardy knew the Almighty took pleasure in man's suffering, he could steel himself to endure wrong. It is 'Crass Casualty' and 'dicing Time', however, that rule our lot; they are 'purblind Doomsters', and it is mere chance whether we are fortunate or unfortunate. The poem heralds the part to be played by 'the whimsical god . . . known as blind Circumstance' in Hardy's fiction, and the recurrent onslaught on the blindness of the First Cause which followed in *Poems of the Past and the Present*.

Two sonnets emphasize the insignificance of humanity within the immensity of the universe, 'In vision I roamed' faintly anticipating *Two on a Tower*, and 'At a Lunar Eclipse' hinting at more than *The Dynasts*. The 'ghast heights' of 'taciturn and drear' space in the former make any earthly spot seem home, and the long distance separating lovers a trifle. The second poses the question whether the shadow on the moon is

> the stellar gauge of earthly show,
> Nation at war with nation, brains that teem,
> Heroes, and women fairer than the skies.

So much, it seems to say, for 'Heaven's high human scheme'.

Nature's indifference to heredity is the subject of 'At a Bridal'. The poet thinks of dream children that might have been born to

him and one who has just married, but realizes that in nature there
are no high aims such as they might have had, and that generation
proceeds according to unalterable law. The tendency to read autobiography into hypothetical circumstances conjured up by Hardy
for dramatic purposes in some of these early poems can be quite
misleading. No evidence has been found to indicate that any
passionate attachment disturbed the busy programme of cultural
pursuits, study, and literary dedication which he undertook during his later years in London. He may certainly have been thinking
of Eliza Nicholls when he wrote 'The Musing Maiden', 'From Her
in the Country', and 'Her Confession', but 'Revulsion', in conjunction with 'At a Bridal', suggests very forcibly that Hardy was
interested in neither love nor marriage, however much he could
frame words 'to fetter some unknown spirit' to his 'in clasp and
kiss'. Significantly in 'Her Reproach' (written in 1867), the poet,
like the poetic hero of *Desperate Remedies*, is reminded of Milton's
line on the writer's pursuit of fame (the 'last infirmity of noble
mind'), asking

> Were it not better done as others use,
> To sport with Amaryllis in the shade,
> Or with the tangles of Neæra's hair?

Apart from this, the most important of the dramatic poems are
four surviving 'She, to Him' sonnets of 1866, all that remain of a
'much larger' series. It is an ageing, disappointed woman who
speaks or reflects; in the second sonnet she imagines that when
she is dead her lover may be reminded of her by somebody else's
feature, accent, or reflection, and think with a sigh 'Poor jade!'
without realizing that the thought in those two words (everything
existing only as it is perceived) had been a whole life to her. In his
adaptation of this to *Desperate Remedies* Hardy makes clear that the
capitalized emphasis of 'Whole Life' was intended to convey her
'single opportunity of existence'. Like Swinburne he felt passionately that, since 'no man under the sky lives twice, outliving his
day', no one should be caused heedless suffering or deprivation. It
is the keynote to the tragedy that threatens the heroine in *Desperate
Remedies* and repeatedly overtakes the heroine of *Tess of the d'Urbervilles*. The effect of Time's tyranny in 'She, to Him' is more dominant in 'Amabel'. Hardy had been shocked when he saw it in Mrs
Martin in London, and may have been most impressed by it in a
poem by Béranger which he read in Bagehot's essays.

Although he later professed to regard 'A Young Man's Epigram on Existence' as 'an amusing instance of early cynicism', Hardy thought that, in expressing the irony of a life in which we are for ever learning the lessons of experience too late, it formed a fitting conclusion to *Time's Laughingstocks*, his third volume of poems. 'A Young Man's Exhortation', which urges us to avoid care by indulging in enjoyment and illusion, is nothing but a piece of cynical posturing. All is as we see it; 'aspects are within us' and 'who seems most kingly is the King'. In his later years Hardy wrote poems in the same strain, on the iris-bow of illusory hope and beauty. In them the poet assumes a role, whereas the authentic Hardy of the London years is like the Hardy of 'In Tenebris' who knows that 'if way to the Better there be, it exacts a full look at the Worst'. Cynical humour blends delightfully with worldly truth in the satirical irony of 'The Ruined Maid', an early dialect poem which remains unequalled. The more earnest Hardy will be found in 'The Two Men', where two of equal age, ability, and early advantages, but of contrasting character and aims, are judged ultimately to be equal failures by the world. Hardy, averse to the 'science of climbing', sympathizes with the first, a man like Clym Yeobright who renounces 'the Market's sordid war' and devotes himself to higher aims, the furtherance of Truth and Purity, plain living, and altruism.

Whether by accident or design, 'Domicilium', the one surviving poem of an earlier period, is reminiscent of the plain-statement style in which the maturing Wordsworth excelled. Hardy's poems of 1865–7, however, show little sign of imitation; they are evidence, rather, of the astonishing fact that a young poet realized almost at the very outset that he had to forge his own style and resist beguiling rhythmical exercises, giving sense priority over sound. Concentrating on precision of thought, Hardy is sometimes elliptic and awkward. His studies in inventive diction clearly had a practical aim; 'indwell' exemplifies his arbitrary daring. Such coinages frequently occur in his later poetry, sometimes for the worse; among them will be found idiosyncrasies more unfortunate than 'outfigure' and 'fitless' in 'Her Definition'. The sustained simile with which this sonnet ends and that which permeates 'Her Confession' have their counterparts in Shakespeare's sonnets; they recall an Elizabethan manner, but they are drawn from life and not from Heliconian springs. Significantly, while rejecting his rhythmic fluencies, Hardy can take an image from Swinburne and adapt it most realistically and sensitively to a particular human situation: in 'Rondel' (*Poems and Ballads*, 1866) joy is 'a vane that veers'; in the third of the 'She, to Him' sonnets, the ageing speaker, faithful to her old love, is

> Numb as a vane that cankers on its point,
> True to the wind that kissed ere canker came.

Some of these early poems may have been written at Higher Bockhampton. 'The Bride-Night Fire', a narrative based on Dorset tradition, is entirely in dialect. Far less subtle and artistic than 'The Ruined Maid', it originated in humour of obviously masculine appeal, and, not surprisingly, was the first of Hardy's poems to be published, though not until 1875 and in a bowdlerized form. Rushy Pond may have supplied the setting for 'Neutral Tones', which illustrates more superbly than any other of his early poems the creative genius whereby a particular situation is endowed with a general emotion. The thought and imagery, which haunted Hardy's imagination during 1867 and for some years later (as may be seen in 'An Indiscretion of an Heiress' – drawn from *The Poor Man and the Lady* – and in *Desperate Remedies*), came from Shelley's lyric 'When the lamp is shattered', where the bird's nest wrecked in a storm expresses the desolation which follows disappointment in love. The following lines supply the other imagery from which Hardy's particularities grew to a unified whole:

> Bright reason will mock thee
> Like the sun from a wintry sky. . . .
> Leave thee naked to laughter
> When leaves fall and cold winds come.

Imagery and idea have been translated into setting and individualized situation; the setting could have been almost wholly imaginary. The result is a tone-poem of negative beauty, without parallel in Hardy, Shelley, or any other poet. Hardy would not be the writer he is had he not appropriated imagery informed by ideas from Shelley and other authors.

The theme of 'Heiress and Architect' is that, as Hardy tells us in 'Yell'ham-Wood's Story', 'Life offers – to deny!'. The 'arch-designer' who thinks in architectural terms is the First Cause or Prime Mover; he is unable to depart from 'the law of stable things' (the universe of natural law). The poem proceeds in a prohibitive or reductive manner (as does for a while Hardy's unphilosophical fictional essay 'How I Built Myself a House'), the amenities and joys which the heiress of life requests being denied one by one. Birdsong, scents, and hues cannot be granted, for it is part of the natural law that 'winters freeze' (a Shelleyan symbol of deprivation or adversity which is implicit in 'Neutral Tones'). Ultimately only room for her coffined corpse is allowed. That is final; there is no suggestion of a future.

The incidence of frost as an image of adverse chance or unfulfilment in 'Discouragement', 'Neutral Tones', and 'Heiress and Architect' is a reminder of the casualties of winter which Hardy had observed in the garden and neighbouring woods at Higher Bockhampton. The havoc wrought by rain and frost, or by heavy clustering snow, on branches of shrubs and trees preyed on his mind creatively to such effect that the hopes of three of his fictional heroines are either blighted or unrelentingly exterminated in memorable scenes of wintry extremity, the first of them significantly appearing in his first published novel.

Amid the remarkable variety of Hardy's early poems, 'A Confession to a Friend in Trouble' seems to stand apart. There can be little doubt that the friend is Horace Moule, who from 1865 to 1868 taught at Marlborough College, where he succeeded his younger brother Charles, now a fellow at Corpus Christi, Cambridge. Hardy may have heard that Horace had been the worse for drink during a holiday period; the troubles that 'shrink not' could include the disclosure or allegation that he was the father of an illegitimate child at Fordington. (The story Hardy seems to have told his second wife, that the mother and child – before its birth or after – had been sent to Australia, has an obvious bearing on *Jude the Obscure*.) The subject of the sonnet is most unusual for poetry. The author finds that he has come to accept such news with a shrug or smile, listlessly, feeling that he does not wish to incur pain by expressing interest and sympathy, or by sharing his friend's grief. He recovers, but is guiltily aware of his 'unseemly instinct', now distanced like a murky bird or buccaneer 'that shapes its lawless figure on the main'. The psychological analysis is impressive; the keynote is utter integrity, however discomforting. To this extent the poem is characteristic. It may afford a clue to Hardy's note of 17 July 1868: 'Perhaps I can do a volume of poems consisting of the *other side* of common emotions'.

Walking to and from Hicks's office assisted in his rapid recovery of health, and he soon found, with only part-time architectural engagements, that he had time on his hands. Though he wrote a little more poetry, his previous unsuccessful attempts at publication made him feel that it was 'a waste of labour', and he decided to venture on a novel based on the country he knew so well and 'the life of an isolated student cast upon the billows of London with no protection but his brains'. Its title was to be 'The Poor Man and the Lady, A Story with no Plot, Containing Some Original Verses'; in the end this was reduced to 'The Poor Man and the Lady, By the Poor Man'. Although in his later years he tended to disparage it, he told Edward Clodd in December 1910 that, for its date, it was 'the most original thing' he ever wrote. He was so pleased with its progress by October 1867 that he 'paid a flying visit to London to fetch his books and other impedimenta'. His decision to abandon regular professional work in the city was not encouraged by his mother, and her concern was recalled in Mrs Yeobright's reproaches after Clym's abandonment of a promising career in Paris. Earlier, on 10 September, while visiting Mary, who was now in charge of a small school at Minterne Magna, Hardy sketched Dogbury Hill, an occasion recollected in his poem 'Life and Death at Sunrise'.

The first version of the novel may have been completed by the end of the year; on 16 January 1868 he began revising and making a fair copy of it. During April he read Browning and Thackeray, and took down the exact sound of the nightingale (which he remembered at the end of *Under the Greenwood Tree*; Henry J. Moule described the Hardy cottage as 'a nightingale-besung home'). Copying up was ended on 9 June, and soon Hardy was thinking of writing poetry again, including a narrative of the Battle of the Nile (in the war against Napoleon), the first sign of attraction to a subject to which he was to give recurrent thought until, rather late in life, he fulfilled his ambition in *The Dynasts*. Most of his spare time during 1868 seems to have been devoted to reading, which included plays of Shakespeare, the six volumes of Horace Walpole's *Letters to Sir Horace Mann*, Macaulay, Walt Whitman, and the *Aeneid*, 'of which he never wearied'.

He found time, it is assumed, to visit his favourite aunt Mary at Puddletown, and may well have discussed classical textual difficulties with her husband John Antell, a self-taught Latin scholar who was liable to seek consolation in bouts of drinking (in these respects a precursor of Jude Fawley); he was a frequenter of

Noah's Ark when he visited Dorchester. The thought '*sic diis immortalibus placet*', which occurs near the end of *The Dynasts*, gave this shoemaker and cobbler a certain grim satisfaction for his growing arthritic pains, his depression after fits of intemperance and violence, and his many educational frustrations. At the Sparkses' early in the year, Hardy had probably heard much on the unpleasant experience of Tryphena, the youngest of the family, as a pupil-teacher. She had done so well in the Nonconformist school at Athelhampton that in her last year as a pupil she became the headmaster's monitor or assistant. Her distinct promise was most probably brought to the notice of Mrs Wood or of Miss Elizabeth Samson of Upwey, a relative who frequently stayed with the Woods at Athelhampton Hall. Both could have been interested; they were ardent Congregational supporters of 'British' schools (schools built and maintained by the British and Foreign School Society, specially for the children of Nonconformists). Either could have encouraged Hardy's young cousin to teach, and given her financial assistance when she entered a training college.

In November 1866 Tryphena was engaged as a pupil-teacher at the new National school which had been built in Puddletown at the expense of the local squire, John Brymer of Ilsington House. The Brymers took great interest in this school, visited it frequently, provided prizes, and did everything possible to ensure its success. It is not clear whether Tryphena taught first in the infants' department. In the main school she assisted Mrs Collins, head of the girls' department, who on 16 January 1868 reproved her for neglect of duty. Very indignant at the injustice of this complaint, her parents threatened to withdraw her; they may even have taken steps which brought their grievance to the attention of Mr Brymer, who visited the school next day. As a result Tryphena was transferred to the boys' half of the school, where she taught with the headmaster Mr Collins. She and Frances Dunman had been interchanged, and the school log-book suggests that the headmaster, who was highly conscientious, knew what he was doing, the inspector's report for the previous July indicating that Miss Dunman was unsatisfactory for three subjects, Tryphena for one. Whenever a problem arose or was likely to arise, it was noted in the log-book, either for reference to the Brymers or for raising at managers' meetings. The headmaster's record, chiefly of lessons taught or prepared with his pupil-teacher (whom he usually refers to as his 'monitor'), during Tryphena's pupil-teacher period does not indicate any withdrawal at short notice, as her parents threatened, or any serious teaching problem, or her replacement at any time. Her absence from her mother's bedside, when the latter died about two o'clock in the morning of 2 November 1868, with four others present, including Mr Sparks and two of his older daughters, is hardly surprising. Her mother had been ill for some time; Tryphena must have been fully engaged as a teacher; and, according to a family tradition which has sufficient probability to warrant its mention, she lived during this disturbing period with one of her Puddletown relatives.

The suggestion that she became a pupil-teacher at the Noncon-formist school founded by Miss Samson's brother at Coryates, a remote hamlet west of Upwey, is based on conjecture and a very tenuous, if not suspect, tradition that 'a relative of Thomas Hardy had taught there'. Some years were to pass before he became known as an author, and it seems most unlikely that any mention of him at this period in a neighbourhood hardly known to him would be remembered a century later. It is very doubtful, more-over, whether such a small school would qualify for a pupil-teacher. Tryphena, after completing her pupil-teacher requirements (which meant that, in addition to being of a suitable character, she had completed three years' apprenticeship successfully, the time being determined by her beginning at the age of fifteen), was recom-mended by the regional inspector who had examined her teaching annually, and was admitted to Stockwell College for a two-year course of teacher-training at the minimum age of eighteen. Teach-ing experience in a 'British' school was a normal requirement for admission to this college. Tryphena's acceptance on exceptional grounds supports the view that she did not teach at Coryates, and that she had very influential support from Nonconformists such as Mrs Wood and Miss Samson, the latter particularly, for Tryphena kept in touch with her and visited her home. Miss Samson's continued interest in her work was clearly demonstrated when she visited her at the Plymouth school where she began her appoint-ment as headmistress in January 1872.

Much had happened affecting Hardy's literary career and life in the meantime. On 25 July 1868 he had sent the manuscript of *The Poor Man and the Lady* to the publisher Alexander Macmillan. At the same time he posted him a letter, accompanied by an introductory note from Horace Moule. The letter itemized the 'considerations' which 'had place' when he wrote the novel. One seems axiomatic:

'That as a rule no fiction will considerably interest readers poor or rich unless the passion of love forms a prominent feature in the thread of the story.' The others bear on satire of the upper classes, stressing its tolerability if 'inserted edgewise so to say', as if it were not the main aim of the book. He thought that 'discussions on the questions of manners, rising in the world, &c (the main incidents of the novel)' had become a 'particularly absorbing' subject. Lastly, he was convinced that 'novelty of *position* and *view* in relation to a known subject, is more taking among the readers of light literature than even absolute novelty of subject'. (Such a 'consideration' was to weigh again with him when he wrote *The Hand of Ethelberta*.) The emphasis on 'light literature' takes into account the more farcical incidents of the story, but neither the satire nor the ending was light. Macmillan's reply of 10 August suggests that the tragic conclusion, shorn of its immaturities, did not differ substantially from that of 'An Indiscretion in the Life of an Heiress'.

The story, as told by Hardy to Edmund Gosse, is of a Dorset youth of peasant extraction whose success at school wins the patronage of the local squire and lady. In consequence he is trained as an architect's draughtsman. (His name being Strong, it is clear that Hardy was thinking of himself, Kingston Maurward House, and his apprenticeship with Hicks.) As the squire's daughter falls in love with the young man, he is sent to London, where he assists an eminent architect, and takes up radical politics 'in pique'. The heiress comes to town with her family, and the lovers contrive to meet; but, after driving past while he is addressing a crowd in Trafalgar Square, the young lady is offended by his radicalism, and breaks off relations until they meet by chance at a concert, where, as in 'An Indiscretion', they are so moved by the music that they cannot conceal their love. When, accepting her invitation, he visits her home, he is received by her mother. An angry scene ensues; the mother faints; he throws water over her face, and the rouge runs down her cheeks. He is ejected, and the family returns to Dorset. After a time the 'poor man' hears that she is to be married to the heir of a wealthy neighbouring landowner. He meets her in the church the night before her wedding, and she confesses she has never loved anyone but him. The story as Hardy told it broke off at this point; he could not remember whether she married 'the proposed bridegroom' or not.

Hardy indicates the scope of his satire, wherein lay the main thrust of the novel, in his *Life*:

The story was, in fact, a sweeping dramatic satire of the squi-
rearchy and nobility, London society, the vulgarity of the middle
class, modern Christianity, church-restoration, and political and
domestic morals in general, the author's views . . . being obviously those of a young man with a passion for reforming the
world . . . the tendency of the writing being socialistic, not to
say revolutionary; yet not argumentatively so, the style having
the affected simplicity of Defoe's [which had long attracted
Hardy, as it did Stevenson, years later, to imitation of it].

Following Defoe's example, Hardy's invention in 'circumstantial
detail' as told in the first person was so plausible at times that it
was taken as a representation of the actual, he thought, by the
publisher and his reader. As an example of this he mentions
Strong's introduction to

the kept mistress of an architect who 'took in washing' (as it was
called in the profession) – that is, worked at his own office for
other architects – the said mistress adding to her lover's income
by designing for him the pulpits, altars, reredoses, texts, holy
vessels, crucifixes, and other ecclesiastical furniture which were
handed on to him by the nominal architects who employed her
protector – the lady herself being a dancer at a music-hall when
not engaged in designing Christian emblems – all told so plaus-
ibly as to seem actual proof of the degeneracy of the age.

Alexander Macmillan thought 'the pictures of character among
Londoners, and especially the upper classes', incisive and just in
many respects, but too dark and unrelieved to be true. He con-
trasted the 'utter heartlessness of *all* the conversation' in drawing-
rooms and ballrooms about the working classes with the 'light,
chaffy' manner of Thackeray. Such 'wholesale blackening' was
bound to offend': 'he meant fun, you *"mean mischief"'*. Not that
Thackeray did much good; his mocking tone culminated in that of
the *Saturday Review*, 'paralyzing noble effort and generous emotion'. The story was improbable, and Macmillan questioned
whether the scene in the church at midnight, or the retraction *in
public* of an award by an institution (Hardy still fretting over the
circumstances which denied him part of the RIBA prize) could
have happened. Much of the writing was admirable, the publisher
being particularly impressed by the description of country life and

the Rotten Row scene (in Hyde Park). He enclosed the report of his reader John Morley, and wished to consult 'another man of a very different stamp of mind'. Morley thought that 'the opening pictures of the Christmas Eve in the tranter's house' were 'really of good quality', and much of the writing 'strong and fresh'. In parts there was 'a certain rawness of absurdity' that was 'very displeasing', like 'some clever lad's dream', and the whole thing hung 'too loosely together'. 'If the man is young, there is stuff and promise in him: but he must study form and composition, in such writers as Balzac and Thackeray, who would I think come as natural masters to him.'

Apart from his main literary work little is known precisely about Hardy's Dorset activities during the next year. Towards the end of August 1868 he accompanied his sister Mary to Weymouth, where they took an excursion by steamboat to Lulworth Cove, some details of this outing being remembered early in *Desperate Remedies*. Dancing with his vivacious cousin Tryphena, eleven years his junior, at a Puddletown fête or 'gipsying', as he recalled it in 'In a Eweleaze near Weatherbury', could have taken place the same summer or the next. It may have seemed to kindle romantic feelings ('Love's fitful ecstasies') in retrospect, but, if he was attached to anyone at this time, it was to Catherine ('Cassie') Pole of West Stafford, a lady's maid with the Fellowes family at Kingston Maurward. His future was much too uncertain for him to think of marrying, but she was most probably the local girl for whom, as his sister Kate told Irene Cooper Willis after his death, he bought anticipatively the ring which he eventually presented to Emma Gifford.

In September he wrote to Macmillan, telling him that he had been preparing another story, 'entirely of rural scenes and humble life', but lacked the heart to proceed until he knew what had happened to *The Poor Man and the Lady*. The result of further correspondence was that he collected the manuscript for revision, returned it in November, and visited the publisher in December for a verdict. Macmillan had to refuse the novel, but, finding the author still bent on publication, he gave him an introduction to Frederick Chapman (of Chapman & Hall) in Piccadilly. Hardy's interview with Chapman was not propitious, but he left the manuscript with him. Having received no reply, he returned to London on 17 January 1869. He met Macmillan again, who suggested he should try his hand at articles in reviews; John Morley offered him an introduction to the editor of the *Saturday Review*. Hardy felt he could always turn more profitably and surely to architecture, without giving up his career as a creative writer; it was 'the course he loved' and one to which he felt drawn by 'natural instinct'. He stayed in London, studying pictures at the South Kensington Museum and elsewhere, and reading desultorily until he received the long-expected reply. It was not a promising one, Chapman & Hall's reader having advised against publication, chiefly because the novel needed a more interesting story which would link up the episodes satisfactorily. Yet, after receiving Hardy at the back of his shop, and telling him to observe Thomas Carlyle, the old man talking to his clerk, Chapman offered to publish *The Poor Man and the Lady* if Hardy would guarantee £20 against loss. Hardy agreed, and was promised a contract.

Neither the agreement nor the expected proof-sheets arrived. At the end of February he was invited to call and meet Chapman's reader. Early in March he arrived at the appointed time, and was shown into the back room of the publishers' offices, where he met 'a handsome man in a frock-coat – "buttoned at the waist, but loose above" – . . . his ample dark-brown beard, wavy locks, and somewhat dramatic manner lending him a striking appearance'. It was George Meredith, the poet and novelist, with Hardy's manuscript in his hands. He spoke sonorously, telling him that the firm was willing to stand by its offer, but advising him not to 'nail his colours to the mast' so emphatically in his first book, lest his future be damaged. Hardy could either rewrite the novel, 'softening it down considerably', or, better still, put it aside and write another for 'a purely artistic purpose' with a more complicated plot. The probability is that he did further work on *Under the Greenwood Tree*, his story of 'rural scenes and humble life', before deciding to try Smith, Elder & Co. in April; they rejected *The Poor Man and the Lady* without delay. Early in June he sent the manuscript to Tinsley Brothers, but it was not until September, after asking Horace Moule to call on them, that he received their decision. Not being able to afford the guarantee they asked against publication costs, he instructed them to send the parcel to Weymouth railway station. He had been living for some time at 3 Wooperton Street, near Weymouth harbour, and doing church-restoration work which his employer G. R. Crickmay had inherited from John Hicks, who had died suddenly in February. Hardy had started this work at Hicks's

Dorchester office, the results being so satisfactory that Crickmay, who had not specialized in Gothic architecture, persuaded him to work three months for him at Weymouth in the hope of clearing all the outstanding commitments. His first main responsibility was the building of a new church, all but the tower, at Turnworth, west of Blandford Forum; incidentally he saw Turnworth House, the situation of which he remembered for deceptive purposes in *The Woodlanders*. Hardy hoped that his new appointment would give him time to continue his literary activities, especially in fiction.

He must have found the sea air at Weymouth very bracing. At seven o'clock in the morning, after walking along the promenade, he bathed from the pebble beach towards Preston; he rowed in the bay most summer evenings. Charles Moule came down from Cambridge, and they were rowed into the bay, where, after diving off and swimming around, they had great difficulty in getting back to their boat. During the summer and autumn, when he and a new assistant joined a quadrille class, Hardy wrote a number of poems with imaginary situations in the Weymouth setting: 'Singing Lovers', 'On the Esplanade', 'The Dawn after the Dance', 'At a Seaside Town in 1869' (after hearing the town band play the Morgenblätter waltzes by Johann Strauss), and 'At Waking', the last two on the illusoriness of a lover's imagination, a subject taken up in *Desperate Remedies*, where the hero, a poetic architect like Hardy in major respects, however much he was based on Crickmay's new assistant, concludes that the ideal woman of his imagination is unattainable, until Cytherea appears. In the autumn, discontinuing *Under the Greenwood Tree* and taking Meredith's advice, Hardy began 'the long and intricately inwrought chain of circumstance' which he had planned for his next novel. In this the heroine Cytherea obtains a post as lady's maid at Knapwater, which is recognizably drawn from Kingston Maurward. How far Cassie Pole contributed to her presentation is uncertain; she is said to have been beautiful.

Hardy had decided to incorporate or adapt portions of *The Poor Man and the Lady* wherever possible in his new fiction. He had already developed the Christmas Eve scenes at the tranter's in *Under the Greenwood Tree*; now he took the Knapwater setting and descriptive scenes relative to the heroine's unhappy wedding from the same source. Transfers, as may be seen from their later repetition in 'An Indiscretion in the Life of an Heiress', include some satirical sentiments, notably: 'The truly great stand upon no middle ledge; they are either famous or unknown.' They can be famous only if they are conventional and 'exclusive'; they have to adopt upper-class views and values. Even so, *Desperate Remedies* required strenuous efforts both in preparation and execution. Hardy had read much to gain ideas on plot construction and effects, and was influenced by complication and mystery in the novels of Wilkie Collins, *The Woman in White* and *Basil* particularly; his villain is cast in the same physical mould as Mannion in the latter. Some narrative ingredients may derive from Miss Braddon, a prolific writer who enjoyed enormous popularity after the amazing success of her *Lady Audley's Secret* in 1862. Two of the most critical situations were suggested by George Eliot's latest novel, *Felix Holt*. The first is the dependence of the plot on the part played by a lady's illegitimate son. In George Eliot's story Mrs Transome's tragedy leads to a scene in which she vicariously receives the affection she yearns for from the heroine Esther Lyon. Hardy's adaptation of this is more psychologically complex, and neither intentionally nor essentially lesbian, as is often assumed (as if he were trying to shock Victorian readers and not doing his utmost to secure publication). Miss Aldclyffe's passionate embraces of Cytherea are the expression of a deprived and warped nature, a sudden accession of the love for the heroine's father which fate had aborted. *Felix Holt* could also have given Hardy the assurance he needed for adopting a complicated criminal plot. His achievement was greater than he realized. *Desperate Remedies* has intensely poetic scenes of tragic import, a colourful landscape of such concentrated psychological depth and change that it would be quite an extravagance in any novel, and rustic humour of a distinctly promising vintage, especially in Richard Crickett, the parish clerk. Unfortunately Hardy paid a heavy price to secure publication, resorting in the end to cheap sensationalism and intrigue, scarcely probable and rather crude at times. Even so, it is a disciplined and unusually well-articulated work, with situations which Hardy, thinking they were wasted in a novel which had little future, chose to use again, with great tragic effect, in *Tess of the d'Urbervilles*.

Anxious to complete the novel, he gave up the flirtatious dancing-class he had joined, and returned home at the beginning of February 1870. He had not been there more than a week before Crickmay invited him to visit St Juliot in Cornwall, and make new plans for the restoration of the church which Hicks himself had planned as early as April 1867. Hardy found it inconvenient to go but, after almost completing *Desperate Remedies*, he agreed, on receiving 'a more persuasive request'. After forwarding his manuscript on the Saturday to Macmillan, in whom he felt he had made a friend, he prepared for his journey to Cornwall, leaving home by starlight at four o'clock on the frosty morning of Monday, 7 March.

8

Emma Gifford

With train-changes and stops at intermediate towns, even at villages on the last stage, the journey from Dorchester via Yeovil, Exeter, and Plymouth was slow, and it was not until he had been on the way twelve hours that Hardy reached Launceston, a few miles within the confines of Cornwall. As he walked up the steep hill from the station in the fading light he could not but be impressed by the keep of the ruined Norman castle which dominated this town. For the remainder of his journey, another seventeen miles or more over the hills to the fringe of the northern coast, he hired a driver and conveyance. As the evening darkened he noticed the planet Jupiter and the red glow of distant smouldering fires where land was being cleared for agricultural use; eventually, revolving beams from a distant lighthouse were seen. His impressions were very much as he recorded them near the opening of *A Pair of Blue Eyes* and, later, in his poems 'The Discovery', 'The Wind's Prophecy' and 'A Man was Drawing Near to Me'. He was to stay at St Juliot rectory. Here, after ringing the bell and waiting in the porch, he was received somewhat embarrassingly by a youngish lady of striking appearance, her rosy cheeks and luxuriance of corn-coloured curled hair contrasting with her brown dress. This was Emma Lavinia Gifford, sister-in-law of the rector, Mr Caddell Holder, who had retired to bed with gout; his wife Helen was upstairs attending to him. Before Emma could finish explaining the situation, her sister appeared and conducted the visitor to Mr Holder's room. Emma thought Hardy looked businesslike and older than he appeared by daylight; she noticed his soft voice, his 'yellowish' beard, his 'rather shabby greatcoat', and a piece of blue paper protruding from his pocket. On it he had been sketching nothing architectural, but a poem, he afterwards disclosed.

The church at St Juliot had been left mouldering for many years. Cracks continued to appear in the tower, from which the five bells had been removed; they stood mouth-upward in the north transept. Ivy hung from the rafters of the roof; carved bench-ends were left

to rot; and bats and birds made the ancient building their habitation. For more than three years services had been held in the
National school. The Revd Richard Rawle, patron of the living, had
promised £700 for the restoration, provided the parishioners raised
an additional £200. Holder, who had lost his first wife in 1867 soon
after Hicks's visit, had married Helen Gifford (less than half his
age) in 1868 from her father's home at Kirland near Bodmin in
central Cornwall. Emma accompanied them to St Juliot, to assist in
the rectory and in the neglected parish, where the raising of money
for rebuilding the church was an urgent necessity.

Apart from intervals for meals at the rectory, Hardy spent the
whole of the next day at the church, sketching and taking measurements; his attention was diverted when one of the inverted bells
was tolled for a funeral. Next day he was taken via Tintagel to find
out if slates for the roof could be provided from a quarry at
Penpethy. He remembered that the epicure John Douglas Cook,
first editor of the *Saturday Review*, had lived in these parts in his
later years; the Holders, it seemed, had known him, and he was
buried above Tintagel. On Thursday Hardy accompanied Emma
Gifford as she rode her pony to Beeny Cliff; he was to remember
her drawing rein and singing 'to the swing of the tide' below. In
the afternoon he visited Boscastle, the two sisters walking with
him most of the way before returning; the early evening was spent
in the rectory garden, overlooking the Valency valley which ran
down to Boscastle harbour. Every day, with perhaps one exception, ended with music in the drawing-room, Mrs Holder and Miss
Gifford playing the piano and singing duets. On Friday, 11 March,
Hardy returned home; Emma struck a light six times in her anxiety
to call the servants and ensure that everything was provided
before his early departure. In his later years, when writing his *Life*,
he could not remember, he says, whether 'At the Word
"Farewell"', a poem he liked because it was 'literally true', referred
to his first visit or the next, a statement which makes one wonder
how he could have overlooked one detail in the final verse:

'I am leaving you . . . . Farewell!' I said
    As I followed her on
By an alley bare boughs overspread;
    'I soon must be gone!'
Even then the scale might have been turned
    Against love by a feather,

– But crimson one cheek of hers burned
When we came in together.

The bare boughs show that what took place happened at the end of the first visit, not the second in August. Like 'When I set out for Lyonnesse', the poem 'Ditty', which Hardy wrote soon after his return from Cornwall, leaves no doubt that he had fallen in love as never before. Such lyricism, expressing both the magic and tenderness of love, is unprecedented in his poetry, suggesting he had previously never really been in love, whatever he had imagined or whatever the length of any of his attachments. His friendship with Cassie Pole, like that with Eliza Nicholls before her, would be left to wither, if it had not already waned.

Born at Plymouth on 24 November 1840, Emma was only a few months younger than Hardy. Her parents were both of Bristol origin, her mother being an accountant's daughter, her father, John Attersoll Gifford, son of a schoolmaster. After qualifying as a solicitor, he had practised in Plymouth, to which he returned with his family after five years of married life in Bristol. His mother had spoilt him, and when she came to live with him persuaded him to give up his profession, which he disliked, and live a life of cultivated leisure. Emma, after being given a good education, enjoyed music, singing, and painting, and loved books. In his later years Mr Gifford discovered that he was not nearly as well-endowed as his mother had led him to believe, and he had moved to Kirland, after a short stay in Bodmin, in the hope of cutting down expenses. Such was his style of living that he rented a large, beautifully situated house; his means, however, were so circumscribed that he could hardly keep it in order, and his exigencies were exacerbated by alcoholic excesses. Helen and Emma, too poor to take advantage of all that Kirland might have offered, found it beneficial to leave home and work as governesses. The former then became companion to an old lady who had retired to Tintagel; there she met her future husband, Caddell Holder. Emma had literary aspirations and a poetic spirit that bestowed enchantment on the Atlantic cliffs, coves, birds, waves, seascapes, and gorgeous sunsets; she was fascinated also by the superstitions, legends, and witchcraft of the neighbourhood. There were few people of interest in the area, and the coming of an architect from the outer world, with the early prospects of a new church where she could play the harmonium, was an exciting event. Hardy's literary talent, his love of music, his quick, lively intelligence, and his familiarity with London attracted her; her youthful spontaneity and zest uplifted him. The Holders did everything possible to make his visit a happy one; he had never been a more welcome guest in a cultured household.

Hardy stayed longer (by a day, it seems) than he intended. Without realizing it at this stage, Mrs Holder may have encouraged a romance which would release her sister, with whom her relations were not always cordial, from the restrictions of a remote village. It began on the morning Hardy accompanied Emma to Beeny Cliff; his feelings and the sight of the waves breaking at its feet made him think of 'the tender grace' of the day recalled by Tennyson in 'Break, break, break'. He had yet to learn that Emma was on the point of engagement to a local farmer; when this knowledge came, he felt twinges of jealousy which were soon overcome. He had no doubt of Emma's love, and could exploit his recollected jealousy with artistic detachment in *Under the Greenwood Tree,* and even more in the extremism of Henry Knight in *A Pair of Blue Eyes.* The theme of this novel is already incipient in his note of May 1870: 'A sweet face is a page of sadness to a man over 30 – the raw material of a corpse.' The genuineness of Emma's love is unmistakable in her reminiscences. Looking back through the years, with their frustrations and discords, Hardy affirms this after her death in 'Beeny Cliff':

the woman riding high above with bright hair flapping free –
The woman whom I loved so, and who loyally loved me.

On Saturday, the day after his return home, Hardy went to report to Crickmay at Weymouth, and present his expense account, which came to £6.10s.9d. Soon afterwards he resumed his lodgings and architectural work, which included detailed drawings for the restoration at St Juliot. Not until April did he receive Macmillan's decision on *Desperate Remedies.* Their refusal to publish it made him realize that it was not their custom to produce sensational novels. John Morley had read it, and taken exception to 'the violation of a young lady at an evening party, and the subsequent birth of a child' as a key incident from which the main action springs; he objected furthermore to the scene 'between Miss Aldclyffe and her new maid in bed'. There was much he admired in the book, but he advised Macmillan not to touch it. Knowing that they were not above publishing it, Hardy posted the manuscript to Tinsley Brothers, with a résumé of the last unwritten chapters. Afterwards he wished he had tried Chapman & Hall, thinking that Meredith would have given him expert advice on making use of 'the good material' in his novel.

In 'The Wind's Prophecy', written many years later from an old version of the poem, Hardy draws a contrast between the fair tresses of the one whom the poet is doomed to love as he travels toward the Cornish coast and the looped 'ebon' hair of the lady he loves in the city. Some biographical speculators have made much of this, assuming that a poet cannot invent for artistic purposes, and that the poem as a whole presents autobiographical truth. The contrast may have been suggested by someone Hardy remembered in London, Martha Sparks or Eliza Nicholls, for example; he could have thought of Tryphena Sparks at Stockwell Training College, though her hair was not 'ebon'. It is uncertain whether he ever met her again, or yet knew what had happened to her sister Martha, whom at one time he may have hoped to marry. (So ran a family 'tradition', which originated perhaps a century later, it being said that both mothers resisted the marriage on the grounds of the couple's cousinship.) After being married in November, as a result of her pregnancy, to the butler of the house where she was employed, she and her husband had been dismissed. At the end of May 1870 she bore twins; some years later she and her family emigrated to Australia. Tryphena finished her teacher-training at the end of 1871, settled in Plymouth, and just over a year later, early in 1873, was joined by her eldest sister Rebecca, who had deserted her husband, a Puddletown saddler, not long after their marriage. Tryphena remained there as a headmistress until the end of 1877, when she married Charles Frederick Gale of Topsham near Exeter. Hardy's 'Thoughts of Phena', completed soon after her death, emphasizes his 'unsight', his unawareness of what had happened to her since the earlier time when they may have corresponded.

In May 1870, after accepting William Tinsley's agreement to publish *Desperate Remedies* subject to some alteration (making the 'violation' less evident, it appears) and the advance of £75, Hardy decided to return to London, where again he visited museums and picture-galleries; he thought the presence of Death made Gérôme's *The Death of Ney* a great picture, and the presentation of only the shadows of 'the three crucified ones' in his *Jerusalem* 'a fine conception'. During this leisure period he wrote 'Ditty' and devoted much time to the study of Comte. Blomfield was pleased to see him again, and Hardy helped to finish some drawings for him. He then spent several weeks working for Raphael Brandon, a Gothic architect who was out of fashion and in decline because of his conviction that modern English architecture should be based on English and not French Gothic. The description of Knight's chambers in *A Pair of Blue Eyes* contains many details from Brandon's offices in Clement's Inn. Whether Horace Moule caused any upset in Tryphena Sparks's life or not, Hardy enjoyed meeting him during the summer, when Moule was back in London for reviewing and leader-writing. Hardy sent books to Emma Gifford, and maintained the regular correspondence with her which had begun in March. His own reading included *Mohammed and Mohammedanism* (a work which began as a series of lectures given at Harrow School by the author, Bosworth Smith, son of the West Stafford rector and later one of Hardy's best friends) and much from the Bible, Shakespeare, and poetry in general. The outbreak of the Franco-Prussian war in July created much excitement in the city and in Brandon, who communicated it to Hardy, one curious result being the latter's attendance at a service in Chelsea Hospital, where he observed the tattered banners of war and talked to asthmatic and crippled veterans, some of whom had fought against the French in the Peninsula or at Waterloo.

On 8 August Hardy ended his work with Brandon and travelled to St Juliot at the invitation of Mr Holder. He found Emma dressed in 'summer blue', which suited her complexion far better that her brown dress of March. The summer was unusually dry, and his hosts drove him to picturesque spots along the wild rugged coast, including Tintagel Castle of Arthurian legend, where, lingering too long, he and Emma would have been locked in for the night had they not succeeded in attracting attention by signalling with their handkerchiefs. Hardy saw the old church at St Juliot 'in its original condition of picturesque neglect' for the last time, before the tower, the north aisle, and the transept were razed to the ground. On the first Sunday evening, the ninth after Trinity, he attended service in Holder's other church, at Lesnewth across the Valency valley, and saw the man to whom he had been preferred lighting the candles; Emma, spontaneous and agnostic at the time, was probably his gay informer. It was an occasion he would have reason to remember with bitter irony in 'The Young Churchwarden';

he recalled the Old Testament reading from I Kings on Elijah and the still small voice, in the first section of 'Quid Hic Agis?'. Horace Moule sent press cuttings on the progress of the war, and Hardy realized that the bloody battle of Gravelotte was being fought on the day when, as he and Emma sat reading Tennyson in the rectory garden, he noticed an old horse harrowing in the field below; he was to remember the view, associated with lovers, in his poem 'In Time of "the Breaking of Nations"' during the much bloodier war of 1914–18. The next day he sketched Emma stooping over a tiny waterfall in her vain search for the tumbler lost after picnicking in the Valency valley, where, the fond lover thought in 'Under the Waterfall', it was to remain as a symbol of the sacredness of their love. Three days later, on 22 August, he sketched her sitting cloaked in the rain, with Beeny Cliff in the background, recalling the occasion, with her remark 'It never looks like summer' – after an unusually long spell of dry, sunny weather – in the poem of that title, in 'The Figure in the Scene', and in 'Why did I sketch?'

One sketch by Hardy that summer must have meant more to him than all the others. It was that of the Celtic cross (of a 'wheel-head' type which was commonly referred to as 'a Runic cross' in Cornwall) by which he and Emma sat, he 'white-hatted', she in her old brown dress, as they gazed down over a meadow and across the Valency valley, lost in 'the transport of talking' for hours outside the entrance to the church at St Juliot which had brought them together. The casting of the 'die' and its unforeseen consequences were recalled long afterwards in 'By the Runic Stone', a poem to which the parenthetical note '*Two who became a story*' was subsequently added, with an allusion less, it seems, to *A Pair of Blue Eyes* than to the autobiography which Hardy was preparing.

Hardy's earlier impressions of Emma were confirmed. Above all he was affected by her vitality; she was 'all aglow', he remembered in 'After a Journey; 'so *living*', he wrote in his *Life* (and more emphatically with reference to Elfride in *A Pair of Blue Eyes*). Her courage as she rushed downhill on her pony – a present from the old lady of Tintagel with whom she had stayed while Helen was her companion – astonished him. Her exuberance was refreshing; as he recalled after her death in 'Without, Not Within Her', it could dissipate any anxiety or depression as if it were 'corn-chaff under the breath of the winnowing-fan'. At the time, however, he did not realize what a handicap it could be in a partnership for life that this light-hearted animation, the 'flashing facile gaiety' of 'If you had known', was accompanied by little ability to contribute anything significantly memorable in conversation on serious topics. Such was Hardy's happiness that any inconsequentiality in her conversation was usually taken light-heartedly. One remark, however, possibly a flippant aberrance, wounded and perplexed him at the end of his holiday. It could have been made when they were staying overnight with her cousins at Launceston; the reconciliation which is the subject of the poem 'In the Vaulted Way' could have taken place in the old Market House before he left for the station.

'The Sun on the Bookcase' suggests that any doubts were soon resolved or forgotten; upstairs in his study at Higher Bockhampton, after looking forward to marriage when he has succeeded as a novelist, and thinking he has wasted another day, he asks

> Is it a waste to have imagined one
> Beyond the hills there, who, anon,
> My great deeds done,
> Will be mine alway?

Soon he was revising *Desperate Remedies* to such effect that it needed a fair copy, which Emma wrote for him, instalments being sent to her in the autumn while he completed the work. It was dispatched to the publishers in December with no great expectations, as may be guessed from Hardy's marking in his copy of *Hamlet* on the 15th: 'Thou wouldst not think how ill all's here about my heart: but it is no matter!' Fearing the new terms sent by Tinsley were worse than before, he wrote, asking if the required £75 would be refunded should the publishers' receipts equal their costs, with half of the additional income should the cost be exceeded. Being virtually engaged, and Emma having 'no money except in reversion after the death of her relatives', he had reason to be anxious with only £123 in hand. After a visit to London, where he paid the £75 in Bank of England notes, he returned to Dorset for proof-reading, filling up some of his leisure time by writing down 'such snatches of the old country ballads as he could hear from aged people'. *Desperate Remedies* appeared anonymously on 25 March 1871, and five days later Hardy resumed work with Crickmay at Weymouth. After two reviews, one not too discouraging in the *Athenaeum*, followed by a very favourable one in the *Morning Post*, the novel was damned in the *Spectator*, mainly for the author's daring to suppose that 'an unmarried lady owning an estate could have an illegitimate child'. The reviewer hoped that the author would manage 'better things' in future than the 'desperate remedies' he had adopted as a cure 'for ennui or an emaciated purse'. Whatever he said in extenuation, particularly on the country scenes, could not lighten Hardy's feelings as he returned home on Saturday, 22 April, after buying a copy of the weekly in Dorchester; he sat reading the review on the stile leading to the eweleaze (part of Kingston Park), and wished he was dead. He had not consulted Horace Moule on· this 'venture', and the latter's encouraging review did not appear until 30 September. A third visit to St Juliot in May for professional reasons, the rebuilding of the church having been started after Emma had laid the foundation stone, helped to restore him. It was probably on her advice, reinforced by seeing at Exeter station his three-volume novel listed at half-a-crown in W. H. Smith's remainder catalogue, that he sent commendatory extracts from the reviews to William Tinsley for publicity purposes.

Crickmay's commissions in June and July took Hardy to a number of work sites, including Slape House, Netherbury (near Beaminster), where a large picturesque mill caught his eye; he remembered it three years later when he wrote his first short story, 'Destiny and a Blue Cloak', for publication in America. He must have been working for some time on *Under the Greenwood Tree*, for he had not been long at home in the summer before it was finished. On 7 August, when it was sent to Macmillan, he wrote to the publisher, emphasizing that the story was wholly rural, and referring to the praise he had received from reviewers on his presentation of rural life in *Desperate Remedies*. Malcolm Macmillan, writing for his father, asked for information about this novel, and Hardy replied after collecting 'perfect copies' of the reviews for inclusion. He wrote defensively *vis-à-vis* the *Spectator*, urging that, because they were mere puppets in a complicated plot designed to create mystery to the end, the characters had been wrongly condemned for being unreal or lacking in moral attributes. The argument is quite unconvincing, and Hardy would have done better had he not referred to his first publication. In his report on *Under the Greenwood Tree* John Morley praised the writer's care and delicacy in handling the story, but thought the opening Christmas scenes too long and lacking in sparkle and humour. He did not expect 'a large market for it', but thought it good work, likely to please 'people whose taste is not ruined by novels of exaggerated action or forced ingenuity'. He recommended the author to read George Sand's best work, to turn a deaf ear to 'the fooleries of the critics', as his letter 'proves he does not do', and 'to beware of letting *realism* grow out of proportion to his *fancy*'. The report was sent to Hardy on 11 September in the hope that he would not mind waiting a little longer for a final decision, and with the assurance that the favourable judgement of their trustworthy critic made the publishers feel strongly inclined to accept Hardy's offer. In the meantime he had been thinking of his next novel, and sketching and painting at Higher Bockhampton.

In October he combined professional work with a long holiday in Cornwall. One of his excursions with Emma took him to St Neitan's Kieve, an impressive waterfall which he sketched in a wooded valley east of Tintagel, a visit which he remembered late in his life when he wrote *The Queen of Cornwall*. Horace Moule's favourable review of *Desperate Remedies* encouraged him to ask Tinsley if he would use an extract, together with those already sent, for advertisement. On 14 October he replied to Malcolm Macmillan, stating his willingness to shorten 'the scene alluded to as being too long', and calling attention to the further commendation his first novel had received. Four days later Alexander Macmillan replied. He had read *Under the Greenwood Tree* while on holiday at Brighton, and found much that was charming in it, though the opening scenes were tedious, and the story too slight and unexciting to be popular. As they were fully engaged on Christmas publications, he would like to reconsider the matter in the early summer or spring, if Hardy had not made other plans. Hardy wrote immediately to Tinsley, principally to discover whether he was interested in his 'rural story' or in another, 'the essence of which is plot, *without crime* – but on the plan of D.R.'. He had evidently done some preparatory work on *A Pair of Blue Eyes*, and probably found time to discuss it with Emma Gifford.

Although Tinsley was interested in Hardy's second proposal, he could not raise hopes of financial gain from *Desperate Remedies*. Hardy therefore decided to concentrate on architecture, and continued working during the winter for Crickmay at Weymouth, confident that it was the only way of raising sufficient money to afford marriage. On hearing of this resolution, Emma nobly set aside self-interest, and urged him not to give up authorship, which she felt was his true vocation. After a period at home Hardy moved to London in March 1872 to assist Roger Smith, Professor of Architecture at the RIBA, in designing schools for the London School Board, after the 1870 Act had made elementary education compulsory for all. Moule, when they met by chance on a crossing by Trafalgar Square, advised him not to give up writing altogether. About this time, after a number of inquiries about his account, Hardy managed to obtain a settlement with Tinsley. Although Moule's article had increased sales of *Desperate Remedies*, only 370 of the 500 printed copies had been purchased, earning Hardy a repayment of almost £60. He was pleased with this and, no doubt, with Tinsley's invitation to call at his office and discuss his next book. The two met accidentally in the Strand, where Hardy told him he had a short story ready, and an outline for another in three volumes. The result of this meeting was that Hardy asked his parents to forward the manuscript of *Under the Greenwood Tree*, which he sent to Tinsley without looking at it, and with a message that he wished to have nothing to do with publishing accounts. He was offered £30 for the copyright, and accepted it, not knowing that Tinsley thought it 'the best little prose idyll' he had ever read.

Neither Crickmay nor Hardy was present when the restored church at St Juliot was opened on 11 April 1872. It had cost approximately £1275, £900 being contributed by its patron, who was about to leave and take up his appointment as Bishop of Trinidad, the remainder, including a large donation by Mr Holder, being raised by the parish. Hardy's efforts to restore and retain the old chancel screen had come to nought, the builder having decided 'not to stand on a pound or two' but provide, in Hardy's words, 'a new and highly varnished travesty' of its decaying predecessor.

He now lived at 4 Celbridge Place, Westbourne Park, very near his former abode at 16 Westbourne Park Villas. Late at night in the early part of May he was busy with proof-reading; some evenings were spent in the preparation of drawings for Blomfield, with whom he was 'in frequent and friendly touch'. *Under the Greenwood Tree* appeared early in June, and earned appreciative reviews in the *Athenaeum* and the *Pall Mall Gazette*; Horace Moule's anonymous notice in the *Saturday Review* did not appear until 28 September, however. Although Tinsley was keen, and advertised liberally, sales were never high, largely for the reasons Alexander Macmillan gave in his forecast. Nevertheless, *Under the Greenwood Tree* is a minor masterpiece, and remains as much in demand as ever. It is Hardy's most happy and idyllic novel, and the reason is not hard to seek. George Eliot's praise in *Adam Bede* of rural life in Dutch paintings (hinted at in his sub-title) and her portrayal of the old village choir in 'Amos Barton' had made him realize the fictional possibilities of the Stinsford choir he had heard so much about, and knew so much of as a caroller, in his boyhood. The love story is inseparable from its demise; and its telling, even the awakening of jealousy, is inspired by happy thoughts of the 'young lady in summer blue' who played the harmonium at Mr Holder's services. The humour and wisdom of rural comment help to give this early novel a rare maturity and permanence.

Hardy was encouraged more than ever before to write the three-volume novel he was planning, but he did not come to a final agreement with Tinsley on this until late in July, after being asked on what terms he would write a story for *Tinsleys' Magazine*, to run serially for a year. Hardy thought over the matter, and proposed £200 for this, £15 to be paid for each monthly instalment and the remainder when the three-volume edition appeared, the copyright to return to the author one year after the latter's first publication. Tinsley was surprised at such business acumen but accepted the terms, and persuaded Hardy to promise the first instalment soon enough for the artist to prepare the accompanying illustration for the September number, which was due for publication on 15 August. Hardy foolishly accepted, without considering what pressures he could be under; he had done no more than make notes for 'the opening chapters and general outline' of his story. He undertook to deliver the script for the whole novel three months before its serial completion. It was to be called 'A Winning Tongue Had He'. He must have changed the design of his novel, and it is not surprising that, very late in life when questioned on this, he was unable to see how such a title could have been suitable. The verse containing this well-known line was included in the original third chapter, but replaced in the serial edition which had been appearing anonymously as *A Pair of Blue Eyes*.

After giving Professor Smith notice that he would be taking a holiday in August, Hardy wrote more than the first five chapters required for the first instalment, and left London for Cornwall on 7 August. Except for the opening and the slight change already indicated, the text of the first instalment shows no significant difference from that published today. The biographical implications of this important. They show that Hardy had already met Emma's father at Kirland and seen Lanhydrock House (also near Bodmin), the original (as he hinted in the 1912 postscript to his preface and admitted in June 1920) of Lord Luxellian's home, which he describes in the fourth chapter. Mr Swancourt, the heroine's father, has all the snobbishness of John Attersoll Gifford; his character does not change, and very soon he is to show the penchant for quoting Latin which was characteristic of Emma's father. She may have visited Lanhydrock House before meeting Hardy, and would have had little difficulty in arranging another visit with him; his knowledge of the masters exhibited there suggests as much. The aristocratic lady whom she had known at Tintagel was a Miss R—, almost certainly one of the Robartes family which had owned Lanhydrock for centuries. Emma may have visited the house when she stayed 'some months' not far off with friends at Lanivet, before her sister's marriage. She could have introduced Hardy to her father in the summer of 1870 or in October 1871, and, while at Kirland House, would have done everything possible to satisfy his interest in architecture and paintings by ensuring that he visited this seventeenth-century mansion with its striking barbican and its gallery of paintings.

Hardy travelled to Plymouth on the *Avoca*, a boat belonging to the Irish Mail Packet Company; the voyage was to supply the background for a chapter of his story. He had asked Tinsley to address the proofs to Kirland House, and it was there that he spent the first part of his holiday. He must have checked the proofs and returned them without delay. Already it was clear that his authorial allegiance to his own social status was to feature strongly in his portrayal of the architect Stephen Smith's parents, the mother particularly; her husband is the master-mason to Lord Luxellian's estate, as Hardy's father had been to Kingston Maurward. Hardy and Emma may have been on their way from Lanhydrock to Lanivet, where they were visiting her former friends at St Benet's Abbey, when she, inclined to lameness when tired, sought support against the signpost on the St Austell road, and rested her arms on two of the signs, as if she were, Hardy thought (and remembered in 'Near Lanivet, 1872'), 'like one crucified'. Later, in his absence, she may have said something about his background to her father, possibly in response to his prying after reading *A Pair of Blue Eyes*. In 'I rose and went to Rou'tor Town', a poem ironically written in the same stanza as 'When I set out for Lyonnesse', she is imagined setting out in the morning for Bodmin (its poetic name from Row or Rough Tor, a height on Bodmin Moor), to be struck by sorrow at the 'evil wrought' on him she had loved so truly. Gifford had probably declared or insinuated that Hardy was not socially worthy of the daughter he idolized.

Hardy may have felt some relief when he left Kirland House for St Juliot, where he usually found Caddell Holder a congenial companion, though his health was poor. One day he walked to Tintagel Castle, where he sketched a stone altar which he looked for in vain years later. Much of his time was taken up with the continuation of his novel. Tinsley, alarmed perhaps by the late arrival of the first instalment, wrote an urgent reminder, and Hardy completed sufficient for the second by the end of the month, after an excursion which took him to Brent Tor, north of Tavistock, where he sketched a church on a hill which reminded him of a volcano; he may have been on a visit to Emma's relatives at Launceston.

On 8 September, the fifteenth Sunday after Trinity, he read the 'proper lesson' from Jeremiah at the St Juliot evening service. (It was held in the afternoon, like the service in 'Quid Hic Agis?'. This poem is structured on three readings of the lesson on Elijah and the still small voice from the First Book of Kings, which was 'decreed' by the Church of England for the evening service on the ninth Sunday after Trinity. Hardy had heard the first of these readings during his second visit to Cornwall in August 1870; he had the third in mind in 1916 during the war with Germany, his poem making its appearance on 19 August, the day before the appointed reading. As the lesson contained some of his favourite Bible verses, which he had heard himself mentally reading many times, and particularly as he had recalled it imaginatively in St Juliot Church when he made Henry Knight read it in *A Pair of Blue Eyes*, he could easily have assumed forty-four years later that it was the lesson he himself had read there in 1872, and that it had been read in August. Easter was early that year, and the Sunday for the reading fell on 28 July, ten days before Hardy left London for Cornwall.) He had prolonged his stay a week; Tinsley had written again; Hardy had sent off his script, and promised to have his copy ready in future by the beginning of the month.

After continuing his novel in London, Hardy was invited by Professor Smith to continue his architectural work, another of his designs having been successful in the London School Board competitions. Needing to devote himself fully to *A Pair of Blue Eyes*, he told his employer what his preoccupation had been, and declined regretfully, having enjoyed work with such an 'able and amiable man'. As he did not find London conducive to writing, he returned to Bockhampton at the end of September to complete his novel in good time. After 'a flying visit' to St Juliot early in the new year, he stayed at home until the beginning of June. The last portion of the serial was forwarded on 12 March 1873 for its appearance in the July number of *Tinsleys' Magazine*. Each of the eleven instalments had a full-page illustration by J. A. Pasquier, for whose benefit Hardy had sometimes sent sketches. The three-volume novel, the first to bear his name on the title-page, appeared in the last week of May. Although somewhat improvised at times, often hurried, and patchy in texture, it was altogether no small achievement in the circumstances; in the words of Edmund Blunden, it is 'sketchily beautiful and daringly contrivanced'. Directed by the death theme from the beginning (lines associating love and death from Shelley's 'When the lamp is shattered' being substituted for the 'And a winning tongue had he' verse of Elfride's early song, from 'The Banks of Allan Water'), it has a recurrent poetic imaginativeness which appealed to Tennyson and Coventry Patmore. However much it draws from what Hardy had seen and experienced in Cornwall, and from people he had met, the characters are imagined rather than copied. Emma Gifford was not a weak vacillating Elfride, and there is probably more of Hardy in Knight (a man who stands condemned by the absurd lengths of his uncharitable jealousy) than in the architect Stephen Smith, who was named after Hardy's employer and drawn to some extent from the very confident young man, John Hicks's nephew, whom Hardy came to know when he returned to the Dorchester office in 1867. Some of the rustic humour seems forced, yet the comic rivalry of the lovers at the end heightens the tragic conclusion. Despite its coincidentality this is profoundly moving, and Hardy rightly refused to change it.

At the beginning of December 1872 Hardy had received a letter which had been picked up by a labourer in the Higher Bockhampton lane. He was familiar with the primitive and casual delivery arrangements made by local post offices, but the contents of the letter were most unexpected and gratifying. It was from Leslie Stephen, who had already made his name as a writer and Alpine climber, and was known to Hardy from his articles in the *Saturday*

Review. He had enjoyed *Under the Greenwood Tree*, and discovered its authorship from Horace Moule; it was long, he wrote, since he had received more pleasure from a new author. He invited Hardy to write a story with more incident, though not with a murder in every number (he probably knew something of *Desperate Remedies*, though he had not read it), for *The Cornhill Magazine*. Stephen had been appointed editor in 1871. Hardy must have felt that it would be a great distinction to contribute to the magazine which had first been edited by Thackeray, but he was still busy with *A Pair of Blue Eyes*. A great opportunity to raise his literary status lay before him, and it would be folly not to make the most of it; he probably discussed the prospects with Emma Gifford a few weeks later. Knowing full well the dangers of writing under great pressure for serialization, Hardy had expressed his regret that he was unable to accept the offer immediately, but hoped that, at a later stage, Stephen would consider 'a pastoral tale' he thought of calling 'Far from the Madding Crowd', in which the principal characters would be 'a woman-farmer, a shepherd, and a sergeant in the Dragoon Guards'. The novel idea of a woman farmer may have come from Emma, who had been very interested in one, an old widow, in north Cornwall. Hardy had not time to give the subject much thought; Boldwood does not seem to have been considered, and no one can be certain what part he had in mind, if any at this juncture, for Fanny Robin. Fortunately Stephen was prepared to wait, and hoped that Hardy would call at the offices of his publishers, Smith, Elder & Co., and talk over the proposed novel the next time he was in town.

At home, after completing *A Pair of Blue Eyes*, Hardy had more time to talk with his mother and make notes on stories and folk-rhymes she remembered. He probably thought about his next novel, but decided to take time off before beginning in earnest. The prospect of writing for *The Cornhill* must have outweighed any doubts he felt when he consulted Charles Moule in May on the advisability of devoting himself entirely to fiction. On 9 June, a week after his thirty-third birthday, he travelled to London, where he saw some French plays. Six days later he met Horace Moule and dined with him at the British Hotel. Moule was on his way to Ipswich, where, after an uncertain period which he seems to have spent mainly in London writing articles and reviews, he had officiated as the Poor Law inspector for East Anglia under the Local Government Board for almost a year. Hardy, after showing his brother Henry places of interest in London during the next five days, took an early-evening train to Cambridge, where he dined with Moule at his college (Queens'), and strolled along the Backs with him in glorious sunshine. Next morning they visited King's College, and climbed to the roof, where they looked across the fens to Ely Cathedral, which could be seen gleaming sunlit in the distance. Horace's smile at the railway station remained in Hardy's memory as he left for London, where he caught a train for Bath, on his way to see Emma Gifford, who was staying there with Miss d'Arville, a friend she had met at St Juliot. The poem 'Midnight on Beechen, 187–' presents Hardy's view of the lamplit city from a wooded height immediately to the south, as he sat wishing that his well-beloved were there with him. After a day with her and her friend in Bath and Bristol, he and Emma visited Clifton, where they found by chance in a newsagent's a copy of the *Spectator* with a commendatory review of *A Pair of Blue Eyes* by John Hutton, who had condemned *Desperate Remedies* as an outrage on landed society, and who, realizing what esteem Hardy was now winning, had written to him on 29 April, admitting the severity of his censure in the same magazine. Hardy spent the last day of June looking round Bath for himself, studying architecture more closely and discovering places of historical and literary interest he would have otherwise missed. With Emma he devoted the following day to Wordsworth, making a trip to Chepstow and the Wye valley, where they explored Tintern Abbey, which he found time to sketch. On 2 July he returned home to concentrate on *Far from the Madding Crowd*.

9

Shock, Success, and Marriage

Hardy was happy writing in the bedroom study which overlooked the garden and orchard at Higher Bockhampton. He could meditate on his subject as he walked in congenial surroundings on the heath or in the neighbouring woods, jotting down his thoughts, sometimes, when he had no scrap of paper with him, on 'large dead leaves, white chips left by the wood-cutters, or pieces of stone or slate that came to hand'; he had found that 'when he carried a pocket-book his mind was barren as the Sahara'. The high hopes he entertained are the subject of his poem 'In the Seventies', where he speaks of the 'magic light' that 'certain starry thoughts' threw on his 'worktimes and soundless hours of rest', and of the vision which was unknown to his neighbours and the 'nodders' whom he passed. Not until the end of September did he forward, at Leslie Stephen's request, all he had written, enough for two or three monthly parts in *The Cornhill*. It was sufficient for Stephen to make a final acceptance.

On Sunday, 21 September 1873, Hardy had walked almost ten miles to the sheep fair on Woodbury Hill, an ancient earthwork on the eastern side of Bere Regis, hoping no doubt to find background for a scene in his novel. (Ultimately he combined it with the recollections of Turpin's ride at Cooke's Circus in a dramatic presentation of Troy's ominous return at Greenhill Fair.) Three days later he was shocked to hear that Horace Moule had committed suicide at Cambridge. On the evening before he attended his funeral at Fordington, he sat by Ten Hatches Weir above Grey's Bridge, looking toward the church tower and sketching the chalk mound thrown up from 'the waiting grave' below (a scene recalled many years later in the poem 'Before My Friend Arrived').

Moule had long been subject to bouts of depression and heavy drinking. Nothing is known of the circumstances in which he left Marlborough College suddenly in 1868. If he spent much of the intervening time at home and in London, little is known precisely

111

of his life, though it seems likely that Hardy kept in touch more, and knew more, than any evidence shows. If being the father, or believing he was the father, of an illegitimate child was the tragedy of his life, as Florence Hardy gathered from her husband, this may have been the subject of Hardy's poem 'The Place on the Map', which, very significantly perhaps, was first published with the subtitle 'A Poor Schoolmaster's Story'. Setting and season may suggest Cornwall and the summer drought which he experienced in August 1870, but the poem is fictionally framed, and devised principally as a protest against conventional views on love by the author of *Jude the Obscure*. If Moule had an unfortunate affair with a woman of low repute, it seems absurd to associate her with 'She at His Funeral', though the date assigned to it is 187—. The poem, which could present a wholly imaginary situation, is based on an irony which would appeal immensely to Hardy: relatives clothed in sable stand round the grave 'with griefless eye', while the dead man's sweetheart, in her usual brightly coloured gown, remains consumed with burning sorrow outside the churchyard wall. The church of the accompanying illustration is clearly intended to suggest that at Stinsford.

Moule must have found his employment as a Poor Law inspector depressing, especially after seeing workhouse alcoholics in the last stages of helplessness. After drinking for days in the country, he had been rescued by his brother Frederick, vicar of Yaxley near Peterborough, and suffered from the preying fear that such breakdowns would lead to his dismissal. He knew that his talents had been dissipated, and the thought of Hardy's success and happy prospects of marriage may have dispirited him at times. His hopes of marrying a governess whom Frederick's wife thought highly estimable were dashed when she broke their engagement, convinced that Horace was incurable. She is most probably the person Hardy imagined him addressing when he wrote the poem 'Standing by the Mantelpiece' late in life. It cannot be assumed that he saw the wax of the burning candle form an ill-omened shape as he and Moule talked at night on 20 June. The image probably came to the author of this dramatized scene as a result of associating his visit with Moule to the interior of King's College Chapel the next morning with the fantastic shapes in which the candles guttered, changing continually before wisps dropped off, some of them like shreds of shrouds, when he and Emma attended evening service there in October 1880.

After visiting a number of workhouses, Moule had reached Queens' College, where he often stayed during his working periods, on Friday, 19 September, two to three weeks before Michaelmas Term began. He was so depressed that his doctor arranged for a nurse to be in attendance the next morning, and sent a telegram to Charles Moule, Fellow of Corpus Christi, who arrived on Sunday, the day Hardy made his excursion to Woodbury Hill. After three hours of conversation, Charles began to write in the outer room as Horace retired to bed. He had not been occupied long before his attention was caught by a dripping sound; he found his brother lying on his bed covered in blood. He rushed to the porter's lodge, and a messenger was sent for the doctor. All Horace said when the latter reached his bedside was 'Easy to die' and 'Love to my mother'. The doctor confirmed that he had slashed his throat, and an open razor was found. At the inquest next day a verdict of 'suicide whilst in a state of temporary insanity' was returned. Charles Moule did not recover from the shock for years. In the copy of *The Golden Treasury* which Horace had given him Hardy marked the sestet of Shakespeare's thirty-second sonnet (entitled 'Post Mortem' by Palgrave):

> O then vouchsafe me but this loving thought –
> 'Had my friend's muse grown with this growing age,
> A dearer birth than this his love had brought,
> To march in ranks of better equipage:
> But since he died, and poets better prove,
> Theirs for their style I'll read, his for his love.'

In 1880, after taking Emma to Queens' College, he wrote '(Cambridge) H. M. M.' against the opening of Tennyson's *In Memoriam*, lxxxvii,

> I past beside the reverend walls
> In which of old I wore the gown

and marked the line 'Another name was on the door'. It would be wrong to assume that Hardy's outlook on life was darkened by Horace Moule's death, but it was long before he recovered from the shock his great loss had brought.

As *Far from the Madding Crowd* was centred principally in the large parish of Puddletown, the Weatherbury of the novel, Hardy spent much time there familiarizing himself with rural husbandry, especially in sheep-farming. He met relatives and their acquaintances, discovered much about the old malthouse, kept by uncle John Antell's father, which used to stand almost opposite the home of the Sparks family, and heard anecdotes and sayings which he treasured for his fiction. Time and patience were needed for such rural engagements. One day James Dart, of whom he had heard much as a fiddler in the old Stinsford choir, kept him talking interminably, telling him 'neither truth nor lies, but a sort of Not Proven compound which is very relishable', including the story of a man who spent his last sixpence at the Oak, and kept taking it out of the till when the landlady's back was turned, until he had drunk 'a real skinful'; he was too honest to take any money but his own, Dart added.

During the autumn Hardy helped his father with cider-making for the last time. He had always enjoyed the sweet smell of crushed apples in the crisp air, and remembered the gleaming of the shovel at sunset in *The Woodlanders* as he had done in *Desperate Remedies*. A violent thunderstorm and its heralding early in November supplied the background which he was to use with dramatic effect when Gabriel Oak with Bathsheba's assistance thatches her stacked corn, while her husband and other harvest revellers lie in drunken stupor.

A week or so earlier Stephen had asked whether Hardy could maintain the supply of copy if, instead of making its first appearance in the spring, as arranged, his novel started in the January number of *The Cornhill*, which was due out in the third week of December. Hardy felt that he could, and an agreement was reached whereby he would receive £400 for the serial. He informed Stephen that, in order to ensure that his rustics, though quaint, should appear intelligent and not boorish in any of his illustrations, he had made sketches during the summer of such 'out-of-the-way things' as smockfrocks, gaiters, sheepcrooks, rick staddles, a sheep-washing pool, and an old-fashioned malthouse, which he could send if necessary. While in London (where he stayed at 4 Celbridge Place again) for a few days in December, he met Leslie Stephen for the first time, at 8 Southwell Gardens, a new house in South Kensington, with the pavements hardly laid and the road stones still not rolled in. Stephen had chosen to live there because the surroundings reminded him of his childhood when he played with his nurse in the neighbouring fields. Invited to lunch the next day, Hardy arrived in raw yellow fog, and found Mrs Stephen there with her lively elder sister Anne Thackeray, both draped in shawls. Having studied several of his essays and his graphic history of the French Revolution with keen interest and admiration, he was pleased to hear about Thomas Carlyle, whom Stephen had visited the previous day. When the conversation turned to biblical stories of David and Saul, Hardy was quick to comment on the artistry with which they were presented; 'in a dry grim tone' Stephen advised him to study their presentation by Voltaire.

Hardy spent the Christmas of 1873 in Cornwall, meeting, it seems from 'The Seven Times', Emma at Launceston. (In this poem he recalls the six pre-marriage visits to Cornwall which he remembered in his *Life*; he had forgotten that of October 1871; the seventh combines the two he made to St. Juliot and the neighbourhood after Emma's death.) As he was returning on New Year's Eve, he bought a copy of *The Cornhill Magazine* on Plymouth Hoe, and, not having heard from Leslie Stephen in the meantime, was thrilled to find his story given pride of place at the beginning, with a striking illustration, not by a man as he expected but by Miss Helen Paterson. He sent Emma a copy, trusting it would be a delightful surprise, vindicating her faith in him as a writer; he had never told her how his new story had developed. Soon he found himself in a position which reminded him of crises when he was writing *A Pair of Blue Eyes*, that of having the beginning of a novel in print with little time left to complete the instalment which was due. He worked so strenuously that by February he was able to send enough copy for two or three further numbers. Where Emma spent most of her time in 1874 before her marriage is uncertain; Hardy's memorial of her at St Juliot records that she lived there from 1868 to 1873. She may have stayed with her brother early in 1874, Hardy meeting her at the station, as he recalled in 'The Change'; the date – 'Jan.–Feb. 1913' – and the opening suggest that this is an anniversary poem, and that he spent a week with her in London. She could have spent much time with her father, some with her cousins at Launceston, some possibly with her friends at Lanivet. Nothing indicates that she was invited to Higher Bockhampton, though an uncertain hint has survived from an indirect source that she independently ventured on such a visit. What evidence we have suggests that she already knew the status of Hardy's family, and, unlike her father, accepted it. How his sense of social inferiority weighed on Hardy may be seen from a letter he wrote to Geneviève Smith, wife of the Evangelical rector of West Stafford, a village patriarch of aristocrat descent and a friend of the vicar of Fordington, Henry Moule. He had accepted her invitation to dine with them a few days after his return from Cornwall, and had been waited on by James Pole, butler at Stafford House and father of Cassie, the girl he and Mrs Smith thought Hardy had jilted; the class situation here, with the butler's disapproval of the guest, had a comical side which Hardy was to exploit in *The Hand of Ethelberta*. Two days later he sent his hostess a copy of *A Pair of Blue Eyes* to read, adding that he would be delighted if she found anything in it as pleasant as he had found her conversation; he admitted his handicap, both personally and as an author, from not having experienced 'until very lately' the society of educated women. He had been reminded of Anne Thackeray and her sister.

To write with such candour Hardy must have been impressed by Mrs Smith's sincerity; she was Evangelical like her husband. Her happy disposition and the advantages of her lot in the large thatched rectory were manifest. Her father had been a well-known host and wit in Bath; she had travelled much on the Continent, and, according to her daughter, spoke French like a native; she was a most accomplished singer, and had other artistic gifts. Much of her life had been devoted to the upbringing of a large family and helping her husband in his parish. They had been married in 1836 at Lyme Regis, where she lived with her widowed mother. Very shortly afterwards the Revd Reginald Smith accepted the West Stafford living from John Floyer of Stafford House, with whom he remained a neighbour and close friend for more than fifty years. Hardy later became acquainted with two of his daughters, and formed a lasting friendship with Bosworth, the eldest-but-one of the family, a man slightly older than himself whose integrity and distrust of affectation he admired.

If Hardy was socially diffident, his confidence as a writer must have been fortified by his recognition in America, where, largely through the interest of the New York publisher Henry Holt, *Under the Greenwood Tree* and *A Pair of Blue Eyes* had been included in the Leisure Hour Series of Holt & Williams in June and July of 1873. Their sales encouraged Holt to invite corrections for the issue of *Desperate Remedies*. Though unlikely to gain much financially, Hardy complied, and this novel, for which he saw little future in England, was added to the series in March. When he wrote, Holt had been impressed by the view of one of his readers that the first *Cornhill* instalment of *Far from the Madding Crowd* was 'good enough' to have been written by Thomas Hardy, and asked if arrangements had been made for the publication of the novel in America, stating that it had been announced by another house, but clearly implying a prior claim to publishing it. Hardy informed him that his publishers had arranged for its appearance in America without knowing that he had any preference in the matter, and that in the circumstances he could not interfere. His astonishment can be judged when he received a letter from Smith, Elder & Co., the tone of which hurt his feelings, based on the inference that he had been negotiating independently with Holt & Williams. Replying on 4 March, Hardy sent a full account of his relations with his American publisher, and wondered if he had been the victim of some 'sharp practice'. He thought that, as James Osgood had bought the right to reprint it from *The Cornhill*, his story was appearing in the *Atlantic Monthly*, where he preferred it to be; in fact it was published in *Every Saturday*, which Osgood had sold, from the end of January to October 1874. However, an agreement satisfactory to all parties was reached, whereby it appeared again from June to December in the *Semi-Weekly New York Tribune*, and was added to the Leisure Hour Series at the end of November, shortly after the publication of the book in England. As the *Cornhill* serialization was not completed until the December issue, Hardy had sent Holt, at his request, the concluding chapters in order to expedite his publication of the complete novel. With this, his position in America was established; his next six novels were to appear in the Leisure Hour Series soon after their publication in England.

Dining with Stephen in April, Hardy renewed his acquaintance with the two daughters of Thackeray, whose life had been cut short in 1863; he also met his publisher George Smith and his family. When he dined with them in May he was introduced to his illustrator Helen Paterson and Mrs Anne Procter, wife of the popular writer 'Barry Cornwall'. Hardy was undoubtedly attracted by the former, with whom he discussed details for illustrations to his story; one cannot be certain that he felt quite as 'romantical' about her then as he did in July 1906, when he told his friend Edmund Gosse, apropos of her marriage to the poet William Allingham in August 1874 and his own to Emma Gifford the next month, that 'those two almost simultaneous weddings would have been one but for a stupid blunder of God Almighty'. Written forty years after he and Helen first met, Hardy's poem 'The

Opportunity' dwells on such 'chance' of things, as Browning had done, to the same metre and on the same subject, in 'Youth and Art'. With Mrs Procter, soon to be widowed, Hardy was far more at home; she had known an astonishing number of famous writers and other celebrities over the years, and could tell many anecdotes of them with delightful humour. Hardy drew a youthful portrait of her in Anne Garland, heroine of *The Trumpet-Major*. All was going well for him at the time of their first meeting; both his editor and publisher were pleased with his work, and he continued it with such zeal that it was concluded in July, the last few chapters being written 'at a gallop' to gain time for his wedding preparations. Whatever the fascination of Helen Paterson, it was temporary; he was still ardently in love with Emma, and it was only in after-years, at times of depressing disillusionment, that he indulged in regretful dreams of what might have been with one 'lost prize' or another. It was his dedication to literary work and business – a major preoccupation with him for the rest of his life – that caused Emma some jealousy, as he pressed on with the conclusion of *Far from the Madding Crowd*. 'My work, unlike your work of writing', she wrote in July, 'does not occupy my true mind much. . . . Your novel seems sometimes like a child all your own and none of me.' She regretted that she was not in a position to help him with his literary work. She wished to share and sustain his main interest, without realizing to the full what a long sacrifice it would cost her. Hardy had concluded his story with the shrewd anti-romantic reflection that shared interests are the key to enduring love between those who are drawn to each other. He repeated this conviction in two of his last novels, but nowhere did he express it with more explicit eloquence than near the end of *Far from the Madding Crowd*.

Though he was anxious for the sake of his immediate future to please Leslie Stephen, whose advice he found illuminating at times, his wish 'to be considered a good hand at a serial' was temporary; on this subject he hinted at 'higher aims' in pursuit of which he would make his own artistic decisions. The warnings of his cautious editor to proceed 'in a gingerly fashion' with Troy's seduction of Fanny Robin could have given him little idea of what would happen when the presentation of truth to life in alliance with art brought him into conflict with the Grundyism of the Victorian establishment. In March 1874 he found time to plan ahead, as he was to do again and again before he relinquished novel-writing, for what was to be his major work, *The Dynasts*. 'Let Europe be the stage and have scenes continually shifting', he wrote. This suggests that he may already have regarded prose fiction, however artistic, as a means to an end, his aim being to achieve security and then turn to poetry, his first literary love, including a large-scale drama on the Napoleonic wars.

The 'winning tongue had he' theme which Hardy had originally in mind for *A Pair of Blue Eyes* was obviously brought to life in the role of Troy. No hint of a change of course appears in the former novel, but one may be suspected in *Far from the Madding Crowd*. The hero who wins the reader's sympathy for his endurance and loyalty, and who becomes a foil to such extremes as Troy and Boldwood, is initially presented with unmistakable touches of satirical amusement. There may be artistic intention in this shift of authorial attitude, marking the strengthening of character and purpose which obtains after Oak has suffered disappointment and disaster.

Hardy was already preparing the plan of his next novel; it was to be set aside, but he returned to it when he began *The Woodlanders* more than ten years later. Its background was 'one of those sequestered spots' where 'dramas of a grandeur and unity truly Sophoclean are enacted in the real, by virtue of the concentrated passions and closely-knit interdependence of the lives therein'. Whether Sophoclean or not, the drama of *Far from the Madding Crowd* answers this description more than does *The Woodlanders*. Both novels almost certainly came to Hardy's mind as a result of reflecting on George Eliot's impressive introduction to *Felix Holt*, which presents a 'far from the madding crowd' scene where the shepherd's 'solar system' is his parish, and 'the master's temper and the casualties of lambing-time' are his 'region of storms'. Much of *Far from the Madding Crowd* reveals the 'noiseless tenor' of such a rural life in a 'sequestered' locality, where the uprooting of an old apple tree 'that used to bear two hogsheads of cider' or the installation of an iron pump and stone trough for drawing water from an old well is an exciting event, where five decades have hardly altered the embroidery of a smockfrock 'by the breadth of a hair', and the purposes of the great barn have remained unchanged for centuries. Yet the noiseless world which recalls Gray's elegy in George Eliot's introduction is associated with human agonies, as is Hardy's in *Far from the Madding Crowd*. Her long preamble ends with a profound evocation of a doom-laden house

which is reminiscent of Greek tragedy at its best. The uncommonness of events which disturb parish life in Hardy's ironically
entitled novel is even more sensational (or 'melodramatic' in the
popular sense of the word), straining credulity with Fanny Robin's
painful journey to her death in the workhouse, or with the startling murder of Troy by the maddened Boldwood.

So moving is the story it can bear such strains, but the strength
of the novel lies elsewhere. After reading in the *Saturday Review*
that it was worthy of Shakespeare, Hardy had made a close study
of the Rainbow Inn scene where the rustic worthies of *Silas Marner*
discuss unusual events in the village. He uses the same techniques
with more variety in developing his 'chorus' at Warren's malthouse. The humour of his gossips there and elsewhere has rarely
been surpassed; without it the novel would lose its identity.
Imaginatively it gains even more from a succession of pictorial
scenes, which serve less as settings than as external manifestations
of inner conflict or states of mind in the principal characters. They
are varied, and show unusual observation and imaginative creativity. The gradual extinction of hope in Fanny Robin, for example,
as she makes her way to appeal to Sergeant Troy in the barracks
beyond the river is conveyed in a crescendo of tragic impressiveness by environmental changes which were most probably suggested by the scene in *Middlemarch* when the shrinking of the flat
landscape in 'uniform whiteness and low-hanging uniformity of
cloud' as the snow continues to fall reflects Dorothea's dying hope
of ever reaching those 'clear heights' of intellectual and spiritual
communion which she had expected to share when she married
Casaubon.

For some strange over-cautious reason Stephen published *Far
from the Madding Crowd* anonymously. A reviewer in the *Spectator*
surmised that the first instalment was the work of George Eliot;
next month he was able to reveal the true authorship. After taking
hints from George Eliot for situations and scenes in all his published novels except *A Pair of Blue Eyes*, Hardy had reason for
concern, although Stephen, who had read more than a third of the
novel when he wrote, thought that 'the supposed affinity' resided
mainly in the humorous treatment of rustics by both authors.
When further resemblances between them were pointed out in the
reviewing of *Far from the Madding Crowd* as a whole, Hardy must
have felt even more that the expediency of abandoning the woodland story he had planned, and of making 'a plunge in a new and
untried direction', was justified.

Working happily at home, in and from a familiar environment which never ceased to supply something new in natural observation or in strange and sometimes exciting revelations of local events, past and present, Hardy the writer had prospered as never before. Marriage prospects and growing success in *The Cornhill* and America had been additional spurs. His return to 4 Celbridge Place marks the beginning of a period of uncertainty and experiment in his fiction. There he hastily wrote his first short story, 'Destiny and a Blue Cloak', for the *New York Times*, corrected serial proofs for Leslie Stephen, and resumed acquaintance with theatres and friends. Valuing words and expression more than anything else in drama, he admired the '*still* manner' of Horace Wigan, an actor who did not distract his audience by movement and gesticulation when speaking.

Hardy's marriage took place on Thursday, 17 September, at St Peter's, Elgin Avenue, Paddington, Emma's uncle, Dr Edwin Hamilton Gifford, Canon of Worcester and headmaster of King Edward's School, Birmingham, officiating. It seems strange that the ceremony did not take place at St Juliot, and that its only witnesses were Emma's younger brother Walter, at whose London home she had been staying, and the daughter of Hardy's London landlady. Hardy undoubtedly would have desired the quietest of weddings, and Emma had most probably agreed; she remembered the occasion happily. The day was perfect, 'wearing a soft, sunny luminousness; just as it should be', she wrote. They proceeded to Brighton, staying at Morton's Hotel in Queen's Road, where Hardy wrote to his brother Henry, indicating clearly, as if to emphasize non-discrimination, the minimal few who were present at the wedding, and inviting his family to look out for the announcement which he and Emma had sent to the *Dorset County Chronicle*; they were on their way to Normandy, then to Paris; he hoped to collect material there for his next story, and find a reply at Celbridge Place as soon as they returned.

Emma kept an illustrated diary of their honeymoon holiday. Its concentration of notes suggests that she did not wish to forget any of it; perhaps she thought she was preserving observations which might be useful in Hardy's fiction. At Brighton they walked on the old pier, caught sight of Beachy Head, listened to bands, attended a concert, and visited the aquarium three times. The Pavilion with its exotic architecture and Prince Regent associations was of special interest, and remembered in *The Dynasts*. On Sunday they attended morning and evening service at St Peter's, where Hardy recalled a service he attended there on the first Sunday after Easter in 1864. Outside it was like a Parisian Sunday, with bands, excursionists, and enjoyment almost everywhere they went. The next morning Tom bathed in the rough sea; in the evening they left for Dieppe and Rouen, where they stayed at the Hôtel d'Albion. Hardy remembered this and the view from the cathedral spire, including St Ouen Church (where Emma had been most impressed by the colouring), when he wrote his next novel, *The Hand of Ethelberta*. The diary reveals a painter's sensitivity to colour, and Emma's interest in French food, dress, and bedroom arrangements. In Paris she was delighted with her first view of the Place de la Concorde by moonlight. Hardy used his copy of Murray's *Handbook for Visitors to Paris* as a guide, and they visited the Louvre, the Tuileries, Notre Dame, the Morgue (where Emma found the bodies repulsive), the Hôtel Cluny, the Père Lachaise cemetery (where she plucked an ivy leaf, which she kept as a souvenir, from Balzac's grave), the tomb of Napoleon and the Hôtel des Invalides. They saw *Le pauvre jeune homme* at the Vaudeville Theatre. One day they went by train to Versailles, another, by 'omnibus tramway' along the Seine and over it to the wooded park of St Cloud. Emma was struck by the beautiful flower-shops of Paris, the cleanliness of its streets and of the smoothly ironed and starched white coats of café waiters. Gradually she became aware that she attracted attention; men turned to look at her, and women sometimes passed with 'a short laugh', She began to wonder whether she was *strange-looking* or merely picturesque in her hat. However unusual her head-dress, her appearance was striking; she had a rich complexion, a certain nobility of countenance, set off by ringlets of brightly coloured hair, and she radiated vitality. On 30 September she bade farewell to her 'charmante ville':

> Adieu to the Boulevards. To the gay shops – To the 'gens' sitting in the streets To the vivants enfants To the white caps of the femmes To the river and its boats To the clear atmosphere and brilliant colourings.

London seemed very dirty when she and Tom reached it in the rain next day after a rough Channel crossing. She must have been quickly in touch with her father when they eventually found rooms to rent at St David's Villa, Surbiton, for when they arrived late in the afternoon of 6 October he was there in the garden with her cousin's daughter Annie and a retriever. He may have been staying with his son Walter. He had not come to show his disapproval of Hardy; perhaps Emma had lived with him during the year, and done much to reconcile him to her forthcoming marriage. If the story which Hardy's second wife told is true (and there is no reason to suppose she invented it), that he referred to him in a letter as a 'low-born churl' who had 'presumed to marry into' his family, it must have been at some later period when, becoming maudlin and drinking heavily in his habitual manner to find compensation for the loss of one of his family, he wished perhaps that his favourite daughter could settle comfortably and more respectably in a home of her own. In a happier state of mind, as at the present juncture, he was most probably disposed, despite his snobbish pretensions, to accept a son-in-law who had good prospects and was already winning fame.

10

Leslie Stephen

George Smith was anxious to publish *Far from the Madding Crowd* without delay, and Hardy found a copy of the text awaiting revision when he returned from his honeymoon. He completed the task by 9 October, most of his alterations being made in the opening chapters. Published on 23 November, with ten of the serial illustrations, the first edition was almost sold out by the middle of January 1875, and a second appeared in February with further improvements. A presentation copy of the first edition was sent to Canon Gifford. Although the melodramatic element was noted in some reviews, they were altogether favourable with one egregious exception, which was written by the self-assured Henry James and appeared in the *Nation* on 24 December. He thought the rustic chorus inferior to George Eliot's, and 'everything human in the book' factitious and insubstantial;'the only things we believe in are the sheep and dogs'. Hardy described nature 'with a great deal of felicity', but the novel could have been reduced to half its length. It was clever and superficial, and showed 'little sense of composition'. As this criticism appeared in New York, it may not have come to Hardy's notice for some time; meanwhile he and Emma were delighted to see the novel being read by ladies on trains between Waterloo and Surbiton.

Not surprisingly, Leslie Stephen wished to know early in December whether he would have another story which could be serialized in *The Cornhill* from April onwards. It was too soon for Hardy, however, who hoped that Smith, Elder & Co. would remain his publishers and take over his earlier novels. George Smith felt it was untimely to republish *Desperate Remedies*, but suggested that Hardy should retrieve the copyright of *Under the Greenwood Tree*. In January Tinsley asked £300 for it, together with the remaining stock and the stereotype plates, ten times the sum he had paid for it. It was far more than Hardy could afford; Smith thought the demand preposterous, and the matter was dropped. On 19 December Hardy had seen in the snow-mantled graves at Long Ditton (near Surbiton and the Thames) 'a superfluous piece of cynicism in

Nature'; it was probably about this time that he returned to poetry, in rather low key, with 'A Light Snow-Fall after Frost'. A month later he submitted a rough draft of the first part of *The Hand of Ethelberta*. Still waiting to receive proposals for a new contract towards the end of February, when he was revising this section, he urged his publishers to forward definite terms in the belief that his story would benefit were this distracting uncertainty removed. He accepted a £700 offer for serial and volume production; serialization in New York of the eleven instalments produced an additional £550. Copy for the first was sent off in March, when Hardy watched – with Stephen, it is thought – the Oxford and Cambridge boat race, before packing to make a move into London, which he thought advisable for more effective background description of several scenes in his novel, and in furtherance of his aim to show readers that 'he did not mean to imitate anybody', George Eliot in particular. All Emma's and Hardy's possessions were packed in four cases and boxes, and by 22 March they were living at 18 Newton Road, Westbourne Grove, not far from Celbridge Place and Westbourne Park Villas.

In moving to London, Hardy had a less immediate aim. Marriage had made him realize that, having staked his career on success in novel-writing, he must prepare for future contingencies when he might have to write *à la mode* and produce 'novels proper', presenting 'modern artificial life and manners', to which most of his readers were accustomed. He was to make notes year after year with this in mind when he and Emma visited London during the social season, but he made no significant use of them until he needed to vary the setting of *The Well-Beloved*, the last novel he completed. It was a momentous question for him in 1875; he discussed it with Anne Thackeray, 'who confirmed his gloomy misgivings by saying with surprise: "Certainly; a novelist must necessarily like society!"' It seemed to him that, like Ethelberta, he would have 'to carry on his life not as an emotion, but as a scientific game'. Whether he drew anything for his new novel from *The Poor Man and the Lady* is uncertain, though his subject was to a limited extent the contemporary London of Anne Thackeray and Leslie Stephen. *The Hand of Ethelberta* was to show his readiness to turn away from the metropolis for his background, and a preference for members of the working class. His satire is that of an outsider, and for the most part tempered within 'A Comedy of Chapters', a descriptive subtitle which Stephen, after giving it his approval, decided to omit because he found it suggested a farce without serious purpose.

On 23 March, the day after he and Emma occupied rooms in Newton Road, Hardy received a mysterious note from Stephen, requesting him to call that evening, no matter how late. He found him in his library at the top of 8 Southwell Gardens, which he and his wife Minnie had shared with her sister Anne since 1873; since the birth of his daughter Laura in 1870 Stephen had discovered the joy and relaxation of playing with the very young. Now he was alone, pacing up and down in his slippers and heath-coloured dressing-gown. After discussing arrangements for publishing the first instalment of the *The Hand of Ethelberta* in the July number of his magazine, he wished Hardy to witness his signature – not to his will, as Hardy had first thought, but to a deed whereby he renounced his Holy Orders under the Clerical Disabilities Act of 1870. When this formality was over, they talked about 'theologies decayed and defunct, the origin of things, the constitution of matter, the unreality of time and kindred subjects'. Stephen was a very reticent man. When Edmund Gosse and R. L. Stevenson dined with him that same spring there was so little conversation, even with the chatterbox Anne Thackeray, that they were subdued to silence; he said little all the evening, and they were not offended, for they felt he was essentially 'kind and good'. He was almost eight years Hardy's senior, and already famous as an Alpinist and scholarly author. His choice of Hardy to witness his deed of renunciation indicates a high degree of trust and respect in such a cautious man; their broad-ranging discussion suggests intellectual kinship. To appreciate why Hardy was influenced by his philosophy more than by that of any other contemporary, as he acknowledged, more needs to be known about Stephen's life and thought.

In his home and his upbringing and education Stephen had enjoyed enormous advantages. His father, of Scottish descent, had been knighted for his work in the Colonial Office, which in the course of time, by virtue of his competence and astounding memory for detail, he had virtually controlled. His mother, who had the 'healthiest nature' and outlook on life he ever knew, was the daughter of John Venn, rector of Clapham, a notable member of the Evangelical 'Clapham Sect', who 'swore by Wilberforce' and the anti-slavery crusade. From them Leslie Stephen inherited his keen moral sense and reforming zeal. He was a self-willed but most sensitive child, who could not bear reproof from his sweet and affectionate mother; he loved flowers, and delighted in drawing and listening to poetry, first Southey's *Thalaba*, then shorter poems by Wordsworth, followed by Scott's *The Lady of the Lake* and *Marmion*. So excited was his imagination that he was completely absorbed, and could repeat whole passages; in the end, for the sake of his health, poetry was tabooed and school recommended. His parents moved to Windsor, in order that he and his elder brother Fitzjames could attend Eton as day-boys, without incurring the risk of moral taint as boarders. As members of an Oppidan house, they were treated as inferiors and bullied from the outset. Leslie made progress up the school, but the unrelenting grind of longs and shorts as an aid to the appreciation of classical prosody, and the general poverty of the curriculum, meant that much of his education continued at home. In the end he acquired a considerable knowledge of classical and modern languages. After a period at King's College, London, where he attended lectures to improve his mathematics, which had been neglected at Eton, he was admitted to Trinity Hall, Cambridge, in 1850. It was his father's college as a student and now as Regius Professor of Modern History at Cambridge. Like his son he was ascetic and tenacious, but not without a sense of humour; he was sensitive, and wished he had been 'a real and true man of letters'; his work was marked by precision of thought and expression; his religion was Evangelical in a latitudinarian sense.

At the end of his first year Leslie obtained a first class and a college scholarship; his health was still erratic, but it steadily improved. He took to rowing without ever being a good oarsman, and walked occasionally with his father, whom he and Fitzjames accompanied during the long vacation of 1852 on a tour which included Brussels and the field of Waterloo, Ghent, Namur, Cologne, and Amsterdam. He had chosen to take an honours degree in mathematics, and after much coaching gained twentieth place among the Wranglers in 1854. A Trinity Hall man higher in the list was awarded the fellowship he had coveted, but Stephen stayed on happily. The college expected him to be a good tutor, and, another fellowship falling opportunely vacant, he was elected to it at Christmas, on condition that he took Holy Orders within a year. In the long vacation he had gone to Heidelberg to improve his German. The following summer he was there again, studying his Greek Testament, and finding time to tramp with a friend in the

Tyrol. In the autumn he passed an examination in theology, and was ordained deacon by the Archbishop of York at Bishopsthorpe. He took this step principally to qualify for his fellowship and relieve his father of the burden of supporting him. In 1856 he became the second or junior college tutor, and undertook this work with zeal, winning the grateful appreciation of many students as time passed.

His utter devotion to his college and university was evident in sport. He not only rowed as student and don for ten years from 1852; he undertook the coaching of the first boat with such ardour and success that in 1859 Trinity Hall went head of the river, a feat repeated in 1862. Young enthusiasts carried him shoulder-high round the court. He had acquired strength and amazing stamina, ran frenetically along the river to encourage his rowers, and did as much as anyone to found athletic sports at Cambridge. He set the example by winning first the mile event, then the two miles. In 1862 he walked almost six and three-quarter miles in an hour. Just as he, priest at Ely, was known on the towing-path of the Cam for the large patch of reddish-purple on the seat of his grey flannel trousers, so he and other exponents of 'muscular Christianity' became a byword in the Fens for their fanatical long-distance walks. The physicist John Tyndall and he had joined the Alpine Club in 1858. After traversing the Eiger Joch in 1859, and making several notable ascents in the interim, he made his name in 1861 when he was the first to climb the Schreckhorn, 'the grimmest fiend of the Oberland'. Alpine ascents remained compulsive for most of his remaining life. He was President of the Club for three years from 1865. As a climber he was as cool as he was intrepid; he took no risks. Not until 1861, after writing essays on his Alpine adventures, did Leslie Stephen begin to feel that he could write.

At Cambridge he lectured on mathematics, spent his afternoons yelling at his crew, and seemed to devote most of his evenings talking about the college or University boat. Yet he found time to read much, including books on socio-economic welfare and philosophical works by Kant, Mill, Comte, Hobbes, Hume, Locke, and Berkeley. When he was appointed to examine in the Moral Science Tripos in 1861 he was far better equipped for the post than was generally realized among Cambridge academics. Herbert Spencer's *First Principles* attracted his attention when it appeared in 1862; read by Hardy in 1867, it stimulated his thinking so much that in later years he referred to it as a book which 'used to act . . . as a

sort of patent expander' whenever he had been 'particularly nar-
rowed down by the events of life'. Philosophical thought based on
new scientific truth combined with the biblical exegesis of the
Higher Criticism to undermine Stephen's belief in the miraculous,
so much so that in the summer of 1862 he declined to take part in
college chapel services and was compelled to relinquish his tutorship. He was allowed to remain a fellow, but in 1864, feeling that
the yearly round of college activities had staled, and that Cambridge had no prospects for an agnostic, he decided to start a new
life as a writer in London. He wished to live with his mother and
sister. He had shed his Christian beliefs but not his moral principles,
and proposed to think for himself.

It is typical of Stephen that he decided in 1863 to visit America
while the Civil War was being waged, and judge the people and
the democratic aims of the Northern leaders for himself. He must
have favoured the North for its anti-slavery policy, but pro-
Confederate reports for aristocratic and Tory readers in the south
of England (including the University of Cambridge), and superior
attitudes fostered by travellers from Harriet Martineau to Dickens,
made him suspect that Establishment views were outdated and
biased. He travelled to New England and the South, visited the
fighting-front, met Lincoln and other leaders, and made friends for
life, particularly James Russell Lowell. He was no starry-eyed
idealist, and knew that American statesmen had much to learn,
but he had no doubt that Northern aims and their civilization had
been traduced by provincial British bigotry, and wrote on his
return a long and carefully prepared pamphlet, signed 'L.S.', in
which, regretting that 'the freest nation in the old world' was
alienating 'the great nation in the new', he claimed with every
justification that *The Times* had been guilty of 'foolish vituperation'
and 'a public crime'.

Stephen's main aims as a writer, however, were in philosophy
and literature. His brother Fitzjames, who wrote for the *Saturday
Review*, introduced him to John Douglas Cook, the editor; and so
successful were Leslie's articles that he was given a retaining fee of
50 guineas a year as a wedding present in 1867. (Disqualified by
marriage, he could no longer retain his Trinity Hall fellowship.)
For the *Pall Mall Gazette* he wrote *Sketches from Cambridge, by a Don*,
and for the *Nation* in New York, where his radical views were more
acceptable, a fortnightly letter on English affairs. In *Fraser's Magazine*
and the *Fortnightly Review*, when its editorship was assumed by

John Morley, he was able to write more freely at home. Hardy had no doubt read some of these articles, which appeared in 1873 as *Essays on Free-thinking and Plain-speaking*. One, 'A Bad Five Minutes in the Alps', which appeared in the November 1872 issue of *Fraser's*, undoubtedly inspired the far more exciting and convincing scene in *A Pair of Blue Eyes* when Knight, suspended within inches of death on a slope above a high cliff, is confronted by the eyes of an embedded trilobite fossil which flash upon his visual imagination a sense of man's ephemerality in the periods of geological time. Stephen's contributions to *The Cornhill* began in 1866, and it is strange that such a free-thinker·was made its editor in 1871. The long series of literary essays he wrote for this magazine appeared as *Hours in a Library* in three volumes (1874, 1876, 1879), and exerted a considerable influence on Hardy's choice of reading, undoubtedly extending his interest in such authors as Richardson, Fielding, Scott, Wordsworth, and Crabbe.

The year after their marriage he had taken his wife to America, where they stayed at Cambridge with the Lowells before visiting Boston, New York, Philadelphia, and Washington, which he thought 'about the most God-forgotten place on this earth'. His wife's health being delicate, he spent the summer of 1870 with her by the Thames at Surbiton; a much more strenuous holiday for him followed in the Swiss Alps. At the end of 1874 he chose to read eighteenth-century sermons (which he thought, with a few exceptions, notably two or three by Swift, were 'a desert') merely to provide 'a single paragraph or so' for his projected *History of English Thought in the Eighteenth Century*. Writing on Henry Sidgwick's *Methods of Ethics* for *Fraser's Magazine*, he came to the conclusion that it was 'an everlasting bother about metaphysical puzzles . . . not worth bothering over'. He had begun to fear that Carlyle, the proclaimer of the Everlasting Yea, thought him irreverent. The one person with whom he could enjoy open discussion was John Morley. Soon afterwards he discovered he could philosophize freely with Thomas Hardy. Another of his personal and intellectual friends was George Meredith, whom he first met in Vienna.

On the momentous evening of 23 March 1875 he told Hardy that he had wasted much time on 'systems of religion and metaphysics', and that 'the new theory of vortex rings had a "staggering fascination" for him', an allusion, it seems, to Comte's grand philosophy of a phase-by-phase evolution from religion to a scientific or 'positive' way of thinking and of organizing society, a theory which Hardy was to meet the following year when he studied, and made copious notes on, Comte's *Social Dynamics*, part of Edward Beesly's translation of his *System of Positive Polity*. It includes the notion that progress comes after setbacks, as if it followed loops along its particular orbit, a theory which Hardy accepted, provisionally at least, in two of his essays, 'Candour in English Fiction' and the Apology to *Late Lyrics and Earlier*. He had read some, if not the whole, of Comte's *A General View of Positivism* before he met Stephen, besides philosophical works by authors such as J. S. Mill, who had helped to give Stephen his intellectual freedom. Stephen's influence on Hardy was to be both literary (particularly in the way already indicated) and philosophical; the latter was the more important because it strengthened his assurance in expressing views on life and the universe which were based on scientific thought. Hardy had given intellectual assent to Mill's arguments on the right of the individual to express his views however heterodox and unacceptable, but Stephen's example and utterances gave him the courage he needed at a maturer stage of development to express himself more and more patently in his works. Stephen's admiration was for men who would go to the stake for their beliefs, and he had no time for compromisers such as Jowett, who in practice, it seemed, thought the wordly success of his university students more important then the pursuit of truth.

In the spring of 1875 Stephen took Minnie and their daughter Laura to Cambridge. 'Lord! what a melancholy place it is after a couple of days!' he wrote to his American friend Charles Eliot Norton:

> The whole system and organisation is rotten to the core, though some changes have been made. There is still no decent career for anybody there, and therefore the best men either leave it or run to seed at about forty. . . . And yet Cambridge is a very pleasant place for a man under thirty, and I once thought that I should never leave it. I am uncommonly glad that I did! By this time I should have been half mad or wholly. . . . A few years of such life would cover me over with blue mould. . . .

The same year he took Minnie to the Alps for her health. She died unexpectedly in November, on Stephen's forty-third birthday, and her loss was devastating.

Outwardly Leslie Stephen was rigorously reserved and self-controlled; conjugally, especially in his second marriage, he appears another Victorian to whom his wife was the angel in the house, though his idealizing propensity in the course of time did not preclude a self-centred, irritable, and emotionally demanding disposition. As a critic he distinguished between manly and morbid or effeminate writers. Unlike Hardy, who had chosen a literary career because he preferred life 'as an emotion', he regarded the Shelleyan readiness to 'weep away' a 'life of care' with distaste, however lyrical the poetry that flowed from such self-indulgence. Hardy is most sympathetic towards his heroine Ethelberta when she is in such a mood. His morbidity was to reach the point when he recurrently convinced himself that it is better not to be born. Stephen's admiration went out to what he regarded as the more balanced philosophical spirit of Wordsworth: 'But welcome fortitude, and patient cheer. . . . Not without hope we suffer and we mourn.'

Editing *The Cornhill Magazine* was a sideline, a *point d'appui* which brought in £500 a year and enabled Stephen to reduce his journalism and undertake more ambitious work. He fulfilled his duties conscientiously, but his failure to adapt to changing tastes led to a steady decline in sales, and to his resignation after little more than ten years in office. His recurrent jitteriness towards Hardy on questions of sexual behaviour in fiction revealed not only justifiable editorial anxieties for which he apologized but also his own decided preference for the proprieties. In May 1875 he took exception to the use of 'amorous' in *The Hand of Ethelberta*; in August, to 'the very close embrace' in a London churchyard. Two months later he complimented Hardy on managing 'the rose-leaf incident' without it. So alarmed was he by amorous intrigue in the first version of the opening chapters of his next novel, *The Return of the Native*, that he refused to consider it unless he could see the whole. For a number of reasons Hardy could not comply; he knew that he and Stephen the editor worked on different wavelengths, and, even though his next novel, *The Trumpet-Major*, was sketched for *The Cornhill*, offered it elsewhere. Stephen was interested; with George III 'just round the corner' or almost, it was the kind of historical novel he would have liked editorially, except perhaps for the ending. When he told Hardy that the heroine married the wrong man, and heard that they usually do, his answer was: 'Not in magazines'.

Any doubt Hardy felt over the rightness of his course when he received a dazzling tribute in March 1875 from the poet Coventry Patmore, on the beauty and power throughout *A Pair of Blue Eyes* which would have earned him immortality had it been written in verse, must soon have been dispelled. However flattered he felt, especially in retrospect when he had proved himself as a poet, he must have known that his own versifying ability fell far short of Patmore's hyperbolical contention. He wisely studied prose, reading again Addison, Macaulay, Newman, Sterne, Defoe, Lamb, Gibbon, Burke (a strange assortment), and leaders in *The Times*, and coming to the conclusion that 'the whole secret of a living style', or the difference between it and a dead style, lies in not being too stylistic or mannered, and in giving the appearance of being a little careless at times. The observation of such a principle is more noticeable in his mature verse.

Hardy's recognition after *Far from the Madding Crowd* was such that on 10 May, after joining the Copyright Association, he was selected as one of a deputation presenting the case for copyright reform to Disraeli. The next day he attended a dinner organized at Oxford by the editors of *The Shotover Papers*, and seconded the toast to literature which was proposed by the accomplished verse-writer Austin Dobson. Hardy's later history suggests that he would be too nervous to make a long speech, and that he enjoyed himself more watching the college boat races from a privileged position, an occasion which he remembered distinctly when he wrote the end of *Jude the Obscure*.

In June, on the sixtieth anniversary of the battle, he and Emma visited Chelsea Hospital to meet campaigners who had survived Waterloo. One of them, John Bentley, recalled his experience there very happily as he clasped Emma's waist and punctuated his discourse with 'my dear young lady'. Hardy's paramount ambition grew, but presentation posed an insuperable problem; he thought he might achieve 'an Iliad of Europe' from the outbreak of the French Revolution to the battle of Waterloo in a series of ballads. All he could write at the time was a memorandum which began: 'A Ballad of the Hundred Days. Then another of Moscow. Others of earlier campaigns . . .'. He was busy reading George Henry Lewes's biographical study of Goethe, in whom he had been interested ever since Horace Moule gave him a translation of *Faust*. House-hunting in Dorset took up some of his time; he visited Shaftesbury, Blandford, and Wimborne, favouring the last after listening to organ-practice late at night in the minster. The search for a home outside London remained unsuccessful, but the spell of the music played its part in determining a happy ending for the true hero of *The Hand of Ethelberta*; Christopher Julian's prospective installation as chief organist of Melchester expressed a wish that remained with Hardy until the last years of his life.

On 12 July Hardy and Emma left London for Bournemouth. Emma had invited his mother to join them there; Jemima replied through Kate that she was too busy to leave home, but would like to see her again. Just when and where and how often they had met must raise questions as critical as they are unanswerable. On St Swithin's Day rain kept the married couple indoors, and their frustration made them irritated with each other. Retrospectively, in the poem 'We sat at the window', Hardy regrets that 'two souls in their prime' missed this rare opportunity of cultivating each other, with so much there 'to read and guess' and particularly for him to prize ('to see and crown'). 'Nobody can enter into another's nature truly, that's what is so grievous', the heroine of *Desperate Remedies* laments. Hardy knew this well enough, and felt that he ought to have been more equal to the occasion. The sense of his inadequacy weighed on his conscience, whereas with most men it would have passed like a shadow. There was no rift, just impatience with circumstances and with each other.

The same day they proceeded by steamer to Swanage, where they rented rooms at West End Cottage, which overlooked the town on one hand and the bay on the other. It belonged to Captain Masters, who told them many sea-stories, especially about smuggling. They enjoyed walks over the cliffs and inland, and a number of sea-outings. Whether Emma was able to walk as far as Dancing Ledge beach and further west, along the cliffs to the chapel on St Aldhelm's Head, is doubtful; a walk in that direction is recalled in 'Days to Recollect'. She probably accompanied Hardy south to Durlston Head, as far as Tilly Whim Caves, where he began a water-sketch. The coastal scenery moved her to write 'The Maid on the Shore', a novelette which recalled the Cornish coast and hinterland she knew so well. It was never published, and there is nothing to indicate how much interest Hardy showed in it. Her dependence on the success of his career would undoubtedly make her oppose his sacrificing time on it, had he been so inclined. She probably intended to work at it again, and deferred the task.

Mary Hardy and her sister Kate, now a pupil-teacher at Piddlehinton (preparatory to her teacher-training course at Salisbury in 1877 and 1878), spent two weeks of their summer holiday with them. Mary's sketches show that they made a number of excursions; details of the most notable, a cruise round the Isle of Wight, are found in Emma's diary. Before Mary and Kate set off for home on 13 September, they all picnicked at Corfe Castle, where Hardy surveyed the landscape with a further development of *The Hand of Ethelberta* in mind. It had been a splendid day Emma thought as they drove back to Swanage on the top of a 'bus', listening to jokes, with three horses abreast.

After meeting R. D. Blackmore in London, and reading his most successful novel *Lorna Doone*, Hardy wrote a letter of congratulation in June, saying how absurd it seemed that, considering what he had attempted in *Far from the Madding Crowd*, he had not read it sooner. It contained observations of natural things such as 'the marking of a heap of sand into little pits by the droppings from trees' which he thought only he would notice. Thinking that some rustic humour might appeal to Blackmore when his literary work was hindered by 'troubles and perplexities', Hardy sent him in early November a copy of 'The Fire at Tranter Sweatley's', which had just appeared in the *Gentleman's Magazine* and was about to be published, by arrangement with Henry Holt, in America. (Suitably bowdlerized, it was the first of Hardy's poems to be published; eventually it was entitled 'The Bride-Night Fire'.) Hardy's friendship with Blackmore was short-lived.

He completed *The Hand of Ethelberta* towards the end of January 1876. It had been difficult work, and he did not wish to extend it to a twelfth number, as had originally been scheduled. The serial, illustrated by George Du Maurier, ended in May. The changing background, especially from London to the Swanage area in the later stages, suggests that Hardy was prepared to gamble with improvisational elements. Even had he been familiar with London society (and Hardy maintained that Lady Portsmouth, 'a woman of large *social* experience', had told him that it was the only novel she knew in which the society scenes 'showed people exactly as they were'), he lacked the stylistic ease and readiness of wit to give incisive charm to his satirical comedy. Adapting his mother's pre-marriage plan of being a cook in a London 'club-house', he provides interesting *Upstairs, Downstairs* scenes as a result of presenting 'the drawing-room . . . from the point of view of the servants' hall'. Some exciting entertainment is aroused by the indignation of the heroine's working-class brothers (whose occupations recall those of Hardy's Sparks cousins) at her association with an old aristocratic roué, and their frantic efforts to prevent the family disgrace that would ensue from their marriage. Lord Mountclere's ruse in preventing her escape is adapted from a rustic version in 'Destiny and a Blue Cloak'. The main action is contrived from contemporary philosophical ideas. Ethelberta and her suitors are engaged respectively in a struggle for existence and domination, and the wild duck in an early scene prefigures a heroine who can fend for herself. The Darwinism of the age is reflected and indicted in the worship of Mammon, especially in a scene which reveals the horror of Neigh's knackery business. Ethelberta finds justification for the worldly ambition of her entrepreneurial role against natural instinct in altruistic motives which are supported by reference to J. S. Mill's *Utilitarianism*. Her marriage is one thing in artificial comedy, but *Desperate Remedies* and *Tess of the d'Urbervilles* indicate very clearly that Hardy would have regarded it as tragic in actual life. He may have thought this philosophical admixture would please his editor; it was the kind of subject which held interest for both of them, especially Leslie Stephen, whose works on social and moral welfare owed much to recognition of the Darwinian law of natural selection, to Mill (who was considerably influenced by Comte), and to Comte and his insistence on altruism as the key to social progress. Mill's utilitarianism depends on the conviction that readiness to sacrifice oneself for the sake of others is 'the highest virtue which can be found in man'. Stephen was too wary, however, to think that the contrivance of a plot in accordance with such philosophical principles would appeal greatly to readers of magazine fiction, and he and his publisher were disappointed with *The Hand of Ethelberta*. It was the last of Hardy's novels to appear under his editorship.

Their friendship continued, and in May 1876 Stephen wrote, urging Hardy to resume his 'perfectly fresh and original vein', ignore his critics, and read great authors such as Shakespeare, Goethe, and Scott; he particularly recommended George Sand, whose 'country stories' had a 'certain affinity' with his. It was advice Hardy took to heart. He had, as early as March, informed his publisher that he did not wish 'to attempt any more original writing of any length for a few months', until he knew 'the best line to take for the future'. He needed time to find a home which could give him and Emma greater amenities and independence;

above all, to read, reflect, and gather resources for a novel which would re-establish his position with the reading public. A suggestion that Stephen should publish some tragic poems which Hardy had in mind was not taken up. They met occasionally for a while, but their correspondence was allowed to lapse, much to Hardy's subsequent regret; it was not resumed until after 'a ten years' chasm of silence'.

11

'A Two-Years' Idyll'

By early March the Hardys had left Swanage and taken rooms at 7 Peter Street, Yeovil, in the hope of finding a home in that region. Proofs were soon checked for the issue of *The Hand of Ethelberta* on 3 April, and the novel was more favourably received than Hardy expected. He had been pleased to receive a request for permission to translate *Far from the Madding Crowd* into German, and had also advised George Smith to reach an agreement with the Leipzig publisher Bernhard Tauchnitz for its addition to his 'British and American Authors' series for readers on the Continent. Tauchnitz preferred to issue his latest novel first, but *Far from the Madding Crowd* and most of Hardy's other novels followed. The early arrival of the cheque for *The Hand of Ethelberta* made the Hardys look forward, after a holiday in London, to a tour in Holland and the Rhineland which would bring them to Brussels in time to visit the field of Waterloo on approximately the anniversary of the battle. No light can be thrown on what house-hunting they did, or what places of interest they visited before leaving for London towards the middle of May. They must have liked Yeovil, for in the 1880s, before having Max Gate built, Hardy was tempted to buy a house on Hendford Hill.

Of all the activities that must have been packed in the 'fortnight or so' the Hardy's spent in London nothing is known beyond the fact that the popular Scottish novelist William Black (in whose works George Meredith found nothing but fishing and sunsets) accepted their invitation to lunch with them at the British Hotel, and afterwards accompanied them to the exhibition at the French Gallery, which Hardy had heard was particularly good. On 29 May they went by train to Harwich on their way to Rotterdam. Next morning, as they approached the Dutch coast, Emma was amazed to see 'flat land on a level with the sea', with numerous windmills, and a line of little straight trees by the edge of the water. Hardy thought Rotterdam looked 'over-clean and new, with not enough shadow, and with houses nearly all out of the perpendicular'; to Emma they seemed 'falling forward into the street'. From The

Hague they drove along an avenued road to the red-roofed fishing village of Scheveningen; Emma noted its fine hotels and the white-painted sabots of the villagers; for the philosophical Hardy the grey landscape and the sand dunes which formed a sea-wall above the village were to assume an 'emotional colour' which represented the outlook of 'the more thinking among mankind'.

Throughout the tour Emma made little, sometimes exquisite, sketches in her diary, which is continually enriched with fresh observations; she is interested in menus, domestic architecture and furnishings, foreign dress and customs, life, and the scene, whether in city or country. At Cologne Hardy was disappointed by the 'machine-made Gothic' of the cathedral. As they travelled up the Rhine, he was reminded of *Childe Harold's Pilgrimage* by 'the castled crag of Drachenfels' and the huge fortress of Ehrenbreitstein opposite Koblenz. At Mainz they were impressed by the massive confirmation service in the cathedral, accompanied by music which reminded Hardy of Keble's 'Evening Hymn' at Stinsford. It was becoming increasingly hot, and Emma observed 'a fat English lady' fanning herself at the other end of their long *table d'hôte* in their 'very high class, rich hotel'. At Heidelberg the view from the tower on the Königsstuhl was disappointing, only the Rhine being visible through the mist, glaring, Hardy thought, as if it were 'a riband of blood' serpentining through the atmosphere. Emma wished she had not climbed the rough, slippery steps, and was greatly fatigued the next day. They continued their up-river journey to Karlsruhe, where they attended a fair, and to Baden-Baden, where Emma began to feel very ill; nevertheless, probably for novelistic reasons (Hardy having perhaps read the opening chapters of George Eliot's *Daniel Deronda* in London), they thought it worth while to visit the gaming-rooms. A view of the Black Forest with its 'turmoil of mountains' delighted Emma. At Strasbourg she was so ill that she had recourse to brandy (a flask of which she seems to have brought with her, Hardy having been 'angry about' it at Cologne). The next day they left for Brussels.

On Monday, 12 June, she accompanied him to the field of Waterloo, enjoying the sunshine and breezes, the flowers, and the broad expanse of cornfields. Hardy studied the account of the battle as they reconnoitred, and found time to sketch a plan of the ruined château of Hougoumont at the end of his Baedeker guide to Holland and Belgium. How long they spent in Brussels is not clear from Emma's rather muddled diary, but it gives the impression of at least another day spent on the battlefield, with visits to La Belle Alliance and La Haye Sainte (where a cupboard near the bullet-marked front door reminded her of one at Kirland) and a return walk through Mont St Jean and the village of Waterloo which led to the discovery of the Hôtel des Colonnes, where Victor Hugo had finished *Les Misérables*. The walk to the station was very fatiguing; so ended 'Waterloo day', Emma wrote. The next day she was very tired, and Tom, still anxious to explore, was 'cross about it'. However, they watched women making lace in a factory, drove round the city, and visited the cathedral. Hardy wished to find exactly where the Duchess of Richmond's ball took place on the eve of the battle, but his investigations did not convince him, and he was never to be satisfied that the scene had been accurately located.

At Antwerp, on their way home, Emma made many notes on the religious pictures which they viewed in the gallery; she thought the painting of Christ in God the Father's arms horrible, and one on the martyrdom of saints hideous. At the end of a holiday which proved exciting and memorable, the thought of returning to Yeovil and house-hunting was rather depressing. 'Going back to England where we have no home and no chosen county', she wrote (Yeovil being in Somerset, just outside the northern boundary of Dorset). The prospect was not improved by their 'miserable passage' to Harwich 'on a windy night in a small steamer with cattle on board'. Having recovered in London by the next morning but one (Sunday, 18 June, the actual anniversary of the battle of Waterloo), they set out early for Chelsea Hospital, and were in time to attend the service there before chatting again with John Bentley. For Hardy's satisfaction 'the battle was fought yet again by the dwindling number of pensioners who had taken part in it', over 'glasses of grog' in the private parlour of the Turk's Head.

When Hardy and Emma returned to Yeovil after an absence of more than five weeks, during which they had enjoyed some unusual amenities, the urgency of finding a home with the space, privacy, and furnishings which were necessary for her comfort and his professional advancement was most apparent. They were seriously incommoded by a growing accumulation of possessions, especially books, although they had 'not a stick' of furniture until they went to an auction-sale and bought a door-scraper and a bookcase. Hints from relatives (undoubtedly the Giffords) that they 'appeared to be wandering about like two tramps' had not been forgotten, though Hardy, and Emma too at this stage, felt the irksomeness of being conventional. Fortunately they did not have to wait long before they found an attractive and adequately commodious house to let in a quiet position overlooking the River Stour at Sturminster Newton in the south-east corner of Blackmoor Vale, the country of William Barnes's best dialect poetry. They were able to take possession on 3 July, after making a journey to Bristol to acquire the furniture they needed; this they did in two hours at a cost of about £100.

Although Hardy wrote initially from 'Rivercliff Villa', the house was known as Riverside Villa, as he indicates in his *Life*; this is, in fact, how Emma referred to it in her diary when she made her entry for 3 July. It and the adjoining house (each registered as 'River Villa') had been recently built in comparative isolation above a steep slope overlooking the Stour. Riverside Villa was the more northerly of these semi-detached houses; from the front bedroom, which became his study, Hardy could look directly down the slope to the wooded stream and its eyot; upstream was a high footbridge beyond which rich, open pastoral land was visible. To reach their new home, the Hardys took a side road which ran from near the centre of Sturminster in the direction of this bridge, then followed a track along the upper edge of the rise, on the eastern side of the river, to their garden entrance. The main garden lay on this side of the house; it extended along the front, and was supplemented by a smaller, more secluded one at the back. In summer the river flowed through lush meadowland, past Riverside Villa and the eyot to a picturesque mill half a mile away, and on, under an ancient six-arched stone bridge with its warning of transportation for wilful damage, past the hill on which stood the remains of a castle, once the home of Saxon kings.

In the summer Hardy and Emma often followed the path in this direction (to the left from the front of their house) through a profusion of wild flowers, meadowsweet predominantly, by the side of the bird-haunted river surfaced with crowsfoot and stretches of water-lilies such as those remembered by Barnes when he described the 'cloty Stour' a few miles from Shaftesbury (in lines which remained dear to Hardy, who quoted them in *Jude the Obscure*). Soon after their arrival he rowed with Emma near their home:

Rowed on the Stour in the evening, the sun setting up the river. Just afterwards a faint exhalation visible on surface of water as we stirred it with the oars. A fishy smell from the numerous eels and other fish beneath. Mowers salute us. Rowed among the water-lilies to gather them. Their long ropy stems.

Passing the island drove out a flock of swallows from the bushes and sedge, which had gone there to roost. Gathered meadow-sweet. Rowed with difficulty through the weeds, the rushes on the border standing like palisades against the bright sky. . . . A cloud in the sky like a huge quill-pen.

Hardy's main purpose in choosing a far-from-the-madding-crowd home was to improve his authorial status. To do this and emulate writers such as Sir Walter Scott, George Eliot, and Victor Hugo, he knew that he had to be better informed. Since his bachelor days in London when he read the poets assiduously, his reading had not been very systematic; nor had the note-making which he had begun with the best of intentions. The two note-books which begin with entries from that period are not very reliable chronological guides to his reading. One, dated 1867 and designed initially, it seems, for the inclusion of choice quotations and phraseology, begins with Swinburne's *Atalanta in Calydon*, Shakespeare, Carlyle, Herbert Spencer's *First Principles* (a book of scientific philosophy which may have introduced 'the First Cause' to Hardy), George Eliot's *Adam Bede*, and Trollope's *Orley Farm*. The next item is from Hugo's *Ninety-Three*, a translation which did not appear until 1874. Extracts from other publications show that the majority of the entries which follow were added in the 1880s.

The second notebook begins with the analytical notes and diagrams which Hardy made in 1863 as a summary of Fourier's *The Passions of the Human Soul*. Several quotations from Newman's *Apologia*, the first of which is dated 2 July 1865, precede a single-entry reference to Boswell's 'grand scheme' of class-subordination, which ran completely counter to the sentiments of *The Poor Man and the Lady*. Over 200 follow in the handwriting of Emma Hardy, and the occasional dating indicates no chronological sequence until about 1876, passages from G. R. Lewes's *Life of Goethe*, which Hardy was reading in June 1875, following an entry from the *Daily News* of 27 November 1875. Subsequent entries from the *Saturday Review* and *The Times* of early April 1876 suggest that all this copying-up may have been done at Yeovil, and that his studies there were heavily weighted in favour of the classics, Aeschylus, and the history of Greece, for example. Quotations from the *Fortnightly Review* and the *Athenaeum*, and from J. G. Wood's *Insects at Home*, belong to this period.

The same copy of the *Athenaeum* contains a review of *The Hand of Ethelberta* which advised Hardy to observe 'longer intervals of silence'. 'To novelists, if to any people, *sua mortifera est facundia*', the reviewer continued. Hardy had realized this before he finished his last novel. At Sturminster Newton his note-making became much more extensive and methodical; he copied as he read, his purpose being to revise his memoranda periodically, and to have at his disposal a store of knowledge and ideas from which he could draw continually to enrich the interest of his more-educated and cultured readers. Intrinsically he was acting in conformity with the belief that took the following eighteenth-century mould in Samuel Johnson's *Rasselas*:

> To a poet nothing can be useless. Whatever is beautiful, and whatever is dreadful, must be familiar to his imagination: he must be conversant with all that is awfully vast or elegantly little. The plants of the garden, the animals of the wood, the minerals of the earth, and meteors of the sky, must all concur to store his mind with inexhaustible variety: for every idea is useful for the enforcement or decoration of moral or religious truth; and he who knows most, will have most power of diversifying his scenes, and of gratifying his reader with remote allusions and unexpected instruction.

Hardy must have been encouraged in July by the commendation he received in 'The Wessex Labourer', an essay by Kegan Paul which appeared anonymously in the *Examiner*. He kept a copy, referring to it when he wrote his preface for the 1895 edition of *Far from the Madding Crowd*, where he draws very obviously from one delightful passage: 'Time in Dorset has stood still; advancing civilisation has given the labourer only lucifer-matches and the penny-post, and the clowns in *Hamlet* are no anachronism if placed in a west country village of our own day.' About the same time Hardy heard that an article on his novels had appeared very early in the year in the *Revue des deux mondes*, and requested his publishers to obtain a copy for him. This was 'Le roman pastoral en Angleterre', a long essay which evinced such deep appreciation of his work that Hardy wrote gratefully to the author, Léon Boucher, who replied in November, thanking him for his kind, flattering letter, but holding out no favourable prospect for a French translation of *Far from the Madding Crowd* just then.

Little is known of Hardy's life at Sturminster Newton during the remainder of 1876. How much time Emma found for sketching and painting, dress-making, embroidery, and other domestic refinements remains conjectural, but it can be assumed she did all she could to make her first home comfortable, and that as soon as she had settled she felt the need for a piano. That one was bought about this time appears to be the only conclusion one can draw from Florence Hardy's slightly inaccurate statement of 30 August 1925: 'Our old piano is certainly useless for playing upon. My husband is attached to it as he has had it for so long – over 50 years.' Singing contributed to Emma's happiness, and consequently to Hardy's. Their house stood near a large paddock, and she probably did some riding. They engaged a housemaid as soon as a suitable one could be found, and they seem to have employed a man or youth to do part-time jobs. If so, Emma's brief diary entry on 13 November, 'Notice to Geo—', suggests he was soon dismissed. The fact that Hardy planted a monkey-puzzle tree not only in front of Riverside Villa but also in front of the adjoining house shows that they were on good terms with the neighbours, Mr and Mrs Hallett. Emma's note for 26 October runs, 'Dined at Loundes'. At the end of the month her brothers Willie and Walter came to stay for a few days, and on 14 November she and Tom lunched with the Dashwoods, one of the Sturminster families with whom they became friendly. Charles Dashwood was a solicitor and landowner (a successor of Thomas Henry Dashwood, who had employed William Barnes to copy deeds when he first left school at Sturminster), and it was on this occasion that Hardy met Mr Warry and his wife and daughter. Mr Warry told him how a tenant farmer used to take the heart of every calf that died, stick it full of thorns, and hang it on the cotterel (the cross-bar) of his chimney, in order to prevent the spread of the disease that killed the calf; the next tenant found the chimney smoked because it was choked with hard dry hearts that had been suspended there for the same superstitious purpose. During this period Hardy heard other strange stories, one of a young doctor at Maiden Newton who received a dead baby from its mother in lieu of payment for attendance, and kept it in spirits on his mantelpiece even when he was married.

Another concerned a witch-doctor, who used to attend a fair at Bagber Bridge, and sell toads' legs in little bags, which people wore round their necks as a charm against scrofula, believing that the legs would twitch and effect a cure by 'turning' the blood.

At a small farm on Bagber Common, about two miles to the west, across the fields from Riverside Villa, William Barnes had been born in 1801. Hardy must have been reminded of his poetry and early years by scenes and places in that area, and probably wrote to him, for it was in 1876 that he received a copy of his *Poems of Rural Life in Common English* with the author's 'kind regards and good wishes for his writings'. There are lines in Hardy's poem 'The Interloper' which indicate how, 'by a slow sweet stream', he and Emma sat happily indoors half in the dark reading poetry together. His copious notes for the second half of the year show the studiousness of his reading. It included, in addition to the *Saturday Review* and, less regularly, the *Fortnightly Review* and the *Edinburgh Review*, George Sand's *Mauprat* in translation and Webster's *The White Devil*, which he used for the dramatic heightening of Clym Yeobright's fevered quarrel with Eustacia after his mother's death. In addition he read *The Dialogues of Plato*, edited by Benjamin Jowett, J. P. Mahaffy's *Social Life in Greece from Homer to Menander*, John Addington Symonds' *Studies of the Greek Poets*, and Comte's *Social Dynamics*. Many entries from John Hutchins' *The History and Antiquities of the County of Dorset* suggest that he had acquired the four-volume edition which was to serve as a frequent source for narrative and setting in his fiction, His return to Carlyle's *French Revolution* and his reading of John Morley's study of Robespierre are another reminder of his major literary aim, though the Revolutionary era had to be excluded from his final planning of *The Dynasts*.

About this time he may have attempted 'the outline of a novel' on Elizabeth, Empress of Austria. Many years later, when compiling his *Life*, he attributed this to his 'youthful years'. She was a woman, he wrote, 'whose beauty, as shown in her portraits, had attracted him greatly', and had even 'inspired some of his early verses'. How much he knew of her first visit to London, when he was there just before his marriage, is uncertain; she travelled under an assumed name. A Bavarian princess, cousin of the Wagner-obsessed Ludwig II, she had married the emperor Francis Joseph of Austria when she was only sixteen. Court restrictions and the dominance of her mother-in-law had made her long for a freer life, and though she supported the emperor in crises, and her beauty added to his prestige, undoubtedly helping to achieve reconciliation with Hungary, over which they were crowned king and queen in 1867, she gradually lost all taste for court life. Riding became her passion. After a short stay in the Isle of Wight, where Queen Victoria visited her, she came to Richmond in August 1874 as the guest of the Duke and Duchess of Teck. When she rode with her ambassador in Hyde Park, mounted on the white horse he had ridden at her coronation in Budapest, crowds of admiring holiday spectators were attracted by her equestrian grace and beauty. Her hunting prowess was revealed at the end of the month when she stayed at Belvoir Castle. It was impossible to conceal her identity very long, and soon after her arrival in March 1876 for six weeks of hunting in Northamptonshire, before meeting Queen Victoria again, it must have been widely known and publicized in fashionable circles. Love of the chase brought her to England and Ireland several times, and people talked of her as the empress 'who looked like an angel and rode like the devil'. Hardy wisely destroyed the verses he wrote about this infatuating 'queen and huntress', knowing they were the stuff of artificial romance which was alien to his world. For a similar reason he must soon have realized what a rash undertaking a novel on this fascinating celebrity would have been.

Before the year ended Hardy had decided on his next subject for fiction. Whether Emma accompanied him when he visited London in December, probably to see Leslie Stephen and his publishers, is not clear. He attended a conference on the Eastern Question at St James's Hall, where he heard speeches from Gladstone, Lord Salisbury, and Anthony Trollope, the latter causing some amusement when, on having his coat-tails pulled by the chairman, the Duke of Westminster, for overrunning his time, he turned, requested him to desist, and continued speaking. Hardy and Emma spent Christmas at Higher Bockhampton, one purpose being to form impressions of Puddletown Heath in the wintry gloom for the opening scenes of *The Return of the Native*. Anticipating a need which does not seem to have arisen, in describing the home of the heroine and her father, the old sea-captain, he sketched the ground-plan of a house near the well, remembering the retired Lieutenant Drane and his masts, no doubt. His father was reminded of the Christmas amusement once provided by the hobby-horse at Stafford House, when the village band was playing there, and one of the servants, 'terrified death-white' at the sight of the hobby-horse running about, rushed into an adjoining dark room and crashed into the violoncello of one the players, breaking off its neck.

On 5 February 1877 Hardy wrote, telling George Smith that he had sent the manuscript of his new novel 'as far as written'. He must have received a non-committal reply, for eight days later he wrote to George Eliot's publisher John Blackwood, requesting to know when there would be room for a serial in his magazine. Although he stated he had not written enough to be worth sending, he most probably had no copy of the early chapters, for on 1 March he asked Smith, Elder & Co. to return his manuscript. About six weeks later he forwarded the first fifteen chapters (about a third of the story, he estimated) to Blackwood, telling him to strike out anything he found likely to offend his readers, but doubtful whether such a passage would be found, since the story had been written with 'a partial view to *Blackwood*'. John Blackwood was unable to accept it for serialization in 1877, but read the manuscript carefully. Nothing could be 'more graphic than the description of that awful Egdon Heath', he replied; the rustics and their conversation showed a 'wonderfully real life' but were perhaps 'more curious than interesting'. He thought there was insufficient action in the early chapters, until 'the connection between the villainous Toogood and that she-devil Avice appears and they are run to ground by the indefatigable reddleman'. ('Toogood' and 'Avice' were the original names of Wildeve and Eustacia.) Hardy may have thought then or later that Blackwood had other reservations, for when he offered him his next novel, *The Trumpet-Major*, he described it as 'a cheerful story, without views or opinions' and 'intended to wind up happily'. He asked Leslie Stephen to reconsider the novel, but Stephen wished to have full details of the 'intended development' of the story. He feared that the relations between Avice, Toogood, and Thomasin might become too 'dangerous' for a family magazine unless he could see the whole. This was not ready, and was never sent, Hardy being anxious to secure serialization as soon as possible. His offer to the editor of *Temple Bar* being unsuccessful, he continued with his revision of the story, which was eventually accepted by Miss Braddon for *Belgravia*. It was published in twelve monthly parts during 1878, and Hardy accepted as little as £20 for each. But for additional income from the publication of new editions of his last three novels in 1877 he would have felt rather anxious about his immediate future.

With *The Return of the Native* giving more trouble and taking up more time than he had expected, Hardy's outings with Emma must have been curtailed in the spring and summer of 1877. She probably accompanied him when he walked to Marnhull in Blackmoor Vale at the end of May. It was 'the prime of bird-singing' time, blackbirds and thrushes in particular being audible, pleading rather than singing, with such modulation that Hardy imagined he saw 'their little tongues curl inside their bills in their emphasis'. A bullfinch in a tree sang with the piercing metallic sweetness of a fife. Marnhull is the Marlott of *Tess of the d'Urbervilles*, and Hardy could not have passed through without examining the architecture of the splendid church which overlooks the village, including the original of 'The Pure Drop' inn. Nor could he fail to be impressed here, as elsewhere in Dorset, by the contrast between the large houses of wealthy farmers and the rather primitive, cheap cottages of the poor. The club-dance which he imagined there may have been based on observations at Sturminster, where dancing and sports had been held in a field on Whit Monday, and took place again on 28 June, the anniversary of Queen Victoria's coronation, when he noticed 'the pretty girls, just before a dance, stand in inviting positions on the grass. As the couples in each figure pass near where their immediate friends loiter, each girl-partner gives a laughing glance at such friends, and whirls on.'

Hardy's imagination could play strange tricks, and was partial to the macabre. On this outing to Marnhull he came across 'a hideous carcase of a house in a green landscape, like a skull on a table of dessert'. However beautiful the scene, he was apt to regard it philosophically, as he had done intensively and at length in the opening chapter of *The Return of the Native*. 'I sometimes look upon all things in inanimate Nature as pensive mutes', he wrote on the day of his Marnhull visit. It was an idea he returned to in 'Nature's Questioning', a poem which suggests that he was already familiar with J. S. Mill's views in 'Theism' (the last of *Three Essays on Religion*, published in 1874) on the limited powers of the First Cause and its inability to fulfil its original aims, a supposition which was to find formulation little less than four years later in Hardy's 'Unfulfilled Intention' theory. Such an outlook coheres with the conviction expressed in June 1877 that there is poetry in the unromantic, when Nature's defects (awareness of which is Clym Yeobright's prerogative or handicap in *The Return of the Native*) are 'looked in the face' and transformed into a new kind of beauty by 'the spiritual eye'. In the same vein he writes in September: 'An object or mark raised or made by man on a scene is worth ten times any such formed by unconscious Nature. Hence clouds, mists, and mountains are unimportant beside the wear on a threshold, or the print of a hand.' In June he had found time to reflect on his Napoleonic project in the form of a 'grand drama, based on the wars with Napoleon, or some one campaign. . . . It might be called "Napoleon", or "Josephine", or by some other person's name.'

Visiting Riverside Villa a few years after Emma's death, Hardy remembered gazing through his window down on the river as the rain fell in June 1877, and wished he had turned to see more important things in the home behind him; he regretted that he had not devoted more time to her. This does not imply that they were unhappy. As in 'The Self-Unseeing', where he remembers his childhood ecstasy as he danced to the music of the father he had lost, the thought of 'looking away' brings with it a sense of life's transience and a pang that one cannot make more of what it offers when the time is ripe. This is the theme of 'The Musical Box', in which Hardy recalls returning to Riverside Villa one evening after hours of torrid sunshine; he slows down in his walk, which takes him past 'Stourside Mill' until he can see the dusky house, with Emma, white-muslined, waiting in the porch as bats flit round with whirring wings; her laugh as she hails him blends with the gentle chimes of 'the tuneful box' indoors, but just then, when they were enjoying the 'best of life' and he thought it 'lifelong to be', he was unaware of the spirit which, in long retrospect, he hears and sees, as it sings to 'the thin mechanic air', 'O make the most of what is nigh!' Whichever version of the poem is followed, whether the poet was accompanied as he returned or not, the meaning is the same: in a period of happiness, when we are young or relatively young, we take too much for granted, and assume too readily that such happiness will last the rest of our lives.

The end of June was marked by a most unusual occurrence at Riverside Villa. When the Hardys' housemaid returned at about ten o'clock, after a day's outing with her young man to Bournemouth, they thought she seemed depressed. About half-past twelve, when she thought they were fast asleep, they heard her creep downstairs from her bedroom at the back and go outside. Hardy looked through the back window of their bedroom in the north-east corner of the house, and saw her emerge with a man from the outhouse. The moonlight showed that she was wearing only a night-dress with something round her shoulders; beside her 'slight white figure' the man's form looked 'dark and gigantic'. She led the way to the back door, where Emma, who had rushed downstairs, met her and ordered her to bed. The man vanished. The door-bolts were found to be oiled, and it was evident that he had often stayed in the house. The young woman remained quiet in her room until between four and five in the morning, when she came down, opened the dining-room window, and made her escape. The next day Hardy met her father, who thought she had probably gone to her lover at Stalbridge. During August it was heard that she was expecting a baby. 'Yet never a sign of one is there for us', Hardy wrote wistfully. One cannot but feel that future happiness for Emma and him would have been more assured had they had children.

Although there was no urgency for copy, Hardy decided to send the text of the first two monthly parts of his novel to Chatto & Windus, publishers of *Belgravia*, at the end of August. He offered to provide rough sketches of anything unfamiliar to the artist responsible for the illustrations, and hoped the publishers would like his title. This, in fact, had been chosen for him by the American publisher J. Henry Harper when they met in London to discuss the serialization of the story. Hardy presented a list of the titles he had been considering, and asked Harper which he preferred. *The Return of the Native* was serialized in *Harper's New Monthly Magazine* a month later than in England. Arrangements were made for electroplates of the illustrations to be sent over, but they arrived too late; no illustration appeared before the fourth instalment, and after that no attempt was made to include another. In the autumn Hardy wrote 'The Thieves Who Couldn't Help Sneezing' in fulfilment of a promise made in July to contribute to *Father Christmas*, a children's annual edited by a friend of Roger Smith, the London architect for whom Hardy worked in 1872. His fee was only £9. It is a delightful short story, suspenseful and dramatic, evoking an imaginary past in a lonely wooded part of Blackmoor Vale, with its 'heavy clay roads and crooked lanes', not many miles from Sturminster Newton.

On 25 September Hardy thought it worth his while to attend a fair at Shroton near Iwerne Courtney, where he saw the mimed beheading of a woman in a twopenny show, and a man whose hair grew on one side of his face in another. On his way home he left the road for a more direct route over steep Hambledon Hill, where he found himself in a fog among the earthworks, and was fortunate not to lose his way. 'A man might go round and round all night' in such a situation, he realized. At the end of October he travelled to Bath, where he booked lodgings for his father near the baths and abbey. After taking him there from the station, he accompanied him to the theatre in the evening. The next morning he took him to the baths, and ensured that he was happy with the arrangements for the treatment he was beginning in the hope of curing his rheumatism.

On 8 November, after he had posted the third, fourth, and fifth instalments of his novel to Chatto & Windus, he and Emma had tea at Riverside Villa with Mr and Mrs Dashwood, their closest Sturminster friends. Mrs Dashwood, musical and well-read, kept in touch with Emma, and looked forward years later to seeing the stories which she hoped to publish. Dashwood talked interestingly on the subject of poaching. A poacher whom he defended at the quarter sessions told him, after being allowed until the next meeting of the justices to pay his fine, that he would 'get it out of 'em before then', and poached enough from the justices' preserves in one week to pay the £5 in time. Dashwood's accounts of battues and poaching practices against pheasants made a deep impression on Hardy; weighted with further evidence from other parts of Dorset in later years, they were not forgotten when *Tess of the d'Urbervilles* was written. Four days after this visit heavy rains caused the Stour to flood, and lumps of froth 'like swans' floated below Riverside Villa. Hardy walked down to the bridge, and saw foam accumulated 'like hillocks of salt' against the arches; 'then the arch chokes, and after a silence coughs out the air and froth, and gurgles on', he observed. There was a time when a man came every evening to the ascent in front of the house to watch the colourful western sky. To Hardy, one evening at the end of November 1877, it looked like some vast foundry in which new worlds were being cast.

The vision of 'In the Seventies' still inspired him, and gossips in Sturminster may have wondered how a man with no regular employment could make a living as a writer. A major work on the Napoleonic wars remained supreme among his 'starry thoughts', and he seems already to have decided on a novel relating to a collateral subject. Initial research in preparation for *The Trumpet-Major* is evident in his correspondence with Charles Bingham, rector of Melcombe Horsey and original of the antiquary Parson

Tringham in *Tess*, on the 'threatened invasion of 1803', and in a
note he made in July on a subject which eventually he chose to
treat separately in a short story, 'The Melancholy Hussar of the
German Legion':

> James Bushrod of Broadmayne saw the two German soldiers [of
> the York Hussars] shot [for desertion] on Bincombe Down in
> 1801. It was in the path across the down, or near it. James Selby
> of the same village thinks there is a mark.

Hardy had much to do, and was not without his anxieties. Letters
at intervals to Bernhard Tauchnitz indicate his concern for the
continued publication of his novels in Europe as well as in England
and America. He had corrections of serial proofs to attend to
month by month, and his novel to finish. Even so, he agreed in
January to complete a story by 10 March for Francis Hueffer, editor
of the *New Quarterly Magazine*. He and Emma had come to feel that,
however much they enjoyed living at Sturminster, it would be
more practical and advantageous to live in or near London, and to
be in closer contact with publishers, editors, and a world of
culture. Early in February therefore they went to the capital and,
after devoting several days to house-hunting, agreed to a three-
year lease of 1 Arundel Terrace, Trinity Road, Tooting. While in
London, Hardy wrote to his illustrator Arthur Hopkins (brother of
the poet Gerard Manley Hopkins), giving him hints on the story of
The Return of the Native which leave no doubt that the happy
ending, Thomasin's marriage to Diggory Venn, was not an after-
thought. Soon after his return to Sturminster, he sent him sketches
for the dress and ornamental staff of the mummers in the May
number illustration.

On 5 March Emma and he attended a concert at Sturminster in
which Miss Marsh sang 'Should he upbraid', the most marvellous
English song, Hardy thought, in its power to move an audience.
To him she was 'the sweetest of singers', and he described her
performance in the most poetic prose: 'thrush-like in the descending scale, and lark-like in the ascending – drawing out the soul of
listeners in a gradual thread of excruciating attenuation like silk
from a cocoon'. He commemorated her nearly 40 years later in 'The
Maid of Keinton Mandeville', a poem written as a tribute to Sir
Henry Bishop, who had composed the tune. Two weeks after the
concert Riverside Villa was divested of all its furnishings, and the

Hardys had all their meals at the Dashwoods'. They slept there and, after seeing their possessions on the way in two vans the next morning, left for London. On 18 March, the last day in their home, Hardy had written: 'End of the Sturminster Newton idyll'; at some unspecified later date he added: 'Our happiest time'. Later still, when he wrote his *Life*, he referred to Riverside Villa as the house in which Emma and he spent probably their happiest days. In the poem 'A Two-Years' Idyll', which he wrote no doubt when he came across the earlier comments while preparing his *Life*, he looks back on the Sturminster period as one of romance and hope, a prelude to 'plays soon to come – larger, life-fraught'. If these expectations were not realized, it does not signify that unhappiness and disillusion soon followed. The strength of Hardy's feelings makes him exaggerate; he is too extreme. 'End of the Sturminster Newton idyll' does not imply that he and Emma rated their days there as 'nought' compared with what was to come, nor does the record of their succeeding years tally with the absolute blankness of

> Nothing came after: romance straight forsook
>   Quickly somehow
> Life when we sped from our nook,
> Primed for new scenes with designs smart and tall. . . .
>   – A preface without any book,
>   A trumpet uplipped, but no call;
>   That seems it now.

12
'The FAILURE of THINGS'

Arundel Terrace consists of eight three-storeyed yellow-brick houses, each with a bay-windowed front drawing-room, to the south of Wandsworth Common where the long straight Trinity Road enters the Tooting area. The house which the Hardys injudiciously chose (known as 'The Larches') stood in a rather elevated position and exposed at the northern end, 'where Brodrick Road crosses Trinity Road down towards' Wandsworth Common railway station. The nearness of the station for journeys to and from London was one of the few advantages the house possessed. It had very little garden and privacy; the main door was on the Brodrick Road side, and let in the cold; and Emma soon discovered that they would need more furniture if they were to entertain as they hoped to do, and invite friends and relatives to stay with them.

Hardy's funds were diminishing, and such were his expenses that he felt obliged to undertake short stories, and on three occasions at least to remind, first, his American publishers, and then Chatto & Windus, that they had not sent the expected payments for portions of his serial. 'The Duchess of Hamptonshire' appeared as 'The Impulsive Lady of Croome Castle' early in April in the first two numbers of *Light*, a short-lived weekly founded by Robert Buchanan, and five weeks later in *Harper's Weekly*. Unable to provide Francis Hueffer with a story for the *New Quarterly Magazine* in March, Hardy set to work as soon as he could on 'An Indiscretion in the Life of an Heiress', adapting it, for the most part with little modification, from what was left unpillaged in *The Poor Man and the Lady*, one change being the substitution of Egbert Mayne the schoolmaster for Will Strong the architect. It was finished in June, and appeared almost simultaneously the following month in Hueffer's magazine and five numbers of *Harper's Weekly*.

Serial proofs of *The Return of the Native* continued to demand attention, and Emma probably gave what assistance she could. In April Hardy found time to set down his thoughts on tragedy, on the advantages of the epistolary technique in novel-writing, and once again on the unromantic kind of vision which is indicative of his artistic leanings. The memory of two pictures, one by Boldini in the French gallery of 'a young lady beside an ugly blank wall on an ugly highway', another by Hobbema, and their manner of 'infusing emotion into the baldest external objects either by the presence of a human figure among them, or by mark of some human connection with them', reminded him of his feelings at Scheveningen, and convinced him that 'the beauty of association is entirely superior to the beauty of aspect, and a beloved relative's old battered tankard to the finest Greek vase'. Hardy was expressing what George Eliot had felt when she wrote about Dutch paintings in *Adam Bede*. 'Paradoxically put, it is to see the beauty in ugliness', he wrote. Ten years later he concluded that this defined 'the province' or the function of the poet.

In response to a request from the editor of the *Literary World*, in Boston, Massachusetts, Hardy prepared notes on himself for a sketch in a 'World Biographies' series. He may have consulted Emma, who wrote the copy which was dispatched on 9 May. The final article laid stress on the classical education he had received from a fellow of Queens' College, Cambridge, and on his interest in art at home and abroad. Had he set out to impress less, and adopted Burns's 'a man's a man for a' that' attitude in presenting the facts, he would have been regarded no less highly in America. At the end of the month he made the first of his visits to the British Museum for research on the background for *The Trumpet-Major*. The recollections of Grandfer Cantle in *The Return of the Native* afford evidence of his earlier interest in defensive preparations against Napoleon's threatened invasion. Before 1878 was over he had worked on the poem 'Valenciennes'. His notebook entries for *The Trumpet-Major* continue into 1879. He read contemporary newspapers, magazines, and local histories, and copied an enormous amount of detail on relevant events in Dorset, including George III's visits to Weymouth; on military training, regulations, and encampments; and on period dress for both sexes, especially the ladies. Some lengthy passages at the beginning appear to be in Emma's hand, suggesting that she either copied his notes or occasionally read for him at the British Museum. She probably accompanied him when he made another Sunday visit to Chelsea Hospital, where he was particularly interested in a deaf and palsied pensioner, aged 88, who had served under Sir John Moore, remembered the terrible winter retreat through mountainous country to Corunna, and fought at Waterloo. With others he talked on army discipline, which could mean 300 lashes at a time 'if you only turned your eye', salt being subsequently rubbed on the victim's back, to harden it.

Alexander Macmillan lived in a large house with attractive surroundings at Upper Tooting; he had named it Knapdale after the home of his clan in Argyll. With its rambling passages, its croquet-lawns and trees on the edge of a gipsy-frequented common, it had often been the rendezvous of writers, artists, and many other distinguished people, old and young, 'who seem to have been endowed there with a special gift of laying aside their pomps and vanities and so of enjoying themselves'. On Sunday evening, 16 June, Hardy and Emma were among the Macmillans' guests. Macmillan told him a story he had heard from Mrs Carlyle, of a red-cloaked woman who was regarded as a witch in the region of Craigenputtock Moor. She had fallen in love with a cattle-dealer who visited her father's farm; after their marriage he lived there, undertook its management, and ran into debt. In consequence her father's farm and property had to be sold. The young man left and never returned. After the birth of her baby son, the wife set out to find him, and came back very unhappy on hearing that he was married. Her father died; the boy grew up, and was intended as a schoolmaster. While crossing the moor one night he lost his way, and was buried in the snow and frozen to death. His mother continued to live in a hut there, 'and became the red-cloaked old woman who was Mrs Carlyle's witch-neighbour'. The story would have appealed to Walter Scott or to the younger Wordsworth, and it may seem strange that Hardy, who could think of writing a novel on an empress, did not adapt it for fictional use.

Another friend of the Hardys was Charles Kegan Paul, formerly vicar of Sturminster Marshall, a Dorset village four miles west of Wimborne Minster. There he had combined his church duties with teaching private pupils, two of the most notable being Hallam and Lionel Tennyson, sons of the Poet Laureate. After being Henry King's manager, he had recently succeeded him as publisher. Having lived in Dorset for several years, he had a special interest in Hardy, and keenly appreciated his presentation of 'Wessex' life. When Emma and Hardy dined with him at his home in Kensington Square during the summer of 1878 they met Mr Leighton, father of the painter Sir Frederick Leighton, his daughter Mrs Sutherland Orr (a Browning enthusiast), and Professor Thomas Henry Huxley, to whom they had been introduced at the Macmillans'. Hardy grew to admire him for the fearlessness of his scientific thinking, his modesty, and the warmth of his personality. It was partly owing to Kegan Paul's recommendation that Hardy was elected to the Savile Club, where he made many acquaintances and met Edmund Gosse, who became his lifelong friend. There on 3 August he dined with William Minto, editor of the *Examiner*, before attending the Lyceum with Walter Pollock (who became editor of the *Saturday Review*), to see a last programme by Henry Irving, first in a scene from *Richard III*, then in the role of Jingle from Dickens' *The Pickwick Papers*, finally in a recitation of Thomas Hood's poem 'The Dream of Eugene Aram', to most of the audience a harrowing evocation of a murderer's guilt. To Hardy, who noticed how Irving forgot his part by keeping up one shoulder during his Jingle performance, as if he were still Richard III, it seemed as if Hood's poem was 'the only piece of literature' actors knew outside plays. After the show they found Irving stripped to the waist in his dressing-room, where they drank champagne from tumblers.

It may have been at Kegan Paul's, or by his arrangement, that Hardy received an invitation to visit Kingston Lacy, the home of the Bankes family near Sturminster Marshall. This he did while staying at Higher Bockhampton from the end of August to 9 September. He wished to see particularly its large collection of pictures, some of which he was to remember when he described the long gallery of Stancy Castle in *A Laodicean*. He called on William Barnes at his rectory on the Wareham road outside Dorchester, and dined at West Stafford rectory with the Smiths, whose daughter Evangeline had already sought his advice on some of her fiction. Subsequent developments in their friendship suggest that Bosworth Smith was at home on this occasion; Hardy may have met him when he and Emma were staying at Bockhampton at the end of 1876. A classical scholar, he was probably a friend of Charles Moule, who was at home from Cambridge. Hardy and Moule travelled to the west boundary of Dorset to see Forde Abbey, a Cistercian foundation of great architectural and historical interest. Standing in a secluded part of the Axe valley, it had been much improved in Tudor style by its last abbot Thomas Chard; during the Civil War it had belonged to the Prideaux family, who had employed Inigo Jones to make alterations and additions. The Duke of Monmouth had stayed there, and it had been let to Jeremy Bentham, with whom James Mill, father of John Stuart Mill, had stayed for long periods with his family. It was not open to the public on the day Hardy and Moule chose for their visit, but the owner rushed out as they were leaving, insisted on showing them round, and gave them a 'sumptuous' lunch. With its mixture of architectural styles from the twelfth to the seventeenth century, from the monastic to the lordly and elegant, Forde Abbey may have stirred those initial thoughts from which the theme of *A Laodicean* was elaborated. The day after his return to London, Hardy visited the wreck of *The Princess Alice*, which had sunk with heavy loss of life below Woolwich during his absence, and broke off some splinters of wood as mementoes. One of these he sent to his brother Henry, enclosed in a letter which urged his mother to 'make up her mind' to stay with him and Emma; he would meet her at Clapham Junction.

About this time Emma, looking out of a back window, caught sight of her husband running down Brodrick Road and disappearing into a by-street. He soon returned and explained how, while in his writing-room, he had heard a street barrel-organ playing the quadrille which, at the beginning of his architectural apprenticeship, he had heard Fippard whistle as he capered in Hicks's office. He had always wanted to know the name of the tune; the organ-grinder had shuffled off when he saw him running up, and all he could answer in a foreign accent was 'Quad-ree-ya!' as he pointed to the index at the front of his instrument. Hardy saw nothing registered there but 'Quadrille', and disappointedly concluded that it might have been one of Jullien's forgotten tunes. The incident illustrates the hold on Hardy's imagination which the music of his early years was to maintain. Unfortunately there is nothing to indicate how much music he and Emma enjoyed in London or at home at this time.

No doubt he needed a holiday; he had enjoyed little relaxation for a long period. Jane Panton, daughter of the painter W. P. Frith, saw him for the first time at the Kegan Pauls' in the 1870s, and described him as short and 'frail-looking'. His notebook for the previous year shows that most of the time when he was not writing had been devoted to studious reading. He returned to Spencer's *Principles of Biology*, read Leslie Stephen's *English Thought in the Eighteenth Century* and George Otto Trevelyan's *The Life and Letters of Macaulay*, besides other works and the usual journals and newspapers. Whether he or she selected them, Emma copied up many of the maxims of the seventeenth-century Spanish Jesuit Gracian, some of which are reflected in the truisms of Sir William de Stancy in *A Laodicean*. Nothing, however, in Hardy's multi-farious reading of 1877 (so far as it is recorded in his notebook) affected his thinking more than Matthew Arnold's first volume of *Essays in Criticism*, published in 1865.

The fact that little is entered for 1878 does not indicate that Hardy lived a more relaxed life in London; he had begun a long period of intensive research for *The Trumpet-Major*. The memor-anda he made at Sturminster had a wider but equally practical aim, supplying many an illustration or comparison for *The Return of the Native*. Johnny Nunsuch, adding fuel to the bonfire at Eustacia's command, 'might have been the brass statue which Albertus Magnus is said to have animated just so far as to make it chatter, and move, and be his servant'. One of the reddleman's ruses to deter Wildeve from meeting her is a 'species of *coup-de-Jarnac*'. Notes for these references were drawn for Charles Mackay's *Memoirs of Extraordinary Popular Delusions and the Madness of Crowds*. An intermittent transcription from a passage in Heer's *The Pri-maeval World of Switzerland* (1876) – which Hardy had read in the *Saturday Review* – on the vegetation of the carboniferous period, 'very uniform . . . few forms of plants . . . no flowers . . . mon-otony. There were none of the higher animals; no birds rested on the branches of the trees. . . . The air was sultry and full of vapour . . . the stillness was profound', is repeated in the descrip-tion of the hollow to which Clym Yeobright repairs after quarrel-ling with his mother: 'ferny vegetation . . . quite uniform . . . not a single flower. The air was warm with a vaporous warmth, and the stillness was unbroken. Lizards, grasshoppers, and ants were the only living things to be beheld. The scenes seemed to belong to the ancient world of the carboniferous period, when . . . no bird sang.' One of Gracian's maxims is quoted. References such as those to deaf Dr Kitto, to express Eustacia's abnormal alertness when she first overhears Clym's voice, and to the Pitt Diamond when Christian Cantle conceals the guineas in his shoes, undoubt-edly heighten the reader's interest. Sometimes this form of ac-cessory knowledge seems imposed and supernumerary. Few readers can appreciate what is implied in 'Possibly Clym's face, like Homer's, owed something to the accidents of his situation', and it would not have occurred to Hardy had he not remembered one of the passages he copied from Comte's *Social Dynamics*. Many references come from other sources, including the Bible, though the allusion to the new commandment of Jesus, 'That ye love one another', in Clym as 'an itinerant preacher of the eleventh commandment' originated from J. S. Mill's reference to the text of St John in 'Utility of Religion', another of his *Three Essays on Religion*, when, influenced by Comte, he outlined what altruism effectively demands.

With the slight exception of the last, incidental references are of small significance compared with the creative ideas which came from two essays in particular. The conflict between Hellenism or Greek joyousness and the Christian demand for the subjugation of the senses which is adumbrated in Arnold's 'Pagan and Medieval Religious Sentiment', and which was to break out with dramatic vehemence in *Jude the Obscure*, combined with Walter Pater's thought in 'Winckelmann' to suggest much in the main story of *The Return of the Native*. Yearning to escape a life of endurance and boredom, the young and passionate Eustacia dreams of joy in Paris; she embodies 'the warm and glowing emotions of sense' which Arnold associates with 'the brilliant whirl' of the poet Heine's Paris in the above essay. Repeatedly she is presented as a Grecian figure, almost a goddess. Egdon, which is home to an ascetic altruist like Clym, is her Hades. Their polarization in the opening and concluding scenes reveals the axis on which the novel turns, she the self-seeking queen of the night and the senses, he the man who has abandoned worldly vanity and chosen ideally to help his fellow men. As he preaches on Rainbarrow, the shade over his eyes signifying a blindness in his judgement of human nature, he creates the impression, which Hardy had felt when he heard and watched Mill addressing a Westminster crowd in 1865, of an utterly sincere man for whom the world was not yet ripe. Clym had failed to realize that material needs had to be satisfied before the gospel of Comtean altruism could succeed.

The main question for Pater, and for Hardy, was how the Hellenic ideal, which Goethe had reflected in the second part of *Faust*, could be regained. It implies a unity in man, and 'a concourse of happy physical conditions as ever generates by natural laws some rare type of intellectual or spiritual life'. Contending for this 'makes the blood turbid, and frets the flesh, and discredits the actual world about us', Pater adds. Hardy endorsed this view, but, however much he hoped could be done to liberalize the Church, he did not believe that the 'blithe and steady poise' which Pater and Arnold found in the happy communal life depicted by Theocritus could return. 'That old-fashioned revelling in the general situation grows less and less possible as we uncover the defects of natural laws, and see the quandary that man is in by their operation.' Clym Yeobright 'already showed that thought is a disease of flesh'; his face 'bore evidence that ideal physical beauty is incompatible with emotional development and a full recognition of the coil of things'. In a world where the defects of heredity and Darwinian law call for endurance, the best that can be done is to make full use of human and natural resources for the welfare and increasing happiness of mankind.

Hardy had devoted an enormous amount of time to the subject and composition of *The Return of the Native*. He may have preferred a tragic ending, but did not object to complying with magazine demands; 'Aftercourses' had been clearly in view when he wrote to Arthur Hopkins early in February 1878. The polarization which it produced is at least as significant as the five-act unity of a year's events from one dark night to another. The learning which Hardy concentrated on the aggrandizement of Eustacia results in such a farrago of romantic hyperbole that the 'Queen of Night' is distanced from the scheming girl of the heath. Hardy's attempt to give her tragic elevation is undermined by its excess; when she is referred to as Clym's 'Olympian girl', we are on the edge of the ridiculous. Another weakness is more crucial: the tragedy turns on circumstances which lead to the death of Clym's mother, first her inquiry about the guineas, which can appear only as an unwarrantable accusation of dishonour to Eustacia, finally her apparent rejection when she seeks reconciliation. At both of these points fictional probability is strained to breaking-point. The crossing of the heath by Mrs Yeobright and her death as she broken-heartedly turns back in the torrid sunshine is one of the great features of the book; it works imaginatively on both narrative and philosophical planes, emphasizing the Darwinism of existence in a universe where the individual has little more significance than an ephemeron. The rustics provide a lively introductory chorus, and the tragic finale is no small accomplishment. The work contains much that is poetic and artistic, but perhaps Hardy was attempting something beyond his resources in Clym. His growing sense of the defects of nature had made him bolder, and he must have known that he was inviting criticism when he wrote, with reference to the chance events which wrought his hero's double tragedy:

Human beings, in their generous endeavour to construct a hypothesis that shall not degrade a First Cause, have always hesitated to conceive a dominant power of lower moral quality than their own; and, even while they sit down and weep by the waters of Babylon, invent excuses for the oppression which prompts their tears.

Hardy must have been disappointed in September when he received an offer of only £200 for the publication of the novel in volume form, considerably less than he had received for *The Hand of Ethelberta*. As he did not wish to change his publisher, he saw George Smith the next day and accepted his terms. (It is worth remembering that Smith had offered George Eliot, when she was at the height of her fame, £10,000 for *Romola*.) On 1 October Hardy sent him the sketch-map which was printed, at his suggestion, as the frontispiece. While it clearly takes features from the heath behind his birthplace (Black Barrow being Rainbarrow) and from the adjacent Frome valley, its direction and distances are considerably altered. The novel was published on 4 November, and on the whole its reception was not very favourable. Charges of 'gloomy fatalism' and of passionate scenes suggestive of immorality were raised. Although the poet W. E. Henley recognized its imaginative qualities, he thought the language of the rustics unnatural, as did a number of other reviewers, apparently assuming that a novel needs to be an accurate copy of life in all its particulars. In self-defence Hardy replied that his chief concern was 'to depict the men and their natures rather than their dialect forms'. This was in answer to the review which appeared in the *Athenaeum* on 23 November. One of its sentences must have made all Hardy's efforts seem a mockery: the book was 'distinctly inferior to anything of his' the critic had read. Hardy must have known that typical readers of the age did not wish their dream worlds to be disturbed by uncomfortable or provoking thoughts, but he was amazed to find that critics failed to see or appreciate his deeper meanings. It is no wonder that he woke up before it was light on 28 November, and felt he had insufficient 'staying-power' to hold his own in such a world. The mood continued on New Year's Day 1879, when he wrote:

A perception of the FAILURE of THINGS to be what they are meant to be, lends them, in place of the intended interest, a new and greater interest of an unintended kind.

The question which Hardy already saw looming up, and which was eventually to drive him from novel-writing to poetry, was that of artistic sincerity in unpropitious times. With *The Trumpet-Major* he would be on safer ground.

13

This Way and That

Hardy's ill-fortune seemed to be accentuated by the weather in January. A cold east wind brought rain, which could be heard wheezing through the joints of the buffeted back door, as the poem 'A January Night' testifies. A letter from his father at the year's end had informed him that his mother was unwell but that both hoped to stay with him and Emma soon. On 1 February, hearing that her condition was worse, he travelled in the cold to Dorchester, where he saw his brother advancing with horse and wagonette towards the station entrance as rain fell in the gloom. A lamp at the bottom of the town showed the reins in Henry's hands glistening with ice; the cold east wind entered Hardy's sleeves and chilled him to the elbow as they crossed Fordington Moor; sleet and rain 'shaved [them] like a razor' most of the way to Higher Bockhampton. Hardy stayed two weeks, and found time to visit Weymouth and Portland to re-familiarize himself with settings for scenes in *The Trumpet-Major*. As he told Rebekah Owen years later, he learned many facts about local events at the time of the threatened French invasion from old relatives who had lived at Sutton Poyntz and Preston. On 12 February he made a sketch of the English Channel from Maine Down. His father, whose fund of inherited stories and gossip had grown as his business contacts increased, told him how a hanging at Dorchester in his boyhood had been delayed until one o'clock, the custom being to wait until it was known whether the mail-coach from London had brought a reprieve, and how one of the choir instrumentalists at Puddletown church had copied up tunes during the sermon, as his own father did at Stinsford. He remembered a local rector's son who married a German woman he met as she played her tambourine at Puddletown fair; he became a miller at Owermoigne, where his wife called in a neighbouring fiddler, gave him some gin, and beat the tambourine to his playing, when her husband went to market. Elsewhere Hardy saw a wonderful example of the incongruities which followed church-restoration, when he was shown a fowl-house constructed of material bought at a builder's sale; 'chickens

164

roost under the gilt-lettered Lord's Prayer and Creed, and the cock crows and flaps his wings against the Ten Commandments', he wrote.

It seems almost certain that during this period at Higher Bock-hampton Hardy heard from old James Selby, who worked forty years for Hardy's father and remembered carrying tubs for smug-glers, how smuggled goods were buried at Owermoigne in pits over which apple trees planted in boxes were placed, and that in consequence one of Hardy's most endearing novelettes, 'The Dis-tracted Preacher', a story of smuggling behind Ringstead Bay and Lulworth Cove, appeared in the April number of the *New Quarterly Magazine*, now edited by Kegan Paul. Later in the year he wrote for the same editor and journal an anonymous review of William Barnes's collected poems, *Poems of Rural Life in the Dorset Dialect*, which Paul's firm was publishing. Hardy writes evocatively of Blackmoor Vale, with a reference to the white hart legend which he uses proleptically in *Tess of the d'Urbervilles*; the critical portion which follows is brief but sufficient to express his genuine appreci-ation not only of Barnes's lyricism and truth to nature but also of the country and peasantry he presents. Hardy's promotion by Kegan Paul continued with the inclusion in the same issue of a lengthy and favourable essay on his novels by Mrs Sutherland Orr.

During the year Hardy had been impressed by Matthew Arnold's essay on Wordsworth, particularly by his stress on 'the noble and profound application of ideas to life' as 'the most essential part of poetic genius'. He had pursued such a policy in *The Return of the Native*, with little appreciation from the reviewers, and was to do so more challengingly in his last novels. Among his rather miscellaneous reading during this unsettled period we find Arnold's *Mixed Essays* (1879) and two of Disraeli's novels, *The Young Duke* and *Coningsby*. Even more significant was his acqui-sition of Richardson's novel *Clarissa Harlowe* in eight volumes; when he read it is not known, but had he not done so *Tess of the d'Urbervilles* could not have been created in its present form, and might never have been written.

In the spring he did more work at the British Museum for *The Trumpet-Major*. On his return to London in February, hoping to appear again in *The Cornhill*, he had informed Leslie Stephen of his new project. Once again this cautious editor, who told Hardy that he preferred historical novels like Thackeray's *Vanity Fair*, with historical characters kept in the background, wished to see the story when it reached a more advanced stage. What happened in the interim is uncertain. In May Hardy sent the early part of the story to Macmillan; in June he made overtures to John Blackwood. On 5 July he agreed to its serialization in *Good Words* for £400. On 1 August he invited the proprietor and editor to lunch with him any day at the Savile Club; he had been thinking that Charles Keene, who drew for *Punch* and was said to present soldiers 'remarkably well', would be his best illustrator. He had written to a publishing firm in Philadelphia, asking if it was interested in serializing a cheerful story with a happy ending, but further difficulties were to be encountered before he found an American publisher.

Special recognition came to Hardy in March from the novelist Walter Besant, who invited him to join the Rabelais Club as 'creator of the Native', which he considered the most original, virile, and humorous of 'all modern novels'. In June he attended the International Literary Congress, then a *soirée musicale* at the Hanover Square Club to meet members of the Congress and the Comédie Française; it was such a 'mix-up' he wondered why he was there. During the second week of July he and Emma attended the Macmillans' garden party at Knapdale, where Hardy conversed with Mr White of Harvard University and Henry Holt, his New York publisher. He remembered the party on the lawn and the thunderstorm which interrupted it when he wrote *A Laodicean*. A few days later he attended the funeral of young Louis Napoleon at Chislehurst, and was struck by the profile of Prince Napoleon as he walked past bareheaded, a son on each arm. This sight of Napoleon's nephew helped him enormously, he said, when he imagined the Emperor's appearance in *The Dynasts*.

Earlier, on 21 June, the Hardys had travelled to Harrow to spend a weekend with Bosworth Smith, who had been a master at the school since 1864. The following year he had married Flora Wickham, daughter of one of his father's Winchester and Balliol friends. At the suggestion of the headmaster, Dr Butler, he had built 'The Knoll', a four-storeyed boarding-house where he established his own traditions as housemaster, encouraging hobbies and an interest in gardening and wild life. Hardy probably knew the story of his first memorable adventure as a naturalist, when he was a young boy at a school in Blandford. He set out on a wintry afternoon, with snow on the ground, to take eggs from a raven's nest high in a tree on Badbury Rings; he had to fasten nails in the trunk to climb, and remove them as he descended, the operation taking two and a half hours and being successfully completed when it was almost dark. Hardy noticed a raven and a barn owl in his aviary at Harrow. Bosworth's elder brother was staying with him; he died relatively young and was already an invalid. Hardy noticed his 'churchyard cough', and how he kept repeating it, despite his wife's protests, to please the baby, with that 'extraordinary nonchalance about death' that 'so many of his family' showed. Emma and Hardy attended service in the chapel on Sunday, and were moved by some of the memorial tablets to boys who had died at the school. In the evening they went round the dormitories with their host. 'One boy was unwell, and we talked to him as he lay in bed, his arm thrown over his head. Another boy had his room hung with proof engravings after Landseer. In another were the two K——s of Clyffe [in the "Egdon Heath" country]. In another a big boy and little boy – the little boy being very earnest about birds' eggs, and the big boy silently affecting a mind above the subject, though covertly interested.'

During the latter part of August Hardy stayed a week at Higher Bockhampton, where he was then joined by Emma. They spent a few days visiting different places in Dorset, then took rooms overlooking Weymouth harbour, where Hardy's mother visited them. With her they continued Hardy's mission of inspecting settings for some of the later scenes in *The Trumpet-Major*, including Portland and Upwey, where he made a close study of the mill. Very probably, while in the vicinity, he visited the site of the sulphurous spring near Radipole (specifically mentioned only in the serial), where he imagined the meeting between George III and the heroine; in the meantime it had developed into a 'spa-house'. Unfortunately it was so wet and windy while the Hardys were at Weymouth that they were unable to enjoy their stay as much as they had hoped.

John Collier was chosen to illustrate *The Trumpet-Major* in *Good Words*, and Hardy forwarded the first four parts at the beginning of September, promising the next two within a week, to give him sufficient time for his work. He did some final research at the British Museum in November, and the novel must have been completed early in 1880, the year of its monthly serialization on both sides of the Atlantic. Collier was pleased to receive sketches from Hardy, and appreciated his collaboration in pursuit of accuracy. Proud of the moral wholesomeness of his magazine (implied in its title), the editor, the Revd Dr Donald Macleod, requested the change of a lovers' meeting from Sunday to Saturday, and the avoidance of 'swear-words'. Hardy obliged, knowing that the text could be restored when the novel appeared in book form. This happened in October. Although it was well received, sales were disappointing.

By Hardy standards *The Trumpet-Major*, though carefully prepared and written, and still popular, is no more than a moderately successful novel. Its unity depends on the invasion alarm, which was shifted from 1804 to 1805 to ensure continuing suspense, but its effectiveness suffers from the lack of both a great single action and characters of stature. The heroine's repeated vacillation, and the hero's continual self-sacrificial promotion of his less-deserving brother's claim to her, become rather tediously provoking. Hardy wisely combined the ordinariness of life with the uncommon events of a time fraught with momentous issues; and his time-sense, which is recurrently communicated from the opening mill-scene onwards, gives another dimension to little things such as the volunteers' pikes in a church; or it creates poignant resonance, notably in the references to Stanner's death and the silencing of the trumpet-major, each on a bloody battlefield in Spain. The comic element is much to the fore, but it is traditional and artificial rather than indigenous to Wessex, and the Derriman episodes are rather too farcical. Anne Procter, who recognized the youthful presentation of herself in Anne Garland, always maintained that the heroine married the wrong man. Had he accepted the story, Leslie Stephen would probably have not objected on this occasion.

After returning from Dorset in September the Hardys had dined out 'here and there'. As Emma had never seen the Lord Mayor's Show he took her to view it from the windows of the *Good Words* office in Ludgate Hill, where she thought the surface of the crowd below looked like a boiling cauldron of porridge. To him it seemed as though individuals were lost in the mass, forming a monster which threw out 'horrid excrescences and limbs into neighbouring alleys'. After narrowly escaping being crushed to death by a surging crowd during his first sojourn in London, he must have been glad to survey it in safety. Only a few months later he made a note on London at early dawn, after a sleepless night, partly from an eerie sense 'which sometimes haunted him, a horror at lying down in close proximity to "a monster whose body had four million heads and eight million eyes"'. One Sunday in November

Hardy and Emma were the guests of W. P. Frith, a painter renowned for his crowd scenes. In his studio they met Miss Braddon, whom Hardy always liked to meet, and Sir Percy Shelley, son of the poet, with Lady Shelley; they were introduced to Byron's Ianthe, the 'young Peri of the west' to whom he dedicated the first two cantos of *Childe Harold*. Muffled up in black and furs, she was now 'a feeble beldame' who 'talked vapidly of novels, saying she never read them – not thinking them *positively wicked*, but, well . . .'.

On a very foggy evening in December the inaugural dinner of the Rabelais Club took place at the Tavistock Hotel, and Hardy attended it in the dimly lit brumal atmosphere of a room where the fire, the only cheerful object, was concealed by a dull crimson screen. The only person who came in evening dress 'looked like a conjuror dying of the cold among a common set of thick-jacketed men who could stand it'. Among those present were Walter Besant 'with his West-of-England sailor face and silent pantomimic laughter', Sir William Frederick Pollock, senior master of the Supreme Court of Judicature, Sir Patrick Colquhoun, and Charles Leyland of Philadelphia, some of whose gipsy tales Hardy had heard at the Savile Club. 'Altogether', he wrote, 'we were as Rabelaisian as it was possible to be in the foggy circumstances, though I succeeded but poorly.' Colder weather came in the New Year, when the poem 'Snow in the Suburbs' was probably written. A thaw set in towards the end of February, but one springlike evening a few days later Hardy noticed a man skating round the edge of the pond near Trinity Church schools at Upper Tooting.

In February 1880 George Smith gave a dinner at the Continental Hotel, and there Hardy met Matthew Arnold, Henry James, and young Richard Jefferies. Arnold gave the impression of having made up his mind on everything, though he told Hardy he was only 'a hard-worked school-inspector'. Their conversation turned to Henry Moule, whose death had been announced, and Hardy's memories of the changes he had brought during his exceptionally active ministry at Fordington. He was reminded of Arnold's association of energy and genius (in 'The Literary Influence of Academies'), as he indicated when he wrote to Handley Moule, Fellow of Trinity College, Cambridge, after reading a report in a Dorset paper of the sermon he had preached at his father's funeral. In March he and Emma made the first of a long series of afternoon calls on Mrs Procter, at Queen Anne's Buildings, which lasted almost until her death. They frequently met Browning there, and

Mrs Procter made both of them very welcome. Later in the month she and Hardy lunched with the Tennysons in Belgrave Street. When they arrived, Hardy noticed Mrs Tennyson 'lying as if in a coffin', but she rose to welcome him and presided at the table. Tennyson, who was much more amusing than his portraits suggested, said he liked *A Pair of Blue Eyes* best of all Hardy's novels, and both he and his invalid wife invited him warmly to visit them in the Isle of Wight.

By this time Hardy was planning *A Laodicean*. Earlier in the year he had written 'Fellow-Townsmen', a story rather like the abridgement of a novel on the cruelty of chance which appeared in the April number of the *New Quarterly Magazine* and serially a little later in *Harper's Weekly*. Before he and Emma left England for a holiday, Hardy attended the Derby race at Epsom, and dined at a number of clubs, where he met Lord Houghton, not for the first time, Henry Irving, the artist Du Maurier, the painter Alma-Tadema, and the comedian J. L. Toole, who imitated a number of actors. Others he met in the summer included T. H. Huxley and the sculptor Thomas Woolner. At their meeting in July Lord Houghton introduced him to James Russell Lowell, the American minister in London whom Hardy thought a charming man, without creative genius as a writer. Later in the year, when Lowell consulted him on the proposed copyright treaty between America and Britain, Hardy recommended one revision.

He had been in touch with Arthur Henry Lock, a Dorchester solicitor, hoping that he could obtain a site for building his home there. He had agreed to Harper & Brothers' offer to serialize *A Laodicean* not only in America but also in England, where it was to appear in the first London number of *Harper's New Monthly Magazine*, at £100 for each monthly instalment on both sides of the Atlantic, a much higher rate than he had ever received. A draft of the first, which was due by 1 October, was ready in June, when Hardy proposed to meet his illustrator George Du Maurier and discuss it with him. He had hoped to engage Helen Allingham (née Paterson), but found she no longer illustrated books. John Henry Harper came over in July to help with plans for launching the European edition of the new magazine, and met Hardy and Du Maurier. A week or so later his London representative, R. R. Bowker, accepted Hardy's invitation to Arundel Terrace. He was received in 'a pretty parlor' by Mrs Hardy, 'with her Kensington-stitch work, and her pet cat', and found her 'an agreeable young-

ish' lady, 'immensely interested in her husband's work'. Then
Hardy came down, 'a quiet-mannered, pleasant, modest, little
man, with sandyish short beard, entirely unaffected and direct',
who told him he had great difficulty in remembering 'the people
and incidents' of his stories, his wife looking up such details for
him when necessary.

On 27 July they left for Boulogne. After seeing the cathedral at
Amiens, which seemed unfortunately to belie its loftiness, they
made for Normandy, where they stayed at the seaside resort of
Etretat. Here Hardy swam so long that he felt certain his 'frequent
immersions' were initially responsible for his continued illness in
the autumn and winter. At Le Havre Emma thought the landlord
and landlady of their hotel looked sinister; the waiter and the
chambermaid behaved oddly; the bedroom floor was painted
blood-red, and damage to one of the walls suggested that a
struggle had taken place. Hardy suddenly remembered that he
had told the man who recommended the inn when they were
travelling from Etretat that he carried his money in bank notes.
When they searched the room they found a small door behind the
curtains of one of the beds, with much lumber and another door
beyond. Having piled their trunks and portmanteau and jammed
them tight between the bedstead and the door, they lay down and
waited, keeping the light burning for a long time. Nothing happened, and they woke to a bright sunny morning. This sequence of
events may seem to have the preliminary ingredients of crude
imaginative fiction followed by the obvious bathos of a de-
romanticizing skit, but many intelligent people with heightened
suspicions would have behaved similarly in the same circumstances. Hardy was glad to exchange the 'fast life' of Trouville,
where they stayed at a fashionable hotel, for Honfleur. On a steep
hill behind this town they saw in the gloom of a gusty afternoon a
Calvary tottering to its fall. Hardy thought the crudely painted
figure of Christ seemed 'to writhe and cry in the twilight: "Yes,
Yes! I agree that this travesty of me and my doctrines should totter
and overturn in this modern world!"' After a few days at Lisieux
and Caen, they returned to London by the way they had come.

Hardy spent a week or two in Dorset during September, his
conversation with his parents on leasehold and freehold arising
from his wish to buy a site for a home in or near Dorchester. The
death of his uncle James in March may have made him feel the
need to be near his parents; Mary was now a headmistress in

Dorchester, and Kate, after completing her college course at the end of 1878, taught (and played the church organ) at Sandford Orcas near Sherborne. He returned the revised proofs for the first instalment of *A Laodicean* from Weymouth, informing Mr Bowker that the next two parts would soon be ready. It was probably while going to the Macmillans', and returning, one rainy evening in the early autumn, that he saw the disconsolate lovers of 'Beyond the Last Lamp', a human scene which impressed him so deeply that he recorded it in this poem about thirty years later, long after adapting it to a scene in *Tess of the d'Urbervilles*. On 16 October he and Emma left Tooting for a week at Cambridge, where they stayed at the University Arms Hotel. After the first day or two he began to feel 'an indescribable physical weariness'. Evening service at King's College Chapel reminded him of Milton's 'dim religious light' and Wordsworth's 'music . . . Lingering – and wandering on as loth to die' high up in the fan-traceried vaulting; above all, of his visit with Horace Moule, particularly as the candles guttered and simulated shrouds. The Hardys spent much of their time with Charles Moule and his brother Handley, who was soon to became principal of Ridley Hall.

Hardy was so ill when he reached home that he had to postpone immediate engagements and decline Lord Houghton's invitation to Fryston. A surgeon who lived opposite was called in, and diagnosed an internal haemorrhage. In her distress Emma consulted the Macmillans, who sent their doctor; he confirmed the diagnosis, said the case was serious, and gave instructions that Hardy was to stay in bed. A dangerous operation (most probably for kidney stone) was then deemed necessary; the only alternative was for the patient to lie for the first few weeks 'on an inclined plane' with his feet above the level of his head. Hardy chose this course, and determined to continue his novel, knowing that, should he die at this juncture, Emma would not be well off. The fourth of the thirteen instalments which were to appear from December 1880 to December 1881 was still to be finished when he became bedridden, and from November to the following April Emma acted devotedly as his amanuensis and nurse. It was a most strenuous and demanding time for her, and she responded 'bravely', as Hardy acknowledged years later.

Early in December he had sought the honour of sending Queen Victoria a copy of *The Trumpet-Major*; he informed her secretary Sir Arthur Ponsonby, after it had been forwarded, that in collecting material for the book he had met an aged villager who remembered seeing George III. Shortly afterwards he sent Charles Moule a copy of *Under the Greenwood Tree*, which he had promised long ago, thanking him and his wife for the pleasure Emma and he owed them when they were at Cambridge. January 1881 was extremely cold and damp, and fine driven snow crept in, filming the window-panes of Hardy's room inside and out. At one time, in the passage downstairs, it was sole-deep, Emma reported. After a while articles such as keys and an umbrella began to rust; footwear became mildewed. Edmund Gosse was one of their visitors. Maggie Macmillan called in March, and it was while she and Emma were admiring a gorgeous sunset after tea in Hardy's bedroom that she suggested angling the mirror so that he could enjoy it with them, a device which he remembered in *Jude the Obscure*.

Hardy had time to think. Almost inevitably he reflected again on the presentation of the war with Napoleon, imagining it first as a great drama, then as a 'Homeric ballad', with Napoleon a kind of Achilles, then, for the first time, as a drama with action which was mostly automatic, though seemingly motivated. The death of George Eliot just before Christmas set him thinking about Positivism, a great influence on her fiction; he concluded that if Christ had been included among 'the worthies' of Comte's calendar, making his humanitarian creed appear Christian, thousands more would have been ready to accept this 'new religion'. Arnold's essay 'The Literary Influence of Academies', which he had read more than once in recent years, made him reflect on provincialism in literature. As he was to explain in his 1912 general preface to his novels and poems, and as he knew already from the relative success of some of his novels, *Far from the Madding Crowd* especially, an author needs to be intimate with life in a particular region to write with assurance and true imaginative feeling. He had re-read Arnold's 'Pagan and Medieval Religious Sentiment' the previous winter, and felt that his 'imaginative reason' was the clue not only to style – seeing into the *heart of a thing* or pursuing realism imaginatively – but also to the goal of a thinker faced with the apparent irreconcilabilities between science and religion and the kinds of heterogeneity in the contemporary world which are illustrated in *A Laodicean*.

By early April Hardy had improved to such an extent that, but for a cold east wind, he would have been walking outside. He could now sit with his feet on the mantelpiece over a fire and write, as he informed his friend George Greenhill, a mathematics teacher at the Royal Artillery College, Woolwich, while busy with the twelfth part of his story. On 10 April he went out for the first time since October, on a drive with Emma and his doctor. Later in the month he wrote at length to Kegan Paul, expressing his indebtedness for another commendatory article on his novels, and taking care to tell him politely, without denying that he came from labouring stock (as Paul had written), that his father was probably the last of the old master-masons, and the fourth, as far as he knew, of a direct line of master-masons, all of whom had employed 'journeymen masons'. Two days after finishing his novel, he and Emma called by appointment on 3 May for a consultation with the eminent surgeon Sir Henry Thompson, a fine painter who was greatly interested in the arts, even to the extent of wishing to write a fine novel. Such an enthusiast would undoubtedly have wished to chat with Thomas Hardy. As he had his own telescope, and was the keenest of astronomers, their conversation at some stage may have reawakened an interest which, fortified by other events, was to lead to Hardy's next novel. A few days later Hardy walked, for the first time alone, on Wandsworth Common; here the closing lines of Gray's 'Ode on Vicissitude' came to him, and it is ironical that, at almost the time when the sun and air reminded him of the poet's 'opening Paradise', he should have elaborated his indictment of the First Cause in his Unfulfilled Intention theory. Having had no difficulty in extending their lease for another three months until midsummer, he and Emma spent the latter part of May searching for a house in Dorset. Eventually they found one at Wimborne which would suit them temporarily at least; they moved into it on 25 June. It was agreed that life in the country would be better for Hardy's health and inspiration, and that it would be sensible to restrict their sojourn in London to a few months each year. Tooting had brought mixed fortunes; it had enabled them to make new friends and discoveries in London, but it was for ever associated with pain and struggle. Suffering had made them feel, with Wordsworth, that 'the glory and the dream' of earlier days had faded.

Published in book form by Harper & Brothers towards the end of November, and by their London publishers at the beginning of December, *A Laodicean* was received with moderate approval at best; the London edition was soon remaindered. It had proved to be about one-third longer than was guaranteed (and a disappointment to the American publishers), but the fee for the book was increased proportionately, to Hardy's surprise and delight. Even with an architect as hero, affording him ample opportunities to draw from his own professional experience, it is hardly to be wondered at that he thought of the advantages of provincialism in the course of dictating it, its setting outside London being in an area of England he did not know at first hand and in parts of western Europe which he and Emma had merely visited during two holiday tours. Why he chose the site of Dunster Castle in west Somerset for the location of Stancy Castle, a building which is initially half ruin and finally burned down, is a question made more baffling by its clear identification on the map of Wessex which Hardy later prepared. The story is made suspenseful by devilish intrigue, the villain having Satanic and Mephistophelian associations. In contrast to *The Trumpet-Major*, it is 'A Story of To-Day', the question it raises being how wholeness of vision is attainable in the increasing diversification of Victorian England. Such heterogeneity is found in styles of architecture, in the beliefs and rituals of religious sects, above all in the achievements of engineering and technology in a country of ancient architectural splendours and traditional values. Like George Eliot in *Daniel Deronda*, Hardy is more positive in finding romance or poetry in 'science, steam, and travel', but the general question of reconciling disparates through the 'imaginative reason' remains unanswered; it is merely parroted at the end.

Hardy's future was unsettled in more ways than one. Whatever advantages London offered to an ambitious author, he had begun to feel, even before his illness, that the call of Dorset was stronger. At Arundel Terrace he had experimented with two widely different fictional subjects. An assured way ahead was not clear, and much depended on chance inspiration. The problem of how to satisfy his genius and achieve commercial success remained, but Hardy was a resourceful writer; he was not weighed down with misgiving, and would take, for the immediate future at least, the current as it served.

14

At Wimborne Minster

The chief feature of Wimborne Minster, a small market town in east Dorset, is the Norman church with its magnificent towers, its jack-clock (remembered perhaps in *The Dynasts* as an image of human beings automated by the general Will), and its chained library. The Avenue, in a lower-lying area by the Rover Stour, and near the station, was new when the Hardys lived there. Lanherne, a detached house of convenient size for them, had a conservatory (from which they viewed Tebbutt's Comet on the night of their arrival) and an excellent garden, with many flowers fully in bloom when they settled in. There were ripe strawberries and cherries, currants and gooseberries almost ready, and peaches and apples to look forward to. At the end of the garden stood a carriage-house and stables, which Hardy let rent-free to Frank Douglas, a young Scotsman who was studying land-agency (the management of landed property) in the area.

In her correspondence with Emma, usually from Sandford Orcas where she taught, Kate Hardy's uninhibitedness is a sure sign that relations between Emma and the Hardy family continued to be friendly. She came to see her and her brother one day in August. 'Come to meet me mind and make a fuss about my coming. I hope you've got some cake', she wrote. A wagonette was hired at the George, and all three were driven past the avenued approach to Kingston Lacy as far as the prehistoric hill fort of Badbury Rings, the tower of Charborough Park being visible beyond the Stour valley. The postilion had much to say about his driving experiences, the owners of Kingston Lacy and Charborough House, and the arrival of judges for the assizes when he was at Blandford. Hardy was interested to hear how the first judge on his way to Dorchester stopped to robe himself at the King's Arms, Puddletown, and was met on Yellowham Hill by the sheriff and javelin men. Kate wrote in September to thank the Hardys for their birthday present of a cape, saying that, on Mary's advice, she was going home to see her father (now about seventy), who may have been nervously distressed at the prospect of playing in a concert organized by the Smiths at West Stafford. He not only played but sang.

Henry J. Moule stayed with the Hardys before they left on 23 August for a holiday in Scotland, and was keenly interested in Emma's suggestion that he should illustrate a book on Dorset which her husband could write. Finding no rooms available in Edinburgh, as a result of extra bookings for Queen Victoria's review of the Volunteers the next day, Hardy and Emma took a train to Roslin, and found accommodation at the Royal Hotel. Despite the rain they visited the castle and famous chapel, then went on to Hawthornden, home of the early seventeenth-century poet William Drummond. They then spent a few days in Edinburgh, where they were driven round by a 'good-looking and ingenuous cabman', some of whose traits contributed to Farfrae in *The Mayor of Casterbridge*. After being 'laid up with colds' at Stirling, they continued their way to the Trossachs, 'across Loch Katrine, by coach to Inversnaid, down Loch Lomond, and so on to Glasgow', not without recollections of poems by Wordsworth and Scott's *The Lady of the Lake*. On their return journey via London they visited Windermere and Chester.

Hardy corrected the proof-sheets for *A Laodicean* in book form as he sat below long trailing shoots of the vine on his stable wall during a sunny September spell, the leaves casting a green light on the paper. By early autumn he must have completed his two Christmas stories, 'Benighted Travellers', set on the north Devon coast, and 'What the Shepherd Saw', a tale of four moonlit nights originally on the downs south-west of Salisbury; for the revised version in *A Changed Man*, Hardy transferred the key setting to the Devil's Den, a trilithon about two miles west of Marlborough. The first of these stories appeared in the Christmas supplement of a Bolton weekly through the agency of Tillotson's Newspaper Fiction Bureau; both were published in America, the first by arrangement with *Harper's Weekly*, the second with other Christmas stories which were all pirated from English Christmas numbers. Both suggest that Hardy had made a steady recovery since his illness at Tooting, and was working in accordance with fictional principles which he had formulated in July: 'The real . . . purpose of fiction is to give pleasure by gratifying the love of the uncommon. . . . The uncommonness must be in the events, not in the characters; and the writer's art lies in shaping that uncommonness while disguising its unlikelihood, if it be unlikely.' In October he agreed to supply a serial story for the *Atlantic Monthly* in 1882; developments soon to follow show that he had decided to write *Two on a Tower*.

As Hardy must have realized, Tebbutt's Comet and the prospect of another Transit of Venus in December 1882 had created excitement in the astronomical world. Not surprisingly, the serialization of his story in America and London was scheduled to end at that time. A story in a tower (he thought of the Hardy monument on Blackdown) had appealed to him in 1878, but for the present plan he may have been indebted to Maggie Tulliver's innocent comment on astronomers in *The Mill on the Floss*: 'they live up in high towers, and if the women came there, they might talk and hinder them from looking at the stars'. The tower in Charborough Park had given him a location which he was to disguise by introducing a tower of simpler design on a site suggested by the memorial obelisk on Weatherbury Castle, a wooded hill ringed with earthworks three miles east of Puddletown. He re-read R. A. Proctor's *Essays on Astronomy*, received useful information on lens-grinding and telescope-making from the engineer W. C. Unwin, and completed an ingenious application to inspect the Royal Observatory at Greenwich, especially 'to ascertain if a hollow memorial pillar, with a staircase inside', could be adapted as a small observatory, and how it could be roofed 'so as not to interfere with observations'. No evidence has been found at the Royal Observatory that the projected visit was made, nor does Hardy imply that it was. The account in his *Life* ends with 'An order to view Greenwich Observatory was promptly sent'; it is given merely as 'an amusing experience of formality'. Everything suggests that he obtained the assurance he required elsewhere, very possibly from Sir Henry Thompson, who was to become his lifelong friend.

During the autumn George Douglas, whose first volume of poetry had been published the previous year by Kegan Paul, came to visit his brother Frank, who told him that an author in whom he might be interested lived at Wimborne; he could not remember whether his name was Hardy or Harvey. Indirectly George, who had written an appreciative sonnet 'To the Author of "Far from the Madding Crowd"' when Hardy lived at Upper Tooting, discovered that he was the author of *The Trumpet-Major*. Douglas was born in 1856 at Gibraltar, where his father had served as a captain and married a Spanish lady; his great-great-grandfather had been an admiral. At Harrow his tutor had been Bosworth Smith, for whom he had a high regard. His education had continued at

Weimar, then with a French family at Fontainebleau, before he
entered Trinity College, Cambridge, where he graduated in history
in 1877. With the death of his elder brother in the Zulu war, he was
now heir to a baronetcy and a large estate by the Teviot near Kelso.
Before settling there, this young man was spending much of his
time travelling in Europe. With Frank he called on the Hardys the
next day, and found he was breaking their routine. Yet he was
received with 'the utmost kindness' and soon was alone with 'the
great man'; later he believed that Hardy was at 'the summit of his
career as an artist' and also 'at his best and happiest' about this
time. His talk, mainly on literature, was 'light and cheerful', and he
was 'robuster and less over-weighted by care' than he ever saw
him again. Douglas succeeded his father as fifth baronet in 1885,
and spent much time developing his estate and his interest in
Border folklore. His authorship continued in both prose and verse;
he lectured and wrote articles; and he remained a friend of the
Hardys, meeting them frequently in London. Though he thought
that *Tess* and *Jude* were artistically inferior to *The Return of the Native*
and *The Trumpet-Major* because of their 'special pleading', he believed that Hardy at the age of 80 was the greatest of our novelists
and poets.

A relatively restful period had helped Hardy to recover, but he
must have found life at Wimborne dull after a time. In October
1881, at Kegan Paul's suggestion, he had been appointed representative of the Society for the Protection of Ancient Buildings, to
advise when necessary on matters concerning the minster. He may
already have met the local architect Walter Fletcher, who acted also
as a county surveyor and a land-agent. The year ended brightly for
the Hardys when, after meeting several of their friends in London,
they attended Canford Manor ball as guests of Lord and Lady
Wimborne. They had one genial neighbour in Henry Tindal Atkin-
son, a county judge who 'took care they should not mope if
dinners and his and his daughter's music could prevent it'. He was
highly esteemed locally as a reciter and Shakespearian actor, and it
may have been he who persuaded Hardy to join a group which
met at members' houses to read Shakespeare. Hardy soon found
these readings a trial, and his attendances did not last long. His
amused aloofness is to be seen in the notes he made on meetings in
February 1882: 'the wealthy Mrs B. impassive and grand in her
unintelligence, like a Carthaginian statue. . . . The General reads
with gingerly caution, telling me privately that he blurted out one

of Shakespeare's improprieties last time before he was unaware, and is in fear and trembling lest he may do it again'.

At the end of 1881 Hardy's attention had been called to resemblances between the story of *Far from the Madding Crowd* and Arthur Pinero's new play *The Squire*, immediately after its first stage performance at St James's Theatre. He himself had prepared a stage version of his novel entitled 'The Mistress of the Farm' in 1879, and allowed J. Comyns Carr to adapt it further. The final version had been submitted to the managers of St James's Theatre in the summer of 1880 but eventually rejected. The actress Madge Kendal, wife of one of the managers, had told the story, it was later disclosed, to Pinero, who knew nothing about Hardy's novel or play. A letter of protest by Hardy in *The Times* and the *Daily News* was followed by controversy and explanation, the publicity of which led to the production of *Far from the Madding Crowd*, first at Liverpool and elsewhere in the provinces, then in London. Comyns Carr had seen his opportunity, and prepared a new text, not entirely to Hardy's satisfaction. Accepting Carr's invitation, he and Emma attended its last Liverpool performance at the Prince of Wales Theatre on 11 March. On their way back they saw *Romeo and Juliet* in London, two tickets having been sent by Henry Irving's secretary at Hardy's request to the Savile Club. *Far from the Madding Crowd* was staged at the Globe Theatre for several weeks, and it was after attending rehearsals, and the funeral of Charles Darwin in Westminster Abbey, that Hardy attended the first performance on 29 April.

Any elation which this undoubted success brought to Hardy must have been tempered with irritation that his copyright protest had provoked charges of plagiarism in *The Trumpet-Major* and *A Laodicean*. In the first he had copied a militia drilling-scene from Gifford's *History of the Wars Occasioned by the French Revolution*, not knowing it was taken from A. B. Longstreet's *Georgia Scenes*. In the second Sir William de Stancy's racing past had been copied from 'The Turf' in an 1833 number of the *Quarterly Review*; subsequently Hardy shortened it and gave it a dialectal slant. Late in the year he consulted the secretary of the Copyright Association on the question of protection when a namesake's 'Two Roses', which he described as 'wretched ungrammatical verses', was published over his name in the magazine *London Society*.

A battue in January 1882 did not endear neighbouring landowners to Hardy. He heard that pheasants had been driven into a corner of a plantation and shot wholesale as they flew up, 700 in a single day; 150 were found fallen from the trees the next morning, and he imagined them in the moonlight, fluttering and gasping as the hours of torture passed. He preferred to find friends in the Dorset Natural History and Antiquarian Field Club, which had been formed very largely owing to the initiative and enterprising zeal of William Barnes. It usually met in Dorchester; but arranged outings to places of interest. Such excursions sometimes provided Hardy with knowledge which could be turned to imaginative gain in his Wessex fiction. He attended a meeting in September 1882 at Milton Abbas to hear Barnes talk on the abbey. From this, from Hutchins, and from other sources, including Horace Walpole's letters, he discovered how Joseph Damer of Came House married the Duke of Dorset's daughter, bought Milton Abbey after becoming the first Earl of Dorchester, and built a mansion by the Abbey church, creating grounds by the removal of many of the old monastic buildings, the tombs and their bones, and the adjacent village. Making inventive use of traditional superstitions which arose from such wormy circumstance, Hardy wove (about 1890) 'The Doctor's Legend', a story clearly designed to be told by a member of the club (the Wessex Field and Antiquarian Club of *A Group of Noble Dames*) but left uncollected after being published in the States.

After a number of interruptions, *Two on a Tower* was completed by early September. Some of it had been conceived with the high-spirited nonchalance that characterizes 'The Levelled Churchyard', a poem suggested possibly by the Milton Abbas visit and certainly with London recollections. Written in 1882, with thoughts of what could have happened when tombs were disturbed for the restoration of the minster at Wimborne, the original version of this fancied protest in hymnal verse contained the type of verbal impropriety which the general had stumbled into at a reading of *The Tempest*. During March Hardy had tried to purchase a freehold site for the building of his home on Stinsford Hill; Lanherne had already proved to be 'rather too near the Stour level for health', as he wrote to Gosse the following December. Early in July he had written for *Harper's Christmas* a short imaginary story, which became a local tradition, of Napoleon's reconnaissance landing at Lulworth Cove. During the latter part of September he and Emma travelled on coaches to Salisbury, across to Axminster in Devon, and back via Lyme Regis, Bridport, and Dorchester, where they found time to visit William Barnes at his rectory. Unfortunately, Hardy left few observations on this extensive tour, his surviving notes being restricted to the sufferings of one of the horses from Axminster to Lyme (Emma 'with admirable courage' being ready to intervene and walk the remainder of the way, but for the anger of the other passengers, who wanted to 'get on'); to an encounter at Lyme with 'a cheerful man who had turned his trousers hind part before, because the knees had worn through'; and to a conversation with an old man on the Cobb who did not think long an operation for cataract that had lasted more than three-quarters of an hour, and was like having a red-hot needle in the eye.

Hardy's note on the holiday he and Emma spent in Paris during October is more revelatory; it suggests that Emma took pleasure in some forms of domestic activity, and enjoyed preparing meals from the fruit and vegetables grown at Lanherne. They embarked at Weymouth for Cherbourg, and rented a small *appartement* near the left bank of the Seine, where they stayed a few weeks, away from the English and American tourists, living in Parisian bourgeois style, buying their groceries and vegetables, and dining out at restaurants. Although the weather was uncertain, and they caught colds, they visited Versailles and various parts of the city, and devoted time to the study of pictures at the Louvre and the Luxembourg.

Two on a Tower was published at the end of October. Encouraged by private commendations, notably one from Kegan Paul on the 'marvellously comic touch' of duping the bishop, Hardy persuaded his publishers to advertise it as 'the story of the unforeseen relations into which a lady and a youth many years her junior were drawn by studying the stars together; of her desperate situation through generosity to him; and of the reckless *coup d'audace* by which she effected her deliverance'. His hopes that this would boost sales were disappointed; it probably increased the criticism, one reviewer regarding the novel as an insult to the Church, a charge which Hardy thought he might repudiate by stressing the heroine's religious feelings and pointing out that 'one of the most honourable characters in the book' is a clergyman. The boldness of the plot is reinforced in later editions by dating and unequivocal emphasis which make it clear that the passionate embrace which led to Lady Constantine's pregnancy occurred when she and her lover knew that their first marriage was invalid. The tricking of the infatuated bishop is the work of her brother, whose role as a villain, like that of Dare in *A Laodicean*, is hinted at in his smoking, as it was to be in the more Satanic role of Alec d'Urberville. One result of agreeing to write a novel of more restricted length than usual was that Hardy had little scope for his rustic chorus; after a very humorous choir practice near the opening, its role is perfunctory except at one critical point when their comments make the young astronomer realize for the first time that he is in love. If the story does serve to emphasize that 'two infinitesimal lives' are of greater significance than 'the stupendous background of the stellar universe', it has to be said that rarely in the action are the human and stellar emotionally or imaginatively integrated. Reminders of the heavens come in recurrent imagery, nowhere more effectively than at the end, when the astronomer, returned from all his observations in the southern hemisphere, is shocked at the ageing of Lady Constantine, whose hair, once 'darkness visible', was 'touched here and there by a faint grey haze, like the Via Lactea in a midnight sky'. The ending is one of Hardy's most effective, and the novel, with its altruistic slant, contains some fine writing, often succinct and deeply impressed with biblical overtones. A tragic victim of chance, Lady Constantine is not dishonoured; she is one of Hardy's most attractive heroines.

When Emma heard the sad news of her brother-in-law's death at St Juliot rectory in November, Hardy was reminded of the geniality of one who had suffered ill-health with fortitude and good humour. He recalled the romance of his meetings with Emma, and strange stories which Caddell Holder told from his experiences, in addition to a Mephistophelian legend which he heard from an aged parishioner of a local parson who, after imbibing freely, fell from his horse as he was riding up Boscastle Hill. When he called 'Help me up, Jolly!', a dark figure with a cloven hoof appeared and tossed him up on his horse 'in a jiffy'. During a night of terrific lightning and thunder this 'worthy ecclesiastic' was missed, never to be seen again.

The early months of 1883 were a busy period for Hardy the writer, with miscellaneous results. In January he completed one of his most successful short stories, 'The Three Strangers', for *Longman's Magazine* and *Harper's Weekly*. Towards the end of February he sent 'The Romantic Adventures of a Milkmaid' to the editor of the *Graphic*. This Mephistophelian story, in which Baron von Xanten acts as if he were the gentlemanly prince of darkness referred to in *King Lear*, or 'the Prince of Sin' in Hardy's 'Reminiscences of a Dancing Man', was written hastily. A moral ending was over-elaborately contrived for magazine requirements, although the tale was originally sketched to end with the disappearance of the baron and the dairymaid in the style of Arthurian romance. Ultimately the Swenn (the Frome) valley setting was changed, probably because Hardy did not wish his fantastic tale to be associated in any way with *Tess of the d'Urbervilles*. Much time early in 1883 was devoted to preparing his essay 'The Dorsetshire Labourer' for the July number of *Longman's Magazine*. Hardy's travels of the previous September were undertaken partly to ensure that his earlier impressions of rural life were brought up-to-date. He emphasizes the individualities of the peasantry, their ability to find happiness despite their poverty, and the changes which were taking place, with more frequent migration and steady depopulation. Some of the best descriptive passages were to find their place in *The Mayor of Casterbridge* and *Tess*. The study marks an important turning-point in Hardy's fiction; in future his labouring poor are no longer used merely for comic relief. From Whittle onwards they not only enlist the reader's sympathy; they become central figures in major novels.

In the winter Hardy and Emma attended first aid lectures, at one of which he observed ironically, beyond the skeleton in the window, children outside dancing to band music. On a walk to or from Corfe Mullen, he and the county surveyor Walter Fletcher were shown a stall inside a stable where a smuggler had been killed one night when the house was an inn. The road-contractor occupant whom they were visiting told them that if an old horse were stabled there on certain nights, it would cry like a child at about two in the morning, when the smuggler was killed, and be found in a lather of sweat. As if to provide another example of life stranger than fiction, the Hardys' servant Ann came in one day in March with the news, which was verified, that when a local carpenter, a short man, found the coffin he had made was not long enough and a bystander jocularly remarked that he might have made it for himself, he agreed and dropped dead instantly.

During May and June, after he had written to the psychologist Havelock Ellis, thanking him for the generous article on his novels he had contributed to the *Westminster Review*, Hardy and Emma spent some time 'on and off' in London. They lunched at Lord Houghton's, where they met Browning and the novelist Rhoda

Broughton; they met Browning again at Anne Procter's, and, later, George Smith. In the evening Hardy attended a Rabelais Club dinner in honour of Henry Irving, who was leaving for America. The next day he was one of Edmund Gosse's distinguished guests at the Savile Club. Shortly after this event he and Emma had left Wimborne, and were living in Dorchester.

15
Gosse, Dorchester, and *The Mayor*

Like Hardy, who was nine years his senior, Edmund William Gosse was a precocious child who had been assumed dead at birth. His mother, of Bostonian ancestry, died when he was only seven. His father Philip, an outstanding marine zoologist and an ardent member of the Plymouth Brethren sect, 'satisfied himself in *Omphalos* that he had refuted the theory of evolution before it was enunciated by Darwin, and had proved that the whole world was created in six days according to his fundamental beliefs. Edmund was dedicated to the Lord, and everything possible was done to shelter him from the snares and corrupting influences of the wicked world. Early happiness came to Willy when, after gloomy periods in London, he left with his parents for long periods by the sea. He was at Weymouth in 1853, when his father collected more than 4000 specimens of marine life along the Dorset coast for aquaria and Regent's Park zoo. (When he discovered this as late as 1920, Hardy remembered being taken to Weymouth at the time by his father, and wondered whether Willy had brushed against him in the street.) In 1854 the Gosses spent two months at Tenby; the next year they were in Devon and Dorset from March to September.

In 1857, soon after his mother's death, Edmund and his father left London to live near Torquay, Devon. Three years later Philip Gosse married a Quaker related to the Gurneys of Norfolk; she was a landscape-painter, formerly a pupil of Cotman. In the summer of 1861 she took Willy in a barouche to see the Gurneys at Earlham; the young boy found himself in 'clover' such as he had never 'dreamed of'. Literature had been forbidden fruit, though his father had encouraged him to read Michael Scott's *Tom Cringle's Log* for its geography. At a boarding-school in Teignmouth he acquired a taste for poetry and verse-writing. By November 1865, when his father took him to London to meet Charles Kingsley, whose assistance was sought to secure his appointment at the British Museum, Edmund's knowledge of languages had been

extended to Scandinavian, as a result of the help and encouragement he had received from the Danish scholar Elise Otté, who,
after moving to Torquay in 1863, had become friendly with the
Gosses. When he applied for the post on his seventeenth birthday
he claimed to have a speaking-knowledge of German, skill in
writing French, ability to read Greek, Latin, and Italian, and a
'rudimentary acquaintance' with Danish and Hebrew. He began
his appointment as a cataloguing transcriber at the Museum in
January 1867. There he found time to read much seventeenth-
century literature; in his lodgings with Anne Buckham, one of the
Brethren and a friend of his father, he read more poetry, particularly by William Morris and Swinburne, to the second of whom he
wrote, requesting an opinion of his own verses.

Gosse was an affectionate son; he kept little concealed from his
father, to whom he wrote at the end of 1867, hoping that he would
finance the publication of a volume of his poems. Though Philip
Gosse remained adamant in giving precedence to godliness in all
things, he was not averse to Edmund's pursuit of poetry, and
showed critical intelligence by pointing out how the lure of rhythmical sonorities could result in vagueness and verbal clutter. Gosse
heeded his father's advice, but was only 21 when *Madrigals, Songs
and Sonnets*, his joint venture with John Blaikie, son of a City
wine-merchant, was published at his father's expense in a very
limited edition. Only twelve copies were sold but, after meeting
Swinburne and Dante Gabriel Rossetti, he was adopted as the
youngest of the Pre-Raphaelites. It was at the painter Ford Madox
Brown's home that he met two pupils, Theresa, sister of Hamo
Thornycroft, and Ellen Epps, whom he was to marry in 1875.

In 1871 Gosse spent a holiday in Norway, where he bought a
volume of poems by Ibsen. The following year he accepted invitations to Denmark and Norway. Before visiting Denmark and
Sweden in 1874 he had written articles on Ibsen which appeared in
the *Spectator* and the *Fortnightly Review*, and one on the Danish
theatre in *The Cornhill Magazine*; he had also given his first public
lecture, on the 'ethical condition' of the Scandinavian peoples. To
his father, who was convinced that the second coming of the Lord
was at hand, when the saintly would be received in heaven, this
interest in Ibsen was tantamount to being in league with Satan. By
this time, however, Edmund was capable of answering him point
by point, confident that he could look after his own salvation.
Early in 1875 he was to write an essay introducing Swinburne to

the Scandinavians, in which he maintained that the poem 'Hertha' proclaimed 'a pantheism which is at least as comprehensive and reasonable a creed as any other now presented to the human faculty of faith'. His supreme ambition was still to be a poet, and his first independent volume of poetry, *On Viol and Flute*, published late in 1873, was well received, particularly for its 'colour and melody'. The poems were replete with sensuousness and fashionable romantic imagery, chiefly on the ecstasies of love.

Eventually Ellen Epps, whose sister was the wife of the painter Alma-Tadema, agreed to marry Gosse. After their honeymoon in Cornwall, they lived at Townshend House, Regent's Park, a home full of art treasures and curios, while their owners, the Alma-Tademas, were on holiday in Italy. Later in 1875 Gosse's familiarity with a number of European languages helped to secure him an appointment at the Board of Trade, where he worked happily in close contact with the poet Austin Dobson at a salary of £400 a year, considerably beyond what he had received at the British Museum. After house-hunting all the winter before the Alma-Tademas returned, the Gosses rented a house overlooking the Regent's Canal. Here, at 29 Delamere Terrace, not far from Townshend House or from where Browning lived, they soon made a regular practice of receiving their friends, including Thomas Hardy.

Gosse belonged to the Savile Club by 1877, and met Hardy there often after his election in 1878. Their first meeting must have been as early as 1874, probably when Hardy was in London just before his wedding; Gosse would have been most eager to meet the author of *Far from the Madding Crowd*. In 1912 he reminded him that, assuming they lived two years longer, their friendship would have lasted 40 years; in a radio broadcast soon after Hardy's death in January 1928 he referred to their 53 years' friendship. He had visited Hardy during his long illness at Tooting, and, after reading *Two on a Tower*, had written, suggesting lines from Richard Crashaw's poem 'Love's Horoscope' for the title-page. The dinner Hardy attended at the Savile Club on 25 June 1883 was a special occasion in honour of the American novelist William Dean Howells. Gosse's other guests included his great friend Hamo Thornycroft, the young sculptor with whom he had spent idyllic holidays on the Thames; Dobson, who had to leave early; George Du Maurier; William Black; and the sculptor Woolner, who had much to say. Hardy and Thornycroft had 'a nice talk about country folk'.

In several ways Gosse and Hardy were complementary and antithetical. Gosse was a socializer and ready conversionalist who quickly made friends. His career had brought him into contact with eminent writers and artists at home and abroad, and he deliberately sought the acquaintance of famous people. He loved social engagements and appearing as a public lecturer, but being in the limelight made him grow rather vain; ultimately he preferred to associate with people of eminence. He became an excellent host, and Henry James admired his 'fine rich gossip'. He was nervously excitable, and sometimes irritable, but habitually he was genial, showing a great sense of the ridiculous and a gift for pleasantry. As a writer he showed prodigious spontaneity and resourcefulness from an early age, excelling in painterly description. His verse became smooth and fluent, and the best of it remains forgotten or underprized. His ranging criticism made him regarded as the English Sainte-Beuve. Happily married, with children, he was now enjoying the 'summer' of his life. With her artistic gifts, friends, and relatives, his wife's life was so satisfying that he was able to fulfil his commitments and ambition with little let or hindrance. He had lost his faith, and did not believe in Providence, though he wrote on *Jude* as if he were an orthodox Christian.

Gosse was Hardy's first guest in Dorchester. He arrived by train on Saturday, 21 July, and was taken by Hardy to his home in Shirehall Lane (or Glyde Path Road). The approach was through a small archway and along a passage. Gosse told his wife Nellie that the house would rejoice her heart; it was 'most queer' and 'rambling', 'built on ever so many levels at ever so many periods'. Of it a townsman had said, 'He have but one window, and she do look into Gaol Lane.' Gosse, wishing to talk with Hardy, found Emma effusive but kindly. Henry J. Moule came in, and after high tea the three men walked about the town, which Gosse thought bright, clean, and full of life, soldiers from the two barracks – cavalry and infantry – giving it a foreign air with their colour, marching, and bugling. When Moule left he and Hardy continued their walking in streets busy with shoppers, and then, by moonlight, under the chestnut avenues around the town. On Sunday afternoon the two walked through cornfields to Winterborne Came, to hear William Barnes preach in his eighty-third year. Gosse thought him a wonderful figure with his white silky hair flowing down and mingling with his equally white beard and moustache. After the service they heard school children practise hymns. They then walked nearly a mile to the rectory on Wareham road, where they stayed four hours, Barnes showing them his picture collection; as in 1874, when Kilvert visited him with the vicar of Fordington, his drawing-room walls were most probably 'almost entirely covered with small oil paintings from floor to ceiling'. Much to Gosse's regret, he chose to talk on philology and British antiquities rather than on his own poetry.

About two weeks later Hardy attended the death-bed of his friend T. W. H. Tolbort, Barnes's former pupil, the outstanding linguist whose promising career as Deputy Commissioner in the Bengal Civil Service had been cut short by consumption. Tolbort had hoped to see his work on the Portuguese in India published, but within five days of his return to Dorchester from Algiers, where he had spent the winter, fits of violent coughing proved fatal. In his obituary notice for the *Dorset County Chronicle* Hardy recalled their friend Horace Moule.

Hardy had wished to leave Wimborne for a drier and more bracing air; his immediate purpose was to attend to the acquisition of a site for a home designed by himself and built by his brother Henry. It was not long before he had leased from the Duchy of Cornwall an acre and a half on the Wareham road, and was consulting Henry and his father on building possibilities. Digging in the chalk for the well and foundation-laying soon disclosed 'Romano-British urns and skeletons', which Emma at first thought ominous. From late November onwards Hardy spent much time overseeing building operations. By the early part of the month he had managed to complete 'Our Exploits at West Poley', a story of more then usual length which he agreed to write in April for publication in America. This was a cautionary tale for boys, of caving adventures in the Mendip Hills, ingeniously structured to create surprise, alarm, and heroic example. Much of Hardy's spare time was spent in the Dorset County Museum, after its removal at the end of 1883, under the curatorship of his friend Henry J. Moule, to its present premises in High Street, above St Peter's. Here, in the notebook entitled 'Facts', the first entries in which were made at Wimborne, he recorded unusual and exciting incidents from old newspapers and local histories and biographies. From such readings, especially in early numbers of the *Dorset County Chronicle*, *The Mayor of Casterbridge* began. On market days he was struck by the affluence of farmers and the plight of country labourers, some seeking employment, others intent on emigration, a contrast which is a feature of this novel and of 'Interlopers at the Knap', a shorter story which he completed early in 1884 for the *English Illustrated Magazine*. The knowledge that Moule had accepted the curatorship in 1883 confirmed Hardy's wish to live in or near Dorchester. For its official opening on 1 January 1884 the museum had been transferred from the house in Trinity Street which Moule and his family subsequently occupied; Hardy often visited him there.

With no garden to sit in, Emma could no doubt find much of interest for a while in what Dorchester had to offer. She accompanied Hardy on outings to Higher Bockhampton and to the site of their prospective home, and she resumed painting to good effect, with pictures of Glyde Path Hill and the hangman's cottage, and impressive copies of early paintings by Henry J. Moule, notably of the bootmaker's shop at Lower Bockhampton and of the upper end of Higher Bockhampton lane from the edge of Puddletown Heath. Welcome visitors included Mary and Kate Hardy, both of whom were now teaching in Dorchester; Mary had for some time been head of the National School for girls in Bell Street (now Icen Way), where Kate had recently been appointed mistress of the first class. One day in the autumn Bosworth Smith had called with his father and sisters Evangeline and Alice to see the novelist in his 'nice house'. Even so Emma must have been pleased in January 1884 when she could visit the winter exhibitions in London with her husband; she was probably with him when he met Henry James, Gosse, Thornycroft, and Alma-Tadema, who was most interested in the Romano-British remains which had come to light on the Max Gate site (spelt 'Mack's Gate' at first, after the toll-gate and the keeper who had lived in the cottage near it on the opposite side of the road). There must have been many more; when the main drive was made, skeletons of five Roman soldiers in a row were decapitated, Hardy told William Archer.

The Hardy who came to Dorchester at the beginning of his forty-fourth year had matured. Although he soon realized that 'every error under the sun seems to arise from thinking that you are right yourself because you *are* yourself, and other people wrong because they are not you', he was more determined than ever not to accept tradition and convention at face value. It would be interesting to make lists of 'things which everybody thinks and nobody says' and of 'things that everybody says and nobody thinks', he wrote in August 1883. So, without dismissing love (for without it life offers only 'a scene that lours . . . and then, the Curtain'), his poem 'He Abjures Love' states his resolution no longer to suffer a romantic lover's illusions and disquietudes – the 'lover's love' which he declared at the end of *Two on a Tower* as less to be prized than 'loving-kindness' – but to see life as it really is, rating neither 'the common rare' nor 'the gray hour golden'. On 26 April 1884 he observed the illusion created by lamplight in the High Street, when he saw four girls, itinerant musicians, whom he had noticed during the day, transformed by gleams from silver-ware in a shop window; their brass ear-rings had become golden, the face of one, a cherub's, and that of another, an angel's. He made this observation not long after thinking of the possibilities of a novel in which antagonism between the parents of a Romeo and a Juliet succeeds in 'separating the couple and stamping out their love'. Both conceptions contributed to *The Well-Beloved*, one to the ending, the other to the opening.

Hardy must have enjoyed health and vigour to cope with his multifarious interests and activities. His two overriding responsi-bilities were architectural supervision at Max Gate from first to last and adequate preparation for his next novel, to which he gave great thought. He had little time to spend on casual encounters, though he was delighted in August 1883 to meet an old man whose father or grandfather was one of the beacon-keepers during the threatened Napoleonic invasion; remains of their hut could still be seen on Rainbarrow. Just before Christmas that year and again on his forty-fourth birthday, he took the opportunity in the evening while he was at Higher Bockhampton of entering the neighbouring wood to register impressions which he was to remember in *The Woodlanders*. The next day he found it necessary to water copiously the trees he had planted at Max Gate on New Year's Eve. In the evening he watched part of the entertainment provided by a circus in Fordington Field. (He could never resist a circus in those days, and attended all that came to Dorchester.) He had become a JP for the borough in April. In May, at a meeting of the Dorset Field Club, he read a paper on the ancient relics which had been unearthed at Max Gate, referring slyly to the 'local Schliemann' Edward Cunnington, whose excavations at Maiden Castle had, it was suspected, been motivated by personal gain, as seems to be borne out fictionally in 'A Tryst at an Ancient Earthwork', which Hardy thought it safe to publish far off in Detroit early in 1885.

The writing of *The Mayor of Casterbridge*, which was begun in the spring of 1884, suffered many interruptions. While on holiday in London during the early summer, Hardy and Emma became acquainted with Lady Portsmouth and her daughters. They attended an evening party at Alma-Tadema's, meeting 'an artistic crowd which included Burne-Jones'; elsewhere, with Mrs Procter, they met Du Maurier, Henry James 'with his nebulous gaze', and Matthew Arnold, to whom Hardy felt much better disposed than he did at their first meeting. In London again at the end of July, he answered a questionnaire which had been addressed to him from Detroit: he preferred to work at night, though daytime was usually advisable; he did not take stimulants 'unless tea can be considered as such'; he liked to remove his boots or slippers 'as a preliminary to work'; he had no fixed hours for writing; and he rarely worked against his will. During August, after watching a performance of *Othello* by strolling players in Dorchester market-field, he visited the Channel Islands with his brother, and it may have been at this time that Emma's nephew and niece, Gordon and Lilian, stayed with her, and she gave the children's party which H. O. Lock, son of Hardy's solicitor, attended in blue velvet, and recollected happily in old age. In October Hardy was the Lord Mayor of London's guest at a dinner for members of the Incorporated Society of Authors. On New Year's Eve he climbed to St Peter's belfry with the ringers, and watched them fix the mufflers before ringing the old year out and the new year in. Emma was too ill to accompany him in March when he accepted a long-standing invitation to stay with the Portsmouths at Eggesford House, their home in Devon. Although given sole possession of the library, he could not settle to work, and spent most of the time driving in the country with his hosts and walking in the park. Lady Portsmouth was ready to provide a house if he and Emma would live near them; he knew that Emma would be pleased to return to her native county, 'but, alas, my house at Dorchester is nearly finished', he wrote. He completed *The Mayor of Casterbridge* a few weeks later, more than six months after agreeing to the serialization of his next novel in *Macmillan's Magazine*.

The frequency of surprise, sensational incident, and suspenseful situation in *The Mayor* suggests that Hardy knew long in advance that it was to be serialized weekly in twenty numbers of the *Graphic* and *Harper's Weekly*. His publishers would undoubtedly seek assurance that the story was complete before they would risk embarking on such a rapid production. Even so, it is surprising how much time elapsed between the completion of this Dorchester novel and the appearance of the first part of its serial on 2 January 1886. Hardy was no doubt pleased to have this major work off his hands in order to attend to the completion of Max Gate and his removal in June 1885. His only new fiction that summer, the short story 'A Mere Interlude', ingeniously contrived though it is, appears to have been written very hastily.

Frequent interruptions, combined with the continual need for exciting events, led to some unevenness in *The Mayor of Casterbridge*. As mere story, two of the events are the stuff of popular magazine fiction; some tricks used to intensify conjecture were removed when the serial version was revised for publication in book form. The style varies considerably, from the somewhat laboured and clumsy to the intensely poetical. Some of the finest effects are produced in vernacular idiom, heightening tragedy in Mother Cuxsom's account of Mrs Henchard's death, and even more in Abel Whittle's description of the rejected Henchard's last days on the heath. Once again Hardy had turned with admiration to narrative art in the Old Testament stories of Saul, and the simple grandeur of biblical prose is echoed here and there at moving points in the story.

Although the main narrative, which begins about twenty years after the preliminary drama of the wife-sale, was imagined in the Dorchester Hardy first knew as a school boy (and it had not changed greatly since), he did not hesitate to modify the setting for artistic reasons, most significantly in placing Lucetta's house by the *carrefour* and market-place where much could be seen and heard; its original was Colliton House, with the bricked-up archway ornamented by a keystone mask which stood in a high adjacent wall along Glyde Path Road near where Hardy lived. There were chronological changes for the same purpose: the coming of 'the Royal Personage' to Casterbridge by road for the last few miles because the railway had not yet been completed alluded clearly to Prince Albert's reception in 1849, two years after the railway reached Dorchester, when he was on his way to lay the foundation-stone for the breakwater which created the Portland naval base; the arched entrance to North Square had been demolished by 1848 at the latest.

Important though these departures from the actual were, they affected the novel less than literary influences. This applies especially to the actions and temperament of Henchard, whose character was at first based on Giles Symonds, the 'hot-headed' town clerk who lived in the original of Mayor Henchard's house in South Street until his retirement in 1892; Henchard's name at first was Giles, not Michael. His personality developed from the character and treatment of King Lear, the temperament of Mr Tulliver in *The Mill on the Floss*, even more from the close analysis of the hero's character and development in Sophocles' *Oedipus Rex* by J. A. Symonds in *Studies of the Greek Poets;* above all (and Hardy has left clues for these in his novel), from Saul in the Old Testament and Jean Valjean, the hero of Hugo's *Les Misérables*. The contrast between Henchard's traditional rule-of-thumb methods and Farfrae's business acumen may owe something to that between Tulliver and the Dodsons; their rivalry assumes important aspects of that which grows menacingly between Saul and David. Henchard with only Whittle to care for him on the heath was undoubtedly suggested by *King Lear* (the old word 'wittol' signifying a fool), but the final phase of his life has more parallels with that of Valjean. Hardy's novel and Hugo's, it is worth noting, begin with crimes or illegal acts by physically strong men who become mayors after being successful in business. Hardy had evidently thought long over situations of great or enduring appeal in literature, and decided to use similar ones wherever they were in accord with his most serious Wessex fiction. In no other of his novels did his creative imagination draw more from literary sources. The result is not only a story of powerful appeal but also the greatest of his characters and, many would add, his greatest tragic ending. Whether superfluous or not, the brief postscript in which Hardy's outlook on life is ascribed to Elizabeth-Jane concludes the novel in the same strain as the final chorus does *Oedipus Rex*.

There are new features in *The Mayor of Casterbridge* which make it rather exceptional among Hardy's novels. It is the only one which is centred mainly in a town; which does not depend on a love-story; and where destiny is the result of character rather than chance in the usual sense of the word. To Hardy, however, character was a matter of chance, depending largely on heredity, as he emphasized in 'Discouragement', one of his earliest poems. The full title ran: 'The Life and Death of the Mayor of Casterbridge, A story of a Man of Character'. Farfrae's Scottish pronunciations were revised by Sir George Douglas for a later edition.

When serialization began Hardy felt apprehensive about the reception of some of the contrived situations and sensational incidents in his story, but took comfort in the thought which he had stated some years earlier, and probably found supported in Trollope's *Autobiography*, that 'it is not improbabilities of incident but improbabilities of character that matter'. The book was published in May 1886 by Smith, Elder & Co. despite the warning of their reader, James Payn, that 'the lack of gentry among the characters made it uninteresting'. It did not sell particularly well, nor were most reviewers enthusiastic, though Henchard was judged 'almost magnificent'. Robert Louis Stevenson, who had visited Max Gate the previous summer, was much more discerning than most readers. Early in June he wrote to say that he had read the novel and would like to dramatize it; 'Henchard is a great fellow, and Dorchester is touched in with the hand of a master', he added.

16

Max Gate, *The Woodlanders*, and Italy

Soon after *The Mayor of Casterbridge* was completed Hardy and Emma were on holiday in London. One evening after visiting the Royal Academy private view, they attended a party given by Lady Carnarvon, Lady Portsmouth's sister-in-law; here Hardy met Lord Salisbury for the first time, and discussed with him the art of speech-making. At another reception there, in the middle of May, when Emma had returned home for a brief period, Hardy, who obviously felt it was to his professional advantage to be known and accepted in high society, found the atmosphere more friendly than on the previous occasion, although he felt that Mrs Jeune, a lively hostess of aristocratic descent whose sister-in-law had married Canon Gifford, was very cool, probably because Emma, her niece by marriage, had not called on her. (A footnote to the letter in which he describes the evening to the latter shows the precautions he felt needed to be taken by the servants when turning on and off the gas.) Three of Lady Portsmouth's daughters, Lady Dorothea, Lady Margaret, and Lady Winifred Herbert who complained about the heaviness of the teapot as she did the pouring, were staying with their aunt, and regretted Emma's absence. Among those Hardy met on this occasion were Browning, and Murray Smith, his publisher's son, who greeted him warmly. The novelist and critic Mrs Oliphant, to whom he was introduced, proved to be 'propriety and primness incarnate', and he felt Emma had lost nothing by not making her acquaintance. They met several friends later at Mrs Jeune's, but at 'crushes' held by Lord Houghton and Lady Galway they knew hardly anyone except their hosts.

At one such crush, when the house was filled with people excited by the rumour of General Gordon's death, a Conservative peeress who had recently 'adopted' Hardy told him that she was ashamed of her party, all of whom looked forward to confirmation of Gordon's murder, hoping that it would be the ruin of Gladstone. Such experiences strengthened Hardy's Arnoldian conviction that history is 'rather a stream than a tree', being turned this way and that by a straw or a barrier of sand. The politicians he met at Lord Carnarvon's made him feel that national affairs could be handled just as well by 'a row of shopkeepers in Oxford Street just taken as they came'. It was while waiting for Emma at the Marble Arch that he observed the roar of London and philosophized on the lives of its people, all caged birds, the only difference being in the size of their cages. The next Sunday he called on Mrs Procter, who was vexed with him and Browning, also present, for sending cards to be attached to wreaths at Victor Hugo's funeral; in the evening he met three prominent Positivists, Frederic Harrison, Professor Beesly, and Dr J. H. Bridges.

The endeavours of these men to promote Positivism for the welfare of the underprivileged and of society in general impressed Hardy, and the friendship which developed between him and Harrison may have begun about this time. Frederick Harrison was a man of considerable ability and distinction; he was a barrister and professor of law who had maintained his keen interest in history and philosophy. Inherited privilege made him acutely conscious of labour and economic problems. Son of a prosperous London merchant, he had won a scholarship to Wadham College, Oxford, from King's College School. At Wadham he was fortunate to be tutored by Richard Congreve, founder of the Positivist movement in England, and took a classical first class degree in 1853. He taught with Tom Hughes and others under F. D. Maurice at the Working Men's College, and made a long and critical study of Comte's philosophical works and aims, which he did not accept in their entirety. Differences with Congreve caused him and other sup- porters of Positivism to secede and form their own organization under Harrison's leadership. In 1880 he became president of the English Positivist Committee; in 1881 he opened Newton Hall in Fetter Lane for their meetings and for public lectures on Positiv- ism, many of which he gave himself. Hardy's letter to him on 17 June 1885 reveals that he and Emma had attended some of them, and that he regretted their conclusion.

Two weeks later they had occupied Max Gate, Hardy having left London a day or two before Emma to superintend the removal. What she thought of this isolated house, almost a mile outside Dorchester, after moving in aristocratic circles, is a matter for conjecture. Not far from the prehistoric mound Conquer Barrow, on a rather elevated site south of the Frome valley, with Stinsford

church and Kingston Maurward beyond, hardly a mile away, and
'Egdon Heath' to the north-east, it must have looked uninvitingly
exposed to an impartial observer. Emma was to find it 'bleak and
cold', as Hardy acknowledged after her death in his poem 'Everything Comes'. Years were to pass before the trees which he planted
were to afford it shelter and a more comfortable appearance.
Facing south-south-west to catch the sun as much as possible
throughout the day, it was protected by a high wall along both the
main road and a road on the eastern side which ran down to the
local railway freight-stop. At the back, along the north-east boundary, a row of pines was planted; a large outhouse, intended for a
carriage and stabling, gave some protection on the north-west.
From this to the south-west corner a dense plantation eventually
provided a dark screen for the house, and a cemetery for its pet
cats and dogs. Half the site lay almost undeveloped on the easterly
or Conquer Barrow side of the house. The area to the right of the
gateway at the front was designed for a sheltered lawn; behind
this, from the side road to the end of the house, a garden for
flowers, fruit, and vegetables was planned; further back, protected
by the row of pines, an orchard. In September 1886 Hardy con-
verted his leasehold into freehold possession, purchasing the
ground at no less than £300 an acre. As it stood outside the town,
Max Gate had to provide its own water and drainage. The indoor
well, pump, and storage tank supplied the most serviceable amenities available, including water-closets upstairs. Water had to be
carried to the bedrooms; there was no bathroom until 1920; and
manual work indoors was so heavy that it was difficult to retain
servants for long periods. Apart from the carriage-house and stable
(which was rarely used, for Hardy never owned his own equipage
or horses), Max Gate afforded little beyond minimal accommodation. Rooms for the domestic staff were provided in the attics; at
the back there was nothing but a kitchen, a scullery, and a small
bedroom, the only one suitably placed for a guest, one of the main
rooms upstairs being used as Hardy's study. In August 1886 Hardy
informed Gosse that they had only a bachelor guest-room but
hoped to have a spare bedroom for a married couple the following
year. Further extensions and improvements were to be made from
time to time to this purpose-built, unpretentious, middle-class
home before its owner died there in 1928.

His first distinguished visitor was R. L. Stevenson, now living at
Bournemouth and seeking a more bracing climate for his health.

To Hardy, who had never met him, his romantic appearance must have been striking. He called in August 1885 with his wife, wife's son, and cousin, on his way to Dartmoor, which he failed to reach after being prostrated with haemorrhages at Exeter. 'What very strange marriages literary men seem to make', Mrs Stevenson wrote after leaving Max Gate. She noticed Hardy's pallor, scholarly appearance, and modesty; she thought his wife '*very* plain, quite underbred, and most tedious'. From this it is clear that some of Emma's eccentricities, notably her garrulous fussiness and irresistible urge to call attention to herself, if not to dominate, were becoming more evident. Writers such as Gosse and Stevenson who came to converse with Hardy found themselves frustrated in her company. No wonder he sought refuge in his work, and preferred a study upstairs. At Max Gate his first was at the east end, over the drawing-room; his next, when he wrote *Tess* and probably most of *Jude*, in the original back bedroom; his last, overlooking Conquer Barrow, was located in the main rear extension.

In September Hardy enjoyed a meeting of the Field Club at Pilsdon Pen, a hill in west Dorset which he remembered in 'Wessex Heights'. Next month he called on William Barnes at his rectory half a mile further out on the Wareham road, and talked with him on old families, particularly the Damers of Came House, near his church. Louis Napoleon was staying with them when Barnes kept his Dorchester school, and Hardy heard how one of his ushers, from Blackmoor Vale, nearly came to blows with Napoleon's nephew, afterwards emperor of France. Barnes was growing weaker every day, and Hardy visited him whenever he knew he was able to talk, as he told Edmund Gosse on receiving a copy of his *Firdausi in Exile and Other Poems* in November. Gosse's inscription showed that he would have dedicated 'A Ballad of the Upper Thames' to Hardy had he thought it worthy of him; Hardy responded by quoting verses from 'Points of View' in *The Woodlanders*, which he had just begun.

Having had little time to plan a new novel within the last year, he had turned to the woodland story which he had intended as the successor to *Far from the Madding Crowd*. After working long hours on it for two or three days, and becoming more and more depressed, he decided to keep to his original plot. His depression continued to the end of the year, when he wondered whether the building of Max Gate had been 'a wise expenditure of energy'; Mrs Stevenson had said in her over-emphatic way that he 'recoiled from' his new home. Hardy's New Year's Eve note alludes cryptically to other worrying factors. He may have known already that the house and its situation did not please Emma, and that, having made few real friends, she regretted settling in Dorchester; he may have feared he had gone too far with sensationalism in *The Mayor of Casterbridge*, the first part of which was to appear in two days. His personal anxieties entered his thought when he wrote in November: 'a tragedy exhibits a state of things in the life of an individual which unavoidably causes some natural aim or·desire of his to end in a catastrophe when carried out'. They may help to explain why Hardy empathized so readily in *The Woodlanders* with a hero who is reduced to zestless passivity when struck by the blows of chance. The question arises how different the hero would have been in the projected novel had it been written immediately after *Far from the Madding Crowd*, when the author, despite his intellectual awareness of the workings of 'crass Casualty', was confident and enterprising, and believed more in the spirit of Gabriel Oak.

His literary zeal did not diminish, however. 'My aim is to intensify the expression of things, as is done by Crivelli, Bellini, etc., so that the heart and inner meaning is made vividly visible', he wrote on 3 January 1886. In March he was thinking ahead to fiction in which 'abstract thoughts' are presented as 'visible essences' or spectres, 'the human race to be shown as one great network or tissue which quivers in every part when one point is shaken, like a spider's web if touched'. The idea of 'abstract realisms' as spirits anticipated *The Dynasts*, but the 'great network' concept had operated significantly, it is worth noting, in the planning of human relationships in *The Woodlanders*, where concatenated effects on a larger scale than is to be found elsewhere in his fiction form 'part of the pattern in the great web of human doings' throughout the world. Though but a minor and freakish feature of the story, nothing exemplifies this more strikingly than the linkage between the American Civil War and Mrs Charmond's death in Homburg.

He must have made good progress with the monthly serialization which began with the May number of *Macmillan's Magazine*, for he and Emma spent most of the spring and summer in London. Early in April and again in May he attended sessions in the House of Commons on Gladstone's Home Rule for Ireland bill, a debate in which he noted that his friend John Morley spoke intelligently with little apparent effect. Hardy saw policy in contention with 'good philanthropy' or humanity, speciously insisting they were one, and recognized that Morley, 'a consummate man of letters' and an uncompromising Home Rule advocate, was out of place in this 'motley assembly'. Recalling Carlyle's *Sartor Resartus*, he observed the contrast between the evening-dress of 'the dandy party', with their eye-glasses and diamond rings, and the plain ill-fitting clothes of the Irish members; another in simple dress who caught his eye was Joseph Arch, the agricultural trade-unionist whose tours in Dorset he had sympathetically presented in 'The Dorsetshire Labourer'. Emma and he stayed much of the time at 28 Upper Bedford Place, so that he could read at the British Museum for *The Dynasts* whenever possible. He met friends and new acquaintances at the Savile Club, but lunched and dined out with Emma, several times at Mrs Jeune's, where they met J. R. Lowell. J. A. Froude (literary executor, editor, and biographer of Thomas Carlyle), the Humphry Wards, the Oxford scholar Walter Pater (who had the air of 'carrying weighty ideas without spilling them'), and many politicians. They attended a huge party at the Gosses', where the chief guest was Oliver Wendell Holmes, 'the intellectual king of Boston' with whom Gosse became friendly in 1884 when he was lecturing in America; he was a small, very bright 'juvenile old man', who told Hardy he did not read novels. A few days later they met at a Rabelais Club dinner, where Hardy talked to Meredith and noted Henry James's 'ponderously warm manner of saying nothing in infinite sentences'. At Sidney Colvin's he met R. L. Stevenson again; elsewhere he met Whistler and Bret Harte. He called on Leslie Stephen, whose approval in April 1885 had seemed to him no better than 'disapproval minimized', and found him 'just the same or worse', making caustic remarks when he really intended to be sympathetic.

Emma and he attended concerts, at one of which music by Wagner suggested to Hardy the 'whistling of wind and storm, the strumming of a gale on iron railings, the creaking of doors; low screams of entreaty and agony through key-holes, amid which trumpet-voices are heard'. Mrs Procter had tea with them, and told many literary anecdotes in her usual way, one of Macaulay and Sydney Smith dining with her; when Macaulay had left, she told Smith he had given Macaulay no chance to talk, only to hear that he had made several opportunities, all of which she had taken advantage of. Another caller was George Gissing, who sought advice on novel-writing, and shortly afterwards sent Hardy two of his novels, *The Unclassed* and the recently published *Isabel Clarendon*, with comments on the impossibility of writing honestly for the Victorian public. Hardy met Browning again at Mrs Procter's, and found time one evening to look for bargains at bookstalls in Holywell Street, as he used to do many years earlier. Before returning to Max Gate he and Emma enjoyed discussing pictures with the Friths.

Besides preparing lectures for his American tour, Gosse had written a great deal in recent years and been appointed Clark Lecturer at Cambridge after Leslie Stephen's resignation. Soon after the Hardys' return he sent a copy of his *Raleigh* to Max Gate; Emma, impressed by its superiority to the usual current literature, proposed to read it to Hardy, who invited him to visit them, suggesting they could spend a day at Bridport, Abbotsbury, or Swanage. He knew that Gosse would wish to see Barnes before his death. Gosse came at the end of August, and the sisters Evangeline and Alice Smith, calling at Max Gate from West Stafford, had 'an old-fashioned cold supper tea' with him and Henry Moule, who entertained the company with ghost stories. Hardy and Gosse visited Barnes and journeyed to Bridport, the setting for 'Fellow-Townsmen', where plans went astray, Hardy remembering guiltily 'that terrible kettle at the Bridport pot-house' and Gosse recalling about ten years later, when he dedicated his *Critical Kit-Kats* to him, how Hardy and he had lost their way in the leafy town, and been so far misdirected that they had lost their train. At Maiden Newton, on the way to Bridport, Gosse had sent home a description of the dying Barnes as he lay grey-bearded in a scarlet dressing-gown, with a kind of biretta of dark-red wool over his long white hair, in a white bed in his study, green tapestry on the wall behind him, rows of brown books around the other walls, and light filtering through plants in the window. Gosse left Max Gate to join American artists, and walk with Henry James, in the Cotswolds. Soon afterwards Hardy dined in Dorchester with the poet Aubrey de Vere at the home of his cousin, the Revd Aubrey Spring Rice. Emma Hardy may have been the last visitor to see William Barnes before he died on 7 October 1886. Four days later, as he recalled in 'The Last Signal', Hardy caught sight of his gleaming coffin as he and it made their separate ways to the funeral in Winterborne Came church. His lengthy article on the deceased poet, beginning with a memorable picture of Barnes 'quaintly attired in caped cloak, knee-breeches, and buckled shoes' on a market day in Dorchester, appeared in the *Athenaeum* on 16 October; another by Gosse, on the same day, in the *Saturday Review*. In a letter referring to this 'graceful article', Hardy touched on the scathing attack which Churton Collins had jealously made on factual inaccuracies in *From Shakespeare to Pope*, a collection of lectures which Gosse had given at American universities and repeated at Cambridge. Still Clark Lecturer, he had experienced the 'most terrible week' of his life; and Hardy, knowing what it meant to suffer from reviewers, encouraged him to bear up. Finding Cambridge loyal to him, Gosse slowly recovered, though he remained conscious of scars which he bore for life.

During October the Hardys enjoyed a week in Devon as Lady Portsmouth's guests. Emma sketched Eggesford House and listened, with less pleasure than Lord Portsmouth, Master of Hounds, who added 'corroborative words with much gravity', having heard it many times, to the story told by his whipper-in of the hunted fox that ran up the clock-case in an old woman's house. In London during December, Hardy noticed a strong Impressionist influence at the Society of British Artists' exhibition, and was reminded of a study by Whistler he had seen at the gallery, when Mrs Jeune, in a rich pinkish-red gown, chatted with him by firelight. A cabman drove him furiously as snow fell to Lady Carnarvon's party. The New Year at Max Gate was uneventful, and he continued *The Woodlanders*, finishing it early in February. Some pictures in this novel are of the Impressionist type, as he noted very early in revising the manuscript text; later woodland settings were imaginatively created to express the tragedy of the human situation. In such he had been motivated by the conviction that came to him in his drawing-room, after looking at the landscape in the painting ascribed to Bonington which Thomas Woolner had given Emma, that 'nature is played out as a Beauty'. He wished his scenes to show the deeper realities, including the 'tragical mysteries' of life. The 'simply natural' had lost his interest; 'the much decried, mad, late-Turner rendering' illustrated his aspirations, and he was to achieve them even more remarkably in his next novel.

In later years Hardy thought that in some respects *The Woodlanders* was his best novel. He liked it because it recalled his mother's country, Great Hintock being Melbury Osmond, as he disclosed to Gosse, and Little Hintock an imaginary hamlet anywhere within two miles of it. Early visits had given it a special fascination; his mother's accounts of its folklore and superstitious practices, even more. He did not need to revisit it for woodland detail; throughout the years Thorncombe Wood at Higher Bock-hampton had supplied all the impressions he needed. Reinforced by Norse imagery of unfulfilment and especially by the sylvan elegiacism of Arnold's 'Balder Dead' (in keeping with the opening lines of Tennyson's 'Tithonus', 'The woods decay, the woods decay and fall, / The vapours weep their burthen to the ground'), the novel is Hardy's saddest. Like Shelley, he found pleasure in sad imaginings; in this instance they were associated with his father, who like Winterborne was 'As one, in suffering all, that suffers nothing'. Hardy's father was now crippled with rheuma-tism; the patience he had shown when things went wrong, or when he was subject to conjugal complaints, remained an example which Hardy's experience had taught him to appreciate. Bowdler-izations in the serial were slight, though Mowbray Morris, the magazine editor, had warned him not to bring Suke Damson into 'too open shame'. The ending, with its suspenseful mantrap ploy, did not satisfy Hardy, and it was not until revising it in 1895 that he was able to disregard the conventional taste of libraries and make it clear that the heroine was 'doomed to an unhappy life with an inconstant husband'. Grace Melbury's story illustrates how mar-ried unhappiness can follow when precedence is given to social values which run counter to humbler but more natural or instinc-tive ties. In this Hardy's life-loyalty to his own family was inherent; he recognized values in them which were higher than the social refinements on which Emma evidently set greater store.

On 14 March 1887, the day before *The Woodlanders* was published by Macmillan, they set off for Italy. Emma kept a full but some-what jumbled diary of their tour, showing her usual appreciation of colour and interest in food, cats, dress, and people; Hardy's notes were to supply subjects for his 'Poems of Pilgrimage'. Almost as soon as they left Max Gate for London the weather changed; they encountered snow as they crossed the Channel, and in France, where it thickened as they broke their journey at Aix-les-Bains. The Palazza Doria in Genoa made Emma recall Méry's *Les Nuits Italiennes* and the song 'I dreamt that I dwelt in marble halls'; the colours of the sea beyond the houses formed a rich mosaic which reminded her of the church of St Ouen which she admired in Rouen. At Pisa they visited the cathedral and baptis-tery, stood on the top of the leaning tower as it vibrated to its pealing bells, and watched sunset, as Hardy imagined Shelley must often have done, from one of the Arno bridges. Lucy Baxter, a daughter of William Barnes, and his future biographer, met them at Florence and took them to lodgings she had booked at the Villa Trollope, where the novelist Anthony had stayed when he asked his brother to sketch a plot which became the subject of his next novel, *Doctor Thorne*. They visited galleries and churches, and saw where Savonarola was hanged and burned.

After seeing the famous ruins of Rome, Hardy began to feel 'its measureless layers of history' lying upon him 'like a physical weight'. He was intent on visiting all the places connected with his favourite poets, and was vexed to discover that he had been in the church of San Lorenzo-in-Lucina during a wedding without remembering that it was the church of Pompilia's marriage in Browning's *The Ring and the Book*. They stayed at a hotel near the Piazza di Spagna and the rooms where Keats had died, and picked violets from the graves of Keats and Shelley in the Protestant Cemetery. One day, after visiting the Vatican galleries and the Sistine Chapel, and sitting again in the Forum, they explored the Capitoline Hill. On his way back from the Tarpeian Rock, Tom was carrying an old painting which he had bought in a slum street when Emma was terrified to see three 'confederate thieves' close on him; she rushed at them with great courage, and they disappeared 'as if by magic'. Next day she was pleased that Tom had received 'two nice letters' from Kegan Paul and Gosse on *The Woodlanders*. On 1 April they visited the Vatican to see the sculptures, and explored catacombs on the Appian Way, the road by which St Paul entered Rome, as Hardy informed his mother on a postcard. Though lined by handsome tombs like those in Père Lachaise, the wide margins of the road reminded Emma of Cornish lanes and her sister, to whom she later sent a postcard.

In Florence, on their return journey, the Arno tumbling over rocks made her recall a Devonshire river. At the monastery of San Marco she thought the face of Savonarola resembled George Eliot's; some of the old frescoes seemed horrid, but she liked the 'brilliant colours' of Fra Angelico's. Hardy had to visit the piazza which was 'the supposed scene' of Browning's 'The Statue and the Bust'; Emma admired the limbs of Michelangelo's nude David, but was doubtful about it as a work of art. They saw Mrs Browning's grave, called on Violet Paget (who wrote under the pseudonym of 'Vernon Lee') and her disabled brother, and visited Fiesole with

Mrs Baxter. When the driver left for a drink, the horse set off 'at a furious pace' for Florence; they were saved by workmen just when crashing into a steam tram seemed imminent. After viewing Siena, they left by train and crossed the Appennines for Bologna and Ferrara. In the plain of Lombardy, on their way to Venice, Hardy recalled Shelley's 'Lines' in *The Golden Treasury* as he gazed at the Euganean Hills. Venice delighted him more than any other Italian city he had seen, despite the poor weather they experienced there at first. Byron's *Childe Harold* was much in his mind, and they visited St Mark's, the Doge's Palace, the Bridge of Sighs, and the Rialto. For Emma the Grand Canal was the 'essence of poetical beauty', and Hardy was displeased at finding their hotel was not on it. They stayed at the Riva degli Schiavoni, which he remembered with other Venetian details in 'Alicia's Diary'. It was while they were on a visit to Browning's friend Mrs Bronson that the beautiful prototype (to some extent) of the Contessa in 'Lady Mottisfont' (one of the stories in *A Group of Noble Dames*) called. The Hardys saw much of Venice by gondola, and did not neglect its pictures and palaces. He remembered it as Shelley's 'sun-girt' city, convinced at last that this is how it had been described (not 'sea-girt', as he once held) in 'Lines written among the Euganean Hills'.

Their first visit in Milan was to the cathedral. The next day Tom went with a young Scottish officer, who was returning from India, to see the bridge at Lodi, where one of Napoleon's earliest victories had cleared Lombardy of the Austrians. In his absence Emma looked round Milan by herself and, after admiring the profusion of statues and flying buttresses on the cathedral roof, descended rapidly lest she should meet some 'rough person', and bought presents, including a tie for Tom's brother. Years later Hardy felt certain that it was while he was on the roof of the cathedral with Emma that 'he conceived the Milan Cathedral scene in *The Dynasts*'. After travelling via Como and the St Gotthard Pass ('the loveliest scenery' for Emma, though she was miserable with a cold), they stayed at Lucerne. They reached Paris early on 26 April, saw the Crown jewels, which chanced to be on show before their sale, and reached London the next day, where they stayed, for most of the time at least, until the end of July.

At the end of April Hardy attended the Royal Academy dinner, and found himself ignored by many known to him who preferred to talk to their superiors. At Mrs Procter's the following Sunday,

when he reported how he had looked at 'the empty shrine' opposite the statue of Ferdinand in the piazza at Florence, and been
told that the bust of the poem used to be seen there, Browning
smiled and said, 'I invented it.' Among the important people
Hardy met were J. R. Lowell at Lady Carnarvon's, A. J. Balfour
and the Chancellor of the Exchequer at a Savile Club dinner,
Matthew Arnold at a Royal Academy *soirée*, and Justin McCarthy at
a House of Commons dinner. On 21 June, Queen Victoria's
Golden Jubilee, he took Emma to the Savile Club (in Piccadilly) to
watch the royal procession. Many distinguished people from the
dominions, and far more from the British upper classes, had come
to London to celebrate this anniversary, and receptions were often
made 'very radiant by the presence of so many Indian princes in
their jewelled robes'. The Hardys participated in the gaiety, attending numerous dinners, luncheons, crushes, and special functions. They were guests at several houses, including Lord Lytton's
and Lady Halifax's; while they were dining at Lady Pollock's, Sir
Frederick told Emma that he had taken part in a quadrille with a
gentleman who had danced with Marie Antoinette; at Lady Stanley's an exciting family dispute took place; at Lady Carnarvon's
Hardy noticed the 'round luminous enquiring eyes' of Lady
Catherine Milnes-Gaskell, the most beautiful of all Lady Portsmouth's daughters. He had formed the habit of jotting down notes
after such occasions, fearing that the time would come when he
would have to write stories of 'modern artificial life and manners'.
Some of the observations he made this year and later enter scenes
in *The Well-Beloved*.

He saw Browning twice again when they visited Mrs Procter,
before and after the Jubilee. On the first occasion Browning was
sleepy, and would break off when telling a story, not knowing
what he was about to say. On the second, annoyance at not being
invited to the Jubilee ceremony in Westminster Abbey gave him
much to talk about. As late as twenty-four hours before it was due
to begin he had received no invitation from the Lord Chamberlain.
The Dean had offered him one of his family tickets, but he could
not accept it, and went off to spend the time with Jowett at Oxford.
He had heard that crowds of 'Court-servants' and 'other nobodies'
had been present. An eminent actor had been sent 25 tickets, while
men of distinction such as the painter Millais, T. H. Huxley,
Arnold, and Herbert Spencer had received none. Browning held
that, as they had been unmistakably snubbed, literature, art, and

science should 'turn republican forthwith', and Hardy thought this an interesting comment on the times.

Why he described his forty-seventh birthday as that of 'Thomas the Unworthy' is unexplained. He had recovered his prestige with *The Woodlanders*, though one reviewer regretted his surrender to the influence of French novels, and more were critical of Fitzpiers's libertinism. He had sent a copy to Swinburne, but preferred to send a new single-volume copy of *The Mayor of Casterbridge* to Gissing. After writing 'Alicia's Diary' on his return to Max Gate, he completed a much more successful Wessex story, 'The Withered Arm'. Hardy was in a confident mood, after having been offered a thousand guineas for his next novel. He could write encouragingly to Gosse, who had suffered from despondency after Stevenson's departure for Colorado, confessing that he himself had known 'the very depths of it', worst of all 'several years ago' but now seldom recurring. He urged him to take a holiday on Dartmoor, and hoped he would find time to show Mrs Gosse the cliffs near Boscastle which he had attempted to describe in *A Pair of Blue Eyes*.

17
Tales and *Tess*

During September 1887, while 'The Withered Arm' was being written, Hardy visited his parents at least twice; the story turns on superstitious beliefs which his mother had inherited and actual events which his father had been told. After being considered too grim for *Longman's Magazine*, it appeared in *Blackwood's*. Recent interest in Browning's 'The Statue and the Bust' promoted the writing of its Wessex counterpart, 'The Waiting Supper', the theme of which Hardy recalled years later in his poem 'Long Plighted'. A West Stafford note for 7 October suggests that he walked down to Stafford House to renew impressions for a Frome valley setting he knew well in his youth, including the waterfall which comments with sarcastic hiss on the passing of time with all that love has offered. *The Mayor of Casterbridge* and more recent stories had given new impetus to Hardy's wish to link all his fiction within a Wessex framework. With this in mind, he submitted a selection of his short stories under the title of 'Wessex Tales' to Macmillan at the end of February 1888, and recommended his reprint publishers Sampson Low, Marston, & Co. to head their list 'Thomas Hardy's Wessex Novels'. *Wessex Tales* appeared in two volumes early in May, and presentation copies were sent to Browning for his birthday, Meredith, Mrs Jeune, and Frederic Harrison. Only five stories were included, the last four being rather long: 'The Three Strangers', 'The Withered Arm', 'Fellow-Townsmen' (considerably revised in the opening pages), 'Interlopers at the Knap', and 'The Distracted Preacher'. To these were eventually added 'A Tradition of Eighteen Hundred and Four' and 'The Melancholy Hussar of the German Legion'.

From early March to mid-July the Hardys were in London and Paris. In the reading-room of the British Museum he thought of souls gliding about screened by bodies, just as at a concert during Jubilee week he had seen 'Souls outside Bodies'. In November he had thought of a scheme for *The Dynasts* in which Napoleon was haunted by an evil genius or familiar; in January he had reflected on the possibilities of novels in which events are 'psychical', not outer or physical 'sensation'. He may have been anticipating the 'stream of consciousness' technique, but probably decided that it would be too experimental and unorthodox to sell. As people and cabs passed where he and Emma were staying in London, he imagined 'a motive, a prepossession, a hope, a fear, a fixed thought forward; perhaps more – a joy, a sorrow, a love, a revenge'. They dined at Mrs Jeune's, where he listened to curious medical stories from Dr Quain; heard the Heckmann Quartet at Alma-Tadema's; and lunched with the second Lord Houghton at Lady Catherine Milnes-Gaskell's. A. J. Munby saw him, 'small, brownbearded, kindly, shrewd', listening to music at the Lushingtons' in Kensington Square. Two days earlier, on 28 April, Hardy had thought of a story ending in failure and suicide, of a young man's struggle to gain a place at Oxford; it was 'something the world ought to be shown' and one of the germs of *Jude the Obscure*.

Leaving London at the end of May, the Hardys spent about a month in Paris, mainly because he wished to do some research (and probably buy books) in preparation for *The Dynasts*. Their many visits included the Salon, where they were arrested by *The Death of Jezebel*, a picture which told its horrible story in a flash; the royal tombs at Saint-Denis; an exhibition of Hugo's drawings and manuscripts; and one of the lawcourts, where they heard some minor cases. For diversion Hardy attended the Grand Prix of Paris at Longchamps, which sounded like Pandemonium as he drew near; the closely packed horses passed 'in a volley', and excited cries of *'Vive la France!'* announced a French winner. When he returned to London he was afflicted with rheumatism for a few days. He and Emma had rooms at Phillimore Place near Kensington High Street, and Walter Pater, who lived near, called occasionally. Among the friends they met was Mrs Ritchie (Anne Thackeray), whom they had not seen for twelve years; she told them that when she called on Leslie Stephen and his wife she felt like a ghost. They called on Lady Portsmouth, one of the few women of rank for whom Hardy felt he would 'make a sacrifice', and saw Ada Rehan in *The Taming of the Shrew*. Still feeling it worth his while to cultivate important people, he requested Lord Carnarvon to recommend him for membership of the Athenaeum Club; he was told that he would be nominated in due course. One night, disturbed by the continuous procession of carts carrying loads of vegetables along the Kensington road to Covent Garden market, he got up to view the scene, which he remembered in 'The Son's

Veto'. Two days before returning home, he dined with Emma at Pater's, where they met a handsome girl who smoked; Hardy noticed her cruel mouth, and decided she was one of those 'interesting women one would be afraid to marry'. His letter late in the year to the novelist Eliza Lynn Linton acknowledges that, though he and Emma met many people in town, they made 'very few real and permanent friends, people in London having a habit of looking upon you as dead if you are outside the 4 mile circle'.

His energy seemed to be inexhaustible. After completing much of 'The Melancholy Hussar', he set it aside to write 'A Tragedy of Two Ambitions' for Harry Quilter, editor of the *Universal Review*. By the beginning of August he was 'up to the elbows' in this, hoping to complete its cold-blooded murder climax and the sequel in a day or two. Five weeks later he was making good progress with 'The First Countess of Wessex', and it may have been during an outing to obtain views of Melbury House, the principal setting for this story, that he found time to visit the old White Horse at Maiden Newton. Emma was as interested as ever in his work, and accompanied him, as she had done the previous summer to Melbury Osmond, where she sketched his maternal ancestors' home at Townsend, near the northern entrance to Melbury Park. On this occasion she stayed outside 'on some steps', sketching the groundwork for a painting of the inn while Tom was shown round the interior by the landlady. To ensure its inclusion in his Wessex, he mentioned it – eventually describing it as a 'fine old Elizabethan inn' – in 'Interlopers at the Knap' for a later edition of *Wessex Tales*, a copy of which he sent to Alice Read, the landlady.

More important was the planning of the Wessex setting for the story which became *Tess of the d'Urbervilles*. On the last day of September he thought of contrasting the Frome valley and its great dairies east of Stafford House with the Vale of Blackmoor and its small dairies. In the afternoon he travelled by train to Evershot, south of Melbury Park, and walked to Woolcombe and Bubb Down, from which he could look over Blackmoor Vale. The thought of the valuable properties his paternal ancestors had owned at Woolcombe and further south reminded him of the prominent motif of family decline in *Tess*, which had been stimulated (as he was to tell Rebekah Owen) after hearing a drunken man at the corner of Durngate Street and South Street, Dorchester, singing 'just such a boast' about the family vault of his knighted forefathers (at Bere Regis) as is heard from Tess's father when he makes his first appearance. As Hardy gazed east and saw High Stoy, the advisability of changing place-names in *The Woodlanders* to make it appear that Hintock House, Mrs Charmond's home, was not based on Melbury House, home of the Ilchester family (the Fox-Strangways) must have recurred to him. He had attempted to disguise it by placing it in a hollow, but fictional names such as Rubdon Hill (Bubb Down) and Tutcombe Hollow could not conceal the real setting for many years. Fearful of causing the Ilchesters annoyance by 'The First Countess of Wessex', he had already taken the first step towards safeguarding himself as much as possible by stating at the end of that story that Little Hintock was several miles to the east of her home at 'King's Hintock Court'. For the 1895 edition, with hardly a change of landscape feature throughout the novel, he substituted High Stoy for Rubdon as 'the axis of so many critical movements' in *The Woodlanders*, and changed many other place-names to suggest that the Hintocks lay in the woodlands to the north.

Early in January 1889 he and Emma spent a foggy week in London, principally to see the Royal Academy exhibition, where Hardy made a close study of works by several of the old masters, and found special interest in Turner's water-colours; 'each is a landscape *plus* a man's soul. . . . What he paints chiefly is *light as modified by objects*.' The visit made him reflect on Turner paintings he had already seen, including *Snowstorm*, and served to renew and intensify the pictorial influence already evident in *The Woodlanders*. Light-effects are a recurrent feature of Froom valley settings in *Tess*, in sharp contrast to the polar scenes imagined conjointly with those Arctic birds at Flintcomb-Ash in whose tragical eyes the tormented soul of Tess is seen to be intensified. Late in the month the landscape-painter Alfred Parsons, who had been commissioned to illustrate 'The First Countess of Wessex', came to Max Gate, and was taken by Hardy around Melbury, where he made his preliminary sketches for *Harper's New Monthly Magazine*. Not surprisingly, with Melbury House artistically and recognizably set at its head, the story in the December issue soon came to the attention of the Earl of Ilchester, who was incensed to find in what premarital light his distinguished ancestor Stephen Fox and the mother of Lady Susan had been presented. Fortunately Hardy was to be on good terms with his successor's family.

Among the books which influenced the construction of *Tess* are *Desperate Remedies*, *The Bride of Lammermoor*, and Richardson's

Clarissa. Hardy had just agreed to a five-year lease of his first published novel by Ward & Downey; although he decided to retain the copyright, he did not think the book had a great future. While revising it for publication, therefore, he decided to use its key situations – that of a heroine compelled by circumstances to forfeit the happiness of her one life in a marriage to which she submits for altruistic reasons – in his new novel. In each the man who is loved returns too late; 'Too Late, Beloved' from Shelley's 'Epipsychidion' was one of the titles Hardy had in mind for his work. The heroine's mental derangement and the murder which ensue were suggested by the more romantic presentation of such events in Scott's novel. In 'The Profitable Reading of Fiction', an essay which he wrote a year earlier, Hardy expressed the aims which activated him in *Tess*. The novel, he claimed, was an art form which should vie with the epic, dramatic, and narrative masterpieces of the past; he refers to 'the old masters of imaginative creation from Aeschylus to Shakespeare'. Life remains the same essentially, and a writer who neglects it for the minutiae of social life or manners is attempting the ephemeral. Its uglinesses should not be overlooked, but greater value must be attached to its higher manifestations. The moral worth of a novel depends, furthermore, on 'the inevitableness of character and environment in working out destiny, whether that destiny be just or unjust'. The essay indicates how impressed Hardy had been by the artistic form of *The Bride of Lammermoor* and the constructive skill of Richardson in *Clarissa*. Had he not read this long epistolary novel, *Tess*, a story in which rape is the precursor of a new life rather than a willed death, could not have been designed as it was. Some of the scenes leading up to Tess's rape are influenced by those which Richardson associates with Clarissa's folly in seeking Lovelace's protection; and evil in both novels has manifestly Satanic overtones. Unlike the victims of rape in Richardson and Shakespeare (Hardy alludes to 'The Rape of Lucrece' in 'the serpent hisses where the sweet birds sing'), Tess recovers and feels 'the "appetite for joy" which pervades all creation'. Hardy rejects Roman heroics and outdated literary attitudes for truth to life, having reached the conclusion he formulated on returning to Max Gate in July 1888: 'Thought of the determination to enjoy. We see it in all nature, from the leaf on the tree to the titled lady at the ball. . . . Even the most oppressed of men and

1a. Thomas Hardy's birthplace, from a drawing made by him

1b. The vicarage, Fordington, showing the tripod for Handley Moule's telescope

2b. Emma Gifford, 1870

2a. Thomas Hardy. *c.* 1870

3b. Leslie Stephen, from a photograph by Julia Cameron

3a. The statue of William Barnes outside St. Peter's, Dorchester

4a. (above) Emma, Nellie Gosse, and Hardy on Weymouth
     pier, 1890

4b. (right) Florence Henniker, from a photograph by Chancellor,
     Dublin, 1893

5a. Max Gate, from
Black and White,
27 August 1892

5b. Hardy's study
about 1900

5c. Max Gate from the
lawn in 1919

6a. (left)
Mary Jeune

6b. (right)
Henry Joseph
Moule

6c. (below)
George Meredith
at Aldeburgh,
1905

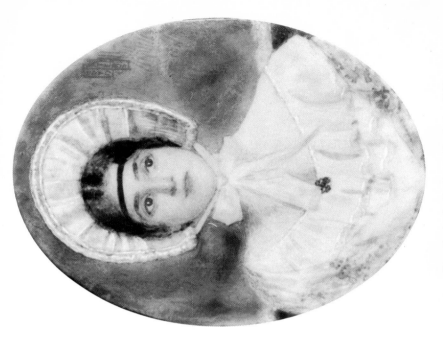

7b. Gertrude Bugler as Eustacia, 1920

7a. Florence Hardy, 1914

8b. The Hardy Players outside Riverside Villa, 9 June 1921

8a. T. E. Lawrence on his Brough motorcycle

animals find it, so that out of a thousand there is hardly one who has not a sun of some sort for his soul.'

Even so, Hardy in April 1889 regarded London as no better than 'four million forlorn hopes'. A letter from J. A. Symonds in praise of *The Return of the Native* made him think of critics who had condemned him for being pessimistic and pagan, but he was 'less and less able' to exclude 'the tragical conditions of life' from his work, and concluded that all comedy was tragedy if one looked 'deep enough into it'. Perhaps tragedy in fiction could help to show 'how to escape the worst forms of it, at least, in real life'. In London with Emma from late April to the end of July, he visited picture-galleries, saw French plays, and attended concerts, luncheon-parties, and dinners as usual. At Alma-Tadema's he met M. Taine, the French philosopher and historian, 'a kindly, nicely trimmed old man with a slightly bent head'. During dinner at the Gosses' he conversed a great deal with Mrs Hamo Thornycroft, and tried to persuade her to attend the dinner of the Society of Authors, where Gosse was to speak the next evening. There Hardy sat next to the poet Rosamund Tomson ('Graham R. Tomson'), whose membership he had recommended. On 14 July, the centenary of the fall of the Bastille, he heard Frederic Harrison lecture on the French Revolution in Newton Hall. One wonders if all was well between him and Emma at this time, for ten days later, at the British Museum, he made a note from the *Oedipus Rex* of Sophocles, 'and if there be a woe surpassing woes, it hath become the portion of Oedipus', as if he had suffered some private sorrow which he could not forget.

At Max Gate his main purpose was to make rapid headway with his new novel, which he now proposed to call 'Too Late, Beloved'. Although his more mature heroine was modelled on Augusta Way, a young woman who worked with her sisters as a milkmaid at Kingston Maurward farm, near the old manor house in part of which they and their parents lived, Mrs Thornycroft was much in mind when he described her, particularly the 'little upward lift in the middle of her red top lip' and the lips and teeth which repeatedly recalled at Gosse's dinner 'the old Elizabethan simile of roses filled with snow'. The 'stopt-diapason note which her voice acquired when her heart was in her speech, and which will never be forgotten by those who knew her' suggests one of Hardy's most distinct recollections of Augusta Way. On 11 July he had recommended 'The Body and Soul of Sue' for his title, 'Sue' being the third name he had given his heroine. This proposal anticipates the subtitle of *Tess of the d'Urbervilles*; Hardy's intention throughout was to present a woman whose intentions had been good, though she is ultimately Alec's mistress and a murderess; innocent in her first 'fall', she gives only her body to Alec in the second. On 9 September Hardy sent off a large portion of his novel to Tillotsons for serial publication in England and in *Harper's Bazar*.

It was not until the first sixteen chapters had been read in proof that Tillotson's editor realized the nature of Hardy's story; he suggested that it be recast and certain scenes omitted. Rather than comply, Hardy suggested the cancellation of his contract, an offer which was accepted with the request that he would provide a short story; in response he completed 'The Melancholy Hussar of the German Legion', and forwarded it in October. Three weeks later his novel was rejected by Edward Arnold, editor of *Murray's Magazine*, who preferred girls to grow up in ignorance of sexual hazards; ten days later, by Mowbray Morris, whose objection must have recalled the danger signals he flashed when *The Woodlanders* was being serialized. By this time Hardy had turned to the writing of short stories, six of which were to appear within a slight narrative framework as *A Group of Noble Dames* in the 1890 Christmas number of the *Graphic*, in accordance with his agreement of April 1889, which gave him the right to publish them abroad and in book form. The stories combined local history, especially from John Hutchins, with traditional scandal and imaginative invention. In November terms were agreed for the serialization of *Tess of the d'Urbervilles* in the *Graphic*, beginning in July 1891. Hardy was very busy. 'The Lady Penelope', another of his new series of stories, appeared in the January 1890 number of *Longman's Magazine*; the same month his essay 'Candour in English Fiction' appeared in the *New Review* as the final contribution to a symposium which deplored the barriers set up by Mrs Grundy. After his recent experience with *Tess*, Hardy was well qualified to write on this subject. Adults believe that the passions in fiction should be proportioned as in life, and as in the great drama of the Periclean and Elizabethan periods, he argued, but 'fancy a brazen young Shakespeare of our time' sending *Othello* or *Hamlet* or *Antony and Cleopatra* 'in narrative form to the editor of a London magazine'. It is not the subject but the treatment that matters. Whatever was to be said for the protection of minors, it does not follow that all fiction should be 'shackled by conventions concerning budding womanhood'. 'The position of man and woman in nature, and the position of belief in the minds of man and woman – things which everybody is thinking but nobody is saying' – should be 'taken up and treated frankly'.

When asked by the editor of the *Weekly Comedy* to express his views on the improvement of stage presentations, Hardy showed that his interest in the subject was keen, considered, and original. His views were not to change fundamentally; they are those of the observer rather than of one who claims expertise in stagecraft. His reply of 30 November 1889 emphasized the unreality of the contemporary stage, which appealed to the eye more than to the imagination. To 'weed away the intolerable masses of scenery and costume', he advocated a kind of theatre in the round with few properties, the spectators sitting 'to a great extent round the actors' and seeing the play 'as it was seen in old times, but as they do not see it now for its accessories'. For Hardy the play was the thing, and anything that came between the spoken word and the imaginative response was to be deplored. In the article 'Why I Don't Write Plays' which he contributed to the *Pall Mall Gazette* at the end of August 1892, he repeated his criticism; it had been made by Addison against contemporary theatre nearly two centuries earlier. Hardy preferred writing novels to plays because the novel gave greater scope at the time for getting to 'the heart and meaning of things', partly because the staging of human passions was subordinated to 'the presentation of mountains, cities, clothes, furniture, plate jewels, and other real and sham-real appurtenances'. The stage should be a conventional or 'figurative' arena, 'in which accessories are kept down to the plane of mere suggestions of place and time'. Late in his life his views had not changed; he practised what he preached in *The Famous Tragedy of the Queen of Cornwall*.

Agreement with Harper & Brothers for the publication of *Tess* and *A Group of Noble Dames* was well in hand when Hardy visited London in January 1890, probably to discuss business matters with Arthur Locker, editor of the *Graphic*. As often happened, his brief stay in the city resulted in 'influenza' and a disincentive to work, but he continued writing 'Noble Dame' stories until March, when he travelled to the capital by train with Emma, principally to meet the Duke and Duchess of Teck at the Jeunes'. On the way he suddenly thought of his cousin Tryphena, and wrote the first four lines of 'Thoughts of Phena', not knowing that she was dying. The poem, completed after her death, shows that Hardy, recalling her lively, cheerful nature, could indulge the dream that she was his 'lost prize', one with whom he might happily have been married. Its subject is not a former love, but the love that might have been. The question of whether his mother would have opposed marriage with a cousin does not occur to him; he is obviously expressing his feelings. 'Love lives on propinquity, but dies of contact', he had written the previous summer, and it is obvious that for him and Emma the golden was turning grey. Mabel Robinson found her most inconsequent, without the intellectual ability to hold her husband's attention; her thoughts 'hopped off like a bird on a bough'. This does not explain why Hardy thought he might have been happier had he married this person or that; his feelings must have been wounded in ways which became increasingly manifest as time passed. At Mary Jeune's crush the most beautiful woman was Mrs Thornycroft with her 'great eyes', but where would the beauty of all these women be, he reflected, if 'put into rough wrappers in a turnip-field'? He was thinking specifically of Tess, as he had been when the memory of the field-women whom he had known in boyhood came back, and he wrote 'At Middle-Field Gate in February'. From this it was but a philosophical stride to altruism, the 'Golden Rule, or whatever "Love your Neighbour as Yourself" may be called', and the vision of mankind as a whole in which the pain of others will react 'on ourselves, as if we and they are part of one body'.

Sir George Douglas stayed at Max Gate during the Easter weekend, and Hardy took him to Barnes's grave and next day to Portland, which was to provide the main setting for his next long story. At lunch the following day several friends were present, including the Misses Fetherstonhaugh of Moreton Hall and Mary Sheridan of Frampton Court, wife of a descendant of Sheridan the playwright and politician. One evening when Douglas was present, Emma read a story by Kipling from a magazine, and nobody could tell what the author was driving at. The Hardys passed the London season from May to July in much the usual manner. They saw Irving in *The Bells*, Bizet's opera *Carmen*, and Ada Rehan in *As You Like It*. At Gosse's they met the young American lady who became Kipling's wife. Elsewhere Hardy met Kipling, and heard much from him on the East, with curious details of Indian life. He also met the explorer Stanley, spent time at police courts, thinking such attendances might supply fictional material, and called on Locker at the office of the *Graphic*, where he learned that the directors objected to certain things in *A Group of Noble Dames*. Emma had to cut short her holiday on account of her father's illness and death near Plymouth, where he was buried. (Her mother died at the end of the following year.) Hardy stayed on to write the epilogue which Ada Rehan was to read at a special performance of *The Taming of the Shrew* on behalf of Mrs Jeune's holiday fund for poor children in London.

The alterations required for *A Group of Noble Dames* were slight, he discovered, the complaint having arisen from reading the unrevised proof which he had already anticipatively amended. In 'Squire Petrick's Lady' several deletions were made against the author's wish, 'by compulsion of Mrs Grundy' or on account of her 'tyranny', Hardy pencilled on the manuscript. Such compromises were trifling compared with the task of emasculating *Tess* for the same directorate, and ensuring consistency throughout a story in which the heroine is tricked into a bogus marriage without becoming pregnant. An amusing change was introduced for the benefit of family readers when the editor objected to Clare's carrying the dairymaids over the flooded lane, and Hardy suggested wheeling them across in a barrow. To one whose highest satisfaction came from independent creative writing, and who loved to gain new impressions for his novel from walks in the Frome valley below Max Gate towards sunset or even at sunrise, this was nothing but galling labour. His dual-purpose text, with revisions and deletions for the serial version indicated in ink of a different colour, appears to have been completed during the autumn.

Fortunately Hardy enjoyed some relief from this drudgery. With Alfred Parsons, who was a welcome guest at Max Gate in August, he and Emma had two memorable outings, the first into Dorchester to see their friend Pearce Edgcumbe's Sir Joshuas and Pintoricchios at Somerleigh Court, which had been built for him almost on the site of a Roman house with tessellated floors, some remains of which were discovered when the foundations were laid in 1862, and at a later period. At Weymouth they lunched at the Old Royal Hotel, where George III and his daughters danced at assemblies. Later in the month Hardy travelled to Paris with his brother, and showed him places of interest, including the Moulin Rouge, where, above cancan dancers grimacing at men, windows showed moonlit graves of 'similar gay Parisians' in Montmartre cemetery, a bizarre visual conjunction which, like that seen during first-aid instruction at Wimborne, had a special appeal for Hardy. In September, on their way to Leslie Stephen and his family at St Ives, Cornwall, the Gosses stayed at Max Gate, Nellie finding it very quiet 'with no little ones running about and shouting'. Hardy hoped to find a country home for them in the neighbourhood, and made efforts to find one as soon as they left and later, all to no effect. Gosse took some interesting photographs with his new Kodak, one of Nellie, Emma, and Hardy on Weymouth pier, another showing Max Gate very exposed to the elements.

In December, after a period devoted to much reading, including several satirists and Weismann's *Essays on Heredity*, Hardy was in London again, staying part of the time with Mrs Jeune. He became friendly with Edward Clodd, secretary of the London Joint-Stock Bank, an author and rationalist who was keenly interested in scientific thought and anthropology. (His home was at Aldeburgh on the Suffolk coast, where Hardy was his guest, with J. M. Barrie and Walter Besant, the following June.) A letter signed by Hardy, Besant, and William Black, testifying to the fair dealing of Harper & Brothers, had appeared in the *Athenaeum* in answer to criticism of the firm by Kipling, who retaliated with 'The Rhyme of the Three Captains'. After being assured by James Osgood, Harpers' representative and head of the London firm Osgood, McIlvaine & Co., with whom he was now publishing, that the American copyright bill would probably become law next July, Hardy was happy to think that the delayed publication of *Tess* would ensure its American copyright and his financial gain.

At home in January 1891 he prepared his final collection of stories for the publication of *A Group of Noble Dames* in one volume. To those recently published in the *Graphic* and *Harper's Weekly* he added 'The First Countess of Wessex', 'The Lady Penelope', 'The Duchess of Hamptonshire', and 'The Honourable Laura' ('Benighted Travellers'). 'The Doctor's Legend' and 'Master John Horseleigh, Knight', which seem to have been prepared for the series, were omitted. The fictional framework was altered, the stories which were told at a meeting of the Field Club being imagined first in a building which was obviously the old museum in Trinity Street, Dorchester, then in the new, where the noble dames take their place in time with the ichthyosaurus and Vespasian's soldiery. The irony of tales which associate deceit, hypocrisy, and cruelty with noble bearing in 'dear, delightful Wessex', where 'honest squires, tradesmen, parsons, clerks, and people still praise the Lord with one voice for His best of all possible worlds' gains by being lightly stressed. Hardy's recent reading had included Voltaire.

In London again toward the end of January, Hardy reported to Emma the attack which William Archer had made on Gosse in the *Pall Mall Gazette* for inaccuracies in his translation of Ibsen's *Hedda Gabler*. What was called 'sunshine' there after cold and snow created effects which he noted with a painter's eye. The sun hung like a red-hot bullet in a livid atmosphere, the light being 'reflected from window-panes in the form of bleared copper eyes, and inflaming the sheets of plate-glass with smears of gory light', while drab snow mingled with liquid horse dung, and 'puddings of ice' floated slowly along the river. After admiring the staging at a performance by Irving, his conclusion that stage illusion would be better without such elaborate scenery was confirmed. The following Sunday Irving and Ellen Terry joined a dinner-party which included Sir Henry Thompson, Justin McCarthy, Lady Dorothy Nevill and many others, at the Jeunes', where Hardy was staying; he remembered the actress Ellen Terry and her appearance in *The Well-Beloved*. Emma and he came to London in March to meet the Prince and Princess Christian (Queen Victoria's daughter) and their two daughters at Mrs Jeune's. In the meantime they had attended a ball given by Mary Sheridan at Frampton Court, and Emma had ridden on horseback for the last time, again on her way to Mrs Sheridan's. During March the 'Druid Stone', which had been found under the garden among ashes and half-charred bones, was moved and erected at the side-road end of the Max Gate lawn. Hardy was giving attention to *Tess* (the heroine of which he had steadily ennobled), to the plot of his next novel, and even to the planning of *The Dynasts*, which he imagined in a dramatic form with a bird's eye view of Europe. On 30 March, while visiting Wool Manor, Emma pretended to faint in order to secure admission and enable Hardy to sketch the two Miss Turbervilles in fresco on the landing while she received attention; he thought the fierce-looking one was like John Antell when drunk at Noah's Ark.

The long hold-up in the publication of *Tess* gave Hardy opportunities to write more short stories. During August 1890 he probably began 'Wessex Folk' (finally published as 'A Few Crusted

Characters'), a collection of very short narratives ranging from the
tragic to his most humorous, which was serialized in the European
and American editions of *Harper's New Monthly Magazine* from
March to June 1891, with a market-day view of Dorchester High
East Street by Alfred Parsons as their headpiece illustration. 'To
Please His Wife' was completed by September 1890; 'For Conscience' Sake' was ready for the *Fortnightly Review* early in 1891;
even in London during April that year Hardy was busy with 'The
Son's Veto'; 'On the Western Circuit' was finished early the following November. London society appealed to him less and less,
and the tendency of some of these stories to stress the inhuman
values created by snobbishness and the craving for class elevation
is significant. Recurrent practice in this briefer form of fiction had
increased its appeal to Hardy, who already had enough stories for
another volume, but became so preoccupied with *The Pursuit of the
Well-Beloved* and other engagements and distractions that nearly
two years were to pass before he found time to assemble them for
publication.

In April 1891, while he was in London hoping to find suitable
accommodation before Emma joined him, Hardy attended Kot-
zebue's popular play *The Stranger*, and thought of all those who
had watched it, including Thackeray; at the Vaudeville he saw
Hedda Gabler in a version which William Archer had helped Gosse
to prepare. He made the acquaintance of the novelist Rider Haggard soon after the latter's return from Mexico, and later received
from him a copy of *Eric Brighteyes*. Among those he met at the
Savile Club were Kipling and the poet W. E. Henley, editor of the
National Observer. About the time that he and Emma succeeded in
finding a flat for the season he heard that he had been elected to
the Athenaeum Club. He had been to hear the famous Charles
Spurgeon preach, and found him a spent force; some weeks later
he could not resist attending a service at St James's, a beautiful
Wren church in Piccadilly, for the sake of his mother, who wor-
shipped there when she lived in London. The behaviour of crowds
at the British Museum made him think ahead to the reign of the
proletariat, when art and literature would be neglected. At a
dinner some weeks after the general election in May the talk was
entirely political – on when the next would be, and the probable
Prime Minister, 'ins and outs', 'Lord This and the Duke of That';
never for a moment did it dwell, he noticed, on the welfare of the
people the politicians represented. He attended lunches at the
Jeunes' with Emma, the first to see their new house in Harley

Street; at the second he sat between 'a pair of beauties'. Clifford Allbutt, a commissioner in lunacy, took him to a large private lunatic asylum, where he 'became so interested in the pathos of the cases that he remained the greater part of the day'. In preparation for his next major novel, eventually named *Jude the Obscure*, he visited Whitelands and Stockwell training-colleges. During August and the autumn he spent much time at Max Gate making a final revision of *Tess of the d'Urbervilles*, mainly to ensure that the text was restored. Two chapters omitted from the serial were printed independently, one as 'The Midnight Baptism, A Study of Christianity' in the May 1891 number of the *Fortnightly Review* (before the serial began), the other as 'Saturday Night in Arcady' in a November literary supplement of the *National Observer*. A section of the latter was overlooked when Hardy restored the text, and not included until 1912.

In September the Hardys were at last able to accept Sir George Douglas's renewed invitation to stay with him at Springwood Park, his home near Kelso. During this visit Hardy's literary interest was chiefly in places connected with Sir Walter Scott; on the way the sight of Lindisfarne glowing in the sunset had reminded him of *Marmion*. Douglas took him to Smailholm and Kelso, Melrose Abbey, Jedburgh, and Scott's tomb at Dryburgh. Smailholm Tower presented a romantic scene; it was the setting for 'The Eve of Saint John', one of the poems of Scott which Hardy prized above all his prose, a ballad which, perhaps more than any other, had a Gothic influence on some of his verse and prose. Douglas noticed how he scrambled with a schoolboy's eagerness to the roof of the tower at Abbotsford; he would not intrude when he found him poring over Scott's death-mask. Emma was interested in the horses at Springwood, and Douglas observed 'a delightful wrangle' when Hardy suggested helping her with perspective in her sketching. On their return journey they visited Durham, Whitby, Scarborough, York, and Peterborough. Weeks later, as a reminder of a visit he had enjoyed, Sir George sent some trees to be planted at Max Gate. Hardy was proof-reading *Tess*. He had made some notes of contemporary significance, the first with Emma and *The Pursuit of the Well-Beloved* in mind: 'It is the incompleteness that is loved, when love is sterling and true. This is what differentiates the real one from the imaginary . . . the Love who returns the kiss from the Vision that melts away.' Comparing his own fiction with that of the American novelist Howells, he observed that 'a story *must* be striking enough to be worth telling'. In reply to the editor of the *Bookman*, he said he was not in favour of giving national recognition to authors, because 'the highest flights of the pen are mostly the excursions and revelations of souls unreconciled to life, while the natural tendency of a government' would be to encourage conformity. In December he received two volumes of poetry from Rosamund Tomson, one 'Concerning Cats', which she had edited, the other her recently published *A Summer Night and Other Poems*, with a frontispiece picture of herself 'in the shadows' of her garden which years later, as his poem 'An Old Likeness' testifies, brought back to Hardy the memory of 'that bright time' when they were happy friends.

Published like *A Group of Noble Dames* by Osgood, McIlvaine & Co., *Tess of the d'Urbervilles* appeared in three volumes at the end of November. With a few exceptions, notably Andrew Lang's, one in the *Saturday Review* (thought to be by George Saintsbury) and, almost inevitably, another by Mowbray Morris, the reviews were highly favourable. Without consciously realizing, as Frederic Harrison undoubtedly did, that the novel allegorizes the spirit of charity, Hardy's key to true Christianity, in an unjust world ruled not by Providence but by the 'god' of chance and consequence, most readers did not question its validity. No previous novel by Hardy had been more popular and sensational, or made such a deep and lasting impression. He received enthusiastic encouragement from friends, including Douglas, whose admiration of Tess extracted from her creator the admission that he had lost his heart to her the more he worked on the story. (Privately Meredith, who placed Hardy among the few novelists he cared for, found the end too depressing except for 'the short scene on the plain at Stonehenge'.) 'The doll of English fiction must be demolished, if England is to have a school of fiction at all', Hardy wrote to H. W. Massingham in acknowledgment of his early recognition in the *Daily Chronicle* that virility in a novel is 'not incompatible with sound morality'. Although the sub-title 'A Pure Woman' created controversy, and the 'President of the Immortals' passage, much misunderstanding, *Tess* roused a sensation in Hardy's favour, and by the New Year his publishers were reprinting 'frantically'. In July 1892, for the fifth edition, he wrote a preface in which he answered several criticisms. Four other impressions of this single-volume edition were printed before the end of the year, and Hardy must have thought his prospects had never been brighter.

18

Florence Henniker

Hardy's professional confidence as a writer is a notable feature of his interview with Raymond Blathwayt at Max Gate early in 1892; equally manifest are the absence of his beard, Emma's evident desire to impress, and her husband's complaisance in offering the information that Tess's wearing of the jewels was her idea (from 'The Maid on the Shore'). Blathwayt noticed at every turn 'pieces of red Samian, rare specimens of ancient pottery, fragments of iridescent glass, most of them discovered on his own ground by Mr. Hardy himself', and on the walls illustrations of his stories by friends, including Professor Herkomer (for the *Tess* serial) and Alfred Parsons, in addition to his wife's watercolours, which went far 'to prove the verisimilitude of her husband's delightful fictions'. Hardy's readiness to flinch in a personal crisis was evident, nevertheless, in London, where he was afraid of meeting 'Saturday Reviewers' at the Savile; one of them might be his libeller, he wrote. His reaction to Mowbray Morris's review in the *Quarterly* gives startling emphasis to his irritation with Victorian readers: 'if this sort of thing continues no more novel-writing for me. A man must be a fool to deliberately stand up to be shot at.' This was in April, after he had written *The Pursuit of the Well-Beloved* for serialization through Tillotson's agency. The idea of this story, 'of a face which goes through three generations', had occurred to Hardy in February 1889.

In February he was delighted to receive a letter praising *Tess* from Mary Harrison, daughter of Charles Kingsley, who wrote novels under the pseudonym of 'Lucas Malet'. Hardy considered *Colonel Enderby's Wife* one of the best to appear in recent years, and told her she was 'one of the few authors of the other sex' who were 'not afraid of logical consequences'. In March she sent him a copy of her latest novel, *The Wages of Sin*. His wish to see her was fulfilled in London early in April, when he called and met her and her sister Rose Kingsley. 'Lucas Malet' made a strong impression; he found her most likable, and noticed her 'full, slightly voluptuous mouth, red lips, black hair and eyes'. Among others he met while Emma was ill at Max Gate were Frederic Harrison, Ellen Terry, Lord Randolph Churchill, and Arthur Balfour. With Sir Francis Jeune (Mary Jeune's husband), who had been knighted in 1891, he attended the Gaiety Theatre to hear Lottie Collins sing her hit-song 'Ta-ra-ra-boom-de-ay' in a burlesque which he thought not nearly as silly as most people assumed.

Towards the end of May the death of his publisher James Osgood caused Hardy to travel to London in advance of Emma. He and William Black rode in a small cortège from Piccadilly to Kensal Green, where tribute was paid in the mortuary chapel to one whose planning included the uniform edition of Hardy's works. With or without Emma, he met once again many people who had come to see the author of *Tess*; society conversation often turned on the question of the heroine's innocence. (He made fewer notes on these occasions than in previous years, and turned to his wife's diaries for many details recorded in his *Life* of London visits in 1892 and later.) At one dinner Hardy found Lady Salisbury very friendly after being 'stiff'; at another the Prince and Princess Christian 'were by this time most affable'. News of his father's illness called him home just after his birthday; he visited him almost every day towards the end, but was not present when he died peacefully on 20 July. Fortunately, her husband being the third life-holder, his mother was allowed to stay in the cottage, though she was often lonely, with Mary and Kate living at the home Tom had bought them in Wollaston Road, Dorchester, a few years earlier.

Hardy's July 1892 preface to *Tess of the d'Urbervilles* reveals a hunger for friendship which Dorchester could not satisfy; with relatively little to do, Emma must have felt it more keenly. Max Gate still stood 'isolated in the fields', and he proposed to add a room for the accommodation of friends. While on holiday a few miles off (at Broadwey, it is assumed), Sir Arthur and Lady Blomfield, whom Emma had met in London a few years previously, called during August, and were taken to see Puddletown church. Early in the month Hardy sat to William Strang for an etching which was to appear in Lionel Johnson's *The Art of Thomas Hardy*. On 5 August he and Emma were pleased to have tea with two American visitors, Rebekah Owen and her elder sister Catharine, now staying in Dorchester, on their third visit to England. Rebekah, a personable lady of thirty-four and a Hardy devotee of the first water, whose memory for detail was such that she often offered factual corrections which he accepted, had secured this appointment very indirectly through a friend who had obtained Hardy's address from one of his previous publishers. After tea her admired author wrote identification notes on some of the Casterbridge places in her copy of *The Mayor*. A week later they had tea again at Max Gate, where they were introduced to Miss Teresa Fetherstonhaugh of Moreton Hall, who invited them to join their picnic party at Bindon Abbey. On 15 August therefore they accompanied the Hardys to places associated with Tess, first the manor house at Wool, where Emma told how she had enabled Tom to sketch the two horrible portraits described in the novel, then Bindon Abbey with its open stone coffin in which Angel laid Tess in the sleepwalking scene. After an afternoon drive with Emma to Upwey and dinner at Max Gate, the Owens invited the Hardys to tea on 1 September. Two days later Emma took them to the Smiths' garden-party at West Stafford rectory. After tea at Max Gate three days later, Hardy walked with them along the Frome valley to Grey's Bridge, then to the milestone of *Far from the Madding Crowd* and *The Mayor of Casterbridge* on Stinsford Hill. On their way to Dorchester after sunset, he paused at Grey's Bridge to show them Ten Hatches Weir, where Henchard prepared for suicide, and a pool beyond, where he (Hardy) used to swim when he was a boy. While he attended the Dorset Field Club meeting the next day at Swanage, Emma took them to see the sailor's cottage where they lived when much of *The Hand of Ethelberta* was written. There was too much about servants in it for her taste, she said. On the subject of travel-writing she admitted that she found it difficult to record her impressions, as she remembered them too rapidly to systematize. After driving one day with the Hardys on a *Trumpet-Major* tour to Weymouth, Portesham (where Admiral Hardy had spent his early life), and Poxwell Hall, the Owens were taken to other Wessex places, including Bathsheba's house and some churches near Dorchester.

While on his way home from Dorchester by carriage on 17 September, Hardy noticed a fire at Stinsford House and, leaving Emma to drive on, change, and continue the journey to Canon Smith's at West Stafford, ran across the meadows to see what help he could give. As it grew dark, flames lit up rooms sacred to the memory of Lady Susan, until the ceilings, and then the roof, fell in the final conflagration. When Hardy left he met his sister Mary in the churchyard, where she had been laying flowers on their father's grave; he then walked directly to the Smiths', where he found that dinner had been delayed almost two hours. Bosworth Smith had taken Emma to see the fire, and Hardy had noticed neither of them. At the end of September he travelled to London on his way to Fawley, Berkshire, where his grandmother had spent the first thirteen years of her life as an orphan. Here and to the north he made notes for scenes in *Jude the Obscure*. On 12 October, after receiving an admission card on request from Macmillan's, he attended Tennyson's funeral at Westminster Abbey, and felt that, despite the impressiveness of this grand and solemn scene, the music and general effect was less deeply moving than the traditional graveside hymn (four verses from the ninetieth psalm) which had been sung at his father's funeral. Not long before the Owens left Dorchester in November, he told them about his Berkshire visit and the view across to distant Oxford, where he imagined the spires gleaming at sunset like . . . 'Like the heavenly Jerusalem', Rebekah added without thinking that her suggestion would be adopted. In London during December, Hardy attended a legal dinner at the Jeunes' (Sir Francis being a divorce court judge), where he heard some delightful stories from distinguished judges. The next day he met many celebrities at a lunch or dinner, including Lady Shrewsbury, Henry Irving, and Hamilton Aidé. On his return he told Henry Moule's daughter Margaret that he had very much enjoyed J. M. Barrie's company. His literary efforts were devoted to the writing of 'The Fiddler of the Reels', which he dispatched to New York on 13 January for inclusion in the 'Exhibition Number' of *Scribner's Magazine* (commemorating the Chicago World's Fair), and to the planning of *Jude*, which engaged his attention on and off until the spring.

For some years romance had been fading from the lives of Hardy and Emma, but about this period their relations became strained, though he did not realize until long afterwards the extent to which they had worsened: she had already begun recording those bitter denunciations that soothed her inner self in times of solitary depression. She was gnawed by jealousy when she recalled the attentions he had received from titled ladies more beautiful than herself, and it hurt her to think that he habitually prolonged his stay at Lady Jeune's, and that she and her daughters were so attached to him. Childless and without any sustained interests, she had too much time to brood until, having allowed her mind to be invaded by a grievous sense of neglect and wrong, her balance of judgement was intermittently destroyed. Outwardly her behaviour did not suddenly change; her eccentricities were more evident to outsiders than to Hardy. It would be a mistake to think there were frequent recriminations; Emma kept much to herself, but she could be acrimonious and sullen, and he was too sensitive not to be aware of the increasing separateness of their lives. He must have realized that the advent of the Owens gave her relief, though it was a trial to listen to what he had heard over and over again as she chattered with inconsequent exuberance and uncontrollable efforts to dominate conversation and play her *prima donna* role. Time given by Hardy to his mother after his father's death may have aggravated tensions, and (judging by the second Mrs Hardy's testimony) it could have been late in 1892 that Emma refused to continue her weekly visits to Higher Bockhampton with her husband, or to receive any of the family at Max Gate.

Before the end of the year she must have read *The Pursuit of the Well-Beloved* serial in the *Illustrated London News*, and seen a parallel between herself and the Marcia whose Junonian face spelt temper, whose family had a social advantage over Jocelyn when they married, and from whose form the illusory Well-Beloved had now taken flight. When Hardy wrote of 'the curse of matrimony' with respect to 'their ill-matched junction', and devised a story in support of the principle that, in marriage, 'healthy natural instinct' and 'not an Act of Parliament' is true law, his inclination to leave her was certain. That Jocelyn should have attempted suicide when the Ideal finally eludes him illustrated the depth of his aversion. A story which had been planned the previous year, to make light of a propensity to imagine married happiness with this person and that, had been soured by Hardy's own feeling on the marriage tie. He had been reminded of this propensity when news of his cousin Tryphena's death reached him, and she had been in his mind when he wrote of the first Avice's death: 'He loved the woman dead and inaccessible as he had never loved her in life. He had thought of her but at distant intervals during the twenty years since that parting occurred. . . .' (A similarly retrospective wish was more strikingly expressed in July 1906, when Hardy was reminded of his former illustrator Helen Paterson, whose marriage to the poet William Allingham had taken place about the same time as his own.) Jocelyn's conviction that his love for the first Avice possessed a 'ground-quality' which derived from the interrelatedness of the islanders, and without which 'a fixed and full-rounded constancy to a woman could not flourish in him', may have arisen from Hardy's reflections on his 'lost prize' Tryphena.

For their London season in the spring and summer of 1893 the Hardys rented the whole of 70 Hamilton Terrace, and brought up their own servants. At Lady Jeune's before they moved in, they met numerous people of repute; elsewhere, at crushes, luncheons, and dinners, the actor Charles Wyndham, Lady Dorothy Nevill, the Duke, Duchess, and Princess May, of Teck. They were especially interested in Frederick Whitehead's picture of Woolbridge Manor, described as Tess's ancestral home, at the Royal Academy view, and Hardy was pleased to receive a photograph of it from the artist. He dined with the author and critic Charles Whibley, and two days later with the zoologist Ray Lankester, at the Savile Club, where he met, among others, Sir Henry Thompson and Tennyson's friend James Knowles, founder of the *Nineteenth Century*; dining elsewhere with Whibley, he met W. E. Henley. Like other successful writers attending the Royal Literary Fund dinner with other guests, he hid his diminished head and buttoned his pocket when the chairman, A. J. Balfour, spoke of the decline of the literary art, and said that as far as he knew there were no living writers of high rank. Among those with whom he discussed exhibits at a Royal Society conversazione were Frederick and George Macmillan, the eminent physician Clifford Allbutt, who had recently been appointed Regius Professor of Medicine at Cambridge, Humphry Ward, Ray Lankaster, and Bosworth Smith. On 18 May he and Emma left Euston for Llandudno, on their way to the Viceregal Lodge in Phoenix Park, Dublin, at the invitation of the newly appointed Lord-Lieutenant of Ireland, the second Lord Houghton, and his sister Florence Henniker.

Lord Houghton and his sister had hoped to meet the author of *Tess* at Fryston Hall, their family home near Pontefract, the previous summer, but the illness of Hardy's father made this out of the question. After his death the invitation was renewed, but this second anticipated meeting had to be deferred when Lord Houghton accepted the Viceroyalty of Ireland. Hardy had received a copy of the Viceroy's *Stray Verses* in January 1893, in acknowledging which he added a note, hoping that his sister's second novel had 'sold out'. Florence Henniker was a talented writer, who developed verse-writing at the age of six; she inherited a charming disposition from her mother, and a sociable nature from her father, formerly Richard Monckton Milnes, a successful poet in his early years, a friend of Tennyson, an admirer of Shelley's poetry, and the foremost promoter of Keats's. With them she had visited Rome at an early age; later, in June 1872, when he had political ambitions, the first Lord Houghton took her to Paris, where she soon became a favourite with M. Thiers, the French President, and his wife. But for delicate health and her marriage to Arthur Henry Henniker-Major, a lieutenant in the Coldstream Guards who was about to leave on the Egyptian Expedition, she might have followed her father's example and become, as Justin McCarthy thought she was well qualified to do, 'the presiding genius of a *salon*'. Her brother had lost his first wife, and she, who had met numerous people of distinction at her father's parties and elsewhere, was acting as his hostess when the Hardys, who had met John Morley, now Chief Secretary of Ireland, when they crossed the Irish Sea from Holyhead, were guests with others at the Viceregal Lodge.

As a novelist Florence Henniker found herself in accord with Hardy's tragic bias and sympathy for the underprivileged; she cultivated his acquaintance in the hope of gaining from his authorial advice. Her interest and charm when they first met, at a time when he had lost Emma's approval, made him feel that she was a responsive and '*intuitive*' woman. She took Emma and the other ladies on outings, while he joined parties to buildings of historical importance and architectural interest in Dublin. He could not resist a visit to the scene of the Phoenix Park murders. At a large dinner party she played the zithern. With Emma, Hardy attended the Queen's birthday review, dined at the Private Secretary's Lodge (where he met J. P. Mahaffy, 'a rattling, amusing talker' whose *Social Life in Greece* he had read at Sturminster Newton), and toured Guinness's brewery, where all were splashed with ale or dirty water on the miniature railway, and Hardy did his best to remove the stains from Emma and Mrs Henniker's clothes. When they left for Killarney, to visit the usual tourist scenes, he received from Lord Houghton a copy of his translations, *Gleanings from Béranger*. Returning to London on 29 May, they met Mrs Henniker on the boat to Holyhead.

Acting promptly on J. M. Barrie's advice, Hardy had dramatized his short story 'The Three Strangers' before leaving for Dublin, and it was now about to be produced as 'The Three Wayfarers' by Charles Charrington, who played the hangman, at Terry's Theatre. Hardy returned to London in time to see the rehearsal, and watched it with Emma, Lady Jeune, and other friends on the opening night. Four other short plays, including Barrie's 'Becky Sharp', completed the short-lived programme, and *The Times* voted Hardy's one-act play 'the best piece of the evening'. It was the season when Ibsen plays were dubbed 'Ibscene'. When Mrs Henniker came up from Southsea, where she was living, to join her brother-in-law and sister Sir Gerald and Lady Fitzgerald, the Hardys, who had already seen *Hedda Gabler* and *Rosmersholm*, went with them to see *The Master Builder*. As a result of meeting General Milman, Keeper of the Tower of London, and his daughter, on the Holyhead boat, they lunched with them at the Tower, and took Miss Milman in the evening to join Barrie and Gosse's friend, the novelist Maarten Maartens, at a performance of the former's farce *Walker, London* which led to their meeting the comic actor J. L. Toole behind the scenes. Hardy had accepted an invitation to lunch in order to meet the author Mrs Pearl Craigie ('John Oliver Hobbes'), who he had heard was 'very pretty', and whom he afterwards thought 'brilliant'. It was probably only a few days before meeting her on 8 June that he found Mrs McFall ('Sarah Grand') waiting in the drawing-room when he returned for tea. Her recent challenging novel *The Heavenly Twins*, which he was soon to read, not only emboldened him in *Jude the Obscure*; it contributed to the story, and influenced his artistic design.

Hardy still had great difficulty in adjusting to the artificial world of London higher society; in this milieu genuine relationships for him were relatively rare, and he writes of 'a great many vain people' known to him and Emma at 'the Academy crush' late in June. The effort to overcome the 'one-sidedness' he felt gave him little pleasure, he told Mrs Henniker, but he would maintain it, and try not to make 'a serious business of unserious things'; he had lunched that day with lots of people, and was to dine at Lady Shrewsbury's in the evening, and lunch on the morrow at the Jeunes', where he really did wish to meet Ada Rehan, whom he had recently seen in *The Taming of the Shrew*. Mrs Henniker had felt it would be to her fictional advantage to know the architectural features of buildings, and he had sent her a book on the subject, after stating what pleasure it would give him to teach her visually in Westminster Abbey or St Saviour's, Southwark, or St Bartholomew's, Smithfield. (The short story they were to write jointly shows that they visited the last of these, at least, with such an aim.) He was equally delighted to write 'the true names of the places' in her copy of *Tess*, and even more when he received some of her verse translations and found special significance in the thought conveyed by one of them of 'a strange and sweet affinity' warming 'two souls in this desert of earth' to such effect that they 'must claim each other'. Such 'mutual influence' explained, he thought, why they had been reading 'Epipsychidion' almost simultaneously, though he regretted that she, a child of the Shelley tradition, had 'allowed herself to be enfeebled to a belief in ritualistic ecclesiasticism', and was to tell her that her future as a writer depended on breaking with conventionality, even if she offended conventional friends, as 'Sarah Grand', a writer with less sympathetic understanding of human nature, had done, and on her saying now 'what they will all be thinking and saying five and twenty years hence'. Mrs Henniker belonged unswervingly to the High Church, and Hardy had to 'trust to imagination only for an enfranchised woman'; he portrayed her in Sue Bridehead before she fell prey to 'belief in ritualistic ecclesiasticism' or 'retrograde superstitions'.

In the latter half of June, Hardy spent a day or two at Oxford in preparation for the final phase of *Jude*, making notes on student celebrations at the end of the academic year and on Commemoration proceedings in the Sheldonian Theatre, where he sat in the undergraduates' gallery while honorary degrees were being awarded. On 19 July he called on Mrs Henniker at Southsea; he was on his way to London, where he had several engagements, one of which was to accompany Lady Jeune (with whom he was staying) and her daughters to see Irving's final performance in Tennyson's *Becket* at the Lyceum Theatre. His last call was on Lady Londonderry, mother of Lady Ilchester; he thought her 'a beautiful woman still', and honoured her loyalty to him in the coming years. When the Duchess of Manchester and Lady Jeune arrived the conversation turned, without his directing it, to marriage laws and the difficulties arising from separation. He probably touched on his own marriage problems on 3 August in a letter to Mrs Henniker, which she discreetly destroyed and which occasioned her reproof when he met her at Eastleigh railway junction on their way to Winchester, where they lunched at the George, attended a cathedral service, and journeyed to the West Hill milestone by which Angel Clare and 'Liza-Lu were imagined to kneel after seeing the black flag raised to announce Tess's execution.

About the middle of August the Hardys were guests of the

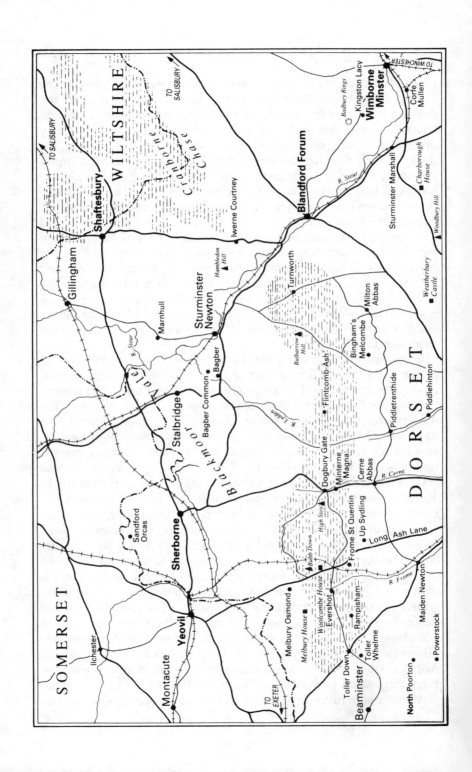

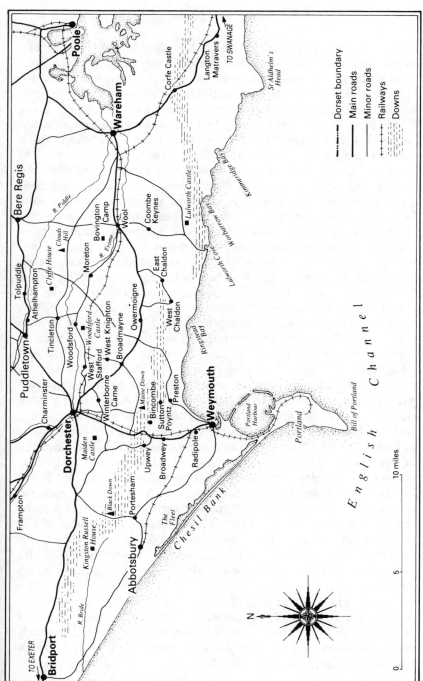

The Hardy Country

Legend:
- Dorset boundary
- Main roads
- Minor roads
- Railways
- Downs

Bridport · Frampton · Puddletown · Bere Regis · Tolpuddle · Poole · Wareham · Corfe Castle · Langton Matravers · TO SWANAGE · St Aldhelm's Head · Kimmeridge Bay · Worbarrow Bay · Lulworth Cove · Lulworth Castle · Coombe Keynes · Wool · Bovington Camp · Clouds Hill · Clyffe House · Moreton · East Chaldon · West Chaldon · Owermoigne · Ringstead Bay · R. Piddle · R. Frome · Athelhampton · Tincleton · Woodsford · Woodsford Castle · West Stafford · West Knighton · Broadmayne · Charminster · Dorchester · Maiden Castle · Winterborne Came · Maine Down · Bincombe · Sutton Poyntz · Preston · Weymouth · Portland Harbour · Portland · Bill of Portland · English Channel · Upwey · Broadway · Radipole · Black Down · Portesham · Kingston Russell House · Abbotsbury · The Fleet · Chesil Bank · TO EXETER · R. Bride

N

0   5   10 miles

Milnes-Gaskells at Wenlock Abbey; they slept in the Norman part of the building. Lady Catherine was as attractive as ever, told humorous stories in the Devonshire dialect as they sat round a lantern in the court, with moths flying about 'as in *In Memoriam*', and alluded to Zola's description of a woman whose presence was 'like a caress'. She made Hardy feel like a father-confessor when she told of her indulgence in a 'wicked, *wanton*' flirtation which had pricked her conscience ever since. When they were tired of walking, she sat with him on the verge of a sandpit, and talked of suicide and whether life was worth living, until they were both quite miserable. In some ways she was a woman after his own heart. When she wrote early in September to thank him for sending her a copy of *The Trumpet-Major*, she had been visiting a poor old man; the experience made her feel that mind without culture was preferable to culture without mind, 'which is what one so often gets in society'. The holiday took the Hardys to Hereford Cathedral, Stokesay Castle, Shrewsbury, and Ludlow Castle, the rooflessness of which Hardy deplored as he thought of its splendour when *Comus* was first performed and *Hudibras* partly written there. Later in the month he spent more time with Douglas in London, where the two may have called on Mrs Henniker and taken her to church. The Owens were in Dorchester when he returned. Rebekah had heard how Emma had been seen at two garden parties, 'got up like "Charlie's Aunt" '. After lunch at Max Gate on 31 August, she left her sister Catharine with Emma, and walked with Hardy to Winterborne Came and down to the remains of Faringdon church, where (as Anne Garland and John Loveday in *The Trumpet-Major* had done) they sat down and talked, their subjects being related to Hardy's fiction. After hearing that Rebekah and her scholarly friend Mary Drisler in New York still thought how unfortunate was the omission of nearly a chapter, on Henchard's unhappy encounter with Elizabeth-Jane at the time of her wedding celebrations, from the English edition of *The Mayor of Casterbridge* – a question she first raised on 6 September 1892 – he promised that he would restore it; his 1895 preface shows that he kept his word.

Hardy's life was too unsettled for him to make progress with *Jude the Obscure*. He had begun it in August, but was too frequently plagued with uncertainties about its reconstitution to make much headway when he had time for it. In September he and Emma planned to visit London to meet Zola, then stay with the Jeunes at

Arlington Manor near Newbury, before possibly visiting Oxford. In November the story was a 'chaos'; in December he wondered whether to continue it, being more disposed just then to write short stories; it was not until the New Year, after he had changed the opening, that it got under way. Earlier he had designed Talbothays, a house for his brother on freehold farmland which the latter had inherited from his father at West Stafford, about two miles from Max Gate; Henry Hardy had expected to marry, but the engagement was broken off and the house let until he and his sisters occupied it in 1911. More recently Hardy had agreed to accept architectural responsibility for his brother's restoration of West Knighton church, an interest and occupation which, like the designing of his father's tombstone and consequent visits to a stonemason early in the year, influenced his choice of Jude's trade. He had also proof-read the stories he had chosen for *Life's Little Ironies*, which was published in February 1894 and so successful after the continued demand for *Tess* that five large impressions appeared before the end of May. Before 1893 ended with carol-singers at Max Gate and listening to the distant muffled peal of Fordington church bells on New Year's Eve, Hardy had completed two stories, one in collaboration with Mrs Henniker, the other with her in mind.

His statement 'I will think over the scheme of our collaborating in the talked of story' in his letter of 20 July 1893 to Mrs Henniker suggests that she had proposed the first of these the previous day at Southsea. After returning from his Wenlock holiday and giving advice, including recommendations for textual improvements, on stories she proposed to publish, he turned his attention to their joint venture in September, first of all suggesting modifications of her sketch, then sending his own outlines. Fearing that his criticism had hurt her feelings, he usually deferred to her judgement and let her write before submitting his comments and proposals. After learning which alternative she preferred, he took the ending in hand and revised the whole. Hardy gives the impression of being hurried and overconfident in his professional decisiveness; 'The Spectre of the Real' contains some of his stock ingredients, and lacks unity of tone. Its romance is offset by hard realism; more specifically, colourful natural scenes contrast with a presentation of common marriage which is almost as cynical and disillusioned as that found in *Jude*. In agreeing to this collaboration, Hardy had allowed his judgement to be swayed by the attraction which his idealizing temperament had given Mrs Henniker; she probably thought her literary association with him would increase interest in her works. In 1894 she dedicated *Outlines* (four stories) to him; later the same year his article on her literary achievement and qualities appeared anonymously in the *Illustrated London News*. After selling the story to an agent, Hardy visited London in December, his last engagement there being its final revision with Mrs Henniker. Almost a year later it appeared in Jerome K. Jerome's *To-Day*. When it was published in 1896, after some revision by Mrs Henniker in an attempt to satisfy public taste, her six accompanying stories in *In Scarlet and Grey* were thought decidedly superior. The *Spectator* judged it to be effective but 'superfluously repulsive', and concluded that Hardy in his later phases (*The Pursuit of the Well-Beloved* and *Jude the Obscure*) was 'hardly a judicious counsellor'. All the wickedness of the story, if it had any, Hardy had prophesied in October 1893, would be laid on his unfortunate head, and all 'the tender and proper parts' attributed to Florence Henniker. The experiment must have taught her that, whatever help and encouragement she continued to receive from him, she had in the final resort to rely on her own judgement.

Early in December 1893 Hardy 'found and touched up a short story called "An Imaginative Woman" '. This suggests that the original, turning on one of those strange events which appealed to Hardy's fictional imagination – an implausible fantasy based on what he had read in Weismann's *Essays on Heredity*, and leading to the suicide of a poet whose last volume had been inspired by his ideal, unattainable woman – had been changed in its setting, and in the conception of its poet, after Hardy's visit to Southsea, near the Isle of Wight. Mrs Henniker had given him a volume of Dante Gabriel Rossetti's *Collected Poems*, and the poet Trewe (originally Crewe, after the family name of Mrs Henniker's mother) was recognizably Rossetti in Hardy's portrait of him and in the obvious reference to 'Severed Selves' in *The House of Life*. This sonnet expresses the affinity between 'two souls' who are 'the shores wave-mocked of sundering seas', an image which came to mind (together with Arnold's in 'Isolation') when, remembering how he and Mrs Henniker had been mistaken for a married couple at the George, Winchester, Hardy wrote 'At an Inn'.

Written years afterwards, the poem 'Alike and Unlike' indicates that Hardy was well aware of the division between Emma and himself when they were on their way to Dublin in May 1893. In

'The Division', written later that year in London, when he continued to address her in his letters as his 'dear' or 'dearest', he
refers to 'that thwart thing betwixt' them; it may have a similar
connotation to that of 'The Interloper', which he described as a
form of madness. Emma's eccentricities were already the subject of
gossip in the Dorchester neighbourhood, but Hardy probably
knew from recurrent outbreaks and oddities of behaviour what
some of her closest friends were soon to suspect, if they had not
discerned it already. What she thought of his neglect of her for the
sake of collaborating with Mrs Henniker, and of the gifts he
received from her – a silver inkstand inscribed 'T.H. from F.H.'
and those 'beautiful large photographs' of his 'most charming
friend' – will never be known. He may have been looking at the
photograph he had chosen, thinking of his starry-eyed infatuation,
when he wrote 'He Wonders about Himself' on 28 November, just
before the thought of Florence Henniker led to the recasting of 'An
Imaginative Woman'. He regarded himself as a puppet, swayed by
forces beyond his control, and wondered if he could free himself to
contribute something towards the welfare of mankind; he could
have been thinking of the novel he had in hand. In September he
had taken Emma to stay with the Jeunes at Arlington Manor, and
found much cheerfulness there. Pearl Craigie had been one of the
guests, and he had walked with her for two hours, during which
she explained why she had turned Catholic, a step which displeased him at a time when his Positivist self was imaginatively at
odds with High Anglicanism. He had lost his 'one-sidedness', but
by the end of the year he felt it was time to give up being 'frivol'
and concentrate on *Jude the Obscure*.

19

Jude and Consequences

When serial publication of *Jude the Obscure* in the American and European editions of Harper's magazine was agreed before the end of 1893, Hardy promised 'a tale that could not offend the most fastidious maiden'. It was still called 'The Simpletons' when the December instalment was published; with the second Hardy reverted to his original title 'Hearts Insurgent', after learning that Charles Reade's *A Simpleton* had appeared in *Harper's*. He would have altered it again, to 'The Recalcitrants', had not sheets for the January number gone to press. Not surprisingly, after planning, replanning, and even wondering whether to continue his story, he found his inspiration and zeal uncertain. In January 1894 he informed Mrs Henniker that he was 'creeping on a little' with it, and becoming interested in his heroine, though she was 'very nebulous'. Almost three months later, finding that 'the story was carrying him into unexpected fields and he was afraid to predict its future trend', he requested Harper & Brothers to cancel his contract. The iron had entered his soul; doubts and hesitations had vanished, and he intended to write for 'men and women of full age', whatever the consequences. The Parnell controversy had made the question of the legality of loveless marriages a public issue, and his resolve to sustain it, either when he began *The Pursuit of the Well-Beloved* or when he decided to fictionalize the topic afresh in *Jude*, may have been fortified by the 1891 article 'Public Life and Private Morals' in the *Fortnightly Review*, which contended that the legal aspect of a marriage union is 'merely its husk and shell' if men and women are bound to each other when they have 'neither love nor sympathy' or are suited 'neither by age nor by temperament'. Nevertheless he agreed to continue his 'conventionalized' serial, one result of the consequent abridgements and modifications being the oversight which led to the 'miraculous' appearance of a boy, as the *Athenaeum* described it, towards the end. For a number of reasons Hardy had too much to cope with while the serial was in hand.

He did not mind diversions. His retrospective stress on cheerful events and amusing stories heard in London at the time seems to emphasize the dullness of his life at Max Gate. At Lady Jeune's he looked forward to taking her two daughters Dorothy and Madeleine Stanley to the theatre, and to lunching at Lady Londonderry's, where he met the Lord Chancellor and other eminent people. He stayed on for his hostess's party, to which 500 were invited, principally to meet Princess Mary and the Duke and Duchess of Teck. Preceding Emma in April, he chose 16 Pelham Crescent near South Kensington Museum ('an instructive place to wander in') for their long seasonal London holiday. At the end of the month he and Edward Clodd spent an evening with Meredith and his son and daughter-in-law at his home near Box Hill in Surrey. Soon afterwards, at Strafford House, Clodd's home at Aldeburgh, he met the novelist Grant Allen and the mountaineer Edward Whymper, who described the tragedy on the Matterhorn in 1865, when he was the only one of four English climbers to survive, a catastrophe which Hardy could remember hearing about when, on his way from Westbourne Park Villas, he reached Harrow, where two of the victims had lived. In London he and Emma attended crushes at the houses of Lady Jeune, Lady Carnarvon, Mrs Pitt-Rivers, Lady Malmesbury, and others. He was surprised to find many fashionably dressed young ladies, Princess Christian among those of the highest rank, at a meeting of the Women Writers' Club; and so moved, as he returned by bus in the rain from a visit to Lady Yarborough's, by the spontaneity of a girl who clutched his arm and kissed him repeatedly for allowing her to shelter under his umbrella, that he could only stare in wonderment at the bus which bore her away from South Kensington. Early in June he and Emma attended the opening performance of a play by Mrs Craigie, and entertained friends at 16 Pelham Crescent. It was rather too much for Emma, who left to recuperate at Hastings while he returned home to check plans for autumn extensions at the back of the house, comprising a new kitchen and scullery, his new first-floor study, with two attic rooms above. After returning with her from Hastings, he and Emma attended more parties, one of them being Lady Spencer's at the Admiralty. Some of the 'famous beauties of the time' disappointed him, but others, among them Lady Powis, Lady Yarborough (remembered with a slight family disguise in 'The Pink Frock'), Lady de Gray, and the Duchess of Montrose, seemed to be 'very beautiful', though he had become tired of talking to people who had little to give in return. He had a long

conversation with a former correspondent of *The Times*, William
Howard Russell, who talked about battles in the Franco-Prussian
war, and related 'a distressing story of a horse with no under jaw,
laying its head upon his thigh in a dumb appeal for sympathy, two
or three days after the battle of Gravelotte, when he was riding
over the field'.

After being recommended by Pearce Edgcumbe, Hardy had
been made a JP for Dorset, and found it more convenient to sit on
the bench at County sessions than remain a Dorchester JP. Such
duties and his Sunday habit of visiting his mother afforded some
relief from the continual task of writing when he was at home. On
his return from London at the end of July he was in pain for a week
as a result of dragging his heavy portmanteau downstairs at
Pelham Crescent, after the departure of the servants with the other
luggage, followed by Emma, leaving him to check that all was in
order before handing over the keys. By this time he appears to
have completed no more than a third of his novel; a sketch made of
'Old Grove's Place', Shaftesbury, on 13 September suggests that he
had reached the halfway stage, and was contemplating the 'Shas-
ton' section. Much remained to be done five weeks later, when he
met Henry Harper on business in London, and dined with Arthur
Henniker, now a major, at the Guards' Mess, St James's. Despite
the building operations, he must have made good progress during
the next two months, for by the end of the year the whole of *Jude*
was in the hands of the serial publishers except a few concluding
chapters, which appear from the manuscript to have been written
in March 1895. He spent a few more days before Christmas in
London, chiefly to discuss the forthcoming uniform edition of his
novels with his publisher McIlvaine. While sleepless one night in
his room off Piccadilly, as he recorded in his poem 'At Mayfair
Lodgings', he noticed a lighted window close by, and wondered
who might be lying there ill. After hearing of her death, he was
convinced, erroneously it seems, that 'one whom he had cared for
in his youth', Cassie Pole, who had married a Mayfair publican,
had lain dying in the room he overlooked.

His main business on returning home was to make initial preparations for the new edition of his works ('The Wessex Novels',
published by Osgood, McIlvaine & Co.). Macbeth-Raeburn,
accompanied by Hardy or following his guidance, had made
sketches for scenes (one for each volume) in and around Dorchester early in December; he resumed in March, probably after his

visit to Boscastle, staying at Max Gate, where accommodation was
still cramped owing to building operations. Hardy prepared his
first Wessex map for the series, and wrote a special preface for each
volume, the first of which, *Tess of the d'Urbervilles*, appeared in
April 1895, the remainder following, usually at monthly intervals,
until September 1896. The first new preface, completed in January,
gave special emphasis to the Wessex background; the second, for
Far from the Madding Crowd, to its old customs. Writing these
prefaces and revising the texts took up considerable time until the
summer of 1896; proof-reading became a drudgery. Revision enabled Hardy to make some important changes; he restored, for
example, the greater part of a chapter to *The Mayor of Casterbridge* in
accordance with his promise to Rebekah Owen, had Farfrae's
pronunciation checked for accuracy, and transferred the setting for
The Woodlanders. The title-page epigraph he invented for this novel
in August 1895 applied more to him than to anyone in the story;
the trees he had planted at Max Gate could not secure him from
storms created by 'ill affin'd' hearts. Although he wrote with ironic
decorum on the marriage question in his preface to this novel, his
later work had emboldened him, and he chose to be more sexually
frank: 'O, my great God! He's had you!' Grace Fitzpiers exclaims to
Felice Charmond; Eustacia surrenders 'body and soul' to Wildeve
(a revision which was withdrawn in 1912, probably because it came
to be regarded as a supererogatory demeaning of the heroine).
Slight changes in *Two on a Tower* afford another example of daring
sexual explicitness in this edition, making it clear that Lady Constantine's son was conceived after she and her lover had learned
that their marriage could no longer be regarded as legal. After
reaching agreement with Macmillan in May 1894, Hardy was additionally busy with the Colonial Library edition of his novels, all
except *Under the Greenwood Tree*, the copyright of which he could
not retrieve.

At the beginning of 1895 Hardy had suffered the embarrassment
of being asked to explain how the purchase of the Max Gate site
from the Duchy of Cornwall came to be misrepresented the previous November in the New York *Independent*. Hardy realized that
the author responsible for this was Rosamund Tomson, 'a London
lady, pretty, and well known in society', who had cultivated his
acquaintance, and gratified her vanity by exhibiting him as her
admirer. This was far from being a pretence at first, the most
cordial exchanges between them having developed by 1891. In her

he thought he had found the ideal 'enfranchised woman', he informed Mrs Henniker on 16 July 1893, telling her how their friendship had foundered as soon as he discovered its purpose. Apart from expressing surprise that she had read some of his letters to others, Hardy never lost confidence in Mrs Henniker; he had thought it prudent to correspond with her husband almost from the outset. His interest in promoting her work continued. His hint to Clement Shorter in April 1894 that her *Outlines* had yet to receive attention produced a full-page portrait of her in the *Sketch*, followed by a review. On 1 March 1895, after supplying the concluding incident, he recommended her short story 'A Page from a Vicar's History' to the same editor; it appeared in the August number of the *English Illustrated Magazine*. Mrs Henniker and her brother (shortly afterwards made Lord Crewe) attended the lunch party given by the Hardys in London on 25 June with many others, including Lady Jeune and her daughter Madeleine, Mrs Craigie, General Milman and his daughter, Mr McIlvaine, Mr and Mrs Maurice Macmillan, and the actor Johnston Forbes-Robertson.

In April the Hardys had stayed with the Jeunes at Arlington Manor, where they met a number of friends, including Lady Dorothy Nevill and Sir Henry Thompson. An excursion was made to the *Jude* country, Emma sketching Chaddleworth Church and describing it as 'Challingworth . . . about 3 miles from Fawley'. For the London season they took a flat at 90 Ashley Gardens, where Hardy's portrait was painted by Winifred Thomson, the hand being completed the following February. Whether the poem 'A Broken Appointment' is to be associated with this period is altogether conjectural; Mrs Henniker's failure to appear, possibly owing to a misunderstanding, convinced Hardy she was not in love with him, as he ought to have known. He wished to return home earlier than usual, but was eventually persuaded to stay on, in order to attend as Edmund Gosse's guest the Omar Khayyám Club dinner in honour of Meredith at Burford Bridge on 13 July. He had already declined invitations from its organizers, Edward Clodd, the President, and Clement Shorter, but must have agreed in the end that it was his duty to be present. Thirty to forty writers and editors, all men, assembled on the lawn in front of the hotel. Meredith had agreed to come on condition that he was not called upon to make a speech. He was in poor health, and did not arrive until after dinner, when he entered leaning on Clement Shorter's arm. Hardy, who looked worn and pallid, spoke first in his praise, and Gissing followed, both recalling the sage advice Meredith had given after reading their first novels. Meredith, who had never spoken in public, was moved to reply briefly, after making a 'chaffing allusion to the fox-like trick' Clodd had played on him; what he said was 'the more rich and heart-deep in that it was unpremeditated'. The evening ended with a rush to catch the train back to London.

Hardy's immediate task at Max Gate was further proof-reading for the uniform edition, and the restoration of his *Jude* manuscript to its original state, a process which he had facilitated by marking all the altered passages and excisions for the serial version in blue ink. 'Curiously enough', he wrote to Mrs Henniker at the time, he was 'more interested in this Sue story' than in any other he had written. At the beginning of September he and Emma enjoyed a week with the archaeologist General Pitt-Rivers and his wife at Rushmore, among the wooded hills of Cranborne Chase, south-east of Shaftesbury. The main events were the annual sports which were held at the Larmer Tree Gardens, and the dancing, chiefly to polka-mazurka and schottische figures, which followed in the mellow moonlight and the illumination of thousands of Vauxhall lamps. When country dances were introduced, Hardy led off with the Pitt-Rivers' beautiful daughter Mrs Grove. Shortly afterwards Gissing was his guest at Max Gate. His observations, rather un-generous and condescending, are a mish-mash of shrewd insights and hasty judgements. He thought Mrs Hardy foolish, restless, and foolish-looking; the cooking was 'of course bad'. On their excursions to 'Egdon Heath' Hardy named wayside flowers inac-curately, and discussed the difficulty he had encountered in de-scribing decently the symbolic incident of Arabella's throwing a pig's pizzle at Jude. Gissing thought there was 'a good deal of coarseness' in Hardy's nature, which was explained by his 'humble origin'. He could not 'let himself go' in conversation, and was uneasy and preoccupied. He was Meredith's 'intellectual inferior', and ran too much after titled people and the kind of society where he was 'least qualified to shine'. Mrs Hardy com-plained of 'being obliged to see more society than she liked', and said how difficult it was to live with people of humble origin, 'meaning Thomas, of course'. It was disagreeable to see a man like Hardy 'so unsettled in life' as a result of being unhappily married, Gissing concluded; far better if he had married 'an honest homely woman who would have been impossible in fashionable society'. Later in the month, while staying at Max Gate, Clodd and William Archer took a midnight walk with Hardy to 'Egdon Heath'.

Towards the end of the summer there was a garden-party at Max Gate; how much Hardy enjoyed it is not known, but with autumn closing in he admittedly became apprehensive about how *Jude the Obscure* would be received. 'Never retract. Never explain. Get it done and let them howl', he resolved, remembering the words of 'a very practical friend' to Benjamin Jowett. He had reason to fear. The story had changed immeasurably since he drew up its first plan in 1890 'from notes made in 1887 and onwards'. Jude, at first named Head, then ironically Hopeson, after Hardy's grandmother (*née* Hopson or Hobson), then Fawley, after the Berkshire village where she was born, was the boy from 'Mellstock' whose early reading, especially in the *Iliad*, coincided with Hardy's; his classical pursuits and later intemperance were suggested by the lives of John Antell and Horace Moule. Little remained of what Tryphena's death prompted in 1890, save some circumstances connected with her teaching at Puddletown. The heroine she had suggested had been superseded by an enfranchised young woman based partly on the author's own heterodox beliefs and partly on his Shelleyan idealization of Mrs Henniker; for Hardy and the hero the 'well-beloved' was 'the sweetest and most disinterested comrade that he had ever had, living largely in vivid imaginings'. Sue's other forenames, Florence and Mary, suggest that the affinity with Jude is based not only on Hardy's with Mrs Henniker but also on that which existed between him and his sister Mary (remembered with their grandmother in 'Marygreen', partly from his first visit to Fawley with her). The educational theme with which the novel originated, and to which Kate Hardy's experience had contributed ('I don't mind if Tom publishes how badly we were used', she wrote in 1882), had been submerged in the marriage question which had driven *The Pursuit of the Well-Beloved* off course. Jude courts death because he has lost Sue, not because his academic ambition has failed. The crucifixion which he and Sue suffer individually arises from the loss of their children. They had believed in the 'Greek joyousness' of natural living, but tragedy had been seen by Sue as God's punishment for sin. The free-thinker succumbs to the High Church 'retrograde superstitions' which Hardy had regretted in Mrs Henniker, and prostitutes herself in remarriage to Phillotson, Jude doing likewise with drunken mockery *vis-à-vis* Arabella. The crucifixion derives from marriages which are unnatural but proper in the sight of the Church. The novel is 'all contrasts – or was meant to be', Hardy told Gosse. By far the most significant is that between the enchantment that distance lends to the lights of Christminster and their dimness when Jude first sees the crumbling colleges in the shadows, the unenlightenment or mediaevalism of the foggy Tractarian centre being ultimately concentrated in the black, windowless walls of Sarcophagus College.

Subject to chance inspirations and changes of plan over a long period, Hardy had not thought out the crux of his plot very clearly. He weakens his anti-marriage case by taking an extreme couple, each foredoomed to disaster by heredity: 'marriage with a blood-relation would duplicate the adverse conditions, and a tragic sadness might be intensified to a tragic horror'. Yet the horror and consequent tragedy are brought about not as the result of this marriage but by little Father Time, son of Jude and Arabella. The story aims at presenting 'a deadly war waged between flesh and spirit', between Arabella's sexual seductiveness and the marriage of true minds in Sue and Jude. The plot is defective in basing the case for true marriage, against the licensed and unnatural, on Jude's longing for Sue Bridehead, who is epicene and instinctively averse to sexual marriage. *Jude the Obscure* (dated 1896), the first of Hardy's first editions in this form and the eighth in Osgood, McIlvaine & Co.'s uniform edition of the Wessex novels, was published in a single volume on 1 November 1895, the day of Sir George Douglas's arrival at Max Gate. The auspices were not flattering, the weather being gloomy, with Emma suffering from an accident sustained while learning to cycle. Hardy was not uplifted by a sense of work well done, but he was quite unprepared for 'the resounding obloquy which was to be its portion'.

The storm soon broke; even Edmund Gosse described *Jude* as a 'grimy' story. A reviewer in the *Pall Mall Gazette* was moved to write mockingly in an article headed 'Jude the Obscene'. On 13 November the *Guardian*, representing the Church, condemned it as 'a shameful nightmare' which one wished to forget as soon as possible, and the London *World* labelled its author 'Hardy the Degenerate'. In the New York *World* Jeannette Gilder claimed that it was almost the worst book she had ever read, and thanked God for writers who had never 'trailed their talents in the dirt'. Hardy had read little of Zola,* but the coarseness of some of his Arabella scenes was attributed to his influence. More favourable reviews were to follow, notably from Havelock Ellis, Howells, and H. G. Wells, but castigation continued from A. J. Butler in 'Mr. Hardy as a Decadent' and from others, including Mrs Oliphant, who, in the January number of *Blackwood's*, considered the novel 'an assault on the stronghold of marriage', and maintained that no book more disgusting, more impious, and more 'foul in detail' had ever come from the hand of a master.

Just what comfort did Hardy receive from his friends? He thought Gosse's the 'most discriminating' of the first reviews, but wrote explanatory letters to ensure that his second, in *Cosmopolis*, was more discriminating. He was pleased to receive Mrs Craigie's congratulations and a long supportive letter from Lady Londonderry. Mrs Grove, who had received a presentation copy of *Jude*, wrote to say she liked it; she could hardly do less. Mrs Henniker, to whom he had hesitated in sending a copy (obviously for religious reasons) may have had reservations, but raised no objections and read with the utmost attention, very quickly requesting the identification of the Oxford worthies who came to Jude's mind when he first visited Christminster; Hardy had already forgotten one of them. He was pleased to receive commendations from Ellen Terry and Chavelita Clairmonte ('George Egerton'), a feminist writer who, like 'Sarah Grand', had stirred up controversy in 1893 (with *Keynotes*, a collection of short stories which came to Hardy's notice when Mrs Henniker sent him a copy for comment); she thought Sue 'a marvellously true psychological study of a temperament' which was far more common than 'the ordinary male observer' assumed. More than anything else, the encomium which Hardy received from Swinburne soon after sending him a copy buoyed him up when defamation was at its worst. 'The beauty, the terror, and the truth, are all yours and yours alone', Swinburne wrote; there had been 'no such tragedy in fiction' since Balzac. Even so, speaking for admirers as cordial as himself, he yearned for 'another admission into an English paradise "under the greenwood tree" '. Later, if not as much at first, it pleased Hardy to think that the outcry against *Jude* had been 'unequalled in violence since the publication of Swinburne's *Poems and Ballads* thirty years before'. His defensive thinking was apt to become confused; at one time he believed he had been 'almost too High-Churchy' (rather than the opposite in his satirical tragedy), and feared that the 'Job-cum-Ezekiel moralist' in him had got the better of the artist. If

Jude preaches, its main text or hope is that Pauline charity will endure when Churches have failed.

Hardy must have savoured some satisfaction when he discovered that *Jude* had been chosen as the book of the year by William Archer in his survey of 1895 publications for the *Daily Chronicle*. Educated at Edinburgh University and then for the legal profession, Archer had begun his London career as a dramatic critic. He soon lost his faith in Christian theology, largely as a result of reading J. S. Mill's autobiography and the novels of George Eliot. In Norway, where he often stayed with his relatives, the taste which he acquired for theatrical realism led to admiration of Ibsen in particular, not only for the technical skill of his drama but also for its emotional appeal and poetry. The first of Ibsen's plays to be produced in London, *Pillars of Society* in 1880, was in his translation. Archer was a rationalist of uncompromising integrity who continued to work for the abolition of censorship in the theatre. Hardy had sent him a copy of *Tess* in October 1892 as a token of esteem for a writer in whom he found kinship of views. As a result of hearing at Max Gate in September 1895 what steps had been taken to have *Jude* serialized, Archer attacked censorship in 'Pandering to Podsnap', an article which appeared anonymously the following month in the *World*. It was not until Hardy discovered that he was not committed to reviewing *Jude*, almost two weeks after its publication, that he sent Archer a copy.

The common association of Zola with *Jude* must have seemed to Emma a slur on her husband's name. Hardy's failure to attend the Authors' Club dinner in Zola's honour on 28 September 1893 was probably due to her intervention. In February 1897 she resisted his working 'hand in glove' with the French novelist in an anti-vivisection crusade which appealed to Mrs Henniker. Hardy told the latter shortly afterwards that she was wrong in assuming he admired Zola; he felt, as he demonstrated in *Jude*, that 'the animal side of human nature should never be dwelt on except as a contrast or foil to its spiritual side'. Much as she was distressed by what had happened, Emma must have felt vindicated. Even if he did not discuss the matter with her, she knew the tenor of his thoughts from *The Pursuit of the Well-Beloved* and the serial version of *Jude*. According to her nephew Gordon Gifford, who was living at Max Gate at the time, she objected strongly to the book, on which she had not been consulted. If there is any truth in the story publicized by Ford Madox Ford that she travelled to London to persuade Dr

Richard Garnett of the British Museum to suppress *Jude*, she must have been at her wits' end; she could have been the one who, setting out on such a mission, said things the poet of 'Wessex Heights' did not wish to hear as she pressed her face against the train window. Jealousies preyed on her mind, but even so her nature seems to have been periodically recoverable; Hardy may well have been thinking of her when, with reference to Jeannette Gilder in the summer of 1896, he wrote of 'the sex that makes up for lack of justice by excess of generosity'. Both seem to have recovered from shocks by early December, when they accepted Forbes-Robertson's invitation, and saw him and Mrs Patrick Campbell in *Romeo and Juliet*, having supper with them afterwards in Willis's Rooms, where Hardy had danced in 1862; 'Reminiscences of a Dancing Man' was written shortly afterwards. *Tess* had been translated into several languages, and *Jude* was selling very well. Unlike his country friends, who depended on press opinion, London society, Hardy found, was 'not at all represented by the shocked critics'.

Hardy had been preparing a stage version of *Tess* for some time. In January 1896, soon after its completion, Mrs Patrick Campbell, as eager to play the leading role as he was to see her in it, stayed in Dorchester and visited Max Gate to discuss its production; for light entertainment he played old tunes on his fiddle to her improvised dancing. Early in February, while Emma remained at home suffering from shingles, he made a brief visit to London for further negotiations on the subject with Forbes-Robertson and Frederick Harrison, and for the completion of his portrait by Winifred Thomson. While at the Hennikers' in Sloane Gardens, he heard an amusing story from Arthur of how he had bought a copy of Byron and struggled manfully through it when his engagement was in view, and never read a line of poetry after his wedding. He was not able to bring Emma for his next visit, and, while she was recuperating at Brighton, accompanied Lady Jeune and her daughter Madeleine to a masked ball at the Crackenthorpes', where he and Henry James were the only two not in dominoes, and 'recklessly flirted with' in consequence.

When Emma had recovered, they brought up their servants to 16 Pelham Crescent, and gave some small parties there. In the meantime, as a result of the outcry against *Jude*, negotiations to stage *Tess* had come to nought. After Hardy had caught a heavy cold and rheumatism, Emma thought it advisable to take him to Brighton.

Back in London, he read the letter in the papers in which Bishop
How of Wakefield professed that he had thrown his copy of *Jude*
on the fire; he was more annoyed later when he discovered from a
biography of the bishop that he was responsible for the withdrawal
of the book from W. H. Smith's circulating library. He was impressed by Miss Gilder's wish to see him for the purpose of
removing any misapprehension for which she was responsible,
but declined to be interviewed on the subject, knowing full well it
could make little difference then or in the long run to the assessment of *Jude*. Some time afterwards he discovered that she was the
strange lady who had drawn near when he was conversing at an
evening party a few days later at the home of an American friend,
and that it was she who suggested inviting him, clearly in the hope
of his being inveigled into a discussion of the novel. As in other
summers, he derived most pleasure from listening with his wife to
concerts by famous European bands at the Imperial Institute. Here
one evening they met, among other promenading friends,
Mrs Grove, with whom Hardy danced a few turns when 'The Blue
Danube' was struck up. Dorothy Stanley's wedding to Henry
Allhusen at St George's, Hanover Square, was their last London
event that summer.

At this wedding Hardy met his friend Mrs Grove again. She was
Dorothy's cousin and a friend of the Hennikers and Lord
Houghton. Soon after becoming acquainted with her at Rushmore,
he had discovered that she wished to reply to an article in the *North
American Review* on why women did not want the ballot. Agnes
Grove was an inexperienced writer, and needed guidance; it gave
Hardy particular pleasure to tutor an attractive lady in the expression of progressive views. He took the finished article in hand,
improved it, and forwarded it himself; when it was rejected, he
advised her to generalize it and keep it for future use, wishing
gallantly that the declined manuscript had been his and not hers.
She had four children, and was prompted by Sue's disclosure to
little Father Time to start an article on what children should be
told. Again Hardy gave much advice and help, taking drastic
action against diffuseness, until he succeeded in having it published in the *Free Review* in two parts, one on the religious, the
other on the physiological, aspect of the question. She had been
such a 'good little pupil', he was pleased to offer her advice. The
result was that, after some publication difficulties and counsel
from Hardy not to be 'afraid of full stops', she succeeded in placing

another article on how to answer children's religious questions. When he read her essay 'Of Women in Assemblies' in the *New Century Review* in March 1897 he congratulated her on being 'more incisive and less diffuse', and told her that if she resolutely criticized every sentence she wrote, and ensured that it contained 'a rounded and complete thought', she would soon be a 'well equipped and facile' writer. Agnes had served her apprenticeship. Shortly before this her husband Walter had succeeded as baronet, and she had become Lady Grove.

In the summer of 1896 the Hardys went on a sight-seeing tour by train which took them to Malvern, where they climbed the Beacon, Emma on a mule, then to Worcester, Warwick, Kenilworth, and Stratford, where they stayed a week. Emma, who had been subject to lameness from her youth, and for that reason had taken to pony-riding, occasionally in Dorchester, went round on her green bicycle ('the Grasshopper'), Hardy trying to keep pace on foot. Just before leaving home he had written a reminiscential preface of great interest, on the choir his father and grandfather knew, for the 'Wessex Novels' edition of *Under the Greenwood Tree*, an inclusion which had been delayed for copyright reasons. He did the proof-reading for this volume at Warwick, and forwarded 'A Committee-Man of "The Terror" ', a short story on which he had been working in London, from Stratford to Clement Shorter. From Coventry he and Emma travelled to Reading, then to Dover, where they had to remain two weeks until she had recovered from a cycling collision. Although he began it at Stratford, it was appropriate that Hardy read *King Lear* there and 'Dover Beach' in his copy of Arnold's *Poetical Works*. They were on their way to Belgium, where they visited many places, 'the Grasshopper' often seeming lost but always turning up sooner or later at railway stations, sometimes when Hardy thought they would be better without it. The brick architecture of Bruges made him pine for the stone buildings he was familiar with in England. At Brussels they stayed 'for association's sake' at the same hotel as in 1876, but found that 'it had altered for the worse since those bright days'. So too had his marriage; 'I ask myself, why I am here again, and not underground!' he wrote to Mrs Henniker from Liège. Brussels was too bustling with people and traffic for Emma to cycle there. They visited art galleries, Hardy being particularly interested in the paintings of Memling, Pourbus, and Rubens. His main object was to visit the field of Waterloo again; the notes he made shortly afterwards on 'Europe in Throes' in three parts, each of five acts, indicate a great step towards the final design of *The Dynasts*. When he returned to England in early October he was pleased to hear from Mrs Henniker that *In Scarlet and Grey* had received good reviews and was selling well. The *Spectator's* attack on their joint story had yet to appear.

No doubt the tour had been generally 'agreeable and instructive', as Hardy told Mrs Henniker; the eight weeks of sight-seeing had afforded relief to him and Emma. In the monotony of Max Gate, each could suffer, Emma's jealousies breaking out at times, and working so much on her that she was not above snubbing him for his peasant habits and origins; there had been times when he sank to the very depths of despondency. Poems written or completed in 1896 show how much he suffered, and how in periods of gloom the whole world changed. 'The Dead Man Walking' emphasizes his loss of joy in living 'of late years', most of all when his 'Love's heart kindled in hate' against him. The 'In Tenebris' poems end with the wish that he had died in early infancy. The gloom was aggravated by the sense of disgrace which afflicted him after repeated critical assaults on *Jude*. In the first 'In Tenebris' he could convince himself that he had no friends left; in 'Wessex Heights' he imagines Mrs Henniker indifferent to him, and is prepared to 'let her go'. Emotional disturbance had falsified actuality, as his letters to her continued to prove; the second Mrs Hardy knew what allowance to make when she stressed that it was 'the poet' who wrote in that way. Hardy did not lose any of his friends; he continued to meet them in London and elsewhere. He appeased his anxious debilitating inner self in poetry, and took refuge in activity, hoping sometimes that the crisis would be resolved. 'Ah, love, let us be true to one another' must have been in mind when he wrote his initials with Emma's by the title 'Dover Beach' in September. The Owens were in Dorchester when they returned, and found when they called at Max Gate that Hardy had moved to his new study overlooking Conquer Barrow, and that Emma was faced with a variety of domestic problems. When he autographed Rebekah's copy of *Life's Little Ironies* and told her that 'The Son's Veto' was his best short story, she disagreed, thinking 'The Three Strangers' much superior. Her failure to bring a copy of *Jude* for his signature was read as a mark of disapproval, and the poem 'To a Lady, Offended by a Book of the Writer's' was the result. Regretting the omission, Rebekah sent her copy with the usual request, but did not receive it until she was back in New York. The trees arranged to be sent in response were very briefly acknowledged on 15 February 1897.

Towards the end of 1896 'The Duke's Reappearance', which may have been written during the year, appeared, like 'A Committee-Man of "The Terror" ', in a Christmas number. At the time Hardy was busy preparing *The Well-Beloved*, a new version of the serial for addition to the uniform edition of his works and publication also in America. It was finished on 24 January. As a result of removing the marriage question by changes at the opening and more lengthily at the end, greater homogeneity of tone and significance on the subject of art were achieved. Artistic idealization may result in creative success at intervals, but when prolonged without interest in the surrounding world is doomed to lifeless results. Hardy was critical of J. H. Middleton, Slade Professor of Art at Cambridge, whom he used to meet at the Savile, because he had lost 'all sense of relativity, and of art's subsidiary relation to existence'. Pierston's release from his particular idealizing 'curse', and a recovery which results in seeing truth without benefit of lamp light and other 'beautifying artifices', are consistent with the principles of a writer who sought to find beauty in ugliness and the unromantic. The revised ending adds a new seriousness to a diverting tale intended to deromanticize the kind of Shelleyan-Platonic idealism which had appealed to Hardy. It is rather like that of Goethe's *Faust*, which, before revealing the dependence of salvation on divine grace, stresses the hero's need to transcend romanticism in schemes aimed at the practical welfare and liberation of mankind. Art divorced from reality in repetitious attempts to express the ideal and unattainable must have seemed effete and indefensible to Hardy when he thought of the practical work and schemes of such people as the late Henry Moule, vicar of Fordington, for the benefit of his fellow-men.

The extraordinary charge by an anonymous reviewer in the London *World* that the most unpleasant form of sex-mania was to be found in 'the Wessex-mania' of *The Well-Beloved* must have confirmed Hardy's resolution to abandon prose fiction, as he probably told Charles Moule, on holiday from Cambridge, during a walk with him at the end of March. The reception of *Jude* had made him realize by October 1896 that he could express unconventional views and feelings in verse without creating much protest. More than anything else it had made him decide to relinquish novel-writing when, as he told Edward Clodd, he had several more plots 'in his head'. He had agreed to write three more stories, but they could wait; the last was finished in 1900. *Wessex Poems*, with his own illustrations, was already in mind; much of it was already written. Writing more verse was as important a further preparation for his main objective, *The Dynasts*, as historical research.

* His notebook shows that in 1886 he read translations of *La Faute de l'abbé Mouret* and *Germinal*. The former, though different in theme and motivation from Hardy's novel, influenced him perhaps more than he realized when he wrote *Tess of the d'Urbervilles*. See D.G. Mason in *The Thomas Hardy Journal*, October 1991, pp. 89–102.

20

To the Century's End

Much to Mrs Campbell's disappointment, Hardy's efforts had turned to the staging of *Tess* in New York. In February 1896 he had asked Harper & Brothers to act as his agent, and had his dramatic version collected from Lady Jeune's, where it had been kept in her husband's dispatch box, and sent to them. After being considerably modified a year later by Lorimer Stoddard in less than a week, it was produced at the Fifth Avenue Theatre with Mrs Fiske in the leading role. On 2 March 1897, the opening night, after a copy of Stoddard's version had been rushed to England, a performance was also staged at St James's Theatre, London, to secure the English copyright, Hardy attending with Mr and Mrs McIlvaine and a friend. Emma, who had suddenly wired to say she was coming to London, stayed overnight at her club, the Alexandra, and returned home without seeing him. The next day he sat to William Rothenstein. Less than two weeks later he received an enthusiastic account of the New York performance and reception from Rebekah Owen, who had attended the first night with her sister. Mrs Campbell still hoped that she would have the opportunity to appear in a London production of the play.

As it was the year of the Diamond Jubilee, accommodation for London visitors was booked early, and Hardy and Emma could secure only temporary quarters. He attended a large dance at Londonderry House with her, and dined with Henry James, Edward Marsh, and others at the Gosses'. For the remainder of the season, they decided to commute from Basingstoke. In this way they met many of their old friends, including Sir George Douglas, heard concerts at the Imperial Institute, where the Vienna Orchestra under Edouard Strauss was playing, saw two Ibsen plays, and visited the latest exhibitions of paintings. When the capital became more crowded, they changed their plans, and chose to seek quieter places in Switzerland. At Berne on 20 June they attended a Jubilee concert with fellow-countrymen in the cathedral. From Interlaken, where the rosy glow of the Jungfrau was visible early in the morning, they went on to Grindelwald and

Scheidegg, then walked to the Wengern Alp, where Hardy was less impressed by the spectacle of the avalanches than by 'the thundering rumble' of those that were invisible. From Lauterbrunnen they returned via Lake Thun to Interlaken, in or near which a view of the Schreckhorn brought Leslie Stephen to mind in association with the thoughtful imagery which later informed Hardy's commemorative poem. A steamer excursion from Lausanne, where they stayed at the Hôtel Gibbon, took them to the Castle of Chillon; another, on Sunday, 27 June, to Ouchy. Inevitably Hardy thought of Byron, but that evening he sat in the hotel garden until midnight, composing the poem 'Lausanne' in honour of the historian who wrote there the last lines of *The Decline and Fall of the Roman Empire* exactly 110 years earlier. Thinking of his own satirical depiction of the Church *vis-à-vis* the marriage bond in *Jude the Obscure*, he made Gibbon ask whether the Establishment was still like that challenged by Milton in *The Doctrine and Discipline of Divorce*, when he proclaimed that Truth 'never comes into the world, but like a bastard, to the ignominy of him that brought her forth'. At Zermatt the black silhouette of the Matterhorn against the stars suggested a poem, but, recalling Whymper, he began another, 'Zermatt. To the Matterhorn', which he finished later. After climbing up to the Riffel-Alp hotel, to which Emma had gone on a mule, and lunching there, Hardy exhausted himself by taking part in the search for a lost Englishman.

By the time he reached Geneva he was so ill that he stayed in bed, where he listened to the playing of a fountain, the same, he remembered next year when he heard of her death, near which the Austrian empress whose beauty fascinated him in his younger days was murdered by an Italian anarchist. (How much Hardy knew of Elizabeth's restless, unhappy life in her last years cannot be assessed. He had doubtless heard of the drowning of her cousin Ludwig II on the edge of the Starnberger See, after his imprisonment for reckless extravagance in the maniacal pursuit of castle splendours in the Bavarian Alps, but, whatever sensational news had reached England of the death of her son Rudolf, the Crown Prince, at the end of January 1889, it is doubtful whether many truthful details of his suicide after murdering his young mistress Marie Vetsera at Mayerling had escaped.) Emma, none the worse for her adventures, visited the cemetery, where she discovered the tomb of the scientist Sir Humphry Davy, one of her collateral ancestors. More orderly than her previous ones, her diary of the tour, from 15 June to 7 July, is vivid and succinct, and suggests that she was in good health and spirits.

The Hardys were soon off again, while Max Gate was being repaired, this time to Wells Cathedral and to Longleat, where they examined the library and the architecture. They then proceeded to Salisbury, where they stayed at the Crown Hotel. On 10 August, after a visit to Stonehenge, which Emma had not seen, they attended evensong at the cathedral, where Hardy underlined the verse from the first lesson, 'To what purpose cometh there to me incense from Sheba . . .? your burnt offerings are not acceptable, nor your sacrifices sweet unto me.' 'The Impercipient' was already taking root. Late that night he watched the moonlight creeping round the statuary of the west front, and concluded that the Close, 'under the full summer moon on a windless midnight', was as beautiful a scene as any he knew; years later, his description of it produced the poem 'A Cathedral Façade at Midnight'. Before August ended, while at Arlington Manor with Emma and many distinguished guests, he visited Salisbury again to meet Madeleine Rolland, whom he had recently encouraged to translate *Tess* into French.

About this time, delighted at having found a poem in *Odes and Other Poems* dedicated to him, Hardy invited the author to Max Gate. This was John Cowper Powys, on holiday at Montacute, west of Yeovil, where his father had been appointed vicar twelve years earlier after a period in Dorchester. Now in his third year after leaving Corpus Christi, Cambridge, Powys travelled by train to Dorchester, then followed the path by the railings of Fordington Great Field. Hardy received him kindly, showed him the manuscript of *Tess*, had tea with him on the lawn, and excited his interest in Edgar Allan Poe's 'powerful and extraordinary' poem 'Ulalume'. John was so pleased with his reception that he invited the Hardys to Montacute. To his 'delighted surprise' they accepted the invitation. He told his family that the greatest living writer was coming, and was very excited when their guests stepped off the train, Hardy wearing a light tweed suit with knickerbockers and black stockings, which reminded him of William Barnes when he walked in stately fashion down South Walk, Dorchester, past Rothesay House, where the Powyses had lived. But for the 'hawk's eye' of Hardy, John would never have noticed the 'odd little creases and criss-cross wrinkles' which frost had created in the mud on the road. He took him to the abbey farm and church, which illustrated, as Hardy pointed out, the ancient practice of building the chancel 'a little askew' to represent the sinking of Jesus's head to one side as he 'gave up the ghost'. There was much to admire in the architecture of Montacute House, the Elizabethan splendour of a historic village built of mellow stone from the neighbouring Ham Hill quarries, as Emma and he were conducted over it by the squire's son and heir.

After completing the short story 'The Grave by the Handpost', Hardy took to cycling. He had bought a Rover Cob, and it was while they were out together in September that Emma had another cycling accident and sprained her ankle. While she was recovering, he enjoyed cycling for a few days in the neighbourhood with Rudyard Kipling, who had recently returned from America, where he had grown tired of living with his wife's relatives, and published some of his best books, including *Captains Courageous*. Hardy had recommended him to the Savile Club. He now lived at Rottingdean near Brighton, and thought he would like to buy a house near Weymouth. They found one at Rodwell, overlooking Portland Roads, but difficulties arose and nothing came of it. This may have been the lonely house which, according to Kipling's biographer, was kept by an elderly lady who, when each tried to impress by telling her privately who the other was, said she had heard of neither, a comment on the relativity of fame which amused both as they returned to Max Gate. Fine weather in October induced Hardy to cycle one day to Wells and Glastonbury, and to Sherborne Abbey on another. He and Emma enjoyed many outings that autumn. His preface suggests that at some time during the year he prepared a detailed plan of *The Dynasts*. The winter seems to have passed quietly, Hardy most probably writing and revising poems for his next publication. On 5 February 1898 he made an anticipatory note, 'Write a prayer, or hymn, to One not Omnipotent, but hampered; striving for our good, but unable to achieve it except occasionally', an idea which he must have met years before in J. S. Mill, though he seems to have thought it original.

Early in 1898 Hardy and many other authors signed tributes which were sent by Gosse to Meredith, and by Gosse and Archer to Henrik Ibsen, for their seventieth birthdays. He gave considerable advice to Lady Grove on the production and publication of a story, which was not accepted, at a time when Mrs Henniker's novel *Sowing the Sand* was being favourably reviewed. In London during most of May and the whole of June, he and Emma occupied a flat in Wynnstay Gardens, Kensington, where they had to be on guard against cyclists when crossing the streets. At one of Sir Henry Thompson's 'octaves' (dinners of eight courses for eight people at eight o'clock) he met Sir William Russell, who had been knighted in 1895, and talked with him again on war experiences. The next morning he heard that Gladstone had died at Hawarden; a few days later he visited Westminster Hall to see him unostentatiously lying in state. Constable & Co. invited him to write an introduction to the works of Henry Fielding, but he declined, feeling strongly that Fielding's attitude towards the peasantry was feudal, and that he would be accused of invidiousness if he were critical of another novelist; the work was undertaken by Gosse. Much of Hardy's time was spent reading for *The Dynasts* at the British Museum, where by chance he came across a passage concerning the battle of Waterloo which suggested his poem 'The Peasant's Confession'. No doubt Emma and he met a number of friends at their clubs, but he did little dining out, after finding (for no disclosed reason) that the practice did not suit him. On returning to Max Gate, they resumed cycling, visiting some places, Weymouth for example, for sketching purposes. Hardy's immediate aim was to complete preparations for an illustrated volume of his poems. Architecture always afforded a strong interest, and he made a cycling tour with his brother in the heat of July along dusty roads over the Mendips to Bristol and Gloucester, at both of which places he attended cathedral services; in Gloucester Cathedral he particularly wished to see for himself evidence supporting the view that the perpendicular style of architecture was 'invented' there. Towards the end of August he cycled to see Major Henniker near Blandford, where the Southern Army was on manoeuvres; at first they had been planned in the Dorchester area, and the Hardys had hoped that he would be able to stay with them. Hardy's visit to Exeter Cathedral had been postponed, but in the latter part of September it became a priority; he was completing his sketches for *Wessex Poems*, and probably had an illustration for 'My Cicely' in view.

Varied in quality and technique, Hardy's pen-and-ink illustrations, copied or original, are with a few exceptions interesting and significant rather than charming; some of the more impressive gain from the use of different tones of wash to create twilight effects. Architectural interiors tend to be linear and flat; human figures are shadowy or dark silhouettes. Some sketches are related to the

Napoleonic war; several are devoted to local scenes; a plain outline of a vase-like container in a surround of radiating lines for the transcendence which 'rayed the distant urn' of the fallen comrades in 'The Casterbridge Captains' was rejected. Altogether 31 were printed, that of the entrance to Stinsford churchyard as the frontispiece, its text 'At mothy curfew-tide / They've a way of whispering to me' linking it with 'Friends Beyond'. Twelve, not always the best, were reproduced as full-page illustrations, the remainder as head- or tail-pieces to individual poems. Whether at the publisher's wish or the author's, five poems were added to the volume: 'The Fire at Tranter Sweatley's', 'Heiress and Architect' (with a full-page illustration), 'The Two Men', 'Lines' (recited by Ada Rehan as an epilogue to a performance on behalf of Mrs Jeune's holiday fund for City children), and 'I look into my glass' (written at the time of *The Well-Beloved*, where its prose counterpart will be found). Only four of the poems in the collection had been previously published: the above 'Lines', 'The Sergeant's Song' (part of it) in *The Trumpet-Major*, 'The Stranger's Song' in 'The Three Strangers', 'The Fire at Tranter Sweatley's' in 1875 and (the original, unbowdlerized version) in Lionel Johnson's *The Art of Thomas Hardy*. A glossary was intended to accompany this poem, but it was not published until a later edition, when the title was changed to 'The Bride-Night Fire'. It looks as if hasty measures were taken by Harper & Brothers to have their London edition ready for the Christmas sales. Hardy had proposed financing this publication, to ensure that his publishers were not 'out of pocket'.

Poems of a predominantly narrative cast take up at least one-half of the volume. Among these are five relating to the Napoleonic war, some of which could have been designed for the ballad sequence which Hardy had imagined as 'an Iliad of Europe from 1789 to 1815'. Among those with Dorchester or Casterbridge settings, one or two may have been earlier intended for prose fiction, including the best of them, 'The Dance at the Phoenix'; 'Her Death and After' suggests a lame attempt to revive Gothic fiction. In its eighteenth-century disguise 'My Cicely' seems to be based on the journey Hardy is said to have made with his brother Henry by cycle to their cousin Tryphena's home and grave at Topsham (some years, rather than a few months, after her death); if so, the poem dramatizes the shock he felt on discovering that his 'lost prize', idealized by memory, had commonly served at the bar of her husband's inn. More remarkable and cheerful, 'Friends Beyond', a dramatized forerunner of 'Jubilate', must have originated from Hardy's visit to his mother on 10 October 1897, when she remembered the story told by Elizabeth Downton, the monthly nurse who attended his birth. Sixteen of the fifty-one poems belong to the pre-novel period of Hardy's life, most of them being composed in sonnet form in 1866. Some, at the very outset, stress fundamental heterodoxies of belief, based on the new scientific outlook. The first and final poems (the latter being taken as either 'In a Eweleaze near Weatherbury' or 'I look into my glass') round the whole, introducing and reinforcing the dominant thought of time and change and chance. 'Amabel' and the 'She, to Him' sonnets turn on the effect of age on beauty and love; 'The Temporary the All' conveys the irony of life which makes us anticipate better things, only to realize in later years, as Hardy had done with a vengeance, that nothing has surpassed all that we thought preliminary to the best. With an utterly sceptical attitude towards the question of whether the Ultimate will have power to dispel 'Earth's old glooms and pains', and reminders of the nighness of life and death, of the Darwinism of nature, and of the complete lack of evidence for belief in Providence or heaven or life beyond death, except in people's memories, Hardy 'exacts a full look at the Worst', as he meant to do.

Wessex Poems shows how his 'spirit for poetic pains' adapted itself to verse with varying degrees of difficulty and skill. The volume was received with little enthusiasm; the *Saturday Review* could hardly have gone further in its condemnation. Lionel Johnson in the *Outlook* thought the title rather cruel to a Wessex which he did not think 'wholly Leopardian'. Hardy valued the praise of friends such as Leslie Stephen, Gosse, and Swinburne, to whom he had sent copies. In answer to Gosse's reply, he ingenuously declared that the poems were lying about, and he did not know what to do with them; more significantly, he recognized that his principle of giving content priority over form would be unpopular in an age when it seemed fashionable 'to view poetry as the art of saying nothing with mellifluous preciosity'. William Archer's phrase 'seeing all the words of the dictionary on one plane', with reference to 'The Peasant's Confession', pleased him; it summed up his policy of drawing his poetic diction from the whole of the English language, including archaisms and dialect words; it may have fortified an intention, which his opening poem seems to declare, of extending the language, wherever he felt it necessary or convenient, with arbitrary coinages, some of which were to prove puzzling, confusing, and even obstinately quirkish.

He probably did not realize how bitterly his wife was provoked by some of the poems. She must have been familiar with 'Ditty', the poem which expressed his love for her in 1870, but whatever satisfaction its inclusion gave her was more than outweighed by the satiric humour of 'The Ivy-Wife', the yearning for another woman in 'At an Inn', the implicit acknowledgment in 'Thoughts of Phena' that he would have been happier with his cousin, regret for a lost love (almost certainly Tryphena) in the histrionic posturing of 'Her Immortality', in 'In a Eweleaze near Weatherbury' (dated 1890, the year of her death), and the 'darling mother' of 'To a Motherless Child', later described as a whimsy, based on a thought which came to Jude and could have occurred to Hardy when he met Tryphena's daughter at Topsham, as he seems to have done. Emma's jealousies sharpened her intuitive perceptions, and she knew that Hardy's longings for the unattainable spelt disenchantment with her. Her friend Alfred Pretor, Cambridge bachelor don, classical scholar and author, whose home was near Weymouth, did his best to assure her that Hardy's poetic memories were fanciful and had no bearing on his present life. Occasionally she may have made allowance for the difference between the imaginative poet who sought refuge in a creative life of emotion and Hardy the man who gave up much time to companion her in cycling excursions and at concerts, parties, and other forms of entertainment in London. Deep down, however, she felt he was unforgivable, at times even detestable. While she lived, and until he read her diaries, he probably did not suspect how much she suffered, or how low he could sink in her esteem.

Emma found it a relief to have her niece, Walter Gifford's daughter Lilian, periodically with her from the summer onwards; a bicycle was provided for her, and they enjoyed outings together. Her brother Gordon came in September, and their presence helped to lessen tensions between their aunt and Hardy, who spent much time cumulatively teaching Gordon architecture. He liked young people, and grew fond of his niece and nephew, who both stayed until the end of the year at least. Emma and he continued to have their principal meals together, but she became more independent. She had furnished both attics, and could live and sleep there happily apart much of the time in her own imaginative world. Just when this partial separation occurred, after the building of extensions at the rear of the house, is uncertain, but in April 1899 she wrote rhapsodically to Rebekah Owen (now settled with her sister in the Lake District, at Belmount Hall, north of Hawkshead) on sleeping in an attic or two, and finding sweet refuge and solace in company with the sun, moon, and stars, and the birds that came to the table provided for them – whenever a hurricane had not sent it flying. She painted and sewed, read considerably, and became ambitious as a writer, attempting poetry and stories with little success. Letters on birds and animals, and an article on cats, were published, and she spoke with such frequency and exaggeration on the extent to which she had helped her husband in writing that it seems to have been thought prudent to destroy the manuscript of *A Laodicean*, which she had written largely at his dictation. Intellectually she does not seem to have advanced; her religious faith had strengthened, so much so that she took Clodd to task after reading the copy of his *Pioneers of Evolution* which he had sent Hardy early in 1897. She strongly objected to the chapters in which he had taken pains to disprove the existence of God and Christ; no evolutionary theory could make her believe that man had not always been man; and, all being limitless, with no permanence of form or time, she saw no reason why, after death, we should not 'rise in *myriads* invisible to such eyes as ours'. She would do all in her power to 'stem the torrent of misery hanging over the next generation'. Her religious ideas were to become more idiosyncratic and eccentric. Plainly her differences with Hardy were not just personal; as a creative writer he had to go his way. They could agree on a *modus vivendi*, but they had little respect for each other's beliefs.

Emma revealed much to her friends. In the above letter to Rebekah Owen her disposition to rule is evident: 'I, too, keep state-apartments but am not permitted to ask anyone to occupy them; a woman's ruling of a house, [*sic*] and friends is far happier for *all*, than a man's.' Thinking of some of Hardy's recently published poems and of *Jude*, she commented: 'He should be the last man to disparage marriage! I have been a devoted wife for at least twenty years or more – but the last four or five alas! Fancy it is our silver wedding this year! The *thorn* is in my side still.' The life of an eminent man's wife was a trial, she lamented, 'except a Browning and a Barrett meet', but, she added, as if it supplied the key to her misfortune, Browning was not an unbeliever. Offering marital advice on 20 August 1899 to Mrs Kenneth Grahame, sister of the artist Winifred Thomson, she says that marriages are occasionally happy, and always so if husband and wife are both Christians. She can scarcely think man capable of true and enduring love; 'perhaps there is no woman "whom custom will not stale"'. At 50, a man's feelings often take a completely new course, his matrimonial thoughts becoming oriental until 'he wearies of the most perfect, and suitable, wife chosen in his earlier life'. She is clearly thinking of herself. Interference from members of either family is often the cause of estrangement, she continues; 'a woman does not object to be ruled by her husband, so much as she does by a relative at his back'. 'Keeping separate a good deal is a wise plan in crises . . . and *expecting little* neither gratitude, nor attentions, love, nor *justice*, nor anything you may set your heart on. . . . If he belongs to the public in any way, years of devotion count for nothing.' What Jemima, aged and failing at Bockhampton, could really do against her at this stage is difficult to imagine; Hardy knew enough to judge for himself. Next March the artist Bertha Newcombe heard much from Emma at Max Gate, and sympathized, as she reported to Mrs Gosse. Emma described how she had first met Hardy, an 'ill-grown, under-sized young architect' whose genius she discovered and encouraged. Miss Newcombe was not surprised that she resented being slighted by everyone 'now that her ugly duckling has grown into such a charming swan', but thought it silly of her 'not to rejoice in the privilege of being wife to so great a man'. Emma's disproportioning of truth in her own favour is obvious; it shows the spiteful impropriety of a warped mind. Once distracted from her obsession, which was yet to result in less sane outbreaks, she could enjoy her own hobbies, and life and company, too much sometimes for Hardy's comfort. Even at her best, her dominating personality was soon evident. 'She asserts herself as much as possible and is a great bore, but at the same time is so kind and goodhearted', Bertha Newcombe wrote.

Mrs Henniker had followed the reviews of *Wessex Poems* with keen interest, and sent Hardy a report on them. He was delighted with her story 'Three Corporals' in the *Idler*, wished it had been longer, and, on discovering that it was mostly a transcript from life, urged her to write a series of true army stories. Congratulations on his poems came from Rebekah Owen, and from the poet Watts-Dunton, friend and guardian of Swinburne, who had lent him his copy. An article on form in poetry by Gosse which had been stimulated by *Wessex Poems* led Hardy to comment on

Browning as '*the* literary puzzle' of the nineteenth century, and ask how 'smug Christian optimism worthy of a dissenting grocer' could be found in one who was 'so vast a seer and feeler when on neutral ground'; he had earlier dismissed Tennyson as 'a great artist, but a mere Philistine of a thinker'.

For the London season of May and June 1899 the Hardys stayed at another flat (no 20) in Wynnstay Gardens. He spent a week with Edward Clodd at Aldeburgh, where the wet weather kept the guests, who included Walter Besant and the Egyptologist Flinders Petrie, indoors telling stories. For his birthday Emma gave him a Bible, and one is left speculating whether he, who never ceased to find it his spiritual mainstay, needed one, or whether she was inspired to think it might make him a true Christian husband. Two days later he spent Sunday with Dorothy Allhusen at Stoke Poges, where, after escorting the beautiful Duchess of Manchester to the poet's grave, at her request, he had to listen to her leisurely recital of Gray's 'Elegy Written in a Country Churchyard' from beginning to end, a feat of memory and endurance which recalled tedious recitals inflicted on him from the Scriptures by a handsome young dairymaid when he taught at Sunday School. Later he attended Pinero's *The Gay Lord Quex* with Clodd, met A. E. Housman, and travelled to Putney to see Swinburne, whom he found engaging, frank, and rather childlike. Perhaps as a result of their conversation, he was prompted to visit with Sir George Douglas the church in which Shelley and Mary Godwin were married. So cheerful and enthusiastic did he find Meredith at his home near Box Hill that he wished he could see him more often. Beyond an enjoyable afternoon at Gosse's, and a midnight ramble by lantern light round Westminster Abbey, after he and some friends had been admitted by the Dean's daughter, little further is known of his London holiday, except that he was rather badly afflicted with 'influenza', which he thought was the cause of an eye affliction from which he suffered recurrently for the rest of his life.

In retrospect Hardy thought that his zeal for cycling reached its peak in the summer of 1899. He never attempted more than 40 or 50 miles a day, and Emma often accompanied him, both feeling fitter in mind and body as a result of vigorous pedalling in the fresh air. A tour in the New Forest region at the end of July had to be abandoned because of the heat; it took him to Southampton, where, missing London orchestral music, he listened to a concert in the pier pavilion, admiring the evening dress of those in front of

him as he sat self-consciously in his cycling attire. A photograph
taken by the Revd Thomas Perkins, perhaps when Hardy and
Emma visited him three weeks later, shows him holding his
high-handled bicycle, with a light modish hat, stiff collar and tie,
loose jacket, woollen waistcoat, knickerbockers, and high, rather
thick stockings. Mr Perkins was the secretary of the Dorset Photographic Club, an ardent anti-vivisectionist, and rector of Turnworth near Blandford; he and Mr Trist, editor of a publication by
the London Anti-Vivisectionist Society, had visited Max Gate the
previous August. Emma and Hardy stayed for the evening harvest
festival service, left the rectory late, and cycled by moonlight all the
way home. Occasionally he would accompany Hermann Lea,
another member of the Dorset Photographic Club, usually by
cycle, sometimes on foot – as he was to do, whenever convenient,
for some years – for the identification and illustration of scenes and
places in the 'Wessex' novels. Emma's free-wheeling exploits were
long remembered in Dorchester, especially as she came down
High West Street in a long velvet dress early in the morning, her
feet on rests attached to the front-wheel fork, and the pedals flying
round and round; no longer the attractive rider by Beeny Cliff
'with bright hair flapping free', she could be equally bold, boyish,
and venturesome. Her oddities were well known; townspeople
tapped their heads as she passed in her world of elation, indifferent to the threat she posed for others and herself. At Max Gate the
lawn was being prepared for croquet; she had a swing where she
could relax, and she taught her nephew Gordon how to paint.

The land on which Stonehenge stood was up for sale, and on
24 August James Milne's interview with Hardy on the best means
of ensuring its preservation appeared in the *Daily Chronicle*. Only
the previous afternoon he had suddenly appeared at Max Gate,
before the letter which announced his coming had arrived, and
talked to Hardy in the garden 'summer-house', the bulk of the
'interview' being based on an article or letter which Hardy happened to have roughed out on the subject, stressing the advantage
of seeing the monument 'in the dusk of evening', as he had
realized when viewing it during the day with Emma in August
1897. On 25 August the Stonehenge scene from *Tess* appeared in
the same paper. Three weeks later Hardy was met there by Sir
Francis and Lady Jeune, and taken by car to their house-party at
Arlington Manor; so fast seemingly was he driven that he thought
cycling preferable.

He had written many poems, having found this form of intensive composition 'so much more consonant' to his 'natural way of
thinking and feeling' (as he told Arthur Symons later, in September 1904) that he was reluctant to return to prose. Poetry gave him
the freedom to write more incidentally, whenever he was in the
mood, on whatever appealed to him. Just recently, confronted by
forms of insect life in the light of his study lamp, he had mused on
the relativity of things and composed 'An August Midnight'. He
refused Gosse's request to write on Zola, believing him to be no
artist but a 'man of affairs' who would have been ready to write on
the statistics of crime or commerce, and had now found himself as
a reformer. Late in November, after staying with Mr de la Fontaine
and another guest at Athelhampton Hall, he had still to finish
'Enter a Dragoon'; it was completed about the same time as his
final prose story, 'A Changed Man', which was sent to Clement
Shorter on 29 January 1900. By this time, knowing that his publishers Harper & Brothers, who had taken over Osgood, McIlvaine
& Co., were in financial difficulties, Hardy was already anticipating publication by Macmillan & Co.

The sooner it began and the sooner it was over, the better,
Hardy had written to Mrs Henniker just before the outbreak of the
Boer War in October 1899; however much he deplored warfare,
none could be more martial than he if it had to come, or 'like better'
to write about it. On 20 October he witnessed the embarkation of
5000 troops at Southampton; he had cycled down to ensure that
Major Henniker received his letter of good wishes but, failing to
meet him and learning that he was to sail with his battalion of
Coldstream Guards the next day, he sent his nephew with it and
was disappointed that Gordon did not meet Mrs Henniker. Late at
night in wind and rain on 2 November he watched a battery of the
Royal Field Artillery marching from Dorchester barracks to the
railway station, and imagined the grief of wives as he witnessed
their farewells. The death in battle of a drummer from a neighbouring village resulted in the poem 'Drummer Hodge'. Much of
Christmas Day was devoted to a sturdy and erudite defence of his
poem 'A Christmas Ghost-Story' (in which a soldier's phantom
upholds the Christmas of peace on earth) against an editorial
which appeared that morning in the *Daily Chronicle*, asserting that
Hardy's soldier was unworthy of the Dublin Fusiliers who had
fought heroically by the Tugela river. Other poems followed, none
more noble than 'The Souls of the Slain', in which the accent is not

on the heroism of the soldiers in battle but on what was memorably kind and honourable in their lives. The suffering of horses in battle, their terror and mangling, preyed on his mind. He followed the fighting keenly, especially the fortunes of the Coldstream Guards, and thought the war would last three years, rather than the three months which had been forecast. In February he shocked his friend Henry Moule by suggesting that, since Christianity had failed to keep the peace for 2000 years, we had better try another religion, Buddhism for example. On Christmas Eve 1900, some time after writing the last of his 'war effusions', he was pleased to inform Mrs Henniker that none of them was 'Jingo or Imperial'.

Hardy had continued to give careful attention to Gordon Gifford's basic training in architecture; early in 1900 he made arrangements for his apprenticeship with Charles Blomfield, elder son of Sir Arthur Blomfield, who had died suddenly the previous autumn, not long before the Hardys had expected to see him and his wife at Broadwey. In London he received a good report of Gordon's progress, met Sir George Douglas and Edward Clodd, and lunched with Mrs Henniker, who was still writing successfully. In the meantime Emma had sprained her ankle – while cycling, he assumed. When he returned to Max Gate, after attending Dorothy Allhusen's large party at Stoke Court and revisiting Gray's grave, she left for London, where he joined her for a few weeks in June. At Max Gate they had a number of distinguished guests: first, the sculptor Hamo Thornycroft and his wife, with both of whom Hardy cycled to Weymouth; then, early in August, A. E. Housman, Clodd, and Arthur Symons, whose recent book of poetry he had enjoyed and whose *Symbolist Movement in Literature* he had found disappointing. With another guest, the eminent lawyer Sir Frederick Pollock, son of the friend he met in the early years of the Rabelais Club, he cycled one day to Portland Bill and back over some rough and hilly roadway, which must have been tiring for one who had just passed his sixtieth birthday. Cycling continued until the autumn, often with Emma, one excursion being to Bulbarrow with Lilian Gifford, Mrs Hardy being driven by Hermann Lea from Mrs Wood Homer's, near Puddletown, because she was too tired to continue the journey on her bicycle.

In October Emma, who seems to have spent long periods in apparent indifference to her relatives, was jolted by news of her sister Helen Holder's illness, and went to nurse her, and to attend to her affairs (with Hardy's advice), at Lee-on-Solent, Hampshire.

How often she had seen her since her marriage is unknown; an undated letter to her from her friend Mrs Dashwood refers to a visit which Emma had expected to make. In her absence Hardy cycled with his niece Lilian, who, not being fond of exercise, found life dull at Max Gate in her aunt's absence. On 9 November he informed Rebekah Owen, who had proposed visiting Dorchester, that Emma had just returned, and that they would be pleased to see her and her sister. When Rebekah arrived, leaving her sister to care for their old maid at Belmount Hall, Emma had gone back to Helen. Writing home skittishly towards the end of the month, Miss Owen told how, chaperoned by Lilian, she and Hardy cycled via Came Park to Ridgeway; later she described her as 'fat as butter' with 'round red cheeks between which the tiny nose is scarcely visible'. One evening, while she was being taken by Hardy, after dark, at her request, along the 'Mixen Lane' of *The Mayor of Casterbridge*, Emma returned; Miss Owen was certain that Lilian's informative letters had brought her back. Rebekah was now staying with the Moules, and hoping to cycle again with Hardy, to see Mrs Sheridan at Frampton Court. Mrs Sheridan, she reported, says that Emma leads him a hell of a life, and thinks her half-cracked; Mrs Moule says she is the devil. Her husband's emphatic 'Poor woman, she is phenomenally plain!' and his outbursts against her general unbearableness may have seemed amusing to his wife, daughter, and guest, but they obviously indicate his sense of a tragic reality at Max Gate. Helen Holder died on 6 December.

Hardy's poem 'A Second Attempt', written, as far as he remembered, about 1900, suggests that he made an effort to achieve reconciliation with Emma. If so, any accord which followed must have been brittle and brief, leaving him with 'pale and hoar' prospects. It may therefore afford a clue to his more remarkable poem 'By the Century's Deathbed', afterwards known as 'The Darkling Thrush', which appeared in the *Graphic* at the end of the year. A wonderful descriptive passage in W. H. Hudson's *Nature in Downland* on the pleasure found in life by the missel-thrush in darkest winter, as he flings out his notes in artless joy, had recalled a poem in *The Christian Year* on the cheerful song of the redbreast in the dreary blast of autumn, an example for the thoughtful seer when he looks darkling ahead. Preferring Darwinian truth to Keble's Christian faith, Hardy reverted to one aspect of his Unfulfilled Intention theory, thinking that the emotional sensitivity of man is far ahead of the Creator's purpose, and that greater happiness is found in instinctive natural life than in the enlightened thinker's. The imagined landscape is a projection of the poet's gloom, and he has little cause for carolling. The bird's song is the expression of 'some blessed Hope', of which he is unaware. The prolongation of the war was depressing, but the word 'darkling' which he subsequently thought more suitable for his title, had deeper overtones; it recalled 'Dover Beach' and what he had in mind when he wrote his initials with Emma's against the title of Arnold's poem in September 1896:

> Ah, love, let us be true
> To one another! for the world, which seems
> To lie before us like a land of dreams,
> So various, so beautiful, so new,
> Hath really neither joy, nor love, nor light,
> Nor certitude, nor peace, nor help for pain;
> And we are here as on a darkling plain
> Swept with confused alarms of struggle and flight,
> Where ignorant armies clash by night.

21

The Dynasts

'Things are as they are, and will be brought to their destined issue.' This reflection from the *Agamemnon*, which had come to Jude at a time of unspeakable calamity, brought some consolation to Hardy, who realized that his stresses were small in comparison with the grief and suffering which the Boer War had brought to many. His principal 'help for pain' was action. Outings and meetings with friends afforded relief; the writing of poetry was even more fulfilling. He hoped to have another collection of poems published in May, but realized by March that he and his publishers needed much more time, especially for publication in America. On Sunday, 27 January, five days after her death, he had written verses in praise of Queen Victoria which were to be printed immediately in *The Times*, and supply the dedicatory opening of this next volume. Shortly afterwards, in a lengthy discussion with William Archer at Max Gate, he spoke among other things on war and pessimism. His belief that war was doomed 'in the fulness of time' because of its 'absurdity' makes his poem 'The Sick Battle-God' look over-optimistic. His own 'practical philosophy' (related, that is, to human endeavour) was melioristic; 'what are my books', he asked, 'but one plea against "man's inhumanity to man" – to woman – and to the lower animals?' He was prepared to concede that there might be 'a consciousness, infinitely far off' striving to express itself though 'always baffled and blundering', and it was on this faintly hopeful note, not nearly as optimistic as the conclusion of *The Dynasts*, that his new volume of poetry was to end.

By the beginning of April the Hardys were ready for a change. Emma did not care for the people of Dorchester, and wished she lived in Devon, which seemed almost a 'perfect' county 'in every way'; local people were 'rougher and more evil-speaking' than Devonians. She may have discovered that local people indulged in malicious gossip at her expense rather than that they were foul-mouthed. Hardy had been plunged into grief by the death of a cat, his very first, which had been killed by the mail-train on the night of 1 April. Three of their cats had suffered a similar fate a quarter of a mile away from home, and 'the violent death of a dumb creature' made him 'revile the contingencies of a world in which animals are in the best of cases pitiable for their limitations'. He looked forward to meeting Sir George Douglas and Florence Henniker in London. There he had to sleep in a basement the first night; Emma did not arrive until more than a week later, staying at the Alexandra Club before they found accommodation at 27 Oxford Terrace. He had seen Irving in *Coriolanus*, dined with Norwegian visitors at the Gosses', attended the private view of the Royal Academy exhibition, where he met Frederic Harrison, and sent Emma advice on the need to wear a black hat and feather in memory of the Queen; 'some women, but not ladies exactly, are in bright colours', he thought it necessary to add. Mrs Henniker had invited them to her house near Windsor. They attended concerts to hear the violinists Ysaye and Kubelik. Hardy's interest in music was on the increase; he wished he had known Sir Arthur Sullivan and Sir John Stainer who had recently died, and felt that the story of the theatre was 'nothing' compared to that of music. He dined with Sir Henry Thompson at one of his 'octaves', and at Maurice Hewlett's met the actress Sarah Bernhardt, who 'talked to him pensively' on her awareness of approaching age, though she seemed 'youthful enough' when he and Emma saw her a day or two later in M. Rostand's *L'Aiglon*. From Max Gate he sent her a copy of Madeleine Rolland's translation of *Tess*, hoping she would appear in a French dramatization of it. In the meantime, despite an attack of 'influenza', he had enjoyed a long weekend at Aldeburgh with J. G. Frazer, author of *The Golden Bough*, the novelist Anthony Hope (Hawkins) and others, sailing in Clodd's boat on the Alde, and walking from Woodbridge two days later to see the rosebush planted by the Omar Khayyám Club on Edward FitzGerald's grave at Boulge. In the intense heat this had proved too much for him, as he wrote, after receiving her greetings, to Mrs Henniker; nor had Emma completely recovered from the influenza which had kept her indoors most of the time in London. After he had attended Sir Walter Besant's funeral at Hampstead on 12 June, they left for home without seeing several friends as they had planned.

On the last Saturday of the month about 100 members and guests of the Whitefriars Club, a London society of journalists and writers, arrived at Max Gate, the ladies' new dresses strewn with dust after travelling the last part of the journey by road in open carriages. Although led by Clement Shorter, the outing had been organized by Charles Hankinson ('Clive Holland'), a writer whose persistent demands for attention, in his zeal to publish articles on Hardy and Wessex, were ultimately to outwear his subject's patience. A marquee had been erected on the lawn for tea, with access from the drawing-room. The visit was brief, and no one realized until long afterwards that the old lady who waved a handkerchief to them after they had passed the end of the Bockhampton road was the author's mother, who, in her eagerness to see this demonstration of her son's fame, had been brought down to the Puddletown–Dorchester road in a wheelchair by Kate and Mary. Hardy's main summer business was the final preparation of his next volume of poems, which he completed in time to welcome Dr Garnett of the British Museum to Max Gate during the third week of August. *Poems of the Past and the Present* appeared in November 1901, about the time of Sir George Douglas's visit to Max Gate and 'Egdon Heath'.

Published by Harper & Brothers in London and New York, *Poems of the Past and the Present* was limited to 500 copies in each country. The London edition, like that of *Wessex Poems*, included a small proportion specially bound in white and gold, and completely gilt-edged, for the Christmas market. It had rather a favourable reception, and a second impression (half for America), with a few revisions, was ready by the middle of January 1902. The volume opens with the Boer War pieces, followed by travel poems, occasioned chiefly by the 1887 Italian tour, with 'Lausanne' and 'Zermatt' from the 1897 visit to Switzerland. The main section is aptly headed 'Miscellaneous Poems'. Most of them were recent, only three, including 'The Ruined Maid', belonging to the 1865–7 period. More common than any other type are those philosophical poems which inevitably came to Hardy's mind as he pondered the 'Overworld' conception of *The Dynasts*, with its emphasis on the blindness of the Immanent Will to human injustice and suffering. One poem reveals him as a proponent of the 'higher criticism'. Pessimism strikes deep notes; it is more personal in 'A Wasted Illness', and deepest of all in 'In Tenebris'. The three poems of 'Retrospect' give a final stress to the main emphases, and of them none is more poignant than 'Memory and I', which asks where now are the poet's youth, joy, hope, faith, and love. Whether Emma Hardy understood the personification of the final answer, or regarded it as a reference to her loss of beauty with age, she probably identified herself with the person addressed in 'Between us now', saw the Valency valley recalled with the transports of love in 'A Spot', and recognized tragic irony in the juxtaposition of retrospective childhood happiness in 'The Self-Unseeing' and the despair of 'In Tenebris'. However impatient with the poet's unsatisfied yearnings relative to the past in 'To Lizbie Browne' or to more recent times in 'A Broken Appointment', she was deeply upset by the way she seemed to be exposed to the world by her husband. His writings could be more faithful, truthful, and helpful, she complained when she wrote to Rebekah Owen on 4 March, imploring her not to accept as anything but fiction the 'moans, and fancies' which seemed to be personal; they were written to please others, or himself, 'but not *me*, far otherwise'.

The previous year had ended with reflective satisfaction for Hardy, after he had enjoyed the artistic composition and rough rustic humour of 'The Homecoming'. He had just publicized his views to an unprecedented extent, and felt assured, on contemplating the contradictions and futilities of various philosophic systems, and the fate of Coleridge, that everyone should 'make a philosophy for himself out of his own experience'. On New Year's Day he drew comfort from the thought that what is called 'pessimism' ('a full look at the Worst') can bring no disappointment but only gain. Replying on May Day to a review of *Apology for Nature*, in which Maeterlinck suggests that nature practises a just morality beyond our ken, he insisted that the difficulty recognized by philosophers such as Schopenhauer, Hartmann, Haeckel, and most people called pessimists, is insurmountable, for pain exists, and nature is either blind to her actions or an automaton unable to control them. To model ourselves on her 'apparent' conduct 'can only bring disaster to humanity'. After reading his friend Clodd's work on the scientist T. H. Huxley, he had expressed the view that the more we know of the laws and nature of the universe, the more ghastly it seems to be, and that, if theology could shed its supernatural lumber and retain only 'reverence and love for an ethical ideal', most thinkers would return to the fold, and 'our venerable old churches and cathedrals' would become the moving sources of moral and spiritual welfare they once were.

Hardy's friend Henry Rider Haggard, the popular romantic novelist, had an agricultural background. He had written *A Farmer's Year*, and was pursuing inquiries which led to the publication of his *Rural England*. In response to his questions Hardy referred him to his 1883 article 'The Dorsetshire Labourer', and wrote notes on more recent changes. The position had almost reversed since 1850 or 1855, farmers finding it difficult to recruit workers, who were now much better off and more migratory, many more finding work in towns. The reason for this, he thought, was that they did not enjoy the security of tenure that the lifehold system had given when it was common. One unfortunate result was the decay of folklore and traditional knowledge of country and people. He could recall when 'the places of burial even of the poor and tombless were all remembered', and the history of parishes and squires for 150 years. 'Such and such ballads appertained to such and such a locality, ghost tales were attached to particular sites, and nooks wherein wild herbs grew for the cure of divers maladies were pointed out readily.' Later, in June, under the pseudonym of 'History', Hardy illustrated his zeal for local history when he wrote three letters to the *Dorset County Chronicle* on the links between Dorchester and the actor Edmund Kean, telling the writer 'Dorset', who proposed to 'turn the hose' on such interest because Kean was the father of an illegitimate child, to turn it on his own 'Christian' uncharitableness.

Limited sales of his poetry and a general slump in his 'few poor' securities may explain why Hardy informed Clodd in May that he had almost ruined himself by buying a new free-wheel bicycle. *Tess* and *Jude* had ensured a continued demand for his novels, and he had no complaints against Harper's, whose 100,000 copies of *Tess* in the sixpenny paperback edition of 1900 had all been sold as part of a general advertising campaign on his behalf. Feeling insecure with a firm in financial difficulties and subordinate to publishers in New York, he had nevertheless resolved to find an independent London publisher when his contract expired on 4 April. He preferred to work with Macmillan, who had included all his novels except *Under the Greenwood Tree* (the copyright of which had not been relinquished by Chatto & Windus) in their Colonial Library, but decided to allow Harper's six months to sell off as much as possible of their stocks. Before the end of March agreement with Frederick Macmillan was far advanced; before the end of July he had sent his revision of the preface to *Far from the Madding Crowd* with alterations to two chapters, in addition to a few changes in *Tess* and *Jude*. During the wet summer he was busy correcting misprints and errors for Macmillan's uniform edition of his books from plates which had been used by Osgood, McIlvaine & Co., then by Harper & Brothers. His anxiety to retain and further enrich his literary association with 'Wessex' was heightened when he found 'The Wessex Novels' omitted from his copy of *Tess*, the first number of the reprint series; the inadvertence was soon rectified.

In January 1902 Hardy had attended the prestigious wedding of the son of the Earl and Countess of Ilchester and the daughter of the Marquess and Marchioness of Londonderry at St Peter's, Eaton Square. If he had not travelled with the bridesmaid Madeleine Stanley, he would not have been able to enter the church, so great was the throng inside and out. Afterwards he managed to speak to the Gosses in the drawing-room of Londonderry House. In the evening he attended the Vaudeville Theatre with Madeleine; next morning they 'sobered down' and attended service at St Paul's. Almost a year later he and Emma were present at Madeleine's wedding to St John Brodrick, Secretary of State for War, at St George's, Hanover Square. In the intervening period, at times of national rejoicing, the Hardys had decided to keep well away from the madding crowds in London. The Boer War had ended on 31 May, and a flag was flown at Max Gate when news of it arrived on Hardy's birthday; Emma was recovering from another cycling accident. The following weekend a massed thanksgiving service was held in Maumbury Rings. Soon afterwards crowds began to arrive in London from many parts of the world, and ceremonial rehearsals began, for the coronation of Edward VII in Westminster Abbey on 26 June. Two days before the expected event the capital was shocked to hear that the king was dangerously ill with appendicitis, that an operation was urgent, and the coronation postponed. There were grave fears that the king would not survive the operation, but it was successful, and the coronation took place in August.

The surgeon chosen at this critical juncture was Frederick Treves, to whom Hardy had written expressing his agreement with what he had to say on the medical care of soldiers in South Africa. Hardy had not forgotten that the first writing-desk he possessed (still in his study at Max Gate) had been bought when he was a boy from the shop in Dorchester where Treves's father conducted most of his upholstery and furniture business. Frederick was very young when he attended William Barnes's school, which he left in 1862 for the Merchant Taylors' School in London. On the sudden death of his father in 1867, his family left Dorchester for the city. After being a demonstrator at the London Hospital, and a field surgeon during the Boer War, he was appointed surgeon extraordinary to

Queen Victoria in 1900. His successful operation on Edward VII won him fame and a baronetcy. Dorset ties did much to increase the friendship that grew between him and Hardy.

Hardy's completion of the poem 'One We Knew' on 20 May 1902 suggests that reflections on the opening of *The Dynasts* had recalled his grandmother's reminiscences of the French Revolution and invasion fears in the south of England. As soon as he could, he set to work on his epic drama, taking time off for outings on his cycle, one to Blackmoor Vale. In the latter part of October he and Emma were in Bath, a city which bore witness to many distinguished people of a historic past. They stayed near where Pitt lived when news arrived of the defeat at Austerlitz that is said to have killed him; looking out very early in the morning, Hardy fancied he could see his emaciated form. He remembered his own earlier visits, to see Emma in 1873 and assist his father in 1877. On Sunday, after attending matins with Emma at Bath Abbey, he joined in evensong at St Mary Redcliffe, Bristol, the church associated with Chatterton, the 'marvellous' young poet who, in Wordsworth's words, 'perished in his pride'. He had cycled over from Bath, possibly to spend time with his cousin Nathaniel Sparks, the violin-repairer who was shortly to send him a violoncello. According to the account he wrote years later in his *Life*, it was in Bristol that, after falling into mud as he was cycling along one of its 'watered streets' and being 'rubbed down by a kindly coal-heaver with one of his sacks', he entered a 'lumber-shop' and purchased a copy of Hobbes's *Leviathan* for sixpence without realizing it was a first edition. Writing to Mrs Henniker a month after making this bargain, he seems to indicate very precisely that the purchase took place in Bath. He had read her account of the rejoicings in Suffolk on Colonel Henniker's return from South Africa, and thought she might like to read the obituary article he had written on Barnes's daughter ('Leader Scott') which he had written for *The Times*.

Hardy's literary preoccupations during the winter may have seemed an adequate reason for resigning from the committee set up to preside over the restoration of Fordington church, but they served as a cloak for his disapproval of departures from the old design towards a more grandiose structure. Lady Grove, who had recently returned from Morocco, hoped the Hardys would visit her at Sedgehill (near Shaftesbury) in February, but Emma was ill and he was confined indoors most of the time with rheumatism. During a period of 'enforced idleness' he had returned to Henry

James, reading his latest novel *The Wings of the Dove*; Emma also read it, and they argued a good deal about what happened to the characters. He was the only modern novelist Hardy could read; 'in small doses' he liked him exceedingly. So he informed Mrs Henniker on 17 March; before the month was over he wrote to thank her for a copy of her newly published *Contrasts*, sixteen short stories which he had read appreciatively. Shortly afterwards he thanked Arthur Symons for the gift of his *Lyrics*, a small book he could carry in his pocket and 'look into at pauses by gates and stiles'. At the end of April 'A Trampwoman's Tragedy', which he had written a year earlier and was to consider his most successful poem, was declined as 'too outspoken' for readers of *The Cornhill*; it was accepted by the *North American Review*, where it appeared in November.

Hardy took Emma to London in May 1903, but she was still poor in health, and returned home in little more than a week. He spent the Whitsun weekend as Edward Clodd's guest at Aldeburgh with Clement Shorter, Flinders Petrie, Henry Nevinson, and others. Not long afterwards Hardy, Clodd, and Shorter were late-night guests at Madame Tussaud's, a visit which made Shorter recall, when he read the final part of *The Dynasts* in 1908, how the three of them had 'pranced about', with Hardy wearing 'the Waterloo cocked hat'. Emma joined him in London at the beginning of June, but was disinclined to go out in the cold, wet weather; she was kept informed about the state of her cats and plants by Bessie Churchill, and returned after about two weeks. During this period Henry Moule, who had been ill in the early spring, was staying with his wife at Max Gate in the hope that the fresh upland air would aid his recovery. After looking forward to having Conquer Barrow and 'the hedge-side track' to Came Wood near him, he found many scenes to sketch in the neighbourhood and benefited from the change. Hardy stayed in the capital until early July, meeting friends and acquaintances at the Savile and the Athenaeum; he had publishing business to attend to, and probably found time for Napoleonic researches. He met Colonel and Mrs Henniker, sat for one of his Rothenstein portraits, and took Lilian Gifford to the Royal Academy *soirée*; the heat had fatigued him, but he enjoyed the crush for the delight it gave her. He attended a party at the Gosses' (17 Hanover Terrace, once the home of Wilkie Collins), but could not accept their invitation to dinner on 10 July. He was anxious to continue work on *The Dynasts* at home.

Wet weather did not seem to diminish the number of uninvited visitors who called at Max Gate, some of whom showed annoyance when they were told in the morning that they could not see Hardy until after 4 pm. He was pleased to see Nathaniel Sparks's son James, who came to finish a bronze medallion of him which he had worked on in 1902. The first part of *The Dynasts* was finished during September. He had intended not to publish it until the whole was completed, but it suddenly occurred to him that this might prove impossible, and he forwarded his untyped copy to Frederick Macmillan, hoping he would be 'inclined to print it' and pointing out that it made a connected whole. He thought it advisable, he said, 'to wait and see' how this part was received before proceeding further. Agreement was soon reached, Hardy accepting a 25 per cent royalty on London sales and 15 per cent on the New York. A thousand copies were ready by December but, in order to secure the American copyright, simultaneous publication was necessary in London and New York, and this was not possible until January 1904. Even more copies were printed in America, where, not surprisingly, the demand proved to be much lower than in England. An appendix giving the contents of the second and third parts, with an eye to future sales, shows considerable divergences from what was to come.

At the proof stage in November Hardy had had to attend to Emma's instructions about payment for deliveries and sending news about her cats and local events. She had gone with her niece Lilian, who had been staying at Max Gate, to Dover. When they crossed to Calais, he wrote very informatively on its Sterne and Shelley associations, reminded her to keep enough money in hand for her return, stressed the necessity also of mentioning the town when she gave her address, and counselled her, wherever she went, to stay near the sea; she could easily catch cold inland, particularly in Paris. On business in London, where it was colder than in Dorset, he still wrote to her. He had been to a service at St Paul's, where the organist Sir George Martin had explained the instrument to him and invited him home to tea; at the Athenaeum he met Henry James, saw Kipling, talked to Humphry Ward, and was introduced to the Vice-Chancellor of Oxford; but for heavy rain he would have visited Lilian's parents in Maida Vale. When he returned home at the end of the month he urged his wife not to winter in Calais; he would be delighted if Lilian returned, but he did not want Emma to stay there alone. Perhaps she would change her mind now that her maid Bessie had decided not to marry but to stay on at Max Gate; they could go away after Christmas, 'not to London, but to some place where influenzas do not abound'.

Just before Christmas Hardy read *The Creevey Papers*, the Waterloo parts of which reminded him of *Vanity Fair*. He was clearly anxious to continue *The Dynasts*, but some of the early reviews, especially that in *The Times Literary Supplement*, made him dubious; if ever he resumed it, he informed Gosse at the end of January, it would be largely owing to his encouragement. There were criticisms of the form and the verse. Writing to Frederic Harrison, he thought his 'Positive view of the Universe' was the unforgivable sin to the anonymous reviewer of *The Times Literary Supplement*. This was A. B. Walkley, who failed to see that Hardy's presentation of the whole was indivisible, and that his cinematic technique of aerial choruses and long-distance views with close-ups of dramatic scenes was a magnificent unifying conception, whatever the initial disadvantages of heavy verse elaborating subjection to an impercipient Immanent Will or keeping close to parliamentary oration. Although weakened by the speculative irrelevance of its conclusion, his preface makes Walkley's refusal to accept the principle that scenes set out in dramatic form are readable as part of an imaginative whole seem little better than perverse and superfluous; it is rather like arguing that Shakespeare should not be read. In his rejoinder Hardy made the mistake of treating the criticism too seriously; Walkley's defensive reply 'The Dynasts and the Puppets' gave Hardy the opportunity to stress his conviction that the main objection to his work arose not from its form but from its philosophy.

More than ten years after sketching a two-act play called 'Birthwort' on the subject of a rural abortion, before realizing that no producer would dare to stage it, Hardy returned to this daring topic when he wrote 'A Sunday Morning Tragedy' in January 1904, a year which brought cruel reminders of the passing of time. 'They are thinning out ahead of us', he wrote when he heard of Meredith's illness, not long after Leslie Stephen's death in February. In March he lost Henry Moule, the oldest of his Dorchester friends; as the burial took place in Fordington churchyard, he noticed Grey's Bridge and the Frome meadows in the bright sunshine. Among the many wreaths was one from Hardy's mother, who was bedridden with sickness. It had been made from flowers in her garden (such as Henry Moule had often admired), and she had sent Mary or

Kate out with a lantern in the evening to gather more greenery for its completion, fearing that it would arrive too late if left until the morning. Hardy visited her often. She died on Easter Sunday, at the age of 90, and was buried at Stinsford. She had suffered much at the end, and wished to die, he wrote to Clodd; there was 'really nothing for commonsense to regret', though regret was inevitable, he added; it was in this spirit that he wrote 'After the Last Breath'. Whatever her feelings, Emma did not attend the funeral. Hardy had Mary's oil painting of his mother photographed by Hermann Lea for inclusion in the *Sphere* and the *Graphic*, and had a hand in obituary notices which appeared in local papers and in *The Times*. He objected to inaccuracies in some reports, including a reference to his mother's 'tiny cottage', using Shorter to inform readers that it was 'an eight-roomed homestead with an acre and a half of land attached', an insistence which sprang from a sense of social inferiority just as much as his affected modesty when he described Max Gate to London friends as his 'country cottage'. Mary and Kate let their furnished house in Dorchester to return to their old Bockhampton home, where they joined their cousin Mary ('Polly') Antell, who had assisted her aunt most of the time since her own mother's death in 1891. Emma became the sole survivor of her family when her two remaining brothers died: Walter, the younger (Lilian's father), in October; Richard, shortly afterwards in Warneford Asylum, Oxford, where he had been an inmate many years. Walter had recently retired from the Post Office, leaving little for his widow and Lilian; Gordon had left Blomfield's, and enjoyed assured prospects as an architect for the London County Council; his sister was left continually dependent on him and the Hardys.

They had stayed at Walter's home in Maida Vale from May to July. Once again Hardy had spent Whitsuntide with Clodd at Aldeburgh. He visited the Gosses with W. B. Yeats, Max Beerbohm, and others in May, with Henry James in June, and the Thornycrofts in July. Gosse had been elevated from one sinecure to a grander one; he was now Librarian of the House of Lords, with longer holidays and even more time for writing. Hardy enjoyed teas with him on the terrace of the House, on one occasion with Lord Salisbury, the Prime Minister A. J. Balfour, and others. He had seen the first performance of Yeats's play *Where There is Nothing* from Lady Gregory's box at the Royal Court Theatre. Emma most probably accompanied him when he attended concerts at the Queen's Hall, sometimes perhaps when he went to

afternoon services at St Paul's, to hear the organ, the most beauti-
ful-toned in the world, according to an eminent European musician. They attended several parties, one at Mrs Macmillan's, and a
very large one at Stafford House, home of the Duke and Duchess
of Sutherland. He did some work at the British Museum, probably
with the resumption of The Dynasts in mind. Emma stayed on
when he returned to Max Gate, waiting to hear that the air from
the Frome valley was no longer polluted by the sewage works.

During August Hardy's cycling tours took him to Yeovil, Wells,
Glastonbury, and Shaftesbury. At Glastonbury he spent 'a romantic day or two' among the ruins, and met by chance the poets
William Watson and Francis Coutts with the publisher John Lane.
Isabella Oppenheim, daughter of the painter W. P. Frith, called at
Max Gate with her daughter in September, and a week or so later
the second part of The Dynasts was under way, Hardy being busy
with the battle of Jena. Gosse came early in October, and was
persuaded to join in some strenuous cycling; 'I don't know when I
enjoyed myself so much', he wrote when he returned. Hardy later
discovered that they had discussed the poems of 'Laurence Hope'
on the very day she committed suicide in Madras from excessive
grief at the death of her husband General Nicolson. Hardy, who
had met her, thought highly of the 'tropical luxuriance and
Sapphic fervour' of her work, and wrote a tribute to her which
appeared in the Athenaeum at the end of the month. Progress with
The Dynasts was hampered by some 'sombre' distractions, the chief
being Emma's illness after her brother's death. Another, related to
this, though it may belong to a later period in a distressful year,
may have been the writing of the poem 'Shut Out That Moon',
which is as much concerned with the effects of age and the death
of loved ones in 1904 as it is with disillusionment in love.

In order to recover lost ground with The Dynasts Hardy declined
London invitations, one from Isabella Oppenheim, another to the
Cornhill dinner from the editor-publisher Reginald Smith. His work
was interrupted several times in 1905. Towards the end of January
he was in London for the dinner given by Gosse at the National
Club. Although he agreed to become vice-president of the Society
of Dorset Men in London, he declined an invitation from the
president, Sir Frederick Treves, to their inaugural dinner, and
made it clear that he was not likely to attend many of their
meetings and functions. Early in April he received an honorary
LL.D. degree at Aberdeen University, staying with the principal

and finding time to visit places associated with Byron's youth. At the Athenaeum, on his way back home, he was deeply saddened to hear of the death of his friend Lord St Helier, formerly Sir Francis Jeune. On 6 May, a week or so after occupying a flat let to them by Lady Thompson (Bosworth Smith's daughter, subsequently Lady Grogan) in Hyde Park Gardens, Emma and he were shocked to discover in *The Times* that Dr Gifford, who had officiated at their wedding more than thirty years earlier, had died. Whether she accompanied him to see Mrs Henniker's *The Courage of Silence* at the King's Theatre, Hammersmith, is uncertain; it can be assumed that she was present at the private viewing of Walter Tyndale's watercolours of the Hardy country at Leicester Galleries. There was much correspondence with Hermann Lea on his forthcoming handbook to Hardy's Wessex with photographic illustrations. In May Hardy had been a guest at the retiring Lord Mayor's banquet, lunched with Gosse at the House of Lords, dined with the Omar Khayyám Club, and attended a conversazione at the Royal Society. In June he visited Swinburne and Watts-Dunton, having a long talk with the former, who told him about a paragraph in a Scottish paper (on the honorary degree recently bestowed on Hardy by Aberdeen University) which stated, 'Swinburne planteth, Hardy watereth, and Satan giveth the increase'; both were rather pleased to think they had been the 'most abused of living writers', one for *Poems and Ballads*, the other for *Jude the Obscure*.

When Hardy visited Meredith in Surrey one afternoon before returning home he found him mentally alert despite his physical disabilities, and opposed to his 'twilight view of life'; he was not told that Meredith thought *The Dynasts* would have been better in prose, but was pleased when he encouraged him to complete it. He probably made progress with it in August, despite having to hunt up letters and record memories in order to prepare a prefatory note on H. J. Moule for an edition of his *Dorchester Antiquities* and provide material for F. W. Maitland's biography of Leslie Stephen. September opened with a visit of about 200 of the Institute of Journalists as part of their 'Wessex' tour. After having tea in a long tent on the Max Gate lawn, they drove off to Bockhampton, Puddletown, Bere Regis, and Wool, where they began their journey back to London by train. In the middle of the month Hardy was Clodd's guest at Aldeburgh for the sesquicentennial celebration of the birth of Crabbe, a poet he honoured as 'an apostle of realism' without exaggerating his aesthetic claims. He forwarded the second part of *The Dynasts* to Frederick Macmillan on 11 October, and wished it was the third. Two editors invited him to write poems for publication on the Trafalgar centenary ten days later, but, as he answered one of them, the second part of *The Dynasts* had pumped him dry, and he could think of nothing on the subject beyond what was printed in the first. Rejoicings in Dorchester led him to think that, keeping to direct lines of descent, his brother and sisters were the only people he knew to be living in the home their family occupied on the day of the battle 100 years earlier.

Part Second of *The Dynasts* was published early in February; of the 1500 or so copies printed, slightly under one-sixth were sent for binding and sale in America, where interest in the subject had proved to be very limited. The concluding scenes lacked the climactic excitement which the battle of Trafalgar gave the first volume, but Hardy was already looking forward to the third, which would, he wrote to Bosworth Smith, be 'crowded with big events'. The reception was generally favourable nevertheless, and Gosse was most enthusiastic; he keenly expected 'a noble and thrilling conclusion', judging the 'poem' to be more of a 'real historical *epos*' than 'anything else in the production of modern Europe', and likely to be 'the most important piece of creative art' of the 'young' century. Arthur Symons thought the political and conversational scenes would have been better in prose, but Hardy argued that the 'contiguity' of 'emotional verse' made his practice as defensible as Shakespeare's use of blank verse for transcripts from chronicles in his history plays.

The London season of 1906 was a busy one for the Hardys. From mid-April to mid-July they stayed again at 1 Hyde Park Mansions, where they entertained many friends and aristocratic acquaintances, including Lady Queensberry, the Crackanthorpes, and Lady Grove. They attended Wagner concerts, plays, private shows, luncheons, and dinners. Before the end of April Hardy heard from Baron d'Erlanger, who composed its music, that the performance in Naples of the Italian opera *Tess* had coincided with an eruption of Vesuvius. When he discussed Wagner's music (of which he preferred the late, as he did late Turner) with Grieg, he compared it, as he had done in 1885, with the sound of wind through trees, iron railings, and keyholes; the Norwegian composer curtly answered that he would prefer the wind and rain. After Hardy had recovered from his inevitable 'influenza', Emma returned to Max Gate for a few days, and suffered her first heart-attack, which caused her to fall while she was gardening. Hardy (who does not seem to have been informed of this) went with the dramatist Henry Arthur Jones to see *Othello*; five days later he and Arthur Symons saw a private performance of Wilde's banned play *Salome*. He signed an appeal which appeared in *The Times* to raise funds for the acquisition and maintenance by the Keats-Shelley Memorial Association of the house where Keats died in Rome. Among the Hardys' subsequent guests were the French portrait-painter Jacques-Emile Blanche and his wife. When Hardy sat for his portrait, the artist noticed his arthritic hands, and fancied the light from a blue sky on a hot June day cast a cadaverously green tinge on his pallid face. Sittings were deliberately renewed by Blanche, in order to continue their discussion of Napoleonic legends in France. Hardy's letters suggest that he was very active. His Napoleonic research continued at the British Museum, and he prepared 'Memories of Church Restoration', to be read in his absence at the general meeting of the Society for the Protection of Ancient Buildings, and subsequently published in the *Cornhill Magazine*. Mrs Henniker's illness had worried him, but he was glad to learn from newspapers, and from General Henniker, that she was making good progress.

He began the final part of *The Dynasts* soon after his return to Max Gate. On 17 August, two days after he and Emma had been shocked to hear of the death of Pearl Craigie, whom they had recently seen in London at Stafford House, he began a tour with his brother to the cathedrals of Lincoln and Ely, the Cambridge colleges, and Canterbury. After this he enjoyed several cycling tours in Dorset and Somerset. He continued to receive books from his friends, and could not resist reading most of them with little delay, though he preferred to take more time over poetry. He was particularly struck by 'A Song against Love' in Arthur Symons' *The Fool of the World and Other Poems*, acknowledging significantly that the conception of love as 'this thing that remembers and hates, and that hurts' was 'as painful as true'. One book he read with special interest was Frederic Harrison's *Memories and Thoughts*, which made him feel that, though a 'meliorist', he could not be as optimistic as his friend, seeing no end in sight to man's love of blood-sports, the counterpart of Darwinian mercilessness among terrestrial animals of the same origin. Nature is *un*moral, he insisted, and this belief is the basis of 'New Year's Eve', a poem published in January 1907 which shows how gloomy his meliorism could be; he assumes in his customary way that man has evolved ethically beyond the intention of a Creator who works by rote, and asserts that, if God had created any joy during the past year on a planet for which one can see no good reason, it was such that no man would ever have wanted it. By the end of October he had reached his most perplexing historical task in the unfolding of *The Dynasts*, how to give a clear presentation of 'that maelstrom of confusion', the battle of Leipzig. On 17 October his poem 'Autumn in King's Hintock Park' appeared under a slightly different title in *Books*, a weekly supplement issued by the *Daily Mail* under Gosse's editorship. Soon afterwards Hardy agreed to become a vice-chairman of the English Association, saying he was appalled by the threat of Americanisms in the press, and instancing the use of 'Hurry up!' for 'Come hither!'

Emma, who walked in February 1907 in a London suffragist procession, had encouraged Mrs Fawcett, leader of the suffragette movement, in November to seek Hardy's support, which he willingly gave for reasons, on women's rights and family questions, so far in advance of his day that it was deemed prudent not to print them. His note to the effect that he completed the draft of Part Third of *The Dynasts* late on the eve of Good Friday (soon after the death of his friend Thomas Perkins) suggests that he followed a habit of mapping every detail in prose before working on the versification. He had been too busy to attend Holman Hunt's birthday dinner. Soon afterwards Emma and he were at Hyde Park Mansions again for another three months in London, where they met G. B. Shaw and his wife, entertaining among other friends the Barries and the Blanches. Hardy attended the *Cornhill* dinner, and met Wells, Conrad, Shaw, Sir Walter and Lady Grove, and the Gorkys at a friend's house. On his birthday he dined at Lady St Helier's. On 22 June, almost two weeks after lunching at the House of Lords with Gosse and others, he and Emma attended King Edward's garden-party at Windsor. There were insufficient carriages to convey all the guests to the Castle, and Hardy walked with Blanche, after a lady had declined a seat next to Emma, thinking her husband looked too frail to climb the hill. There would be nothing remarkable in this but for Blanche's unsympathetic account of Emma with her long green veil and perpetual smile. Whatever truth there is in his statement on her insistence that Hardy could walk, it is not nearly as regrettable as her

ostentatiously dramatic assertiveness in company at his expense
for which more impartial evidence is available. Emma had a habit
of imposing her will on a husband whom she could not always
trust to act the part of a *bourgeois gentilhomme*. There must have
been times when he shrugged it off as a mannerism or reflex action
beyond her control, part of the working of the Immanent Will
which made things what they were. What a tragedy, T. P. O'Connor
reflected, that a man so 'morbidly susceptible and melancholy'
should be married to such a woman. She had told him that her
husband was 'very vain and very selfish'. He needed someone
who would have encouraged him and given him tranquillity; her
'whole bitter purpose seemed to be to discourage and belittle and
irritate him'.

There was less cycling for Hardy that summer, partly because
the roads were much more frequented by cars, principally because
he was held by *The Dynasts*. Llewelyn Powys, who had left
Cambridge at the end of 1906, called at Max Gate without making
an appointment, possibly about this time. He was shown by a
servant into the drawing-room, where he saw a bust of Sir Walter
Scott on top of a tall bookcase, pictures of Shelley and Keats, one
on each side of the fireplace, and a watercolour of Westminster
Abbey painted by Hardy when he was a young man. Mrs Hardy
entered and said she had sent up a servant with a message, but did
not expect her husband to come down. He did, and raised questions about Chaldon, where the young visitor was staying with his
brother Theodore. Hardy asked what career he intended, and
advised him to join the Society of Dorset Men in London. As he
left, Powys was amazed at the courtesy of the famous author in
conducting him to the garden gate, and plucked up courage to ask
what he was writing. With 'a kindly, self-depreciatory, quizzical
glance' at him, Hardy replied, '*The Dynasts*'.

Early in August Sir Frederick and Lady Treves stayed near Max
Gate, and saw much of him and Emma; at the time John Lane and
his wife were at the Antelope, and Francis Coutts and William
Watson were expected. Late in the month the Lanes travelled with
Mrs Hardy to Lyon's Gate, Hardy and Hermann Lea following on
cycles; at Cerne Abbas, where they picnicked, they all visited the
abbey gatehouse and barn; and in one of his jolliest moods Hardy
climbed from Lion's Gate to the top of High Stoy for a view of
Blackmoor Vale. Mrs Kenneth Grahame's statement that the verses
she sent him were written on top of an omnibus evoked the reply

that he could never concentrate on 'inner things' in such a position, his attention being diverted by young women around him 'in
fluffy blouses', a light-hearted admission which has been interpreted as nothing more than an excess of sexual curiosity, though
it is just as venial in a writer with an artistic eye as in a painter such
as Tissot. He did not mind giving up time to correcting and
improving at proof stage Lady Grove's *The Social Fetich*, which she
had dedicated to him, and he was delighted to read Florence
Henniker's new novel *Our Fatal Shadows*, a copy of which she sent
late in September. Most of his work on *The Dynasts* had been
completed, as he informed Desmond MacCarthy, who wished him
to contribute to his new magazine.

On 10 October he sent the complete script to Frederick Macmillan.
Before starting work on the proofs at the end of the year he had
attended Harry Pouncy's 'Hours in Hardyland', with some dramatized scenes from *Far from the Madding Crowd*, in Dorchester Town
Hall, and been taken completely by surprise on receiving Gosse's
'spiritual autobiography' *Father and Son*; it was, he declared when
he finished it, unique and beautifully told, and made him wish for
its sequel. Publication of the final part of *The Dynasts* was held up
until February to secure the American copyright. Despite the
expected cavillings about the verse and the philosophy, reviewers
were more enthusiastic than ever, realizing that the whole had
been brought to a tremendous climax, with, by and large, amazing
control of detail and good sense of proportion. A humorous rustic
scene reminded readers of Wessex scenes in the first part; humorous realism in the second had been allied with horrors of the
Peninsular War. Hardy's cinematic technique was never used to
finer effect than in presenting views of the retreat from Moscow;
and his scenic prose, often his very best, repeatedly reveals admirable economy, imaginative vividness, and sharp poetic intensity.
Aerial choruses throughout sustain a function in which the Pities
play an increasingly important role, and anticipations in both
earlier parts of their hopeful yearning at the end are but a feature of
unity in a work the span of which would exceed the grasp of most
writers. The reading of source-material, French and English, and
his search for detail had been unrelenting. In that search, while
working on the final volume, he had received occasional assistance
from the young woman who became his second wife.

22
Florence Emily Dugdale

In August 1905 Hardy had received a letter from an unknown woman who wished to see him. She had probably expressed admiration of his work and introduced herself as an aspiring writer who had contributed frequently to her local newspaper. Hardy was won by her assurance that she would not take advantage of the interview by publishing an account of it, and answered that he would be at home to her any afternoon of the month provided she made an appointment. The visit must have been postponed until very late in the year, for on 2 January 1906 he wrote, thanking her for the box of flowers she had sent, and assuring her that she had not stayed too long. Years later she said she was taken by a friend and introduced to the Hardys as a distant relative; Hardy did in fact discover a marriage between members of his and her families in the late eighteenth century.

. The young woman who had played her cards so well was Florence Dugdale, the second of an Enfield headmaster's five daughters. She was almost forty years younger than Hardy, and may have been visiting Dorset relatives, her grandmother, after whom she received her second name Emily, living at Langton Matravers before marrying a blacksmith at Wareham. They had moved to the dockland area of Portsmouth, where her father had become a pupil-teacher, qualifying for admission to a college at Battersea which had been founded by the National Society for promoting the education of the poor according to Church of England principles. Here Edward Dugdale was awarded his teaching certificate, and such was the demand for qualified teachers when elementary education had been made compulsory for all, and numerous new state schools were being opened, that it was relatively easy for him to secure appointment as headmaster of St Andrew's National School for boys, Enfield, at the age of twenty three, a position he retained until his retirement at the age of seventy. It called for fitness, energy, stamina, and high endeavour. Even when he had new school premises, overcrowding and instruction courses required strict discipline and systematic planning. Regular inspections, concern to satisfy Church managers, and Sunday School duties added to his cares. He married in 1876, and was ably supported by his wife, who had been a governess at Enfield Court. She was musical, refined, and gentle, and they were devoted to their children, all of whom were educated at National Schools in St Andrew's parish.

Florence left the National School for girls at the age of twelve, and attended a Higher Grade School at the cost of ninepence a week until she was fifteen. Although this type of school provided a secondary education with some bias towards practical skills, her interest was chiefly in literature. She had read a great deal for some years, and loved to walk with her father and their fox-terrier in the neighbouring country. Now, too soon, she read Jane Austen, and was disappointed; she preferred Dickens and R. L. Stevenson, and was soon living romantically in the society novels of Ouida and Rhoda Broughton. At fifteen she was brought into daily contact with some of the harsher aspects of reality when she joined her elder sister Ethel as a pupil-teacher at St Andrew's National School for girls, of which her younger sister Constance eventually became headmistress. The building was crowded and noisy; standards were low; and some severe discipline was found necessary. In addition to six hours' teaching, pupil-teachers had to spend one and a half hours each day receiving tuition from the head. Both sisters were frequently absent with colds, influenza, or sore throats. Florence resigned in March 1897, and completed her statutory apprenticeship elsewhere in Enfield. After being refused admission to a training-college for medical reasons, she began teaching in her father's school the following January, with the aim of gaining her certificate at the end of four years. Assisted by a monitor, she taught the lowest class in a large room overcrowded with other classes, at £85 per annum. Such was the poverty of some homes that the Dugdales had to collect boots and clothing for distribution, and sometimes even send out hot meals. Epidemics broke out every winter, gradually undermining Florence's health; raising her voice to hold her class's attention during disturbances around her weakened her throat. She was in most respects an able teacher, and there were few boys to whom her large luminous eyes and gentle voice did not appeal. She told stories, wrote plays for them to act, and taught them composition. Yet, however rewarding her more imaginative work, frequent illnesses, laryngitis especially, and depression made her yearn to escape the drudgery of school.

She and her elder sister attended conversaziones at the Enfield Literary Union, where in 1901 Florence gave a paper on King Arthur which was ideally inspired by the poetry and morality of *Idylls of the King*. She already shared the children's column in the *Enfield Observer* with A. H. Hyatt, a poet ten years her senior who promoted his personality cult by wearing a cloak and broad-brimmed hat as if he were the local Tennyson. He was a Richard Jefferies enthusiast whose interest in flowers kindled her love of gardening; he also encouraged her to write stories for children. Poor and afflicted with tuberculosis, he could not offer marriage, but she sadly grew up to think he was the only person who ever loved her. He read at the British Museum, and became acquainted with works by a wide range of authors, editing anthologies which brought new writers to her notice. By May 1906 Florence Dugdale's knowledge of Hardy's works was most probably increased rapidly as a result of meeting him and being conversant with the selection of his verse and prose which her friend wished to publish; it appeared as *The Pocket Thomas Hardy* late in the year. Her melancholy disposition and growing agnosticism drew her more to Hardy than to any other living author.

Whether as a result of continual sick-leave or of deliberate deferment, she did not sit for her Board of Education certificate examination until 1906. She passed with special credit in English literature, composition, and the principles of education, and was given the task of teaching the top class and those boys who were about to leave. She gave the latter some lessons on the French Revolution, and probably read some of the poems she thought suitable, such as 'The Ancient Mariner' and the ballad 'Chevy Chase'. She may have had greater discretion than the teacher she presents in the story she began early in 1907, so 'over-keen' for poetry that he has boys gabbling Shelley's 'The Skylark' uncomprehendingly one wearying hot afternoon; but his plight and that of teachers discussing some point in the latest code of regulations issued by the Board undoubtedly express her growing aversion to the tasks of school. She must have corresponded with Hardy, for he had sent her two photographs of himself in September 1906; before the end of the year, after submitting an application in November, she had a reader's ticket for the British Museum, and had begun researches to solve questions which had arisen while he was working at Max Gate on the third part of *The Dynasts*. In March 1907 he insisted that she should not visit the Museum for him unless she was well, and advised her not to accept less than a guinea per thousand words for the children's stories she continued to write for her publishers. Acknowledging her assistance, he suggested at the end of April that she should meet him the following Saturday by the Trajan column in the South Kensington Museum unless it were wet. Later that summer, while still in London, he recommended her, first as a writer of school textbooks and readers to Maurice Macmillan, then as a reviewer to Archibald Marshall, Gosse's successor as editor of the *Daily Mail* literary supplement, emphasizing her skill in shorthand and typewriting. As an expression of his gratitude, he had given her copies, first of the new pocket edition of *Wessex Poems* and *Poems of the Past and the Present*, and then of *The Rubáiyát of Omar Khayyám*. In September he persuaded the editor of *The Cornhill* to accept 'The Apotheosis of the Minx', another story by Miss Dugdale, ending with a slick double irony which may have appealed to an admirer of Hardy fiction, but which may have been recommended by him; he may have revised the text of the story before submitting it. Perhaps he had met Florence, and, after escorting her to the station and watching her until she disappeared in the crowd before boarding the train to Enfield, experienced the feeling which he expressed within the fictional framework of 'On the Department Platform'.

The Dynasts brought Hardy many appreciative letters from his friends. What some of them had to say, and the suggestion which it led him to make when his publisher sent proofs in April of a prospectus for promoting sales of the work, may be gauged from the statement which was added in bold type at the end of the leaflet: 'Many readers who have begun the drama with some hesitation have afterwards assured the author that they found it as exciting as a novel.' Though Hardy was ready to admit shortcomings and wish he had spent more time improving it, he was amused to find before the end of 1908 that, while half the reviewers condemned the blank verse, the other half thought it good, and some who said it was 'mere prose' now thought it 'real poetry'. Recognition at high levels that his epic drama was the peak of his achievement explains why Asquith, the Prime Minister, invited him to accept a knighthood on 2 November, an embarrassing offer over which Hardy found excuses to temporize. Minor honours had been bestowed on him which were privately gratifying but not wholly welcome. In 1907 he had been made president of the Society of Dorset Men in London, an office which he held for two years almost entirely as a distinguished absentee; perhaps not surprisingly, since it was to be published, no time was ever found to read the presidential address which he sent for the May 1908 meeting. A few days later he was made an honorary member of the Dorset Field Club, and genuinely hoped to attend some of its 'delightful meetings'. Invited by Lord Tennyson to take the chair at one of the dinners organized by the Royal Literary Fund, he declined, expressing his convenient self-conviction that he was 'quite unable to preside at any meeting'.

Hardy's first visit to London in 1908 seems to have taken place at the end of April, when he dined at the Royal Academy; an earlier one had been prevented by Emma's bronchial illness. Soon after Dorothy Allhusen had motored with Lady St Helier to see them at Max Gate, and just before he left for London in May, he wrote two letters, one declining to join the committee for a memorial theatre to Shakespeare, on the grounds that Shakespeare was less important theatrically than as a poet to be read, the other requesting Frederick Macmillan to send Lord Curzon a set of *The Dynasts*. As Emma was not fit to manage entertaining in London, he did not take a flat but looked for lodgings. Friends invited him to luncheons and dinners, and he met the Gosses when he dined with several judges and their wives at Lady St Helier's in Portland Place. Emma's visit was postponed while he spent Whitsuntide in the country, first with many distinguished people, including Arthur Balfour and Professor Walter Raleigh, at Lord Curzon's, Hackwood Park, near Basingstoke, then at Lady St Helier's, Poplar Farm, near Newbury. Although Hardy booked a hotel room, Emma did not come to London; they had been invited to dine with the Frederick Macmillans. She was still far from well; her eyesight was failing, and Hardy did not wish her to venture until she was certain her new spectacles were satisfactory. The heat was too tiring for her 'to do anything', he told her, and he would be out twice a week or more at Herkomer's studio; he would rather take her to Cornwall. Before returning to her, he witnessed the unveiling of the memorial to 'John Oliver Hobbes' (Pearl Craigie) by Lord Curzon at University College, and visited Cambridge for the Milton tercentenary celebrations on 10 July. Here he met the Charles Moules and, at Sir Clifford Allbutt's home, Robert Bridges. Before returning home from London he attended the wedding of Gosse's son Philip at the parish church, Kensington, where he sat next to Henry James. Shortly afterwards, at one of the local garden-parties he attended with Emma, he met his friend Bosworth Smith for the last time.

Florence Dugdale had not returned to teaching. After illness in the winter, she had been given three months' leave on the advice of her throat specialist. Earlier, during the Christmas holiday of 1906–7, she had gone to Dublin to act as Lady Stoker's companion, and enjoyed her stay there so much that she may have returned during other holidays. If not, she must have spent a period or more there during 1908. Lady Stoker suffered from an incurable mental illness; her husband Sir Thornley, brother of Bram Stoker, Sir Henry Irving's manager, was an eminent surgeon. They lived at Ely House, an elegant Dublin mansion rich with works of art, ornaments, and furnishings from many countries; it was the most luxurious house Florence ever really knew. She had proved to be very acceptable, and they gave her a typewriter for her literary work, in which they took great interest. Her assistance was given freely, mainly because she liked being with such 'dear, kind friends'; if Sir Thornley Stoker's secretary, who had been appointed because she was a nurse and could help Lady Stoker in crises, needed relief, she went whenever she could. So highly did he appreciate Florence's patient and gentle care of his wife, who eventually had to be placed in a nursing-home, that Sir Thornley left her £2000, an exceptionally generous award, when he died in 1912. How this engagement was initiated in 1906 is uncertain; Florence may have been recommended by the Irish writer Katharine Tynan Hinkson, who lived at Enfield and knew A. H. Hyatt, or, through her, by Mrs Clement Shorter, daughter of the Dublin physician Dr Sigerson, a friend of Sir Thornley Stoker.

In the late spring of 1908 Shorter had all the manuscripts of Hardy's novels bound in accordance with an agreement that he should retain the one he preferred; this was *The Return of the Native*, and the donor's wish that it should not be shipped across the Atlantic was honoured when Shorter bequeathed it to University College Library, Dublin. While in London Hardy corrected proofs of *Select Poems of William Barnes*, an edition which he had been invited to undertake for the Clarendon Press by Professor Raleigh as early as January 1907, when he was too busy with *The Dynasts* to accept the offer. A year later all was clear for an enterprise that must have appealed to him highly; he had selected about 100, almost a third, of the poems. After revising this selection and dividing it into three groups (lyric and elegiac, descriptive and meditative, humorous), with marginal explanations of dialect words (which were printed as footnotes), he forwarded it to the publisher on 2 March. Ultimately copyright difficulties and textual questions created some unexpected problems. Whether or not Miss Dugdale was called upon to help by referring to editions in the British Library, she received an inscribed copy from Hardy when it was published in November. The preface illustrates his critical faculties wonderfully well, and it illuminates one aspect of Barnes's poetry which guided him in his own practice, 'the 'felicitous instinct' with which he preserved the 'naturalness' of his verse against 'further drill' by 'sudden irregularities' among his 'subtle rhythms and measures'.

From early September to late October Emma was again at Calais with Lilian, while Henry Hardy's workmen built a larger new porch and improved one of her attics by adding a dormer window. During that period Hardy visited his sister Mary at Swanage, where she was staying for the sake of her health, lunched with Mrs Sheridan, cycled to Weymouth, where he had tea with Miss Fetherstonhaugh, and joined a Field Club party to see the excavations at Maumbury Rings, where he met the author of *Moonfleet*, John Meade Falkner, and his wife, who had come up from Weymouth; he lunched with them at the King's Arms, and they came to see him at Max Gate six days later. He had planned to cycle to Weymouth with the novelist May Sinclair and her American friend Miss Moss, whose articles on his novels had appeared in the *Atlantic Monthly*, but the outing was prevented by prolonged rain. Francis Coutts came to see him with one of Coleridge's grandsons, and he dined with them at the Antelope. He had met Lady Constance Leslie, whose sister had refused Louis Napoleon's proposal; she had heard that Rebekah Owen had turned Catholic, much to her sister's distress. Bosworth Smith was to be buried at West Stafford. (He had purchased Bingham's Melcombe House, an ancient country manor of great historical interest several miles north of Puddletown, for his retirement. There he had written the essays which comprise his best known book, *Bird Life and Bird Lore*, extended the rockery garden, and arranged the valuable collection of curiosities which had come to him from many parts of the world.) Only when it was obvious that his recovery was impossible, five weeks after an operation in London, was his request to return granted; he reached his home in the evening of 17 October, and died two hours later. Emma was kept fully informed; Hardy sent her money, papers (including a batch of three which he thought Protestant), and news on building progress, the plants, and all the cats. He did not send her *The Times* of 9 October, which contained his article 'Maumbury Ring' (on the excavations and the historic events he associated with it, especially the grisly execution of Mary Channing), as he thought she would probably have seen it. He hoped she would be back in good time for the play on 18 November; a reporter for *The Times* was coming, and he had offered him a bed.

The staging of Hardy which was to become an annual occurrence for several years in Dorchester, London, and Weymouth began almost accidentally when it was decided that an entertaining scene from *The Trumpet-Major*, the party at Overcombe Mill, should follow the lecture 'Napoleon and the Invasion of England' which was given by Hardy's friend, the local historian A. M. Broadley, on 4 February 1908. So enthusiastically was this performance received that three scenes from *The Dynasts* were presented at the Dorchester 'Maie Fayre', and A. H. Evans, producer of the first venture, was encouraged to plan, with Hardy's encouragement and assistance, three additional acts for dramatizing the main story of the *Trumpet-Major* late in the year. In this he played the part of Festus Derriman, with T. H. Tilley, the mayor, as Cripplestraw. News of this dramatic event created considerable interest in London, several critics being deputed to come down and report, among them Harold Child for *The Times*. Hardy attended rehearsals, but influenza prevented him from seeing any of the three performances on 18–19 November; Child stayed at the Antelope on Hardy's advice, and Emma attended the first performance which was interrupted by a thunderstorm. Maurice Evans, the producer's seven-year-old son, who was to become a famous actor, was taken home by her, and remembered how, late that night, she held on to him with one hand while keeping her cape round her as best she could in the wind. So successful was *The Trumpet-Major* that it initiated a succession of plays from Hardy's novels by members of the Dorchester Debating and Dramatic Society, who soon became known as 'the Hardy Players'.

After the completion of *The Dynasts* Hardy found more time for local affairs. Unlike that of the hero of *The Well-Beloved* during a long period of artistic monomania, his persistent interest had been the welfare of the human race, but he was always ready to help with architectural advice, even on guttering. He made careful recommendations for the preservation of St Catharine's Chapel, one of the glories of the Dorset coast on a hill above Abbotsbury, and he was soon to be closely involved in maintenance and restoration work at Stinsford church, his principle being that repairs should be for preservation as far as possible. Experience had taught him too that there was no place in a church 'which so completely controls the singing of the congregation as a west gallery'. He wrote poetry whenever it occurred to him, and must have been pleased in September to send Ford Madox Hueffer 'A Sunday Morning Tragedy' for inclusion in his first number of the *English Review*; Hueffer had read the poem late in 1907, when it was rejected by two editors, and wanted·it to manifest what kind of magazine he intended. One of the books which gave Hardy much pleasure to read was Lady Grove's *The Human Woman*, a collection of essays in which she defended the political enfranchisement of women against the arguments of its opponents. As he wrote when asked to let his name appear as a possible contributor to a suffragist weekly, Hardy did not think that women realized what could follow the attainment of such equality, with probably 'the break-up of the marriage-system', changes in social and religious codes, and legal disputes over the inheritance of property. Somewhat reluctantly, from a sense of duty, he travelled to London to attend a banquet in honour of Milton at the Mansion House on 9 December, the tercentenary of his birth. In January 1909 the Dorset Court of Quarter Sessions made him a governor of Dorchester Grammar School, a position he was disposed to hold because it pleased him to assume that the Elizabethan founder, his namesake, was one of his collateral ancestors.

If the early part of the year was difficult at Max Gate, Hardy secured little relief from correcting proofs for a new edition of his poems. On 1 May he thought it wise not to accept Clodd's invitation to Aldeburgh for Whitsuntide because, he confided, his domestic circumstances made it embarrassing for him to return hospitalities. Though he changed his mind, 'London influenza' prevented his going. He had lost two eminent literary friends: Swinburne, whose funeral on 15 April he would have attended but for rheumatism, and George Meredith, whom he had hoped to visit in the summer after hearing from him in March. Seeing the announcement of his death on a placard, he walked to the Athenaeum and wrote the obituary poem which appeared in *The Times* on 22 May, the day of the memorial service he attended in Westminster Abbey, where he was allotted 'a saintly niche' he felt he desecrated. Fashions have changed; Meredith's interment there was refused, and he was buried at Dorking. As Hardy wrote to Clodd, in the words of T. H. Huxley, Westminster Abbey was a Christian church and not a Pantheon for men of all beliefs; to make room for illustrious writers such as Swinburne and Meredith, a heathen annexe needed to be built. Hardy returned to the cause when he wrote 'A Refusal' in 1924, after the rejection of a proposal to erect a memorial tablet to Byron in Poets' Corner.

Maurice Hewlett invited him to succeed Meredith as President of the Society of Authors, and he instinctively declined, arguing first that the days were over when the appointment could be entirely honorary, then that the position demanded orthodox writers, he being determined on the other hand not to forfeit the right to show the fitness of what was often called immorality or irreligion. Eventually his objections were overcome, and he accepted the post. In a year when he retired from the presidency of the Society of Dorset Men in London without having attended a meeting for two years, he more characteristically refused engagements which would have inconvenienced or embarrassed him. He knew that his craving to write denied him the 'manysidedness possessed by some men', and for that reason refused to consider his adoption as a vice-president at the International Anti-Vivisection and Animal Protection Congress in July. His excuse for declining to contribute to a volume of essays edited by A. C. Bradley was that he was a poor critic. After expressing a disinclination, then refusing, to be a guest at a Whitefriars Club dinner because it meant making a speech, he was so angry weeks later with Clement Shorter, who had invited him, to find his name printed on the programme that he peremptorily refused to go, whatever the consequences. In December he declined the honour of being principal guest at a literary dinner given by the Lord Mayor of Liverpool the following March or April.

One event which Hardy had not wished to avoid was the production of the opera *Tess* at Covent Garden, after its success in Milan. He attended rehearsals, and met Florence Dugdale, hoping to sit with her at the première on 14 July if Emma did not come. When his wife decided at short notice that she would, he consulted Clodd, who suggested taking Florence himself after having a light dinner with her. Finding that she approved, Hardy wrote to Clodd from the Athenaeum, telling him that she would meet him at the

Lyceum Club, and that he would see them if he could during one of the intervals or at the end, urging him also if it were wet to ensure that Miss Dugdale wrapped up well for the sake of her health. Whether she and Hardy met that evening or not, they were to meet several times before November was out. With her kindly disposition and attractive eyes, she had already become fatally fascinating to Hardy; knowing something of Hardy's trials at Max Gate, Edward Clodd was sympathetic. In March she had sent Hardy one of her stories, which he recommended to the editor of *Chambers's Journal*. In September he revised another, on Trafalgar, which he thought read well, and advised her to send it first to the *Daily Mail*, then to the *Daily Chronicle*; it was rejected, but accepted by the second a year later, when Hardy sent it himself to James Milne for publication on Trafalgar Day.

Soon after the first performance of *Tess* he was delighted to receive a suggestion from Clodd that he took Florence to stay with him at Aldeburgh. Hardy said he was very anxious about her health and welfare, and determined to 'get her away to the seaside' to save her from a breakdown. Whatever 'throbbings of noontide' she may have stirred in him, he took a protective, almost paternal, interest in her. Her illness delayed their visit until the middle of August, when the party included William Archer and the historian Professor J. B. Bury, who had received an honorary degree with Hardy at Aberdeen. When Clodd sent Shorter a paragraph from the local paper headed 'Eminent Authors on the Mud', reporting how he, Hardy, and Florence had been rescued after his boat had been stranded three hours, Hardy wrote immediately, urging Shorter not to let the news 'get into any London print' if he could help it; he was anxious that Emma should not know. Florence and he were at Aldeburgh again for the weekend beginning 30 October. The main event at Dorchester was the production of *Far from the Madding Crowd*, the second full-length play which A. H. Evans had prepared with his advice and approval. All the leading London newspapers were represented at the first performance on the evening of 17 November, as Hardy informed Florence the next day. He had recommended Clodd to see it when it was played at Cripplegate Institute for the Society of Dorset Men in London, and was disappointed to learn that he had not been able to find a seat next to Miss Dugdale. In the autumn he and Florence, after visiting Chichester Cathedral, had joined his brother in London, all three then travelling north together to visit cathedrals in York, Edinburgh, and Durham.

Hardy's main literary business in the summer had been the collection and arrangement of poems for a publication which would be in time for the Christmas sales. His title was chosen from Tennyson's *The Princess*; he had first used it when the opening poem ('The Revisitation') appeared in the *Fortnightly Review* as 'Time's Laughingstocks, A Summer Romance'. The volume is another miscellany, containing poems from a period of more than forty years, many of them being published when Hardy was at work on *The Dynasts*. There is a noticeable increase in lyrical verse, though narrative poems, notably 'A Trampwoman's Tragedy' and 'A Sunday Morning Tragedy', are to the fore. The most daring inclusion is 'Panthera', a higher-critical version of the birth of Jesus which Professor Bury had read at Aldeburgh and advised him to print, Hardy in the meantime (as he told his publisher) having taken the precaution of making 'the events a possibly erroneous fantasy of the narrator'. The most evident personal feature is the number of poems on his mother, his old home, and associations with it. Of the poems written in depression in 1896 only 'The Dead Man Walking' is included; Emma could not have missed its inner meaning. Gosse thought the volume most 'poignantly sad', and wondered (as Meredith had done) how Hardy could take such 'a hopelessly gloomy view of existence'. Even so, *Time's Laughingstocks* sold well, and gloomier poems were to come. Significantly among those who received inscribed copies of the work were Edward Clodd and Florence Dugdale; her copy must have been sent in advance, for in the first week of December she gave a paper on the poems to a literary society in Enfield.

In January 1910 Hardy received a visit from the young poet Frances Cornford, who was staying with her husband at Broadwindsor. There must have been times when he considered whether it was wise to continue seeing Florence Dugdale; yet the poem 'To Meet, or Otherwise' shows that she was the antidote to 'sick life' which he was not prepared to forgo. With such feelings, when he had half-finished 'A Singer Asleep', his poem on Swinburne, he travelled with her to visit his grave at Bonchurch in the Isle of Wight, before taking her again to Aldeburgh for the Easter weekend at Strafford House, where he met Edward Whymper (who had been invited at his request) and his wife. Hardy read his poem 'Zermatt. To the Matterhorn', and Whymper marked for him on a sketch of the mountain he had brought the route of the climbers and the spot where four of them had been killed.

Soon after Hardy's seventieth birthday events took a remarkable turn. Emma had not changed. On 24 April 1910, within days of her return with 'an evil cold' from London, where she had failed to find accommodation for the season, she wrote to her new friend Lady Hoare of Stourhead, complaining about life in Dorchester, where recognition had come too late, and saying that she had always expected to live in London, 'with occasional visits to the country'. She was sitting in Hardy's study, from which she was usually excluded, as she had never been formerly; and the thought made her launch out on a diatribe on men in general and her husband in particular. If they had 'good brains', they had little judgement in ordinary matters; they were utterly useless and dangerous as magistrates, but 'to be put up with until a new order of the universe arrives'. 'It will', she ended with almost oracular finality. In London Hardy rented 4 Blomfield Court, a large furnished flat in Maida Vale, where they decided to have regular Thursday afternoon 'At Homes'. At the first of these Florence Dugdale, Florence Henniker, and Mrs Crackanthorpe were present with others, probably Lady Grove and May Sinclair, whom Hardy had invited. Whether Emma invited Florence is uncertain; they could have met at the Lyceum Club when Emma had come up to London to search for accommodation, after Hardy had spent three days in the quest. Both were suffragettes, and seem to have taken to each other very quickly. On 18 June Florence wrote from Enfield accepting Emma's request that she should pour tea for her on Thursday; it would, she said, be a great pleasure and honour to do anything for her. Such high-flown language may seem insincere, but it was typical of Florence's ingratiating style, especially to social superiors. Emma undoubtedly liked playing a *grande dame* role, and invited her new friend to Max Gate. Florence spent a week there from 26 June, while Hardy was in London, discovered how much Emma had written, especially on religion, and took some of her work back with her to type for publication. She had certainly been won over to Emma.

23

Emma's Death

Though only a qualified advocate of women's suffrage, Hardy supported a number of other causes in the summer of 1909 and subsequently. At the request of the barrister novelist John Galsworthy, who wished to use it as testimony before a committee of Lords and Commons, he wrote a letter to *The Times* against the censorship of plays, in which he referred to his abandonment of a plan to dramatize the subject of 'A Sunday Morning Tragedy', knowing that it would not be allowed on the stage. In response to a Berlin professor who wished to present 'the "Weltanschauung" of a few representative men in England and Germany', he stressed almost prophetically the threat posed to vaunted freedom by armaments and 'territorial ambitions smugly disguised as patriotism'. Nearly two years later, although he was not convinced that civilized nations would have recourse to war, he supported a protest organized by Galsworthy against aerial warfare, which could add 'a new hideousness' to it. His humanitarianism in 1909 extended further; he had realized that 'the law of evolution, which revealed that all organic creatures are of one family, shifted the centre of altruism from humanity to the whole conscious world collectively', though he had to admit that vivisection for the welfare of mankind was defensible. Thinking of other issues which made 'the principle of equal justice' untenable, he returned to the subject when the Humanitarian League attained its twentieth year, writing to the secretary from the Athenaeum on 10 April 1910 on 'the application of what has been called "The Golden Rule"', an extension of 'altruistic morals . . . beyond the area of mere mankind to that of the whole animal kingdom' as a *necessity of rightness*. An even wider application of this ideal will be found in his poem 'The wind blew words'.

In May, on the morning after her arrival in London, Hardy and Emma saw a placard announcing the death of Edward VII; it was from the Athenaeum that he and Rider Haggard watched the procession as his body was conveyed to Westminster Abbey. His thoughts on this occasion and three days later, when he saw the

funeral procession from Westminster, were finalized shortly afterwards in the poem 'A King's Soliloquy'. He was still trying to
appease Lady Grove, whom he had offended when he referred to
some of her best *On Fads* essays as 'the nearest to literature', by
giving her what assurances and advice he could on expressions
and sentences to which critics had recently objected. In June he
was delighted to hear that he had been awarded the Order of
Merit, a higher and far rarer distinction than a knighthood, which
he would have found socially embarrassing. More than anything
else, the magnitude of Hardy's achievement in *The Dynasts* had
undoubtedly promoted this act of recognition. Emma later complained, it appears, that he had accepted an honour which she
could not share. They spent Sunday evening, 19 June, with the
Gosses, who had lately returned from a holiday in Italy, and
entertained W. D. Howells, his daughter, and three other Americans on their last Thursday afternoon 'At Home' early in July. On
the 19th, ten days after the appearance of the Birthday Honours
List, Hardy, who had not recovered from another bout of 'London
influenza', was taken to Marlborough House for his investiture. So
nervous was he when he was received by George V that he was
certain he had failed in the customary formalities; he was still
flustered when he rejoined Florence Dugdale, and had some
difficulty in finding the insignia which he had dropped loose in
one of his pockets. Emma, who had returned home with a severe
cold, had arranged that Florence should prepare him for the event
and ensure that the flat was in order before he left for Max Gate.

How often Florence stayed at Max Gate before 'After the Visit'
was published in August 1910 is not known; it records her 'mute
ministrations to one and to all', and ends with the wishful thought
that those 'large luminous living eyes' looked at him as if asking
'by whose strange laws' of circumstance 'that which mattered most
could not be'. She wrote for the *Evening Standard*, in which her
article commemorating Hardy's seventieth birthday had appeared
on 2 June. While interviewing Clodd for a similar feature, she
observed that Hardy was a great writer but not a great man; she
had clearly heard of his shortcomings from Emma, passages from
whose religious essay 'The Acceptors' her mother was to find
'most beautiful and comforting'. In addition to this, she had
promised when she left Emma at the beginning of July to type her
Lyceum Club 'speech' whenever time allowed. After a brief stay at
Max Gate early in August, when she brought 'Blue Jimmy: the

Horse-Stealer' (a story for which Hardy must have provided information, and to which he made some additions before sending it for
publication in *The Cornhill*), she typed 'The Acceptors' and did her
best to secure a promise of publication when it was revised. She
was fascinated by 'The Maid on the Shore', but suggested alterations before typing it. She would begin this when she returned,
she wrote from Aldeburgh, where she and Hardy were staying at
the beginning of September with the Burys and J. G. Frazer.
Immediately on returning home, she continued her letter to
Emma, seemingly to discuss the many improvements the story
required. Whether the Max Gate visit took place or not, others
soon followed.

William Strang was persuaded to sketch her on 26 September,
when he was at Max Gate to prepare the OM portrait which had
been commissioned by George V. Hardy introduced her to his
sisters at Bockhampton, where she had her portrait painted by
Mary, and took her to Maiden Castle, where she picked flowers to
keep in memory of an outing which may have made him more dear
to her. She spent a happy long weekend with Emma in early
October, keen to publish 'The Inspirer', which she thought would
be the most successful of Emma's works. She then proposed to
type 'The Millionaire', but found it needed a 'good plot', and
informed Emma that, if she intended to make a play of it (as she
seemed to remember hearing), she would need to introduce 'some
strong situations'. She had hoped that they would finish 'the
reminiscences' (*Some Recollections*, concluded by Emma on 4 January
1911) next time she was at Max Gate. This was probably about the
middle of November, when Florence had an extraordinary encounter with her. She had felt '*intensely* sorry' for Emma, who was
extremely 'good' to her, but there had always been 'an aspect to
comedy' in the 'menage', she felt. Now she was queerer than ever,
Florence wrote to Clodd, not long before the conclusion of the
Crippen trial at the Old Bailey. (Crippen had poisoned his wife,
buried her remains in the cellar, and eloped with his secretary
Ethel le Neve.) Emma had asked whether Florence had noticed
how extremely like Crippen her husband looked, and said 'in
deadly seriousness' that she would not be surprised to find herself
in the cellar one morning. Miss Dugdale thought it time to depart
before she was asked if she didn't think she (Florence) resembled
Miss le Neve. If Emma spoke with sly black humour (and there is
no reason to think she did), what she said was disloyal and

malicious in the extreme; it testifies rather to one of those temporary mental derangements which created a world of fantasy alive
with malevolence against Hardy. It is part of the tragi-comedy of
their relationship at this time that she had him and many of his
poems in mind when she wrote of the 'non-acceptors' of Salvation:
'Satan's guile is very great; he gets mankind to attribute their
afflictions to God.' She wanted Florence to go abroad with her for a
few months; it would 'have a good effect on T.H.'. Soon afterwards she sent her a collection of verses, hoping they would make
a volume for publication. How desperately Emma depended on
her is clear from the quarrel which shocked Florence at Christmas,
when Hardy wished to take her to Botkhampton, and Emma
insisted his sisters would poison Florence's mind against her. After
this Miss Dugdale became a less frequent visitor; she was as
anxious to avoid 'Max Gate menage' dissension as she was to help
and encourage Emma to achieve some of her literary ambitions.
The quarrel which resulted in the destruction of the Hardy love-
letters (a series Hardy thought 'quite as good as the Browning
letters') may have taken place about this time. Having burned his
letters in the garden, Emma demanded back all those from her
which he had carefully preserved, and consigned them to the
flames. Her anger must have been unbounded.

'A prophet is not without honour, save in his own country and
in his own house.' Rather belatedly the local council decided to
make Hardy an honorary freeman of Dorchester. Postponed several times to suit him, the ceremony took place on 16 November
during Miss Dugdale's memorable stay at Max Gate. The poet
Henry Newbolt was the Hardys' guest, and they all attended the
presentation in the Council Chamber. Local feeling made Hardy
particularly pleased with this honour, and he prepared his speech
meticulously, thinking it most felicitous on paper, though in execution another proof that speech-making was not his forte. He
began by saying that, after taking liberties with the town in his
presentation of Casterbridge, he had enjoyed the freedom of the
borough for a long period. His main thought was on the past; he
regretted the loss of fine old buildings, and the fact that all the
Dorchester people he knew so well in his boyhood were buried,
making elderly people like himself feel that the permanence of
buildings was 'but the permanence of what is minor and access-
ory'. From these elegiac tones he turned to the future, believing
that Dorchester would become residential and, like other provin-

cial towns, lose its individuality, the railway having already made it 'almost a London suburb'. (In his comment on the health-giving advantages of its 'unexcelled' dry atmosphere and subsoil, he was stressing what he regarded as the great compensation for coming to Dorchester and building Max Gate, 'a step' he and Emma 'often regretted having undertaken'.) The presentation was followed by the performance, below in the Corn Exchange, of Mr Evans' *The Mellstock Quire*, a dramatization of *Under the Greenwood Tree* which was repeated in London and Weymouth. From his home, Nether-hampton House, Salisbury, Newbolt wrote a letter of thanks to Emma, saying that the presentation and play had been all the more interesting as a result of seeing them 'from the best point of view, with your Burgundy and your White Cat to start from and come back to!'. (Hardy's white cat Kitsey, his study companion, had been found dead not many days earlier.)

Emma may have felt some elation at the end of the year, when the American fleet was anchored off Portland Roads. Hardy went on board the battleship *Connecticut*, where he invited officers to meet him and his wife at Max Gate. In consequence, on 29 December, after being welcomed on board the English *Dreadnought*, they were taken to a dance on the United States flagship *Louisiana*, to which they were welcomed by Admiral Vreeland. Early in January 1911 Hardy, who had sometimes forgotten Emma's birthdays, remembered Florence Dugdale's, sending her, in addition to a lamp, a copy of Hermann Lea's handbook to the Wessex country of his novels and poems. His visit to Bristol Cathedral and Bath Abbey probably occasioned the poem 'Aquae Sulis'. His cathedral touring continued in April when, after enjoying the company of Clement Shorter and his wife with Clodd at Aldeburgh, he and Florence Dugdale met her sister Constance and Henry Hardy in London, and travelled with them to Lichfield, Worcester, and Hereford.

To avoid 'the Coronation circus', Hardy and Emma did not take a flat in London, but in deference to her self-important wish they attended the reception for the prime ministers of self-governing dominions at the opening of the Imperial Conference in May. Hardy made some brief visits, one to the Royal Academy dinner, where he met Sargent, Barrie, and Kipling, another to the Gosses', where he meet W. B. Yeats and the young novelist Hugh Walpole. He had written on 2 March, regretting that 'unavoidable circum-stances' prevented his acceptance of the Earl Marshal's invitation to attend the coronation in Westminster Abbey on 22 June. Instead, he and his brother, accompanied by Mr Dugdale and his two daughters, Florence and Constance (a match apparently in prospect between Henry and the latter), travelled to the Lake District. They did not call at Belmount Hall to see the Owens, who had thought it worthwhile to travel twice to Dorchester to see the Hardy players in *Far from the Madding Crowd* and *The Mellstock Quire*. Coronation Day was spent pleasantly on Windermere, after visiting the cathedral and castle at Carlisle. At Grasmere, by Wordsworth's grave, Hardy wrote some verses which may have found their final, almost vestigial, form in the opening of 'Lines to a Movement in Mozart's E-Flat Symphony', a poem begun in November 1898. On their way back they stopped at Chester to see the cathedral, and at Rugby to see the school and chapel associated with Matthew Arnold and his father. Hardy and Emma did not seek each other's company; in June she went with Florence Dugdale to Worthing for a holiday, and on her return Hardy travelled by train to Minehead with his sister Katharine, then by coach to Porlock and Lynmouth (where he remembered Coleridge and Shelley), thence by steamer to Ilfracombe. Intense heat made them cut short their plan to tour in south Devon after they had visited Exeter Cathedral.

An inordinate amount of time during the remainder of the year and later was devoted to checking the texts and correcting proofs for the new Wessex Edition of his works, all of which except *The Dynasts* and *Time's Laughingstocks* were published by Macmillan in 1912. Postscripts to prefaces, with occasional footnotes, were added to the prose fiction, but, apart from a few corrections and revisions, the text remained unaltered. By the late October of 1912 Hardy had finished the seventeen volumes of prose; in November he was 'still in the thick of proofs' but hoped 'to see daylight' by Christmas. For this edition he had prepared a larger and more detailed map, which he forwarded in October 1911, with the suggestion that the publisher's cartographer should produce a more artistic copy, decorated with ships and fishes in the sea, for example. About the same time he completed the 'General Preface' for inclusion in the first volume, *Tess of the d'Urbervilles*. Earlier he had thought of dividing the prose fiction into two groups, the second the more superficial and experimental; for the new edition he decided on three, then, with the addition of *A Changed Man* in 1914, on four. The result is that, after the first group, categorization appears increasingly artificial, arbitrary, and unsatisfactory. In the General Preface he discusses his threefold division ('Novels of Character and Environment', 'Romances and Fantasies', 'Novels of Ingenuity'), the universal within provincial settings, his attempts to preserve for his own satisfaction 'a fairly true record of a vanishing life', the basis of his distinction between actual and fictional place-names (as in the 1895 edition), and his philosophy, which was intended to convey impressions rather than a consistent whole, and was not the less valid because it had been condemned as 'pessimistic'.

He had little time for respite, and much of his reading had to be hasty. Although, as he read in his address on receiving the freedom of Dorchester, he thought the 'photographic' reproduction of life an 'inartistic species of literary produce', he found something within the reporterial facade of Arnold Bennett's *Clayhanger* that made him wish to read its sequel. Mrs Henniker's critical reflections on *The New Machiavelli* by H. G. Wells had made him give what attention he could to the novel, and send her on 3 October his views on marriage, which reveal (as *Jude* fails to do) what he thought should happen to the children of divorced couples. Florence Dugdale was staying at Weymouth at the time, and Hardy visited Clodd with her later in the month. In the middle of November Mrs Henniker came to see performances by the Hardy Players of *The Three Wayfarers* and Mr Evans' adaptation of 'The Distracted Preacher'. Whether she stayed at Max Gate or merely visited it (it gave Emma 'so much pleasure to have you here', Hardy wrote in December 1912) is uncertain; she may have booked a room at the King's Arms, where, as he wrote to her on 5 June 1918, he remembered that the last time she dined in 'the large room' was when she came to 'one of the performances of the local society'. During the first week of December he journeyed with his sister Kate and Florence Dugdale to Bath, Bristol, and Gloucester, where he studied the cathedral architecture again before writing 'The Abbey Mason'. Within a few days Mrs Henniker had told Florence (who typed for her) that she had never known Hardy in better spirits than when she was in Dorchester. Florence had found him well and seemingly 'quite gay'; now, she wrote from Enfield to Edward Clodd, he had written to say he was 'most miserable'. 'The Roman Gravemounds' was about to appear in the *English Review*, and she thought what '*monstrous* ingratitude' it was to assert in effect that his white cat Kitsey had been his only friend; he had altered the poem a little in deference to such criticism, but would not change the line which undoubtedly reveals how he felt at times, despite the fictionalism within which he expressed his loneliness at Max Gate. Inevitably he felt it all the more after losing the company of his dearest friends, Florence Dugdale and Florence Henniker. A serious decline in the health of his sister Mary added to his sadness at the end of the year.

Hardy was shocked to hear that his friend Major-General Arthur Henniker had died suddenly on 6 February 1912 of heart failure after being kicked by a horse and sustaining a broken leg. In April his wife sent him a copy of her new novel *Second Fiddle*, which Florence Dugdale (who probably typed it) had told him was 'a very good story'; he thought it one of her best. After remembering two acquaintances who had been lost when the *Titanic* sank six days earlier, he hoped Mrs Henniker was more settled and cheerful. Three days later he completed 'The Convergence of the Twain' for inclusion in the souvenir programme of the Dramatic and Operatic matinée in aid of the Titanic disaster fund. After staying with Florence Dugdale and the Shorters again at Aldeburgh one weekend in May, and hearing from Florence that Mrs Henniker would like a tribute from him for the memorial volume they were preparing, *Arthur Henniker: A Little Book for His Friends*, he sent her the verses 'A.H., 1855–1912', which were, he said, 'not so good as he deserved' but spontaneous and not 'made up'.

At various times from the summer of 1911 onwards Hardy had been advising Hermann Lea on photographic illustrations for his *Thomas Hardy's Wessex* (which was published in 1913), though he could not always remember in what stories places were to be found with fictional names in *A Group of Noble Dames*. Later Sydney Cockerell, director of the Fitzwilliam Museum, Cambridge, who was planning to form a collection of famous authors' manuscripts, visited Hardy and advised him what to do with his. Feeling that it would be unbecoming for him to offer them, Hardy was delighted when Cockerell proposed to take charge of their disposal, though he thought it appropriate to keep *The Mayor of Casterbridge* for the Dorset County Museum. By early October arrangements were made to send *Tess* and *The Dynasts* to the British Museum; a few days later most of the remainder were sent to Cockerell, Hardy agreeing that *Wessex Poems* and its illustrations should be sent to Birmingham, and suggesting *Time's Laughingstocks* for the Fitzwilliam Museum and *Poems of the Past and the Present* for the Bodleian. Cockerell must decide, and he did as Hardy wished. The following April he passed on the information that Hardy would be offered an honorary degree by the University of Cambridge; a month later he wrote to say that the award of honorary degrees had been postponed a year.

By this time Hardy knew that he was to receive the gold medal of the Royal Society of Literature. It was to be awarded on his seventy-second birthday and, as he and Emma had chosen not to book London accommodation 'for the season', the presentation took place at Max Gate. The Society was represented by Henry Newbolt and W. B. Yeats, who travelled by train and found the Dorchester platform empty when they arrived. According to Newbolt, this happened on Sunday, the appointed day. His account was written late in his life, years afterwards, and is less reliable than Hardy's note, which refers specifically to the weekend visit on Saturday, 1 June. Newbolt had been ill, and Hardy had written that morning urging him not to come unless he were better, and telling him that nobody would be present on the Sunday evening but Yeats, 'who is coming this evening because of the inconvenience of Sunday trains'. Newbolt must have caught the train on which Yeats travelled either in London or, more probably, en route. (Travel by train on Sunday from Salisbury would have been absurdly unpractical.) There is reason to think they spent the whole of the Sunday with the Hardys, the poem 'Where the Picnic Was' being based on the memory of an excursion with tea that afternoon on a hill overlooking the 'strange straight line' of Chesil Beach.

Newbolt could not forget the extraordinary evening of the event. Hardy and Emma sat facing each other at the ends of the table throughout an anxious dinner, with the visitors between them, on opposite sides, but too far apart to speak to each other, Hardy asking Newbolt question after question on the architecture of Rome and Venice, while Mrs Hardy imparted to Yeats 'much curious information about two very fine cats, who sat to right and left of her plate on the table itself'. Newbolt thought that Yeats looked like an eastern magician overpowered by a northern witch, and became spellbound by the famous pair of blue eyes, which surpassed all he had seen. At length Hardy rose and looked towards his wife. As she did not move, he opened the door and invited her to leave for a few minutes; for some reason he wished to have no witnesses while the ceremony was performed. Yeats and Newbolt begged she be allowed to stay, but he remained adamant, and she gathered up her cats and train, and departed. While Newbolt and Yeats spoke, Hardy looked more and more apprehensive. After the presentation he drew a roll of paper from the tail pocket of his coat, and read his reply in accordance with the report of the proceedings which he had already sent to London newspapers. In his view Newbolt wasted the best speech he ever made, Yeats wasted a very good one, and he made a bad one as usual, all to an audience which was 'quite properly limited'.

It is impossible to gauge how much Emma wrote in her last years. She once took Hermann Lea up to her attics, and showed him several wooden boxes in which she said her unpublished poems were stored; she also told him that she had inspired *Tess*. Two very small collections of her work, *Alleys* and *Spaces*, were printed in limited editions by Longman of Dorchester in December 1911 and April 1912 respectively, the first comprising fifteen poems, the best of which are inspired by ecstatic delight in nature, the second consisting of religious extracts and pieces in prose which reveal a sure faith based on some original and rhapsodic recasts of Revelation. The end of *Some Recollections* shows that, whatever her tribulations, she could rise above them in the certainty that an unseen Power of great benevolence directed her ways. 'A strange unearthly brilliance shines around our path, penetrating and dis-persing difficulties with its warmth and glow.' Her anti-Catholic zeal had led her to leave Protestant pamphlets in shops and homes, sanguine that they were conveyers of *truth*. During the last months of her life she was taken in a bathchair to services at Fordington church. For several years she had made a habit of inviting the vicar, Mr Bartelot, to tea, initially in the hope that he would save her husband's soul. In the middle of one of her large tea-parties at Max Gate, she started a prayer, to everyone's aston-ishment and discomfort, including Hardy's, who thought 'she must be going out of her mind'. The last took place on 16 July 1912, and many attended, Hardy between two visits to London, the first of which took him to Felixstowe, possibly with Florence Dugdale. In August he took his wife and Lilian Gifford to Weymouth, where they saw *Bunty Pulls the Strings*, a play which he had seen in London with Lady St Helier and Prince Albert of Schleswig-Holstein the previous June.

On 5 September Gosse arrived as expected with A. C. Benson, Fellow of Magdalene College, Cambridge. Benson, a depressive who had often been at odds with his companion, noted how Gosse in his customary grand manner took Emma by both hands and addressed her 'in a strain of exaggerated gallantry, which was deeply appreciated'. Both observed the absurdity of her dress. After lunch in the purple-distempered dining-room which plainly needed redecoration, Gosse persuaded her to smoke, much to Hardy's obvious disgust. Later in the afternoon he had to listen to complaints that her husband was conceited and difficult to live with, kept honours to himself, and wouldn't allow her to have a car. He noticed how Hardy brightened up when they recalled their adventures together about thirty years previously, but found him as sphinx-like as ever, content to leave his 'magnificent genius' unrevealed. In the garden with Benson, Emma ejected seeds from pods 'with little jumps and elfin shrieks'. He went away thinking that she was full of suspicions, jealousies, and 'affronts which must be half insane', wondering how 'the old rhapsodist' could live with the cat, the niece, and such an 'absurd, inconsequent, puffy, rambling old lady' in that shabby, pretentious house behind the dark, overgrown copse. However right he was, he was not very sympathetic.

Though she noticed heart symptoms occasionally, Emma seemed none the worse during the autumn. One day she sat down suddenly at the piano and played a long series of her favourite old tunes, after which she said she would never play again; Hardy remembered this when he wrote 'The Last Performance'. He must have been the authority for the story of their last quarrel in Newman Flower's *Just As It Happened*. He had decided to avoid the 'hurt' of further domestic discord by having all his meals in his study. Just as he had finished his lunch one day she came in, surveyed the remains on the table, and rated him to such effect that his 'passive defence' gave way and 'high words' ensued, much to his subsequent regret. A few days later, in her own world on 22 November, she wrote the lines:

> Oh! would I were a dancing child,
> Oh! would I were again
> Dancing in the grass of Spring
> Dancing in the rain
> Leaping with the birds on wing
> Singing with the birds that sing.

In the afternoon, which was damp and gloomy, she went by car to see her friend Eliza Wood Homer at Bardolf Manor beyond Puddletown.

(Mrs Wood Homer's daughter Christine had been interested in Emma's paintings and verses, but had long been aware of her eccentricities, and knew that her supreme wish was to receive 'the admiration of the world for talents she believed she possessed'; she sympathized with Hardy.) Emma was taken ill the next day, and on the following, which was her birthday, felt very depressed. On the next, Rebekah Owen and her sister called; they had motored down to see *The Trumpet-Major*, a revised version of the 1908 success. Although Hardy advised her not to do so, Emma came slowly down to the drawing-room, obviously in great pain. She had refused to have a doctor, not wishing to submit to the surgeon's knife. She insisted that the Owens' should stay for tea, and suggested they returned on Friday, when they could discuss the play after its two evening performances. Hardy came down when he heard that Rebekah wished to see him; she told him about Lascelles Abercrombie's book on him which she had bought, and promised to bring it the next day, since he had not seen it. After doing so, she returned to her lodgings and found a note from her old friend Teresa Fetherstonhaugh, thanking her for her letter and refutation of Mrs Hardy's 'charges against her poor old patient husband. She is a queer woman and I never thought her quite right in her upper story!' This 'queer woman' had come to the door to see the Owens' car after they had stayed a long time, then climbed back to her bed in the attics.

Next day she consented to see a doctor, who concluded, after she had declined a thorough examination, that she suffered from indigestion. She agreed to Hardy's seeing the dress rehearsal that evening. Early next morning she was extremely ill, and asked her maid to fetch him; she found him working in his study. After reproving her for the untidiness of her collar, he followed her upstairs, and was shocked at Emma's appearance, even more to find that she was unable to answer him. The doctor was summoned, but before he could arrive she died in the arms of the cook, who was trying to lift her. The performance of *The Trumpet-Major* took place in accordance with Hardy's wishes. The Owens attended on both evenings, the first with friends they had persuaded to come down from the Chilterns, the second with Mr Bankes of Wolfeton House, where they had heard him regret Hardy's repeated refusal to accept a knighthood, and express the wish that 'dear old Mrs Hardy' had been made Lady Hardy. At home Hardy had much on his mind, and much to do. Now, like Amos Barton, he could feel that his sympathy with his dead wife had not been 'quick and watchful enough', and begin to relive their life together 'with that terrible keenness of memory and imagination which bereavement gives'. His philosophy must have told him that she had suffered at the hands of 'the Wrongers' far more than his mother had done, and made him realize, as he was to realize yet more keenly, how, whatever he had endured, his stifled love needed pardon for its 'poverty and selfishness'. His rather recent rejection of a small attempt at reconciliation, after Emma had wounded his feelings, now became a continual reproach to him, as he recorded in 'The Peace-Offering':

> And for all I then declined
> O the regrettings infinite
> When the night-processions flit
> Through the mind!

24

Aftercourses

The funeral was not delayed. Emma was buried on Saturday, 30 November, in a grave where Hardy had planned to be interred with her; ironically, it was by the side of his parents and grand-parents, and in eventual proximity to the remaining members of a family from whom she had dissociated herself, distrusting them and scorning their peasant habits and stock. Rebekah Owen attended the funeral with the Leslies (her old friend Margaret, daughter of the late Henry Moule, and her husband, rector of Winterborne Came), and noticed no others present in the lonely churchyard but Hardy, his brother and sisters, a few local people, and 'a deputation from some Dorchester society'. Of the Giffords, only Lilian came, and she arrived too late for the service. The words on Hardy's wreath, 'From her lonely husband – with the old affection', meant more to him than they could convey to others, even to Rekebah, who thought the inscription the 'one outspoken word of a silent man', or to Teresa Fetherstonhaugh, who later wrote to her, 'What beautiful and well chosen words . . .'. During a period of conflicting thoughts and emotions, expression had come to him that was both apt and sincere.

A post-mortem examination revealed that Emma had died from impacted gallstones leading to 'internal perforation' and heart failure. However much Hardy felt he was to blame for neglect, and however regretful he must have been that nothing he said at the end could have comforted Emma, he had only to consider his more recent trials and tribulations to realize at times that his bereavement was tempered by a sense of relief. His sister Kate came to help in household management, and was assisted for a day or two by Florence Dugdale, who had planned a holiday at Weymouth, and found on arrival a telegram from Hardy announcing Emma's death; she had expected to see *The Trumpet-Major* that evening. He soon felt composed enough to begin poems evoked by her loss, the earliest including 'The Sound of Her', verses on the screwing down of her coffin lid which he was later persuaded not to publish, and 'Your Last Drive'. 'Tolerance' shows how comforted he was to remember his refusal to assert himself at times when he had thought it better not to submit to Emma's accusations and censure; it was the only consolation he felt with respect to her, though he knew he had been disdained for his passivity. Much of his time was soon taken up in correcting proofs of the *de luxe* American edition of his works (published in a very limited edition in 1915, with his signature on an inserted leaf), and Florence returned to help him. The sadness of thought which came to him when he had time to reflect on the past sometimes found expression in verse; 'The Prospect' contrasts his wintry surroundings in December with the garden party of July, and ends with the wish that he too were buried at Stinsford.

Nothing Hardy wrote on unpleasantnesses between Emma and himself suggests that his disclosures to his friends were unrestrained or vindictive. The charitable way in which he writes of her at this time to Mrs Henniker is typical: 'In spite of the differences between us, which it would be affectation to deny, and certain painful delusions she suffered from at times, my life is intensely sad to me now without her'; saddest, he went on to say, when he took the walk she used to take 'every evening just before dusk' at the top of the garden, 'the cat trotting faithfully behind her', and at times when he half-expected 'to see her as usual coming in from the flower-beds with a little trowel in her hand'. A month later Florence Dugdale reported that he looked well and cheerful, and had, according to his sister Kate, regained 'the same happy laugh he had when he was a young man'. Unfortunately, loneliness in the evenings led him to read and keep returning to his wife's 'voluminous diaries', until Florence began to think he would ultimately believe that all the 'bitter denunciations' of him which she had recorded from about 1891 until a day or two of her death were justified. Lilian had returned, after rushing up to London to sell her aunt's clothes, she continued; she did not think she would be a success in the house, for she also was imbued with ideas of Gifford grandeur, and of vulgarity in Hardy's relatives. (Lilian must have heard a good deal against him when she was at Calais with Emma, for she was certain he could not have been a great writer but for her 'dear aunt's influence'.) Florence Dugdale's feelings were quickly roused; she had learned much, and she now sympathized deeply with Hardy. She ended her letter to Clodd with a reference to the loneliness he had preferred to endure when he spent long evenings in his study to avoid 'insult and abuse'. It may have been cruel and in atrocious taste for her to write in this way, she admitted, 'but truth is truth, after all'.

Reading Emma's happy account of her early life, from childhood at Plymouth to the years of pre-marriage romance at St Juliot, in *Some Recollections* may, more than anything else, have made Hardy decide to revisit those places and other scenes of his courtship days. He set off with his brother on Thursday, 6 March, staying at Boscastle, his intention being to see the rectory at St Juliot the next day, the anniversary of his first visit in 1870. Florence remained at Max Gate, taking the precaution of having a loaded revolver in her bedroom, for fear of a night marauder in such an isolated place. She knew that Hardy had dismissed Emma's abuse of him as unwilled, the effect of hallucinations, and had made much of her virtues, particularly her strict Evangelicalism and her humani-tarianism (which Florence thought must apply to cats). She had realized as never before how unselfish and deeply affectionate he was. Only the other night he had produced one of those 'diabolical diaries' from his pocket and read her a passage in which Emma had said how right her father had been in his estimate of him (adding, after some adjectival abuse, 'utterly worthless'). Now, she continued, Hardy was on his way to Plymouth, to find the grave of the same father, who had addressed him in a letter as 'a low-born churl' who had presumed to marry into his family. All would be well, his sister Kate had commented, provided he didn't pick up another Gifford down there. He had gone, he said, for the sake of the girl he had married, and who had died more than twenty years ago. She had now become his 'late espousèd saint', Florence tartly observed.

Revivification of a past which may have seemed prospectively enchanting from its remoteness and its contrast to the more recent sequel proved to be a painful experience when Hardy saw Boscastle and its harbour, the Valency valley, Beeny Cliff, the rectory and the church at St Juliot, and other places he had known in company with the young woman who had brought so much happiness into his life. Truly he had cause to think with Dante that (in Tennyson's words) 'a sorrow's crown of sorrow is remembering happier things'. More than once he wondered what had possessed him to come; he did not stay long. Writing to tell Florence he would be back on the following Tuesday, he spoke of the cruelty of events which had begun 'so auspiciously' and 'turned out as they did', and hoped that she would not suffer physically as Emma had done mentally.

In Plymouth, on the return journey, after calling at Launceston, he arranged for a tablet to be placed in St Juliot Church in memory of her who had played the organ there and laid the foundation stone for the new tower and aisle. Thoughts and feelings inspired by the places he had just visited were the source of some of the finest of the 1912–13 poems which were written as '*Veteris vestigia flammae*'. The line 'The woman whom I loved so, and who loyally loved me' had the same qualified time significance and tragic sincerity as 'with the old affection' on Hardy's wreath. Recollections of days which were a joy in no wise deflected him from sheer honesty in this elegiac series; all was past amend, and Emma was beyond praise or blame, love or indifference. Certain poems or features of poems were influenced by *Some Recollections*, and many more were to be written as a result of his journey and visits to her grave or places where they had lived, few more poignant than 'During Wind and Rain', based primarily on Emma's memories of her family at Plymouth, and 'Where three roads joined', the title of which implies a tragedy as predestined as that of Oedipus.

Writing and proof-reading were interrupted late in April for a visit to Florence Dugdale and Mrs Henniker at Southwold, where he met Meredith's cousin S. M. Ellis, the biographer of Harrison Ainsworth, a novelist whom Hardy read in his early years and for whom he expressed great admiration. From Southwold it was but a short distance to Aldeburgh, where Hardy conversed with Clodd on Emma's delusions and a manuscript she had written in which the heroine inspired her husband's novels. At the time he was having Max Gate redecorated and repaired; later a conservatory was added to the drawing-room. In June he received his honorary Litt.D. at Cambridge, where he stayed with Cockerell, lunched with Dr Donaldson, Master of Magdalene and Vice-Chancellor of the University, and dined in hall after the ceremony with H. M. Butler, Master of Trinity, whose invitation to respond to the toast he had declined on the score that he was an unpractised recluse who had been lately bereaved. Florence was back at Max Gate, and among the earliest visitors were Clodd and Shorter, who were introduced to Hardy's brother and sisters at Talbothays (to which they had recently moved. Hermann Lea had been living at their old home since February.) Clodd was so impressed by Henry and his two sisters that he thought it a shame Hardy had allowed his 'half mad wife' to keep them and their mother (whom Evangeline Smith described as 'hospitality itself') from Max Gate. After staying there in September, Mabel Robinson had little doubt that Hardy and Miss Dugdale were engaged. He had to be on his guard to ensure that Lilian or Kate was in the house when Florence was there. When a maid left a few years earlier because she was pregnant, he was blamed locally; it was even said that he kept a mistress named Florence Dugdale in London. (Years later, when she was a parlourmaid at Max Gate, Ellen Titterington heard some less malicious gossip from an old chimneysweep who had known Hardy's first wife: she had written all his books, and Hardy had kept her locked in the attics. Rightly or wrongly, Ellen inferred that the first Mrs Hardy convinced the old man on the question of authorship, because he ended by saying, 'Thomas has wrote no novels since her death, so there!')

Hardy had spent a most interesting weekened with Sir Sidney Colvin, formerly Director of the Fitzwilliam Museum, who had come to Max Gate on his way to Colyton, Devon. His mission was to discover whether Hardy would collaborate with Sir Edward Elgar in the production of an opera based on one of his works. For Hardy the prospect was exciting, and a number of possibilities occurred to him. From Max Gate on Sunday, 20 July, Colvin wrote to tell Elgar that his 'embassy' had been successful, the 'old man' being keen to co-operate. He had proposed three alternatives: 'a light and whimsical peasant opera' from *The Trumpet-Major*, a tragic one with striking picturesque and dramatic scenes from *The Return of the Native*, or another drawn from a section of *The Dynasts*, preferably 'the hundred days' (ending with the battle of Waterloo), which offered 'big cosmic forces (choruses, perhaps invisible, of the Pities and the Years) as well as historic personages and events'. Hardy was delighted and would like to discuss the question with Elgar, Colvin reported, convinced, as they all were, that such a joint work 'would have a huge effect'. Eight days later Hardy sent another proposal to Elgar; he had been thinking of *A Pair of Blue Eyes*, which 'would furnish all the voices, and has a distinct and central heroine, with a wild background of cliffs and sea'. Sir Edward said he would read the books, but, whatever the reason, nothing came of the idea which had clearly appealed to Colvin and elicited Hardy's enthusiastic response.

Although Gosse assumed that he must have been disappointed when Robert Bridges was made Poet Laureate, Hardy was too realistic to entertain high expectations for himself, knowing that his heterodoxies made him an unlikely choice; the poem 'God's

Funeral' alone would have damned him, he said. After visiting Blandford to meet John Lane and help him to discover facts about the early life there of the artist and sculptor Alfred Stevens, he sent off copies of twelve uncollected stories, including 'The Romantic Adventures of a Milkmaid', for publication. When he was revising proofs near the end of August, he informed Sir George Douglas that, though they were 'mostly bad', he had been compelled to include them in his 'set of books' because pirated and badly printed editions of some of them were circulating in America and being imported into England. Ten thousand copies of *A Changed Man*, were published by Macmillan in October, in addition to an American edition by Harper & Brothers, and the reviews were surprisingly favourable. Hardy had chosen not to include 'An Indiscretion in the Life of an Heiress' because he considered it a 'pale shadow' of the original, and thought he might find it 'amusing' to attempt a restoration, aided by memory and a fragment of *The Poor Man and the Lady* which was still in existence.

During the earlier part of the autumn Hardy seems to have been left in charge of Max Gate, one result being that some of Emma's 'animal pets' died, strayed, or were killed, much to his regret. He received short visits from friends, including Frederic Harrison, and he continued to write poems. At the beginning of November, when he was made an honorary fellow of Magdalene College, he stayed with the Donaldsons and was pleased to appear in his doctoral scarlet; after the chapel ceremony he spent an agreeable evening with A. E. Housman, Sir Clifford Allbutt, and other friends. In London, at a special preliminary showing for the press, he had watched an American film of *Tess*. In Dorchester, at a rehearsal of *The Woodlanders*, another Evans dramatization, he was much impressed by the performance of Gertrude Bugler, a girl of only sixteen, as Marty South. The gift of *Memories of a Vicarage* from its author Handley Moule, Bishop of Durham, delighted him, though he wished for more abundant detail on the past; as soon as he had read it, he sent it to his sister Mary, who had been born on the same day as his old friend. Just before Christmas he wrote a long letter to Mrs Henniker, telling her that Sir Hubert von Herkomer was taking shots for a film of *Far from the Madding Crowd*, and enclosing a half-page from the *Sphere* which contained 'To Meet, or Otherwise', perhaps in the hope that she would guess that the girl of his dreams was Florence Dugdale.

On the anniversary of her aunt's death Lilian Gifford had

presented a lamp to Hardy with the affectionate note, 'It is more than a year ago I renamed you "Daddy-Uncle" and that is what you are to me, and God bless you.' She and Florence had been helping to manage at Max Gate, but not very amicably. Writing to Clodd on New Year's Day, Florence announced her intention not to enter into the 'compact' she had revealed to him in the summer if 'the niece' stayed permanently; the question had to be settled in a week, or she would go home for good. However fond of Lilian he was, Hardy soon made up his mind, and Lilian went, financially compensated after he had raised her annuity from £13 to £52. Emma had left little apart from £220 in Plymouth stock, which he included in the much larger investment he made for Lilian's security. Florence returned home to prepare for her wedding, leaving behind Wessie (Wessex), the wire-haired terrier puppy she had recently acquired when he was only a few months old. At eight o'clock on the morning of 10 February 1914 she and Hardy were married by special licence in Enfield church with only the minimal three assisting in the function: Henry Hardy, Mr Dugdale, and his youngest daughter Margaret, a student whose training in domestic science was being financed by Florence from her Stoker legacy. With wise foresight, Hardy had done everything possible to ensure that the church was not besieged by reporters and photographers. After lunch and champagne at the Dugdales', the married pair left for Max Gate. The news was soon in all the papers, and congratulations poured in, one from Henry Stone, who had been one of Hardy's colleagues at Blomfield's. Of those most familiar with the couple, only Mrs Henniker and one other were taken by surprise. In his reply to Frederic Harrison's congratulations, Hardy said it was the modest hope of his wife and himself that 'the union of two rather melancholy temperaments' would result in cheerfulness, 'as the junction of two negatives forms a positive'. On 4 March Teresa Fetherstonhaugh spent 'a delightful time' with them at Max Gate, where she noticed the flowers in the drawing-room and the new conservatory. She thought Florence dear and gentle despite her melancholy mien, and she had never seen Hardy so relaxed and happy.

Florence's habit of attracting birds, soon after her marriage, by hanging up pieces of meat in the trees was noticed by one of the Max Gate servants, who was led to believe she was writing books on the subject for children. However indirectly, this surmise must have originated from her collaboration with the artist E. J. Detmold.

She had provided informative and descriptive accounts to accompany his watercolour illustrations in two books, first, *The Book
of Baby Beasts* in 1911, then, *The Book of Baby Birds* in 1912. For the
latter Hardy had supplied at least one poem, 'The Yellow-
Hammer'; 'The Calf' in the former was attributed to him by Florence's
sisters. A third volume in the series, *The Book of Pets*, was undertaken during the first year of her marriage; the manuscript of the
quatrain heading the chapter 'About Lizards' shows that it was
written by Hardy, who probably helped to improve some of the
other verse inclusions.

Although the marriage was not without convenience to both
parties, it was promoted by Florence's personal and literary devotion and by Hardy's desire to find the kind of domestic relationship that had been denied him for years. He undoubtedly felt, and
continued to feel, a protective solicitude for his wife's health and
welfare. He did not ask for much, he once told Florence, only a
little affection. For a honeymoon which was taken 'in slices' he
took her first to seaside resorts in Devon, then, after attending to
repairs and gardening requisitions at Max Gate, to London. In May
they spent a week at Cambridge, where they met the new professor
of English literature, Arthur Quiller-Couch, and several of Hardy's
friends, including the oldest, Charles Moule, now President of
Corpus College. They enjoyed hospitality at colleges and elsewhere, finally at Girton, where they had tea with Miss Jones and
members of her staff. At an afternoon service in King's College
Chapel, Hardy's thoughts turned to two previous visits, with
Emma in 1880 and Horace Moule in 1873. (Shortly afterwards he
did his best to assure Mrs Henniker that vivisectors would avoid
torturing animals, when she expressed disgust that Prince Arthur
of Connaught had opened a new physiological laboratory at Cambridge, and wished some mad woman would burn it down.) His
interest in the Giffords, which was to persist (more and more to
Florence's annoyance), led to an excursion by car to Plymouth with
Hermann Lea (who was to drive them hundreds of miles from 1914
to 1916, always at Hardy's expense; he enjoyed being 'alone' with
him, because it was only then that the 'simple' side of Hardy's
character came to the fore). They spent two days finding the graves
of Emma's parents, and Florence found the search a melancholy
business. A few days were spent in London during June at Lady St
Helier's, where they dined with Mr and Mrs Winston Churchill;
they also visited the Macmillans and Gosses. Keen to retain links

which were more than half a century old, Hardy attended the
RIBA dinner, though all the members he had known, except the
vice-president and the younger Blomfields, had passed away.
Early in July he and Florence, with Charles Whibley and his wife,
were the guests of Sir Henry and Lady Hoare at Stourhead in
Wiltshire, with its beautiful lake and surroundings; Florence climbed
Stourton Tower for the extensive views, and her subsequent letters
to Lady Hoare found a ready response.

On their return to Max Gate, much time was spent collecting and
arranging poems for a new volume. Sir Frederick Macmillan had
suggested a new, *de luxe* edition of Hardy's works, but priority was
soon given to the publication of the poems, Hardy choosing
'Satires of Circumstance' for the title from that of a short series of
satirical sketches which he felt had to be included because they had
been published in 1911 and would be expected in the new collection. Produced from notes which he had made about twenty years
earlier, they may well have appeared at odds with 'Poems of
1912–13', which he rather shrank from publishing, though, as he told
Mrs Henniker, he felt they provided 'the only amends' he could
make. Among other poems recalling Emma and Hardy's visits to
Cornwall were 'When I set out for Lyonnesse', the Proustian
'Under the Waterfall', 'Self-Unconscious', 'The Re-Enactment' (thinly
fictionalized), and 'In Front of the Landscape'. The more miscellaneous included 'Wessex Heights', 'God's Funeral', 'Beyond the
Last Lamp', 'A Singer Asleep', 'The Coronation' (a fantasy on that
of George V), and 'The Abbey Mason'. 'After the Visit' and 'To
Meet, or Otherwise' were paired near the opening for the sake of
Florence, and the volume was planned to end with the poet's
tribute to both his wives, following the symbolical 'Exeunt Omnes',
which was written on his seventy-third birthday, when he wondered how much longer he had to live. Before the collection
reached the publishers England was at war, much to Hardy's
surprise, and before publication of the volume in November the
war-song 'Men Who March Away' had been added as a conclusion
more in keeping with the times.

Florence was easily depressed, and her copy of *Satires of Circumstance*, inscribed to her 'in all affection', made her feel profoundly
sad, as she confusedly assumed that her husband and the poet
were identical selves. Though he denied having written a despondent poem for eighteen months, she could not rid herself of the
thought that he was 'utterly weary of life', and wondered whether

he would have published the volume if she had been 'a different sort of woman, and better fitted to be his wife'. So she wrote to Lady Hoare five days after writing to sympathize with Rebekah Owen on the loss of her sister, and alluding, it seems, to the death of Alfred Hyatt, 'the only person who ever loved me – for I am not loveable'; nobody in the world, she told Miss Owen, cared whether she was happy or sad. She was the victim of her feelings, high or low (especially in her letters), and could plunge into depths of misery.

25

In Time of 'the Breaking of Nations'

Although 'Channel Firing', written in April 1914, might appear premonitory, Hardy was quite unaware of German aggressive planning for imperial aggrandizement, and still believed that western civilization had reached the age of reason. This streak of evolutionary optimism was extraordinarily bold for one so usually guarded in outlook. When Galsworthy wrote to him in June 1911 on aeroplanes as a military menace, Hardy declared himself an extremist in thinking it 'an insanity that people in the 20th Century should suppose force to be a moral argument'. The poet of 'The Sick Battle-God' and of the ending of *The Dynasts* had not changed by July 1914, when few realized that the assassination of a prince at Sarajevo could be used by designing militarists to precipitate a war which, as a result of one alliance after another, would quickly involve most European powers and eventually the USA, last more than four years, and cost millions of lives. It was to make Hardy regret that he ended *The Dynasts* as he did, and have consequences that caused him to regard the future almost with despair. As a result of the invasion of Belgium (a neutral country) and France at the beginning of August, England, quite militarily off-guard, was obliged to declare war. Two weeks later German merchant seamen, who had been trapped in ports, were imprisoned at Dorchester, which was full of troops (mostly drunken, Hardy reported to Clodd). So too was Weymouth, a port of embarkation over which moving searchlights were visible at night from Max Gate.

In response to a summons from the Cabinet, Hardy attended a meeting of British writers, including Sir James Barrie, Newbolt, Galsworthy, G. M. Trevelyan, Robert Bridges, John Masefield, Gilbert Murray, Arnold Bennett, and H. G. Wells, at Wellington House on 2 September, to consider how they could best serve the allied cause. He remembered how the sun shone in from the dusty street as they sat 'full of misgivings' round a large blue table, and the streets 'bustling with soldiers and recruits' as he left London in

the evening. His 'Men Who March Away', written almost immediately afterwards for publication in *The Times*, was so popular that,
with no copyright restrictions, it was widely reprinted. A mani-
festo with the signatures of Hardy and 51 other authors soon
followed. In October, fully convinced of German malfeasance, he
wrote 'England to Germany', the sonnet 'On the Belgian Expatri-
ation', and a letter of protest against the bombardment of Rheims
Cathedral. Towards the end of the year he sent 'An Appeal to
America on Behalf of the Belgian Destitute' to the *New York Times*;
William Watson's sonnet 'To America, Concerning England', a
plea against neutrality which had already appeared in the *Evening
News*, earned his highest admiration when he saw it for the first
time more than three months later in *The Times*. Granville-Barker's
abridgement and adaptation of *The Dynasts* had been produced at
the Kingsway Theatre from 25 November to the end of January
1915 as a further boost to the war effort. Although he attended a
rehearsal, Hardy was not fit to return to London for the first
performance, when he was represented by Florence, who sat next
to John Masefield and his wife, and was introduced to H. G. Wells.
When they saw it in December, he was much more impressed by it
than he expected, and was delighted to learn that it had been seen
one afternoon by Mr Asquith, the Prime Minister. Hardy contributed generously to the April sales of manuscripts which were held
each year during the war for the maintenance of the Red Cross
ambulance service. A rather consoling universal truth about war
occurred to him in 1915 when he remembered a rural scene in
Cornwall forty-five years earlier during the Franco-Prussian war,
and wrote 'In Time of "the Breaking of Nations"'. He referred to it
later when he claimed to have 'a faculty . . . for burying an
emotion' in his 'heart or brain for forty years, and exhuming it at
the end of that time as fresh as when interred'.

Lilian Gifford's return to Max Gate for Christmas revived
Florence's easily kindled suspicion that she would resort to
'mischief-making tactics' in the hope of living there permanently.
In her postscript to Hardy's letter of 11 February she assured Clodd
that their first year of married life had *really* and *truly* been very
happy. In fact, she had felt lonely at times, missing the friends she
used to have, especially at Mrs Henniker's, where she had spent
weeks; there was nobody in Dorchester like the people she used to
meet there, and Hardy did not wish her to repeat Emma's mistake
of making too many local calls. So she had written to Rebekah

Owen, who sent her two guineas to buy a present for her wedding anniversary, and came down to see her in April, when Hardy mapped out a tour for them under the guidance of his sister Kate. He preferred to stay at home, and work in his study. During March sciatica made Florence wish he would take her to Bath for treatment; he would particularly enjoy the visit if Frederic Harrison were at home, she thought. In the end she decided it would be 'too cruel' to drag him away from his poetry. Early in May she accompanied him to London, where he sat to Hamo Thornycroft for 'a model of a head which the sculptor wished to make'. At the end of the month she underwent an operation for nasal catarrh, choosing to go alone because Hardy was usually unwell if he stayed more than a few days in the city; he urged her not to come home too soon because of the cold winds, and told her he did not mind paying the additional expense. She paid for the operation at least, and remained a week in a nursing-home, established by Sir Frederick Treves in Welbeck Street, before spending a few days with Lady St Helier and returning home. On 10 June she and Hardy motored with Hermann Lea to Bridport, Lyme Regis, and Torquay, returning for the night to Exeter, after having tea with the writer Eden Phillpotts and his wife, and viewing their beautiful garden; the next day they looked round the cathedral and came home via Honiton, Chard, and Crewkerne. On the 27th they visited the tithe-barn at Cerne Abbas, the first time he had seen the interior since examining it for a scene in *Far from the Madding Crowd*. In July, while staying in London at Lady St Helier's, they met Mrs Henniker and paid a long-promised visit to Sir Frederick and Lady Treves at Richmond; Hardy sat again to Hamo Thornycroft. After he had attended the funeral at Stinsford of his old friend the banker Douglas Thornton of Birkin House, they received visits at Max Gate from Sir Henry Hoare, who motored with Charles Whibley from Stourhead, and from Professor Flinders Petrie, whom he had not seen for several years. Late in August Florence sold books, including autographed copies from authors, at a garden bazaar which was held at Kingston Maurward in aid of the Dorset Red Cross. The house and estate now belonged to Cecil Hanbury, whose wife was the daughter of John Symons Jeune, the late Archdeacon Gifford's brother-in-law.

Although the will he made in 1922 shows that Hardy and Florence had not ruled out the possibility of having a child, he had probably given thought to the question of succession before his sisters, in the absence of Florence when she was in London for her operation, urged the importance of ensuring that Max Gate and the bulk of his estate passed to some Hardy relative. The most obvious candidate was Frank William George, who, after working in a Dorchester bank and another in Bristol, had been called to the bar at Gray's Inn. He had volunteered to join the forces at the outbreak of war, and been made a lieutenant in his Dorset regiment after Hardy had supported his application in March. Soon afterwards he came to see Hardy and Florence, and they took such a liking to him that he was regarded as their heir (though Gordon Gifford was not without hope of being next in succession). In August 1915 the Hardys were shocked to hear he had been killed at Gallipoli, after distinguishing himself in action against the Turks. He was 'almost the only, if not the only, blood relative of the next generation' in whom he had been interested, Hardy wrote to Mrs Henniker (as if Nathaniel Sparks's sons were no longer in favour). He and Florence visited his widowed mother and sisters at Bere Regis, offered financial assistance, and bade farewell to a brother who had been given only three days' leave after serving eleven months in Flanders and France; another brother was in 'the front line of trenches'. How Frank's departure and the news of his death affected his home on the edge of 'Egdon Heath' is the subject of Hardy's poem 'Before Marching and After'.

Hardy's main solace continued to come from retiring to his study either to write poetry or read a selection from the books his friends and admirers sent him. The young writers of *vers libre* who thought everything wrong with poetry before they arrived struck him as extraordinarily ignorant of the art of verse they slighted because it was too familiar or hackneyed. He was very keen that Harold Child should distinguish in the book he was preparing on him between his *essential* and *accidental* works, the first being his verse (including *The Dynasts*) and the second his prose, which he preferred rather misleadingly to regard as written by force of circumstances and not from inclination. He found he was becoming less capable of writing on demand, but, although when asked for a poem in celebration of the forthcoming Shakespeare tercentenary he claimed that age was making him less energetic and the war had destroyed 'spontaneity for ideas disconnected from it', his poetical efforts, often stirred by thoughts of the past, did not diminish. From the sheets of his four volumes of poetry, which the publishers sent at his request in July, he soon prepared a selection for the small volume they had discussed publishing after the war; it appeared in their Golden Treasury series in October 1916. A subject referred to him by Sir Sidney Colvin in the summer of 1914, on where Keats and his artist friend Severn landed on the Dorset coast when they were on their way to Rome, was remembered at the appropriate time in 'At Lulworth Cove a Century Back'. Hardy's concern for biographical truth with reference to himself was yet to come to a head. When Sydney Cockerell agreed to act as one of his literary executors soon after the outbreak of war, he thought he would send him dates for reference should any 'preposterous stories' arise requiring factual correction, but declared little interest in posthumous opinions of himself when he would be sleeping 'quite calmly' at Stinsford. 'My reminiscences: no, never!' he declared in answer to the question when he would begin writing them which came from Sir George Douglas towards the end of 1915.

On returning from Melbury House, where he and Florence had stayed with Lady Ilchester (her husband being at the Dardanelles, near where Lieutenant George was killed), Hardy learned that his sister was gravely ill. She died of emphysema a few days later, on 24 November, when Florence wrote to Rebekah Owen, 'She was the kindest sister-in-law to me. Never one unkind word or look', and contemplated the strange irony of her burial next to Emma, who had died almost three years previously; 'You know how things were between those two', she added. Kate was annoyed when Hardy and Florence refused 'even to the last moment' to see Mary after her death and kiss her. When he heard the words of the psalm read by Mr Cowley, the vicar of Stinsford, from the Book of Common Prayer, 'I held my tongue, and spake nothing; I kept silence, yea, even from good words', he thought none could have been more appropriate to his sister, who never defended herself, 'not from timidity, but indifference to opinion'. Immediately after her funeral he upset Henry (who had not fully recovered from a stroke which had incapacitated him early in the year) by refusing to go to Talbothays and meet all the relatives. Soon 'Logs on the Hearth', composed in memory of his sister, had its sequel in 'Looking Across', a poem in which Hardy thinks successively of the four members of his family who lay buried at Stinsford. What Florence must have felt when she read the concluding verse, before or after publication, can easily be imagined:

Tired, tired am I
Of this earthly air,
And my wraith asks: Why,
Since these calm lie,
Are not Five out there?

By the end of the year, when he had made a will which ensured that no more than a due share of his estate passed to his second wife, Florence found Kate 'nice' again. She then jumped to the conclusion that the recent exhibition of a Dodsonian trait in Hardy's brother and sisters was due to poverty and maternal sacrifices when they were young, and explained, she told Rebekah, why the first Mrs Hardy quarrelled with them. Her correspondence with Lady Hoare at the opening of 1916 suggests, however, that Hardy had seen his childhood in a different light at Christmas; and that, mindful of the European slaughter, he had turned nostalgically back in 'The Oxen' to the old rural superstition of a Christian faith he had once shared with his departed sister.

Though Emma's quarrels belonged to a distant past, Hardy could never forget them. In January 1916 Florence referred to the diaries which she had found 'full of venom, hatred and abuse of him and his family', adding parenthetically 'which he burned', as if they had been destroyed long ago. He had a new companion in Wessex, the wire-haired terrier she had acquired late in 1913; although an excitable and quarrelsome disturber of the peace at Max Gate, and probably unwelcome at first, he had won Hardy's affection, so much so that he now kissed him goodnight before he was carried off to bed. February brought special occasions, when Hardy sat to Rothenstein, who was staying not far away at Moreton, and when Sydney Cockerell came for a weekend. The weather was cold, and Hardy had begun his winter habit of sitting with a shawl round his head all day in his study. Sometimes he and Florence had soldiers to tea, and were surprised to find how many pro-fessions the khaki uniform could conceal. It was a time of great shortages, when, as Hardy wrote to Gosse, old shoes had to be cobbled, coals put on fires 'as it were with sugartongs', and cider drunk in wineglasses. He was pleased when Cockerell accepted for his wife's use the well-cushioned bathchair he had bought prin-cipally for the Max Gate handyman to wheel Emma to Fordington church when her health was failing in 1912. In the evening he and

Florence read aloud the lectures *On the Art of Writing* which Quiller-Couch had sent; a month later, after reading a copy of H. C. Duffin's study of the Wessex novels which he had received from the author, Hardy qualified his gratitude with regret that his poetry, to which 'half his writing life' had been devoted, had been ignored. In London about this time Florence was impressed by Thornycroft's sculpture of his head, which she saw at a private view, and interested in the Red Cross sale of manuscripts, where she discovered that Hardy's had raised over £70, 'In Time of "the Breaking of Nations"'' alone fetching £17. She was disappointed to miss George Bernard Shaw and his wife, and the Burys, who had called at Max Gate. They were followed by Reginald Smith and his wife in May. Hardy's seventy-sixth birthday seemed a puny matter when news arrived on 3 June of the battle of Jutland, and fears were roused for friends in the British fleet; subsequently it was learned that Mr Cowley's brother-in-law, Captain Prowse of the *Queen Mary* (commemorated in 'The Sea Fight'), had been lost with his ship and crew.

It was a relief for Florence when Hardy found time for outings. Household management, which she never found easy, reviewing, secretarial work, and reading to her husband in the evenings left her little time, even for writing and expressing her feelings to Rebekah Owen; her letters to Lady Hoare were more concerned with Hardy's literary work. The threat of air raids and his ingrained fear of catching 'influenza' kept Hardy away from London, but he was pleased to make country excursions in favourable weather with Hermann Lea. The first of the year 1916 may have been the one they took to Racedown, the house where Wordsworth had lived with Dorothy when his poetic greatness was beginning to emerge. Hardy's visit with Florence and his sister Kate to Riverside Villa, Sturminster Newton, must have been exciting and memorable for all three. He had not seen it for nearly forty years, and the result was three more poems, 'Overlooking the River Stour', 'The Musical Box', and 'On Sturminster Foot-Bridge', all reminiscential, though two are mainly descriptive, with felicitous images of a moorhen darting out and 'planing up shavings of crystal spray' and of swallows flying like 'little crossbows animate' or 'arrowing' off and dropping like stones by the river. (Some three years later, when he discovered that Robert Lynd was the reviewer who had deemed lines from the last of these poems about as musical as a milk-cart, Hardy wrote to him without mincing matters and pointed out that the words echoed 'the clucking sound of water when blown up-stream into holes on the bank'; after that the poem was printed with '(Onomatopœic)' below the title.) Towards the end of the month, after seeing *Wessex Scenes from 'The Dynasts'* performed by the Hardy Players at Weymouth, where the theatre was crowded (with many wounded service men attending) to raise money for the Red Cross and for Russian casualties, the Hardys visited Lady Ilchester and her young sister-in-law Lady Londonderry at Melbury House. Other excursions took them to Swanage and Bridport. They attended a large tea-party at West Stafford rectory, where Alice Smith noticed how 'genial and mellowed' his 'kind, gentle little wife' and his London literary friends had made him, and how he looked forward to the production of *Wessex Scenes from 'The Dynasts'* in Dorchester. Whatever his poetry suggests, Hardy's zest for life was evident.

How his poetry was apt to repeat his 'Looking Across' strain may be seen in the conclusion of 'Quid Hic Agis?', which appears to have been written when he and Florence were preparing to visit St Juliot. They broke their train journey at Launceston, where they called on Emma's cousins, to one of whom he had written when he sent a copy of *Satires of Circumstance* in November 1914, explaining how an unfortunate mental aberration had made his wife 'cold in her correspondence' with her friends and relatives, changing a nature which had been 'most childlike and trusting'. After examining the tablet to her memory in St Juliot Church, they met accidentally Hardy's old friends the Stuart-Wortleys at Tintagel, where their holiday was spoilt by an occurrence at church. They had sat by a passage to seats in the transept in order to view the nave as Emma had painted it, when the vicar requested them to move to the back in order to make room for the choir as it entered. Hardy was annoyed, but found some consolation in listening to a psalm sung to Smart's fine old tune 'Wiltshire', which recalled Sundays at Stinsford in his boyhood. The vicar, he thought, looked indignant when they walked out at the beginning of his sermon. Florence hoped the Tintagel visit would produce 'an Iseult poem', and her interest in the subject may have sown the long dormant seed from which *The Famous Tragedy of the Queen of Cornwall* grew. At Plymouth she endured another protracted search for Gifford burial stones.

Two publications which interested Hardy in the summer were

Gosse's *Inter Arma: Being Essays written in Time of War*, a birthday present from John Symons Jeune which Florence read to him in the evenings, and J. W. Mackail's British Academy lecture on Shakespeare. One idea which the second of these elicited, that Shakespeare 'puts into his ordinary folk's mouths sentiments that they would have expressed if they could', though they 'never could have in this world', with the addition that we must be grateful when we see what realistic writing 'is coming to', reflects what Hardy achieved with his rustics, and was criticized for, in some of his best novels. Though he saw little hope of an end to the war, he could be excited by news of successes, such as the bringing down of a zeppelin near London at the beginning of·September. After visiting a large German prisoners' camp in Dorchester, including a hospital where many lay helpless with wounds, not far from another filled with English casualties, he sent some of his German books for their library. In the late autumn he was happy making a Barnes selection, and writing an introduction to it, for Humphry Ward's *The English Poets*. Clodd's *Memories* brought relief to him and Florence; they had been so alarmed when they heard that he was about to publish his reminiscences that Florence had sounded a warning note at Hardy's suggestion, but they found no revelations in the book to which they could object, and she pronounced it 'dull'. After reading Wells's war novel *Mr. Britling Sees It Through* to Hardy, she informed Mrs Wells that she had not seen him more moved 'over any book for ages', and wished they were in London and could 'see something' of her and her husband. In December Hardy was busy with rehearsals for the postponed Dorchester performance of *Wessex Scenes from 'The Dynasts'* in aid of the Red Cross; the result was a heavy cold which prevented his seeing it with Barrie and Cockerell. So crowded was the town with officers and their families that Barrie stayed with the Hanburys at Kingston Maurward and Rebekah Owen at Weymouth. Writing to her afterwards, Florence retracted all she had said against Cockerell, realizing how false her earlier impressions had been. In October she had seen a hateful look in his eye, and loathed him; a week later she complained of his arrogance and his wish to take charge of everything, Hardy included.

Florence had reason to be pleased with Cockerell. In February 1917 she received from him *The Poor Man and the Lady* ('a good portion' of the manuscript) bound in light blue morocco as a wedding-anniversary gift; about ten years later Hardy felt it ought not to be preserved, and she allowed him to burn it on his study fire. Cockerell had probably convinced him, as he had suggested a year or more earlier, in December 1915, that with his (Hardy's) assistance she was capable of producing Hardy's biography. At first she seems to have assumed she could do this by a process of interrogation, and she made lots of notes. When she reached the account of Hardy's leaving home for London she inadvertently typed 'April 1917' for 'April 1862', a clear indication of when she was working. By the end of July, however, this method was abandoned, after Hardy had agreed to enlarge on the notes and write his reminiscences in full. For the later years of his life, on which he had preserved more and more documentary evidence, she was to give him more assistance, possibly agreeing with him on what was worth preserving, then typing up, and submitting the typescript for his revision. All this remained a close secret, though Cockerell was kept informed of progress. By June 1918 the year 1895 had been reached, and all Hardy's first drafts of notes on the period from 1840 to 1892 had been burned. This work was to continue into the post-war years. Cockerell must have pleased Florence in the spring of 1916, when he suggested to Hardy that, instead of allowing his poems to be issued by Clement Shorter in privately printed pamphlets, either he or Florence could undertake such publications. Hardy was delighted to leave this work to his wife, and poems were published singly or in small groups at intervals by the Chiswick Press, Cockerell usually checking the proofs; in the last years of Hardy's life a few were printed by Henry Ling of Dorchester. The first in the series, the poem 'To Shakespeare after Three Hundred Years', appeared in August 1916. Of this, 50 copies were printed; thereafter the number was reduced to 25. War poems were prominent in 1917.

Nothing made Hardy more sad about the war than the sight of 'amiable young Germans' under guard at Max Gate, where they were sent from the prison in February 1917 to uproot trees for the enlargement of the kitchen garden, a small operation testifying to food shortages throughout Britain as a result of submarine warfare. In full agreement with the principles of a memorandum to promote international peace, he declared at this time a view which he had held for twenty years, that 'nothing effectual will be done in the cause of peace till the sentiment of *Patriotism* be freed from the narrow meaning attaching to it in the past (and still upheld by Junkers and Jingoists) – and be extended to the whole globe'. At a time when allied fronts were under severe pressure Hardy re-sponded to a Government appeal by writing his rather Words-worthian sonnet 'A Call to National Service'. To promote the war effort, distinguished politicians and writers visited the battle zone in France; Hardy would have accepted the invitation he received from John Buchan to accompany Sir Owen Seaman and Sir James Barrie had he been ten years younger. In July he and Florence fulfilled their promise to stay with the latter at Adelphi Terrace, where Hardy had worked as a young architect. There, overlooking the Thames, with Wells, Shaw, Arnold Bennett, and Barrie, they watched the searchlights wheeling across the sky to detect enemy aircraft, their only illumination within being candles, in accordance with black-out regulations. Hardy talked a lot, according to Bennett, and argued against the merits of Tchehov's stories because they told nothing unusual. Barrie noticed his happy demeanour and the change Florence had wrought in his face; it was the last thing he would ever forget, he told her after Hardy's death. In London during the preceding weeks she had become friendly with Louisa Yearsley, wife of her leading specialist.

In February she had taken Kate Hardy, who had not been to London for thirty years, with her to attend her sister Margaret's wedding at Enfield to Reginald Soundy, a young lieutenant in the Royal Flying Corps who had been given ten days' leave from active service over the western battlefront. The next day, when Hardy had been taken to Plymouth ('to gaze, once again, I suppose, at the house where SHE was born', Florence wrote), they brought the married couple to Max Gate. Florence's epistolary indiscretions continued, especially to Rebekah Owen, though in April she added in a letter to Lady Hoare, after stating Hardy's objection to autographing his books because some people were requesting it for commercial reasons, the admission that she could not persuade him to autograph some of her own first editions of his works. In July she complained that a long course of inoculations for nasal trouble, with 'periodic visits' to London specialists, would cost her hundreds of pounds, all of which would be paid for if she were a Gifford. Near the end of the year, when she was trying to resume her literary work but finding too much of her time engrossed in letter-writing, inoculations, and worry over her parents' health, she realized how querulous she had become, and begged Rebekah ('Betty') to burn her injudicious letters. She had been much hap-pier in the summer, when, after they had stayed at Barrie's, she and Hardy had visited first Lady St Helier, then Mrs Henniker, who were both so warm and friendly that she thought them 'perfect', and could not conceive why 'the first Mrs Hardy' had disliked them so much. Her admiration of Florence Henniker's dress suggests hidden aspirations which neither Dorchester nor Max Gate could satisfy.

Apart from his visit to London, the year was not outwardly very eventful for Hardy. Whatever Florence felt, he enjoyed a visit from one of his first wife's cousins, Evelyn Gifford, who was staying with her cousin Mrs Hanbury at Kingston Maurward and was very like Emma in appearance. He and Florence read Gosse's *Life of Algernon Charles Swinburne* with pleasure, but it was particularly gratifying to receive books dedicated to him from Siegfried Sassoon and John Galsworthy. The homage of younger writers, poets especially, which was to become increasingly evident, was beginning to emerge. Sassoon had been assured by his uncle Hamo Thornycroft that his request to dedicate *The Old Huntsman and Other Poems* would delight 'True Thomas'. As Hardy did not know what hospital he was in, after being wounded on the western front, he sent his appreciation via Thornycroft (who was knighted shortly afterwards in June); he did not know how he could bear the suspense of war but for the sustaining power of poetry, he wrote. Galsworthy's novel *Beyond*, which the Hardys were sorry to end, arrived at the beginning of September. Hardy had received from a distant cousin on his mother's side, a Childs, an oil painting by Eastlake of his great-great-uncle, which bore a strong likeness to her husband, Florence said, and probably set in train the thought which led to his very imaginative poem 'Family Portraits'. The first three or four weeks of August were devoted to collecting and arranging poems for his next publication. In October, still bent on discovering Gifford homes and graves, Hardy was taken with Florence to Plymouth, after calling on Eden Phillpotts and his wife at Torquay; being reminded of 'Drake's Drum' at Plymouth, he wrote to Newbolt, saying that he had always wished he were a Devon man when he was down there, and thought that Phillpotts had 'worked out' Dartmoor in his novels. The end of the year was darkened when a letter arrived from Sir Henry and Lady Hoare to announce that Henry, their only child, had died of wounds in Alexandria. Hardy's reply shows his scholarly aptitude for the right quotation; he remembered what Lord Clarendon wrote in his *History of the Rebellion* on the death of Lord Falkland at the battle of

Newbury: 'If there were no other brand upon this odious and accursed War than that single loss, it must be most infamous and execrable to all posterity.'

Moments of Vision was published at the end of November. Though not the longest of Hardy's volumes of poetry, it contains more poems than any other, almost all of them being written in recent years. In many his thoughts were with the dead, members of his own family and, most of all, Emma. The collection ends with 'Poems of War and Patriotism' and two 'Finale' poems, 'The Coming of the End' and 'Afterwards', the first on the terminating of happy periods in his life with Emma, with her sudden death as its climax, the second on his own death and the range of natural interests which had maintained their hold on him. He did not expect much notice to be taken of these poems, he wrote; 'they mortify the human sense of self-importance by showing, or suggesting, that human beings are of no matter or appreciable value in this nonchalant universe'. Reviews were numerous and 'friendly enough', however, but he thought nearly all of them 'deplorably inept, purblind, and of far less *value* than the opinion of one's grocer or draper'; he remained disappointed that attention was not given to poems on which he set great store, particularly 'Near Lanivet'. Florence, who received a presentation copy inscribed 'to the first of women' gloomily concluded that readers would feel Hardy's second marriage had proved to be 'most disastrous', and that his one wish was 'to find refuge in the grave with her with whom alone he found happiness'.

Alternation of extreme moods such as Wordsworth recorded in 'Resolution and Independence' –

> As high as we have mounted in delight
> In our dejection do we sink as low

– was typical of Florence. How delighted she must have felt when Mrs Sheridan paid a New Year visit and, clasping her hand while Hardy had gone upstairs to fetch his faithful old friend a book, told her she had made her husband happy, and that the title of his book, *A Changed Man*, applied to him, for 'she remembered his *careworn* look, and knew what his life *used* to be'. Soon afterwards, when Mrs Sheridan died, only a week after Mrs Shorter's death on 6 January 1918, Hardy was stoical; he knew of no consolation. On hearing soon afterwards from Isabel Smith, the publisher's widow, that she had found the manuscript of *Far from the Madding Crowd* and proposed to have it auctioned at Christie's for Red Cross funds, he was delighted and sent his immediate approval. At the end of January *The Mellstock Quire* was performed to raise money for sending gifts to the Dorset Regiment in Mesopotamia; Hardy attended a rehearsal and, being dissatisfied with the execution of 'The Triumph' dance, not only demonstrated steps and position-ing very spryly but took a violin and showed in lively style how it should be played. Reminded of contemporary spiritualism by the receipt of Clodd's *The Question* at the beginning of February, he wrote: 'What a set-back this revival of superstition is! It makes one despair of the human mind. Where's Willy Shakespeare's "So noble in reason" now!' So he must have felt in December 1916 when he read Sir Oliver Lodge's *Raymond*, the testimony of a 'poor dear amiable' scientist after losing his son in the war, with examples of evidence for life after death. The war news was depressing, but Hardy appeared 'wonderful' to Florence; he was 'a true sunshine giver' with 'that inner radiance of his'. He was in the course of answering questions which came from Gosse while preparing his essay on Hardy's poetry for publication in April, and agreed that the use of 'revolutionary' was correct if Gosse had in mind his avoidance of 'the jewelled line' in poetry because it was 'effeminate'. On the day of the Red Cross sale he sat with Florence in the garden at Higher Bockhampton, to which they had cycled, and looked up at the window of the small room where he had written *Far from the Madding Crowd*. She had hoped that the manu-script would fetch £400 to £500, and was disappointed when she heard it had sold for only £235.

In February Hardy forfeited the goodwill of Rebekah Owen, whose enthusiasm for his works had delighted him a quarter of a century earlier; she had remained loyal and kept up a correspon-dence with both his wives. For their wedding anniversary she sent Hardy a valuable book on western Dorset which she would have gladly kept, and Florence an 'extra size' standard weeping rose; then she sent her copy of *Moments of Vision* for the customary autograph. Having established a principle not to sign except for charity, Hardy stubbornly refused to make any concession to one who was probably his most knowledgeable and steadfast reader. Explanations, and the return of the book, were left to Florence. Rebekah was 'disgusted'; she remembered that she had always paid expenses for the return of her books, and had given generous presents to both wives, Florence especially. Hardy (she wrote as if soliloquizing) had made a fortune but hated giving anything; Margaret Leslie was right in saying that he was mean in not giving her one of his books. 'As his first wife was fond of saying', Rebekah continued, it showed his peasant origin. 'Yet he *always* seemed so particularly glad to see me', she remembered, before ending almost anathematically, 'Peasant blood! How the Old Testament and Shakespeare despise a churl!' She did not relent, and it was not until Hardy's eightieth birthday approached that, after hearing from Florence, she made any effort towards reconciliation. Hardy stuck to his principles. In November 1922, when he received half a dozen of his books from a total stranger, with the request that he inscribe 'To Lady Sackville – Thomas Hardy' in each, and in all the volumes that were to follow, he took counsel with Sir Frederick Macmillan, informing him of the alternatives he had adopted. The result was a letter to the effect that he would not sign without payment of a fee for charity, in this case half a guinea for each, to be given to the Dorset County Hospital, of which he was a governor; he could not inscribe a book as if it were a presentation copy unless he were the donor. Lady Sackville met his wishes to the full.

After recovering from a severe chill and violent cough in May, Hardy had several visitors, including Cockerell, and Lady Ilchester and her mother, from whom he learned that Mrs Fortescue and her husband, the military historian whom she first met by the Druid stone at one of Emma's tea-parties, had been staying with them at Melbury House. About this time Hardy officiated as JP in the adjudication of several food-profiteering cases, 'the only war-work I was capable of', he wrote. His seventy-eighth birthday brought him many congratulatory letters, the most prized coming with a poem from his old friend Charles Moule. Late in June Dorothy Allhusen stayed at Max Gate, and attended service with him at Stinsford church. Next week he was pleased to receive from Sassoon a copy of his *Counter-Attack and Other Poems*. Other visitors included Sir Frederick Treves. During the summer, among those who had tea with the Hardys, few could have been more remarkable than John Cowper Powys, who must have looked forward to meeting one whose tragic vision of life he admired. He had known Dorchester well in his boyhood, when his father was curate at St Peter's. In recent years he had made his reputation in New York, and much more widely in the States, as a lecturer, a writer on literature, and a novelist; he had also been an eloquent supporter of the allied cause against Germany. Each summer he came to England; after being rejected for national service, he devoted much of his time to lecturing on war aims or for recruiting purposes. In a letter to his brother Llewelyn in Kenya, Powys instanced the 'little things' Hardy talked 'gaily and cheerfully' about, and described the gravity of Florence with 'her hair parted Madonna-wise and a very responsible air'. His host had characteristically chosen, it seems, not to talk on serious matters.

In the autumn Hardy and Florence took several short cycle rides, one to the scene of 'The Revisitation', another to 'Egdon Heath'. He must have followed the final stages of the war with some excitement, but only a minor success in the Middle East, away from the main battlefront, moved him to write. This event, the occupation of Jezreel in September, would have been of little significance to him but for the associations it raised with Old Testament stories of Elijah, Ahab, Jehu, and Jezebel which had haunted his imagination since boyhood. The war was decided in France, where, after desperate attempts to break an allied line which was fast being reinforced by the influx of American troops, the Germans were now falling back. An armistice was signed on 11 November. Hardy's greatest poem on the conflict, 'And there was a Great Calm', was written two years later, specially for *The Times*, where it appeared on the anniversary of Armistice Day. He had come to the conclusion in September 1918 that if, as was predicted, the present war was 'merciful' in comparison with what was to come, it would be better to let western civilization perish. He could only hope; the problem was to ensure that war did not begin again.

Siegfried Sassoon stayed at Max Gate just before Armistice Day. He arrived in the evening, and found Hardy and Florence shy at first. Hardy's voice was 'worn and slightly discordant' until he overcame his nervousness; then it was 'unrestrained, gently vivacious, and – when he spoke with feeling – finely resonant'. In the candlelight, with his large round head and immense brow, he looked 'frail and rather wizard-like', reminiscent of the Max Beerbohm caricature, though more like a bird. They talked much on poets and poetry, and Hardy was enlivened by Sassoon's exuberance; his mind was always 'open to the ideas and speculations of the young'. Siegfried's impressions were confirmed at later meetings, but already he knew he had been in touch with 'the simplicity of true greatness'. It was impossible to imagine Hardy 'talking for effect'; he was 'adroit at declining to be drawn out by visitors angling for oracular utterances'. 'He was, in fact, a wise and unworldly man who had discarded intellectual and personal vanity.' He was not melancholy despite 'what Meredith called his "twilight view of life"'. The 'time-trenched face' of this 'life-seer', as he sat in the firelight with one arm round Wessex, was 'genius made visible'. Sassoon had come to invite him to write a poem in Edward Marsh's 'Little Book' of contributions from contemporary authors. Hardy inscribed 'In Time of "the Breaking of Nations"'.

26

Age and Youth

Although Hardy at his best was still as intellectually alert as ever, infirmities of old age were beginning to tell. His eyes were continually affected by 'rheum', and he forgot things said or done, and people he had seen or heard from, within a day or two. Yet the memory of his early life, stimulated by the writing of his memoirs, was miraculous, Florence thought; she could not help comparing him none the less with the man who was so 'wonderful' when she first met him, when he was writing *The Dynasts* and his mind was 'luminous'. Younger writers admired his work, and were pleased to visit him, however varied their impressions. Charlotte Mew, whose poetry he liked, visited Max Gate in December 1918; she talked all the time and was glad to stay, 'a pathetic little creature', Florence thought, who did not appeal to Hardy at all. H. G. Wells, who continued to send him copies of his novels, came with his mistress Rebecca West in January 1919, while they were staying at the Royal Hotel, Weymouth; and the American poet Amy Lowell, who had visited Max Gate at the very beginning of the war, sent him her *Can Grande's Castle*; her argument for 'polyphonic prose' reminded him of the rhythmic manner of R. D. Blackmore and 'the ever and anon style' which critics once ascribed to Bulwer-Lytton. When John Middleton Murry requested him to send a poem for his first issue of the *Athenaeum* in April, he was confident that younger contributors would wish to sail under Hardy's flag. Again, at the opening of 1920, when he sent him a copy of his essays, *The Evolution of an Intellectual*, Murry maintained that the younger generation of men who had passed through the embittering ordeal of the war had no champion equal to Hardy; he admired hardly any other writer, according to Sassoon. Just over two weeks later Llewelyn Powys wrote to his brother John, describing Hardy as he had found him, probably late in 1919: 'a very old, dapper country gentleman moving about quickly, jerkily like a sparrow or Tom Tit, unaware that I had ever seen him before or was in any way connected with literature'.

Max Gate still lacked modern amenities. Lighting was restricted to lamps and candles, and the coal shortages of the war period continued throughout the winter. During the influenza epidemic of early 1919, which they were spared, the Hardys could hardly keep warm by the fire in his study, where they breakfasted before his letters were typed or they worked jointly on his biography. Old letters were still being sorted out; there were nineteen years still to be done in February, and Florence intended to arrange the correspondence under initials. The previous day she had heard 'shouts of laughter' from the drawing-room, where Hardy was entertaining Lady Ilchester and her fifteen-year-old daughter, to whose rescue she came by interposing, when she saw her turning white, as he reached the climax of the gruesome story of Mary Channing's death by burning. A week or two later Granville-Barker, an authority on the stage, after a distinguished career as an actor, producer, and playwright, called with Helen, his second wife, an affluent American author whom Florence found very attractive and charming. At the beginning of May the Hardys stayed a few days with Sir James Barrie in his London flat, where they met three poets, J. C. Squire, W. J. Turner, and Sassoon, the last of whom brought 24 copies of the first number of *The Owl*, a miscellany to which Hardy had contributed 'The Master and the Leaves', a poem he had written in 1917. The copies were to be autographed by all the contributors, and Sassoon, who knew that Hardy was 'chary of bestowing his signature', was happy to obtain merely his initials. Hardy and Florence enjoyed the Academy preview despite the crowds, and met at Lady St Helier's the Archbishop of Dublin, with whom he discussed Coverdale's translation of the Psalms and the inferiority of the Latin Vulgate in some of them. At the Gosses', where they met George Moore and Mr and Mrs John Drinkwater, he was reminded of Sunday evenings he had spent there before the war. With Barrie at the Royal Academy dinner he was so saddened by the absence of the many members and guests he used to meet there that he did not wish to attend another.

On his birthday he carried out what he had long intended, travelling with Florence and Kate by car along the old road which their progenitors had followed to Salisbury, past Woodyates, the old coach-inn where George III and his family used to stop for breakfast on their way from Weymouth, and via Harnham Hill, where Constable had painted his view of Salisbury Cathedral. By an odd coincidence they were looking round the cathedral at the very time the bishop called to see them at Max Gate. It was not until October that Sassoon was able to present him as a birthday tribute a bound collection of the autograph poems he had collected from 43 younger poets (G. K. Chesterton among them), with a felicitous foreword by Robert Bridges which Graily Hewitt had beautifully transcribed at the request of his friend Sydney Cockerell. The gift suddenly brought home to Hardy what an impression he was making on 'the contemporary world of poetry', and he was so touched that he wrote a letter of thanks to each contributor. A curious late addition from J. M. Murry, written as if after Hardy's death, elicited the reply that he hoped to be buried at Stinsford, as if the thought had crossed his mind that he might after all be given more honourable burial elsewhere.

In June Hardy heard from Sir Frederick Macmillan that the 'Mellstock' *de luxe* edition which was proposed before the war was to be published in 37 volumes, each limited to 500 copies. He sat for an etching by Strang at Max Gate, and added two or three names to his Wessex Edition map. The etching appeared only in the first volume, and the map in the second, of *Tess of the d'Urbervilles*, which appeared in December 1919, the remainder following at intervals in 1920. Hardy's signature appeared on a preliminary leaf in the first volume, and the paper throughout was watermarked with his initials. He was quick to calculate that this edition would make him £2775 richer. He sent a short addition to the preface of *Wessex Tales*, and made very slight alterations, to reduce topographical concealment, in *A Pair of Blue Eyes*, all of which were less significant to him than the inclusion of 'Should he upbraid' (the song which had delighted him and Emma at Sturminster Newton) in the old family ditties sung by the heroine in the third chapter. Apart from the pages which were altered in this novel, he did not wish to see any proofs; he was tired of his prose fiction, though, as he told Cockerell, it was 'woefully in need of a revision'. With poetry it was different; he was more than ready in January 1920 to revise the proofs of the last seven volumes in the series, comprising *The Dynasts* and four volumes of verse. In 1919 he completed the proof-corrections of his collected poems for a one-volume edition corresponding to that of *The Dynasts*; the last two volumes of his published verse, *Satires of Circumstance* and *Moments of Vision*, were also added as a single volume to the Wessex Edition.

For Hardy most of the remainder of 1919 was rather uneventful. In the summer he received two volumes of poetry from their authors, Sassoon's *Picture Show* and Middleton Murry's *Poems: 1917–18*. Florence visited her parents at Enfield and Lilian Gifford at the mental home in Essex to which she had recently been sent. Hardy persuaded the Wessex Saddleback Pig Society, honorary membership of which he had accepted, to take action for the more humane transport and slaughter of 'so intelligent' an animal. He contributed a poem to J. C. Squire's new review, the *London Mercury*, and was astonished to discover from his article in the *Hibbert Journal* how conversant his friend Sir George Douglas was with the works of Goethe. He encouraged him to write more on Spanish literature, and later sent him a copy of *Far from the Madding Crowd* in Spanish which he had just received, in order to discover its merits as a translation. He was pleased to receive the £1000 which Macmillan had negotiated with an American film company for the rights to *Tess*, and actively interested in promoting the filming of some of his other novels through the same channel. He even made speeches, the first no more than a vote of thanks to the Bishop of Salisbury, in fulfilment of a promise to Mrs Hanbury and her father Mr Symons Jeune, when a children's Red Cross memorial hospital was opened at Swanage. More important for him was the speech he made on 2 December when he opened 'The Mellstock Club', a war memorial which was built at Lower Bockhampton almost on the spot where Robert Reason's old shoe-making shop stood when he was a boy. Though brief and not without humour, his address was full of local history and memories. Later in the month, it seems, Sir George Douglas made his first visit since the war, and spent one of the most delightful evenings he had known for years; he found that the Hardys were reading Samuel Butler's *Notebooks*, his life by Festing Jones, and short stories by Tchehov. A week before Christmas Florence found the parsimonious Hardy mending his trousers with a packing-needle and string; he had worn them for twenty years, and thought they would last another ten. After placing a sprig of holly on his grandfather's grave on Christmas Eve, he was confident he saw a ghost clad in eighteenth-century dress; it said 'A green Christmas', and vanished when he followed it into Stinsford church. Two days later he declined the invitation which William Lyon Phelps had sent him to visit New England with Florence, and give the first of the memorial lectures at Yale to a student who had been killed in the war. On New Year's Eve he posted his best wishes to his old Cambridge friend, the philosopher McTaggart, telling him he had lately become impatient with scientific philosophy; after what Einstein had written, the universe seemed 'to be getting too comic for words'.

In February 1920, after his doctor had warned him not to travel by car along the neglected highways, Hardy went by train with Florence to receive an honorary DLitt from the University of Oxford in the Sheldonian, where he had sat unrecognized among the students in 1892. They stayed with Sir Walter and Lady Raleigh, where they met Bridges, Masefield, and other friends, and lunched at Arlington House, the home of Archdeacon Gifford's widow and two daughters. Of these, Evelyn, 'his bright and affectionate cousin by marriage', died not long afterwards; he remembered taking his last leave of her in the rain outside the Sheldonian after the degree ceremony. The welcome of the students made a deep impression on him; it was some relief to them that Oxford had at last honoured the author of much besides *Jude the Obscure*. For the occasion the University dramatic society played Granville-Barker's adaptation of *The Dynasts*, slightly revised by its former stage-manager A. E. Drinkwater in consultation with Hardy, and now stage-managed by Charles Morgan, whom Hardy had permitted to make what production changes he thought fit, recommending the restoration of two scenes (one the burial of Sir John Moore) which had to be omitted after a few performances at the beginning of the war because they caused distress to listeners who had lost relatives in combat. Morgan, a mature student who had served in the navy and been a prisoner-of-war in Holland, met the Hardys at the station, and they were driven at Hardy's request on a sight-seeing tour of the city before being taken to the Raleighs'. He remembered how easy Hardy made it for him to act as his escort, and thought he looked 'prodigiously old', although he was alert and sprightly: his neck had 'the thinness and his brow the tightness of great age', and his eyes seemed to be those of a man still young 'who had been keeping watch at sea since the beginning of time'. Then he was reminded of a bird, 'a small bird with a great head'.

Early in January Florence had attended the Hunt Ball at the Hanburys', and there had been exchange visits between the Hardys and the Gosses, who had stayed at the Gloucester Hotel, Weymouth. Such was Hardy's devotion to the memory of Keats that, though visits to London were almost out of the question, he consented in March to join the national committee for acquiring the house in Hampstead where the poet had lived. Later in the year he wrote 'At a House in Hampstead' for inclusion in *The John*

Keats Memorial Volume which was published on 23 February 1921, the centenary of the poet's death. Early in April he searched for a poem at Murry's request, and found one, written in 1915 or 1916, which was appropriate for the *Athenaeum* of 30 April; this was 'The Maid of Keinton Mandeville', a tribute to the composer Sir Henry Bishop, who had died exactly sixty-five years earlier. At the wedding of Harold Macmillan (one of his publishing firm) and Lady Dorothy Cavendish, which Florence and he attended at St Margaret's, Westminster, on 21 April, Hardy was one of the witnesses, and sat next to Lord Morley, whom he first knew as Alexander Macmillan's reader. It was his last visit to London, and he and Florence stayed in Barrie's flat, in the same building where he worked for Blomfield almost sixty years earlier. About this time he read *The Letters of Henry James*, after reading a review which called attention to the malignity of the author's comments on writers including himself. James had described him as 'the good little Thomas Hardy' and indulged in some very haughty and self-satisfied remarks on *Tess*, especially the vileness of the heroine and the abomination of its style. Hardy noticed how this condescending and dismissive author referred contemptuously to Swinburne and Meredith, and reduced Kipling to 'the great little Rudyard'. On 9 May Florence wrote to Paul Lemperly, an American collector of rare books who had sent them bacon toward the end of the war, telling him that she and Hardy were about to walk to Talbothays and back. Staffing expenses were very much on her mind; the gardener, cook, and housemaid cost £10 a month, and board and laundry 'a great deal more'. A few days later they took Kate Hardy with them to Exeter, calling on the Granville-Barkers at Sidmouth, where they were staying until Netherton Hall, a seventeenth-century house not far from the coastal region of west Dorset, was ready for them to take up residence in the summer. (Here they were to live in style, with liveried servants, sending their car from time to time to fetch the Hardys from Max Gate.) At Exeter the Hardys attended a cathedral service, the music and singing of which moved the author so much that he wished to be a cathedral organist more than anything else in the world. At the end of the month he heard from Charles Moule that his brother Handley, Bishop of Durham, had died; it was the last letter he received from Charles, who died almost a year later, at the age of 87.

On his eightieth birthday the Society of Authors, of which he was president, sent Sir Anthony Hope Hawkins (the novelist 'Anthony Hope'), John Galsworthy, and Augustine Birrell to honour Hardy at Max Gate. The occasion was pleasant, but a lively lunch and many messages and visitors made the day tiring for Hardy, thrilled though he must have been to receive congratulations from the King, the Prime Minister, and the Lord Mayor of London. (The illuminated address from the Society did not arrive until August.) Barrie came the following weekend, and was taken to Stinsford (where Hardy was to be buried, he noted), and to Barnes's rectory and church. On 7 June Hardy was made an honorary fellow of the RIBA. At the beginning of July Mrs Henniker was on holiday at Weymouth, and enjoyed some outings with the Hardys despite the wet weather. The poem 'A Wet August', which adverts to sunshine half a century earlier at St Juliot, suggests that the weather was much the same when Florence's mother, after an illness, was making good progress at Weymouth, and the poet Robert Graves and his wife stayed one night later in the month at Max Gate, while cycling from Oxford to Devon. Hardy told them about the Norman font which, after the bowl and other fragments had been found under rubbish in the churchyard, was about to be restored with a new base in Stinsford church, in accordance with his professional advice. Graves noticed how cluttered the drawing-room was with furniture and ornaments, and listened to jokes against bishops whose episcopal tones at the Athenaeum his host mimicked. On hearing that one of Graves's poems was in its sixth draft, Hardy said he had never made more than three or four, lest the poem should lose its freshness.

During several months of the year Florence read all six of Jane Austen's novels to him; in August, when *Emma* was being read, he was amused to realize how many characteristics he and the spoilt self-caring Mr Woodhouse had in common. On 2 September he received a copy of *The Waggoner, and Other Poems* from Edmund Blunden, a young poet and critic in whom he was to see a likeness to Keats when they met in 1922; characteristically he acknowledged the gift without delay and with the assurance that he preferred 'to read the poems slowly'. By the end of September Hardy had completed 'At Lulworth Cove a Century Back', a poem which associates Keats's landing there while on his way to Rome with the composition of the sonnet (written in 1819) 'Bright star! would I were steadfast as thou art', which scholars and biographers since 1848 had been led to assume, as a result of Severn's erroneous inference, that Keats had written soon after returning on board. Hardy's craftsmanship found another outlet at this time in designing and composing the Dorchester post office memorial to employees who had fallen during the war. He was one of more than 200 friends who had subscribed to a bronze bust of Edmund Gosse (by Sir William Goscombe John, a former pupil of Sir Hamo Thornycroft), which was commissioned in honour of his seventieth birthday the previous year. Owing to the illness of A. J. Balfour, who was to present it, this grand ceremony had to be postponed until 9 November 1920, when it took place at his home, and neither Florence nor Hardy was able to attend.

Dorchester had its excitement too, with the first post-war stage-performance of a Hardy story in the Corn Exchange. This was the dramatization of scenes from *The Return of the Native* (for which Hardy provided the words of 'the mumming play of St George'), by Alderman T. H. Tilley, a former mayor of the town and an enthusiastic member of the Hardy Players. It was repeated in London at the Guildhall School of Music in January, when Gertrude Bugler won Arthur Symons' praise for her outstanding performance of Eustacia. Rebekah Owen, whose enthusiasm for Hardy's works now exceeded her regard for their author, had come down from the Lake District for the Dorchester production, and had reason to notice his interest in the young local actress rather than in her. On Christmas Day, after the singing of carols outside on a clear starry night, the mummers' play was acted in the Max Gate drawing-room, Henry and Kate Hardy being in the audience. After refreshments in the dining-room Hardy and Florence chatted with the players and the singers (a small group who had sung the carols when *The Mellstock Quire* was performed in 1918), chiefly on earlier performances by the Hardy Players, with amused references to the recent failure of the electric lighting, when Clym and Eustacia had to sit in the dark until candles were brought. Hardy asked Gertrude if she would raise her visor for him, as she had done for Clym; then he invited other players to say what the next play should be. Before she left he indicated his own wish when he suggested to Miss Bugler that she would prefer *Tess*. Perhaps, like Mr Tilley, he knew that the novel was not yet highly favoured in Dorchester. Florence, who discovered that the other members of the company were becoming a little upset because Miss Bugler won almost all the applause, noticed how 'very gay' Hardy was at the party. Next day she found him writing a poem 'with great spirit', always 'a sign of well-being with him', she wrote, adding, 'Needless to say it is an intensely dismal poem.'

During the remaining few days of the year Hardy twice met his well-prepared interviewer Vere H. Collins of the Oxford University Press. He had already been interviewed by him in April, and submitted to further questions from him in October 1921 and August 1922. He explained passages which Collins had found obscure in his poems, and told him that he liked Trollope, who, it had been thought, would be the greatest of the early Victorian novelists, but found Dickens too much of a caricaturist, and thought Thackeray too satirical. As he was leaving the dining-room on 29 December, Collins gazed reflectively on the picture of Emma Lavinia Gifford. She was one, he afterwards concluded, 'with whose influence, direct and indirect, on the life of her husband, there must be connected so much of the anguish and sadness, and the philosophy, and the beauty' of his works; he felt certain that Hardy's experience with her confirmed and darkened his view of life.

Despite the changes and modernizations since Emma's death (they included a bath in August 1920, and a telephone for Florence), Max Gate remained a haunted home for Hardy, and he must have been thinking of it in the present and the future when he wrote 'The Two Houses', the poem he found and sent late in the year for publication in the *Dial* at the request of the American poet Ezra Pound, now Paris correspondent for this New York magazine. A great admirer of Hardy's poetry, Pound sent at or about the same time inscribed copies of his last two volumes of poetry, *Quia Pauper Amavi* and *Hugh Selwyn Mauberley*, the assessment of which Hardy realized needed 'considerable deliberation'. When he received another request for a poem in March 1921, he gave his considered views. It was difficult to criticize Pound's verse unless he knew his objective; was it to be read 'only by the select few'? Though old-fashioned himself, he did not rank Pound among those recent poets who seemed to 'aim at obscurity'; he thought 'Homage to Sextius Propertius' a 'very fine and striking poem' and obviously felt the 'racy satire' of *Hugh Selwyn Mauberley*, while wondering whether it ought not to have been aimed at a larger reading public. Pound's admiration did not wane. Nobody had taught him 'anything about writing since Thomas Hardy died', he wrote at the end of 1934. 'Now *there* is a clarity. There *is* the harvest of having written 20 novels first', he observed on reading Hardy's *Collected Poems* in 1937.

As he approached death Hardy's philosophical certitude diminished. For years he had assumed that the dead had no further existence except in people's memories. He thought he had seen a ghost in Stinsford churchyard, and could not reject belief, or hope, in the possibility of Emma's spiritual existence, or his sister Mary's, as he shows in 'He Prefers Her Earthly' and 'Paradox'. After his attention had been drawn in December 1920 to Alfred Noyes's contention that his (Hardy's) philosophy projected 'the Power behind the Universe' as 'an imbecile jester', he wrote to him at length, insisting on his repeated representation of 'the Cause of Things' as 'neither moral nor immoral, but *un*moral', and protesting against recurrent misrepresentations which made the public think he really believed 'the Prime Mover to be a malignant old gentleman, a sort of King of Dahomey'. Finally he admitted that 'the Scheme of Things is, indeed, incomprehensible', a wise conclusion quite at variance with his consistent dogmatism of more than thirty years. How far he had changed is clearer in a passage he wrote only a few days later, where he stated that he had no philosophy, 'merely what I have often explained to be only a confused heap of impressions, like those of a bewildered child at a conjuring show'. It was his misfortune that people continued to treat all his 'mood-dictated writing as a single scientific theory'.

Florence told Cockerell that she married Hardy to express her devotion and 'to add to his comfort and happiness'. She had done this immeasurably. She typed his poetry and most of his correspondence, and had given him enormous assistance in the preparation of his 'biography'. Their life had by and large become a happy literary partnership; they read and discussed a long succession of books and subjects, and she spent hours in the evenings reading to him. Inevitably she welcomed changes from routine: local outings (to the Hanburys, for instance), guests at Max Gate, and excursions to London. She stayed happily there at Mrs Henniker's in December 1920, and again the following April, when she visited her dentist for teeth extraction; 'what with railway and coal strikes and other things', Hardy did not know when he would be in London. He depended so much on Florence that, when she sacrificed a visit there in December 1922, because he had suddenly caught influenza, he said that if 'anything happened' to her he would 'go out and drown himself'; after resorting to his usual antidote, two glasses of champagne twice a day, he soon recovered health and cheerfulness.

In his declining years he maintained a businesslike interest in promoting sales of his works, and new editions, at home and abroad. When Madeleine Rolland informed him at the beginning of 1921 that a revised edition of her French translation of *Tess* was likely to appear, he was more than pleased; he was ready to encourage her to translate another of his novels, especially *A Pair of Blue Eyes*, and particularly keen to have some of his poems appear in French. Later he sent her explanations of dialect words in *Tess*. In November, while making a strong case for the publication of his uncollected poems, though 'by no means anxious to rush into print again – quite the reverse, indeed', he suggested to Sir Frederick Macmillan that readers would like them in an additional Mellstock volume, and informed him that many younger poets would gladly pay more for his *Collected Poems* and *The Dynasts* in thin-paper editions. In support of this recommendation he instanced *The Oxford Book of English Verse*, which had doubled its sales when produced in this less bulky form. Not content with this, he suggested ways of increasing sales in the United States, on the strength of what he had heard from American professors, one of whom said that people out there were like children who read whatever was 'put before them'. His publishers usually accepted his advice.

In April, about the time Florence's sister Margaret Soundy came to stay at Max Gate with her son Thomas before returning to Canada, Hardy read Lytton Strachey's *Queen Victoria*. When he wrote to thank the author for this gift he said that his enjoyment of it derived less from the subject than from the genius with which it had been treated; he had often wished that a more interesting personage, such as Mary Stuart or Queen Elizabeth, had been chosen. Strachey's comments on the domination of Victoria by her mother, the Duchess of Kent, confirmed the account Hardy had heard from his mother of how Victoria had been pulled down into her seat by the Duchess when, on her way to Melbury House in 1833, she stood up to gain a better view of the applauding by-standers. Sir James Barrie and his secretary Lady Cynthia Asquith stayed one night in May. They sat talking with the Hardys at the tea-table until seven, their host making no conversational effort to impress, and merely keeping to the point. Florence looked strained; she was worried about Hardy's health and his refusal to see a doctor. At dinner Wessex was allowed to walk about the table and contest every forkful from Lady Cynthia's plate to her mouth. She heard much about him, how he loved to hear the wireless, and had bitten the postman three times, with the result that letters were no longer delivered at the door. Next morning Hardy took his visitors to his study, which to Lady Cynthia seemed the one room that had character. It was simple, bare, and workmanlike; the walls were distempered 'an unusual shade of coral pink', his old violin hung above the bookcases, and a framed wage-sheet (his father's or grandfather's) stood on the mantelpiece. They then took a long walk to the churchyard where Barnes was buried, Hardy striding on as if he were a young man, and quickening his pace as they climbed up Conygar Hill. Afterwards they visited his birthplace; 'that lovely honeysuckle cottage', as Lady Cynthia described it, was empty and closed, but Barrie used a ladder he found in long grass to open an upper window and climb through, reappearing as he opened the door and bowed to Hardy, whose feelings as he explored the house can be judged by the final stanzas of 'Silences':

> But the rapt silence of an empty house
> Where oneself was born,
> Dwelt, held carouse
> With friends, is of all silences most forlorn!
>
> Past are remembered songs and music-strains
> Once audible there:
> Roof, rafters, panes
> Look absent-thoughted, tranced, or locked in prayer.
>
> It seems no power on earth can waken it
> Or rouse its rooms,
> Or its past permit
> The present to stir a torpor like a tomb's.

Middleton Murry came and stayed one night at Max Gate shortly before Hardy's eighty-first birthday, which was marked by the receipt of a first edition of Keats's 1820 poems, with an address, organized by St John Ervine and signed by more than a hundred younger writers, testifying to his greatness as a novelist and poet, and ending, 'We thank you, Sir, for all that you have written . . . but most of all, perhaps, for *The Dynasts*.' It is interesting to note that *Under the Greenwood Tree* appeared among the best of his novels, to the exclusion of *The Woodlanders*. Among Max Gate visitors in the summer were Siegfried Sassoon, John Masefield and his wife, and, for the first time, Walter de la Mare, whom Hardy found 'delightful'; 'I am getting to know quite a lot of the Young Georgians, and have quite a paternal feeling, or grandpaternal towards them', he wrote to Mrs Henniker, telling her that the Galsworthys would be calling next week on their way to London. Masefield came again in October, with his wife and the model of a full-rigged ship which he had made for Hardy and named 'The Triumph' in his honour; they were on the way to the Galsworthys' in Devon.

Shortly afterwards by coincidence Hardy and Florence completed reading *To Let*, the last novel (and the best, he thought) in *The Forsyte Saga* trilogy. He was sorry that it had ended, he wrote to Galsworthy, though he did not care very much for the characters; his wife had found Soames 'a touching figure', and he thought the death of Jolyon Forsyte 'a remarkably good dramatic stroke'.

The Hardys had enjoyed some memorable outings by car. They had seen the Granville-Barkers at Netherton Hall in April and June, and been taken by Cecil Hanbury of Kingston Maurward, a week after Hardy's birthday, to watch the Hardy Players in scenes from *Far from the Madding Crowd* followed by T. H. Tilley's 'An Old-Time Rustic Wedding' (from *Under the Greenwood Tree*, with songs and dances) among the castle ruins at Sturminster Newton. Hardy joined the actors when they were having tea at Riverside Villa during the interval between their matinée and evening performances. When he heard from the owner that Gertrude Bugler (who took the parts of Bathsheba and Fancy Day) was likely to stay with her, he remembered her in the role of Eustacia, and suggested she should sleep in the room where he wrote *The Return of the Native*. Exactly a week later the same programme was given at Bingham's Melcombe (where Hardy's friend Bosworth Smith had come home to die in 1908), the first play in the ancient courtyard, the second on the bowling-green. The afternoon was hot and tiring; there were crowds of people, and the Hardys avoided publicity as much as they could. Twelve days later, with Colonel Inglis and his wife Ethel from Weymouth, they travelled to High Stoy; Mrs Inglis had become one of Florence's best friends in recent years.

Making scenes in Dorchester for a film of *The Mayor of Casterbridge* was of much greater interest to Hardy at the beginning of July than to the inhabitants, though he met the actors outside the King's Arms and drove with them to Maiden Castle, where they prepared another scene. About this time he attended morning service at St Peter's, where special arrangements were made to sing one of his favourite hymns, Bishop Ken's 'Awake, my soul, and with the sun' to Barthélémon's setting. His interest in the composer years earlier had led him to make notes on his life, and sketch three versions of an imaginary story. This and the St Peter's service combined to inspire the sonnet 'Barthélémon at Vauxhall', which was written to appear in *The Times* on 23 July, the anniversary of the composer's death in 1808. In the same month Hardy opened a bazaar in aid of the Dorset County Hospital. In the evening he was taken to see the dancing in the Borough Gardens, where 'The Lancers' was included at his request; the music of the naval band could be heard at Max Gate when he returned in the light of a full moon. There were happy occasions for him at Stinsford church early in September, the first being when he stood as godparent to the Hanburys' daughter Caroline; his gift to her was a parchment manuscript of the poem 'To C.F.H.' in a silver box. Three days later, at the evening service, memories were movingly evoked when he heard Bishop Ken's 'Glory to Thee; my God, this night' sung to Tallis as in his boyhood days. He had preserved a local newspaper cutting which announced that Gertrude Bugler would soon be married in the same church to her cousin, a Beaminster farmer and war captain who had won the Military Cross. Later in the month and in October Hardy sat to the portrait-painter Walter William Ouless.

27

Late Drama and
T. E. Lawrence

1922 opened unhappily for the Hardys. In November domestic staffing difficulties had left them no alternative, it seemed, to housing Mrs Dugdale's former housemaid (now Mrs Stanley) with her demobilized husband and their young son. She was engaged as cook and he as a factotum. By Hardy's habitual standards they were extravagant, and kept up roaring fires in the kitchen, much to his vexation; the boy was noisy, and never succeeded in endearing himself as Wessex had done. As soon as he went to school he caught a heavy cold, in consequence of which Hardy (so he believed) was prostrated two or three weeks with a severe chill and a recurrence of the bladder inflammation from which he had suffered intermittently since his long illness at Upper Tooting. So ill was he that Florence's sister Eva, a trained nurse, was called in. Before he was able to go out for the first time on 13 February, Florence herself was 'down with influenza'. While he was ill in bed Hardy thought long on a preface to his forthcoming volume of poems. The verse was sent off to Macmillan on 23 January, and the preface was submitted to Cockerell for advice just over three weeks later. Cockerell advised him to omit nothing, and generously proposed to read the proofs, an offer which Hardy was pleased to accept, partly because his eyesight was weaker, partly because he had become increasingly aware that familiarity with the text made him more blind to misprints. He accepted two verbal improvements, and decided to abridge the whole wherever he could.

He preferred to head his preface 'Apology', since it was primarily a defence against the recurring charge of pessimism which his poetry had provoked, based as it was on the 'In Tenebris' assumption 'that if way to the Better there be, it exacts a full look at the Worst'. Hardy was an evolutionary meliorist who accepted the Positivist belief in altruism, and was annoyed that his Positivist friend Frederic Harrison, a strong evolutionary optimist, had publicly declared that nearly every inclusion in his *Collected Poems* of 1919

357

could be headed 'Memento Mori'. He was just in time to take issue
also with J. M. Hone, a Catholic whose article in the *London
Mercury* of February 1922 criticized his heterodoxy; it might have
been written by 'an old-maiden teacher in a Sunday school in
Victorian times', Hardy wrote to Cockerell. Only incidentally did
he state in his apology that, in pursuing 'the real function of
poetry, the application of ideas to life (in Matthew Arnold's familiar phrase)', he had presented not a systematic view, but only 'a
series of fugitive impressions'. After preparing the reader for the
miscellaneity of his collection, he considered the hazards of poetry
in an age when reviewers were apt to judge a volume by selections
of the worst or weaker passages (he had not forgotten a review of
Satires of Circumstance); he then argued that poetry and 'essential'
religion, which often 'modulate into each other', must change in
accordance with scientific truth, advances being made not in a
straight line but rather, as Comte had suggested, 'in a looped
orbit'. His hope was that, whatever the setbacks caused by the age,
they were temporary, a drawing back *pour mieux sauter*.

Apart from its preface, *Late Lyrics and Earlier*, which was published in May, is slightly larger than *Moments of Vision* and the
longest of all Hardy's single volumes of poetry. Only a small
proportion of the poems had already been published. About half
had been written in recent years, and the remainder stretched back
over a long period, two ('A Young Man's Exhortation' and 'Dream
of a City Shopwoman') being written in 1866. If few are really
outstanding among Hardy's poems, the general level is high, and
the collection was favourably received. Hardy had copies sent to
Lytton Strachey and John Buchan, the latter of whom loved the 'flute'
notes, and thought he had reached 'the very heart of seventeenth-
century melody'. Yet a late reviewer in the *Spectator* found the
contents 'almost all more or less the raw materials of poetry' from
an author who could 'really descend to extraordinary ineptitudes'.
Several poems were devoted to recollections of Emma, but Florence
was probably now reconciled to the fact; she does not appear to
have been upset by the volume. A number undoubtedly arose
from reminiscences evoked when Hardy was engaged in writing
his *Life*, among them 'The Passer-By', in which he imagines Louisa
Harding recalling her romance, and 'A Two-Years' Idyll'; one or
two, as a result of reading *Some Recollections*, and one at least, 'The
Sailor's Mother', from proof-reading his fiction. Of few pieces
could it be said that they are overweighted with pessimism. 'Sur-

view', which concludes the volume, is one of the saddest, the expression of a contrite man of conscience recalling times when he had failed to live up to one aspect or another of the Pauline charity which was his ideal. Had he suffered and been 'kind withal' as much as he might have done with Emma, he seems to be asking.

Sir James Barrie stayed at Max Gate one night in April, and Hardy was taken on 24 May, the day after his poems were published, to see Riverside Villa once more. A less happy experience came two days later when he found his birthplace sadly neglected, and wished never to see it again. Early in the month, after being placed top of the list of recommendations forwarded by Barrie, rector of the University, he had been awarded *in absentia* the honorary degree of LL. D. at St Andrews, and had received a presentation copy of Harold Monro's poems, *Real Property*, and a further volume (the third) of *A History of the Great War* by John Buchan. Shortly after his birthday he attended a tennis party at the Hanburys', and wished Mrs Henniker had been present to identify several of the guests. One of many friends who visited Max Gate in July, she stayed at the King's Arms, and was taken to Blackmoor Vale, Sherborne, and more of *The Woodlanders* country. Edmund Blunden, who had sent Hardy a copy of his *The Shepherd, and Other Poems of Peace and War*, arrived with Sassoon, who later brought E. M. Forster. Invited to lunch at Max Gate the next day, Forster found Mrs Hardy full of misgivings about the cook, who had just arrived; Hardy seemed cheerful, though he dreaded visits by interviewers and American ladies, and disliked the disturbance created by passing charabancs with conductors shouting ''Ome of Thomas 'Ardy, novelist'. Forster was taken by his host through the matted ivy, over the graves of ancient Romans, he was told, to see where the Hardy pets were buried under the spindly trees, and hear how cat after cat had been killed by trains; later they watched an amateur performance of *A Midsummer Night's Dream* on the lawn at Trinity rectory. In August, at the age of eighty-two, Hardy managed to cycle with Florence to Talbothays and back. Newman Flower, the managing director of Cassell's, who had spent his boyhood days in Blackmoor Vale, came with his wife and son, and took them to Sturminster Newton and back via Dogbury Gate on 11 September. Hardy climbed to the topmost point of High Stoy with Flower, thinking it might be the last opportunity he would have of gazing over a landscape he had known since he travelled with Mary and his parents, when he was a young boy (as he remembered in 'Under High-Stoy Hill'), along the road below after visiting his mother's relatives and friends at Melbury Osmond. Even as Wordsworth, when about to leave the Lake District for the first time, imagined what 'local sympathy' he would feel at the end of his days, Hardy's soul must have cast a 'backward view', a longing, lingering look on 'native regions' that had remained dear to him for his mother's sake. He could now draw satisfaction even from walking across Boucher's Close at Stinsford to the eweleaze stile on which he had sat and read the crushing *Spectator* review of *Desperate Remedies*.

A handsome edition of Shelley's *Epipsychidion* from Roger Ingpen, the receipt of which elicited the disclosure that he had always thought the line 'Sweet Benediction in the eternal Curse!' the 'greatest compliment ever paid to womankind', gratified Hardy in the summer of 1922, when he had been worried to learn that Vere Collins had been invited to translate for publication in England *Thomas Hardy, penseur et artiste*, the work of Frank Hedgcock, a lecturer in French at Birmingham University. He disapproved with such insistence that finally the venture was given up. His main objection was that it was biographically misleading, his fiction being frequently interpreted as autobiography; it was also outdated, appearing in 1911 and paying insufficient attention to the poetry which had occupied more than half of his writing career. He took no exception to the critical part of the book, some of which he thought excellent, but maintained that 'the untruth is never overtaken by the correction'. Collins agreed to ensure that, as a result of omissions and revisions, no false impressions were given, but Hedgcock soon judged it was better not to allow the translation to proceed. To ensure future accuracy in a second edition of his *Thomas Hardy: Novelist and Poet*, numerous corrections and revisions were sent to the American professor Samuel Chew, one emendation eliciting Hardy's confession that he had read none of the Brontë novels except *Jane Eyre*. He was pleased no doubt in early September when Mary Webb sought permission to dedicate her fourth novel *Seven for a Secret* to him, and described him as 'the greatest exponent of the wild human heart since Shakespeare'.

Brigadier-General J. H. Morgan, Commissioner of Control in Berlin, visited Max Gate early in October, and recalled how Hardy talked, as they crossed the meadows on the way to Stinsford churchyard, on 'the eternal riddles of human destiny, chance, free will, immortality'; the conversation then turned to religion and the

Church of England. On the last subject Hardy said, 'I believe in going to church. It is a moral drill, and people must have something. If there is no church in a country village, there is nothing. . . . I believe in reformation coming from *within* the church. The clergy are growing more rationalist and that is the best way of changing.' When questioned whether the clergy were not guilty of 'casuistry in subscribing to articles in which they did not believe', he disagreed; he regarded it as 'a necessity in practical reform'. As he laid flowers on Emma's grave, he affirmed his belief that Church liturgy was 'a noble thing'. So too were the psalms of Tate and Brady. 'These are the things that people need and should have.'

November was rather a busy month. Dorothy Allhusen, who had always been a favourite with Hardy, came over with her daughter Elizabeth, but stayed, as Mrs Henniker had done, at the King's Arms; the Hardys, it seems, were conscious of their social inferiority and of their modest accommodation at Max Gate. All four had a delightful time, however, and enjoyed motoring excursions to Dogbury Gate and elsewhere. Soon afterwards Hardy was immensely pleased to learn that he had been awarded a fellowship at Queen's College, Oxford. Whether he showed much interest in Mr Tilley's production of *Desperate Remedies* is doubtful; Mrs Bugler was unable to participate owing to a miscarriage, and he had expressed his sympathy by sending her a silver vase and a bouquet of pink carnations. Rebekah Owen came down to see the play, but it is not certain that she met Hardy. As the anniversary of his sister's death approached, Max Gate seemed to become depressing, Florence thought. It coincided with Emma's birthday, 24 November, and fell three days before the anniversary of the latter's death. 'What a revenge, did she but know it!' Florence reflected, well aware that a birthday so often forgotten in Emma's lifetime was now unforgettable and unforgotten. On 27 November Hardy noted, 'E's death-day, ten years ago. Went with F. and tidied her tomb and carried flowers for her and the other two tombs.' In retrospect it seemed to Florence that Emma's death marked a clear division in her own life, as if she had leapt 'from youth into dreary middle-age'. On 17 December she could hear 'ghostly strains' in the drawing-room, where Hardy played a Christmas hymn on the 'pathetic old piano' which had for many years been a source of great delight to her predecessor. It was a relief for her to spend the early days of the New Year at Nether Woodcote, Epsom, with Mrs Henniker, who had been ill in the autumn.

Like many others, Hardy was moved by the conviction of Mrs Edith Thompson for the murder of her husband. On 6 January 1923, three days before her execution, he completed the poem 'On the Portrait of a Woman about to be Hanged', sending it a few days later to John Squire, and asking whether the *London Mercury* was 'too moral to sympathize with a wicked woman'. Squire was pleased to publish it in the February number, and subsequently dedicated his *American Poems and Others* to Hardy. The death of Katherine Mansfield, Middleton Murry's wife, grieved the Hardys, but they sustained a greater loss when Mrs Henniker died. She had remained a loyal friend since he first met her in 1893, and a correspondent with whom he could discuss his affairs and interests more openly and trustfully than with any of his other friends. 'After a friendship of 30 years!' he wrote on reading the announcement of her death in *The Times* on 5 April. Realizing their biographical interest and value, she had taken steps the previous November to ensure that all his surviving letters to her were bequeathed posthumously to Florence.

Acknowledging the gift of *American Poetry 1922* from Amy Lowell, Hardy had expressed the view that Edna Millay was the most promising of the younger poets in the States. When the latter turned to drama a few years later he claimed to be one of the first 'on this side of the Atlantic' to appreciate her poetry, which he obviously preferred to her drama. On this subject he had some decided views, an old one, which he divulged to Granville-Barker in 1922, being that the pit should be level with the stage, forming an extension which would enable the audience to see 'all round' the actors. In March 1923 he was working on *The Famous Tragedy of the Queen of Cornwall* (a play begun not long after his visit to Tintagel more than six years earlier), expecting to have it produced by the Hardy Players in November. In this he carried out an idea which occurred to him when he saw *Hedda Gabler* in 1891, 'that the rule for staging nowadays should be to have no scene which would not be physically possible in the time of acting'. Whatever may be said of its literary merits, Hardy's play is a technical triumph, observing the 'unities' more strictly than was the custom on the Greek stage.

Evidently finding that household affairs and assisting Hardy in various ways was taking up too much of her energy and time, Florence sought secretarial assistance, and was fortunate in March to appoint May O'Rourke, who lived in Dorchester and was able to give three half-days a week and longer when required. Max Gate was still isolated and wind-swept, despite the trees, the new secretary observed; and she soon learned that Wessex had to be obeyed when he insisted on her accompanying his master and mistress to the green door in the side wall of the garden, after Florence had selected the right stick and readjusted Hardy's scarf for their afternoon walk. Another newcomer was Colonel T. E. Lawrence, who, on 29 March, made the first of his many visits on a Brough motor-cycle, after his friend Robert Graves had made an appointment for him; he had come from Bovington Camp on 'Egdon Heath', where he had continued his endeavour to escape the penalty of fame by concealing his identity and serving as Private T. E. Shaw. He became a great friend of the Hardys, but, however much they learned about him, it is doubtful whether they realized what an insecure and enigmatic character they welcomed.

Lawrence, like his four brothers, was illegitimate. His father, an Anglo-Irish landlord, deserted his family for the governess, a Scottish girl who was known as 'Miss Lawrence'. Thomas Edward, the second son, was born in Wales. The new family eventually settled at Oxford, where all the boys were educated at the High School. Often beaten by his strict mother for his wilful behaviour, Thomas ran away from home when he was seventeen, and joined the Royal Artillery. His Welsh birth helped him to gain admission to Jesus College, Oxford, where he made a special study of the Crusades, which led to examination of castles in England, Wales, and France. In 1910 he won first class honours and a demyship at Magdalen College. The knowledge of the Middle East which he subsequently acquired when assisting in the archaeological surveys of C. L. Woolley helped to qualify him for his rather sensational and quixotic role in helping to free the Arabs from the Turks during the 1914–18 war. A daring reconnoitre led to brief captivity at Deraa, where, after refusing to surrender his body to the Bey, he was handed over to the guards and flogged until he submitted to their brutal lusts. Questions have been raised on the extent to which his subsequent career was dictated by the will to subdue the flesh through hardship and manual labour, or by the fear that his illegitimacy, and that of his brothers, would become known. These are but two considerations in the attempt to solve the imponderable complex of Lawrence's life of self-abnegation. A more overriding factor seems to be his hatred of publicity, a rooted, almost recluse-like desire to possess his soul in peace, and develop his own interests. At Max Gate he had glimpses of the kind of life for which he thirsted. He was to find it again at one of the remotest stations in India.

After the war he refused all the honours he had been awarded, and higher ones which George V wished to bestow on him. At Versailles he did all he could for the Arabs, and felt his country was dishonoured when they were not given their independence. A research fellowship enabled him to retire to All Souls, Oxford, where he wrote an account of the Arab campaign, the first version of *Seven Pillars of Wisdom*. After assisting Winston Churchill at the Foreign Office until he was satisfied that the Arabs had been honourably rewarded, and refusing the post of High Commissioner in Cairo, Lawrence chose to conceal his identity as aircraftman John Hume Ross in the Royal Flying Corps. He had told Graves in 1919 that he had intended to pursue such a course as soon as he was satisfied that the Arabs had been given a fair deal. Short of stature and medically unfit, he would never have been accepted but for orders from the Air Ministry, Sir Hugh Trenchard in particular. At Farnborough, where he studied photography, he was recognized by some of the officers, and news of his whereabouts was leaked to the press. He was informed that in the circumstances he could no longer stay in the RAF unless he accepted a commission and assumed his true name; he refused and was discharged. Not until March 1923 did he succeed in joining the Royal Tank Corps at Bovington Camp, and there he was protected from bullies by his friend John Bruce. He could escape his carnal-minded companions when he raced about the country on his motor-cycle, or at Max Gate, or, from the autumn of 1923 but only when off duty during the day, at Clouds Hill, which he rented at half-a-crown a week from a kinsman, later High Sheriff of Dorset. This derelict brick cottage, in a thicket of laurel and rhododendron, with arms of oaks and a huge ilex stretching over it, was very damp, and only the top two rooms were made habitable, the lower being used for lumber and firewood. In this *pied-à-terre*, as his friend E. M. Forster described it, he found a haven where he could read or write, or listen, as he loved to do, to records of classical music. He hated his 'squalid camp'. Eventually, in August 1925, he was allowed to join the RAF which he liked, and was transferred to Cranwell.

Lawrence's third visit to Max Gate took place on 26 May 1923, coinciding with that of Walter de la Mare and his wife, Roger

Ingpen's sister; Hardy had informed them that a prince was coming, after discovering that Lawrence was Prince of Mecca. A week or so later the Granville-Barkers brought Max Beerbohm and his wife, whom Hardy had not seen for years. Among the books he had recently read were two from their authors, Wells's *Men Like Gods* and Masefield's *King Cole, and Other Poems*. A few days after going on board the *Queen Elizabeth* to meet Admiral Fisher (not for the first time on a battleship off Portland) and Sir John and Lady Robeck, Hardy and Florence were taken by car on 25 June to spend two nights at Queen's College; it was the last time he slept away from home. At Salisbury they stopped to look at the cathedral and the training-college which his sisters had attended and he had used as a setting in *Jude*; time was found for an even more important *Jude* setting, Fawley, his grandmother's village in Berkshire. They reached Oxford punctually, and were taken to have tea with the provost. Next day, after they had been shown round the colleges, and lunched with the fellows and their wives, Hardy in his doctoral robe was photographed with his colleagues in the fellows' garden. Ever keen to revive memories, he had requested to be taken first to the spot where he could survey the High Street which he described in *Jude*, 'with its college after college, in picturesqueness unrivalled except by such Continental vistas as the Street of Palaces in Genoa', then to the Shelley memorial in University College. Later in the day they were driven, after calling at Christ Church, to the Masefields' at Boar Hill. Hardy impressed his escort Godfrey Elton not as a man 'much occupied with books' but as 'an elderly country gentleman with a bird-like alertness and a rare and charming youthfulness'. On the way back to Oxford he expressed a wish to see the Martyrs' Memorial and New College cloisters; by an error of chance he and Florence were taken to the college chapel, where, as the evening service was about to begin, he preferred to stay listening to the soaring voices of the boys' choir. Their return the next day via Winchester and the New Forest, where they lunched in a grassy glade, concluded one of Hardy's happiest and most eventful outings during his last years.

Far less congenial in prospect was the visit of the Prince of Wales for lunch at Max Gate on 20 July. Servants from large houses in the neighbourhood were brought in for the occasion. Hardy had been invited to meet him at the new drill hall he opened for the Dorset Territorials, and drive home with him. From Stinsford the Prince's party had been diverted north of Dorchester to Lower Burton, so that school-children massed on the green slopes of the North Walk could see him as he entered from the Sherborne road. Hardy had told Kate and Henry that they could see him on the route above Stinsford Hill, or at Max Gate, as he arrived and departed, from 'the bedroom behind the jessamine'; the Union Jack could be flown at Talbothays if they wished. Never was Hardy so exposed to public gaze as when driven with the Prince from the drill hall down High West Street and along South Street and Prince of Wales Road to Max Gate. In addition to stewards of the Duchy of Cornwall, the guests included, among others, Lord Shaftesbury, Admiral Sir Lionel Halsey, and Sir Godfrey Thomas. It was a very hot day but, thanks to the easy and friendly manner of the Prince, what might have been a very exhausting event passed off pleasantly, Hardy wrote. *Vitae post-scenia celant* runs the title-page epigraph of *The Hand of Ethelberta*: not until the visit was over did he hear of an incident which would be appropriate in such a novel at a higher social level. The Prince had gone upstairs to prepare for lunch, and Florence, waiting below, saw his waistcoat thrown at the equerry on the landing, and heard, 'It's too damned hot! Wear the bloody thing yourself!' Before leaving to visit some of his Duchy farms, the Prince talked in the garden with Hardy, who seized the opportunity to say how much Florence and he would like to own the small paddock behind it; it was soon acquired from the Duchy, part of it being used for keeping poultry. Next day the Hardys called at Talbothays, and Kate thought they were still 'highly strung'.

Visits and outings of a more relaxing kind followed during the summer and autumn. On the afternoon of the Prince's visit the Hardys motored to Portland Bill to have tea with Dr Marie Stopes in the lighthouse, where she lived. While in lodgings at Came Rectory during the last week of the month, Sassoon and Edmund Blunden visited Max Gate; on 29 July they had tea there with Colonel Lawrence. During August Hardy read *Seven Pillars of Wisdom*, and made its author proud 'with what he said of it'. Other visitors included young Ralph Bankes and his sister Daphne from Kingston Lacy, Cockerell and his son Christopher for a weekend, John Drinkwater and his fiancée Daisy Kennedy (who played Hardy's violin), and, when they had left, H. G. Wells and Rebecca West. Lawrence, who admired Hardy's poetry, *The Dynasts* above all, and cared less for the novels, enjoyed the 'cheerful calm' of hearing him 'thinking aloud about life'. What they discussed can be gauged from his letter to Robert Graves in early September:

'Napoleon is a real man to him, and the country of Dorsetshire echoes that name everywhere in Hardy's ears.' There was 'an unbelievable dignity and ripeness' about him, as he waited 'so tranquilly for death, without a desire or ambition left in his spirit'. That same month Hardy and Florence lunched with the Ilchesters at Evershot, and, with Lawrence, at the Granville-Barkers' in Devon. Admiral Fisher and his brother, the historian H. A. L. Fisher, came to lunch, and E. M. Forster called. By this time Hardy had completed sittings for the portrait-painter R. G. Eves; soon they were to begin for Augustus John, whom he met at Kingston Maurward. Florence and he were especially delighted when their old friend Lady St Helier came by train from Newbury to see them on 3 October; it was the last time she and Hardy met. When he heard that Cockerell had bought his Augustus John portrait for the Fitzwilliam Museum, he said he would *far* rather have had that happen than receive the Nobel prize'. (Speaking of this picture in June 1927 at the Granville-Barkers', he remarked, 'I don't know whether that is how I look or not – but that is how I *feel*.') In November Florence had the unusual pleasure of being taken out by Lawrence in his sidecar.

At the end of August Hardy had sent the manuscript of *The Famous Tragedy of the Queen of Cornwall* to Macmillan, even suggesting a paperback edition for so short a work. He included two illustrations, one an imaginary view of Tintagel Castle which he had drawn with 'infinite care' and a masterly touch for a man of his age, the other of the great hall where the whole action takes place; Granville-Barker, whose advice he had sought on staging improvements, thought it would be of great benefit to readers of the play. As soon as proofs arrived, Hardy was at pains to ensure that the agreement was in order, and that the copyright terms for the publication of his works by Macmillan at home and in the States would be satisfactory after his death. On his advice *The Queen of Cornwall* was published on 15 November, almost two weeks before its production began in Dorchester. It appeared in hard covers bound in green cloth, the front attractively illustrated with an encircled portion of Hardy's view of the castle in gilt, the jacket presenting a facsimile of Hardy's title-page manuscript in full. The text was more workmanlike than inspired, and the scene in which Iseult the Whitehanded (Iseult of Brittany) pleads with Tristram was drawn from several passages between Elfride and Knight in *A Pair of Blue Eyes*, first when he leaves her in Cornwall, then when

she follows him to his chambers in Bede's Inn. Memories of Emma
are associated with both Iseults. Iseult of Cornwall is his 'lily-rose';
the corn-brown hair and the white robe of Iseult the Whitehanded
recall her portrait, and her last words with reference to Brittany
allude to happiness in Cornwall before Emma knew what 'pended'
her elsewhere. In arranging it as 'a play for mummers', Hardy, as
the ending of his preface to *The Dynasts* implies, hoped that it
would be produced in a subdued, almost monotonic manner,
especially by the Chanters, a chorus of spirits from ancient Cornwall, to suggest a dream re-enactment conjured up by Merlin.
Archaisms and a simple ruggedness of diction go far to fulfil the
aim of suggesting characters of an early period in contrast to the
Victorianism Hardy found in presentations of the subject by Tennyson, Swinburne, and Arnold.

Although he was not very fit, he decided to attend a rehearsal of
the play by the Hardy Players with Harold Child, who had come to
write a report for *The Times* of the first performance two evenings
later. This was attended by Sidney Cockerell and Colonel
Lawrence, who took Florence with them after dining at Max Gate.
Hardy attended the matinée next day, 29 November, with Florence
and her friend Mrs Inglis, and found John Drinkwater present with
Daisy Kennedy. The play was followed by two light dramatic
sketches, the first being 'O Jan! O Jan! O Jan!', which Hardy had
written, with additions, from recollections of 'a little operatic piece'
played in Dorset homes about 1844–7, and which Lawrence described as 'a blessed piece of foolery to give our poise back to us';
the second was T. H. Tilley's version of the old St George play,
for which his wedding scene from *Under the Greenwood Tree* was
substituted when the programme was given in London on
21 February.

Friends kept dying one by one: Viscount Morley, Hardy's first
reader, in September; Sir Frederick Treves at Lausanne early in
December. On the penultimate day of the year Bernard Shaw and
Mrs Shaw, who were staying at Bournemouth, lunched with their
friend Lawrence at Max Gate, and spent several hours with the
Hardys. On 2 January 1924, a very wet day, Hardy attended
Treves's funeral service at St Peter's, and followed in the procession to the cemetery, where the casket was buried in a small
white grave; his thoughts returned to his early years, when his
sister Mary attended the same school as Treves, and his first
writing-desk was bought from his father's shop. His memorial

poem 'In the Evening' appeared in *The Times* three days later, and a revised and extended version, in the annual publication of the Society of Dorset Men in London, of which Treves was the first president.

As a result of watching *The Queen of Cornwall*, Hardy soon made revisions and an important extension, one scene being divided by the insertion of a new one to make clear how Mark's suspicions that the strange old harper was Tristram were confirmed. Rutland Boughton was already keen to set it to music, proposing the addition of songs from Hardy's poems to relieve the tragedy a little. Hardy did not object to changes of that kind, but insisted that all the words of the text were to be his own. Boughton's aim was to make an opera (a 'music-drama') of the play; he enlivened Max Gate in June 1924 by playing some of the music, and even more by the extremism of his Communist notions. When he saw the wealthy classes, he sometimes thought 'there was nothing for it but the pistol and knife', he said, inviting Florence, who was taken aback by the violence of his talk, to join the party and live more independently. Owing to a chill Hardy was unable to travel with her, Lawrence, Cockerell, and Mr Watkins, founder and secretary of the Society of Dorset Men in London, for the first performance of the opera in the Assembly Rooms at the Glastonbury Festival, but he saw it there six days later, on 28 August, with Florence. There was no room for an orchestra; Boughton accompanied on a piano; and Lawrence had not been altogether impressed, though reviewers in general were warm in their praise.

A controversy stirred up by the publication of George Moore's *Conversations in Ebury Street* made Hardy almost ill with worry in March. He may have remembered that Moore had dismissed *Far from the Madding Crowd* as 'one of George Eliot's miscarriages' many years earlier, but he could only deduce what he had recently written about his work from the robust article 'Wrap Me up in My Aubusson Carpet' which Middleton Murry published in his defence in the *New Adelphi*, and from another by H. M. Tomlinson in the *Weekly Westminster*. Thanking Murry for his 'brilliant little article', Hardy said he knew little of Moore and his works, and could not understand why the press spoke of him with 'bated breath'. 'Somebody once called him a putrid literary hermaphrodite, which I thought funny', he added. He felt that those whose participation in the original conversations had been used to bolster up the author's spite and affected superiority – and they included Gosse, Granville-Barker, and de la Mare – were placed in an unfortunate position, and were timid not to protest. Moore had described Hardy's prose as the worst of the nineteenth century, his popular novels as 'ill-constructed melodrama, feebly written in bad grammar', and his poetry as 'old tin pot' stuff. Murry's 'smashing criticism of that ludicrous blackguard' was supported by *The Times*, Hardy noticed with relief on 1 April.

Later in the month Hardy received some interesting information from Granville-Barker on the actor Kean's association with Dorchester, which helped him to draft a brief description of the theatre where he had acted, for entry in the visitors' book at the china-shop on its site in High West Street. Florence had proposed to read Emily Brontë's *Wuthering Heights* to him, but he would have none of it, after reading parts himself which he disliked intensely for their 'unrelieved ugliness'. Leslie Stephen's *Some Early Impressions*, sent by his daughter Virginia Woolf, one of its publishers, was of special interest in June, and much more satisfying than Ernest Brennecke's *Thomas Hardy's Universe*, which seemed like 'a treatise on Schopenhauer'. Florence was delighted to receive a copy of *Saint Joan*, inscribed to her from George Bernard Shaw. At Clouds Hill on 22 June she and Hardy met Lawrence and E. M. Forster, who was staying there. On 1 July the Balliol Players came to perform *The Curse of the House of Atreus*, an English version of Aeschylus's *Oresteia*. Hardy had suggested that the students performed in Maumbury Rings, but admitted that it would be more convenient for him if the drama were enacted on his lawn. Theatrical properties were brought on a motor-lorry which was not very reliable, while the enthusiastic players cycled down, among them Walter Oakeshott, who played the part of Orestes, and became rector of Lincoln College and vice-chancellor of Oxford University. Granville-Barker came over for the occasion. While having their strawberry and cream tea after the play, the students clustered round Hardy, who enjoyed chatting with them.

It was the centenary year of Byron's death, and Hardy had re-read essays on him, those by John Morley and Matthew Arnold in particular, noting his enmity towards a society which measured man by his estate and not by his spirit. With Balfour, Asquith, and others, he, Gosse, Kipling, and Newbolt were co-signatories to a letter which appeared in *The Times* on 14 July, urging the propriety of a memorial to Byron in Poets' Corner. In rejecting this appeal, the Dean of Westminster referred to the poet's 'dissolute life' and 'licentious verse'. Hardy countered with 'A Refusal', an imagined soliloquy in light couplets by the Dean which ends with horror at the thought that Shelley and Swinburne, two poets more highly esteemed by Hardy, might next be recommended.

Early in August, after motoring one day for lunch with the Granville-Barkers at Netherton Hall, he and Florence had several visitors, Sassoon twice, and Lawrence twice, the latter's second visit on the same day as that of H. M. Tomlinson and his wife. Late in the month Hardy found his sittings to the Russian sculptor Sereg Youriévitch (interrupted by his excursion to the Glastonbury Festival) so tiring that, although he enjoyed conversing with him, he resolved not to sit again to any artist. When invited early in September to supply a Christmas poem for a New York publication, he felt quite unequal to it, but Florence remembered seeing one he had roughly scribbled in pencil and forgotten; after a search he found and completed it for Harold Macmillan, who cabled it across the Atlantic. Known later as 'The Paphian Ball', it appeared in the December number as 'The Midnight Revel', and Hardy received $500 for it. Later in the month Lady Ottoline Morrell, on a tour of Dorset and neighbouring counties, called, and John Drinkwater sought permission to dedicate his poems *From an Unknown Isle* to him. It was a time of great anxiety for Hardy and Florence. After staying overnight in London with the neurologist Henry Head and his wife, with whom Hardy had corresponded over a selection from his works which they completed for publication in 1922, Florence was taken to the surgeon James Sherren, who discovered that what had been diagnosed as a glandular swelling was a cancerous growth. Arrangements were made for its removal at the end of the month. It was decided that Hardy was too frail to accompany Florence, and that he needed to stay at home for the sake of Wessex, who, his mistress wrote, would have broken his heart had he been deserted by both. After a miserable morning Hardy and Wessex accompanied her to Dorchester station. Next morning Miss O'Rourke was shocked at the change in his appearance, and it was an enormous relief when the first telegram came to assure him that the operation had been successful. Cockerell's visits to Florence at the Fitzroy House nursing-home and his letters to Hardy were a source of great comfort to both. Henry Hardy, with a chauffeur to assist him, was delighted to fetch her in the car he had bought that summer, but it was after dark on 9 October when Florence reached Max Gate, to the unspeakable relief of

Hardy, who had waited long outside in the watchful state of suspense he communicates in 'Nobody Comes'.

It was probably because the showing of an American film of *Tess* in Dorchester had revived local interest in the novel that Hardy was asked whether he could provide something for the Hardy Players to perform in the winter. Some knew that he had been keen for *Tess* to be staged; they may even have heard of the dramatized version he had made thirty years earlier. Though professing some reluctance, he must have been pleased when it was agreed that this should be performed, and gratified to learn that Gertrude Bugler, after the birth of her daughter, was able to participate and would play the central role. When he took Florence on 22 October to see the barn at Kingston Maurward farm, where he had heard ballads sung in his boyhood, memories of the milkmaid Augusta Way, Mrs Bugler's mother, whom he had seen there in the late 1880s and recalled imaginatively in *Tess*, must have sprung to mind. The following Sunday they were taken to the manor house at Wool with the mural paintings of the two ugly Turberville dames above the staircase landing, to observe a rehearsal of the tragic honeymoon scene, with Dr Smerdon as Angel, and a later one with Norman Atkins as Alec; Hardy attended other rehearsals at the Corn Exchange. The play attracted considerable interest in London. Barrie and Child came to the dress rehearsal on 24 November, and Sassoon and Forster to the first performance; Lawrence met them in the theatre, while Hardy sat in the wings. Next day Cockerell, Sassoon, and the Hardys attended the matinée, and had tea with the players; in the evening Cockerell went again, and met Frederick Harrison, manager of the Haymarket Theatre. On the final evening Sybil Thorndike's husband, Lewis Casson, and the secretary of Basil Dean, managing director of Drury Lane, were present. Rebekah Owen came on the 27th with a friend, but did not have an opportunity to speak to the Hardys, although Florence had hoped to see her 'for a few minutes'; Hardy had more important visitors and business. When Miss Owen wrote from her friend's at Bath the following June, Florence made it clear that Hardy could not see her; the heat and visitors had been too exhausting, and the doctor had ordered a complete rest. Though Florence said she would see her if she cared to come, Rebekah concluded she was no longer welcome at Max Gate. She seems to have spent most of her remaining life in Italy. From Rome she wrote sympathetically to Florence when she heard

of Hardy's death, and it was there that she died eleven years and a
month later.

Although the Hardys were unable to attend any of the three
performances of *The Queen of Cornwall* in the New Year at Hill
Crest, the Masefields' home outside Oxford, they saw Boughton's
operatic version of it to the music of a full orchestra on the
afternoon of Saturday, 25 April, in the Winter Garden Theatre at
Bournemouth. Before this performance they were received by the
mayor and mayoress; later they were entertained by Sir Dan
Godfrey, the conductor.

So well had Mrs Bugler realized Hardy's conception of Tess in
her moving performances at Dorchester that, although he knew
Sybil Thorndike (who had won great acclaim at the New Theatre in
the title role of Shaw's *Saint Joan*) was keen to play the part, his
allegiance remained with her; but for her there would have been
little future for his play. He knew that Frederick Harrison wanted
her to perform in his theatre, and he was unwilling to have his
dramatization altered, as managers and critics had suggested, for
Mrs Casson's benefit. Lady Forbes-Robertson was also eager for
the role. Such was the position at the end of November 1924, when
Hardy must have been on the edge of nervous exhaustion after
attending a series of exciting rehearsals and performances. Another
demanding day followed when *Tess of the d'Urbervilles* was staged
at Weymouth, in the Pavilion Theatre, on 11 December, and he
and Florence watched the matinée, dined with the Mayor at the
Gloucester Hotel, and felt they had no choice but to stay and watch
the evening performance. The strain of all these events, with
continual concern for Hardy's health, and duties at Max Gate at a
time when several guests were entertained, told inevitably on
Florence after her operation. In allowing the little attentions he had
paid to Mrs Bugler in her dominant theatrical role to prey on her
mind, stirring up much deeper jealousy than ever afflicted the
players, she could not discriminate between Gertrude Bugler in
actuality and the actress who absorbed her husband because she
was Tess's 'very incarnation', as he described her to Sir Frederick
Macmillan, on hearing that an edition of *Tess* with woodcuts by
Vivien Gribble was proposed.

In his more rational moments Hardy began to wonder whether
he was acting wisely in encouraging Mrs Bugler to act in London,
hinting this uncertainty in a letter to her, and fancying that her
husband would agree with him. With her in mind, and almost

certainly at this juncture, he wrote 'An Expostulation', which begins:

> Why want to go afar
> Where pitfalls are,
> When all we swains adore
> Your featness more and more
> As heroine of our artless masquings here,
> And count few Wessex' daughters half so dear?

The allusion to Augusta Way and her sisters at Kingston Maurward farm is clear at the end of the poem, in 'the kine-cropt vale / Wherein your foredames gaily filled the pail'. Mrs Bugler preferred to leave everything to his discretion, and all seemed settled when Sydney Cockerell arrived at Max Gate in January 1925, and soon discovered how despondent and worried Florence was because Hardy appeared engrossed in making preparations for Gertrude's matinée appearances at the Haymarket. On 12 January, the last day of his visit, Mrs Bugler came for lunch; Hardy wished her to hear some prefatory dialogue he had added to the play, and a revision of the ending, in accordance with the novel, as in the original draft. He had forgotten that it was his wife's birthday. Soon Florence panicked at the thought that he would insist on seeing Gertrude perform in London, without regard to his health; she even imagined that his attention would create a scandal. Early in February she was so distraught that, after sending a telegram, she visited Mrs Bugler at her home in Beaminster without informing him, and used all her resources to persuade her to forgo her immediate ambition; Gertrude was young, and would have chances later on. What Florence said illustrated the workings of her heightened imagination even more perhaps than Hardy's infatuation. She was convinced that he had written poems inspired by Mrs Bugler; one was on an elopement, which she had destroyed. Mrs Bugler thought matters over very carefully, and finally found her high hopes outweighed by anxiety not to create disharmony at Max Gate, coupled with growing concern about leaving her baby daughter and her husband. Then, feeling they would think her ungrateful, she wrote to Hardy and Harrison renouncing her agreement. In his reply Hardy mentioned the possibility that Sybil Thorndike might be free to play the part later in the year, but was quite certain that no London actress could come nearer his imagining of Tess than she had done.

Shortly afterwards, however, he wrote to Sybil Thorndike, stating his unwillingness to make further alterations to his version of the play. Tensions over *Tess* for a lengthy period reduced him to a weak and nervous state. Near the end of May his wife reported to Charlotte Mew how, when a voluble lady came to tea and was 'in the midst of a perfect *spate* of egotistical nonsense', Hardy jumped up and left, much to the indignation of their guest; Florence found him lying on his study sofa, feeling 'absolutely exhausted'. (This behaviour may indicate how he had come to feel at the prospect of seeing Rebekah Owen.) Eventually he reached satisfactory terms with Philip Ridgeway for the production of *Tess* in Barnes. On 3 August he suggested that he wrote to Mrs Bugler if he still had difficulty in finding 'a good Tess'. Within days Gwen Ffrangcon-Davies had accepted the part, and soon she was proposing slight modifications of speeches and entries, which he accepted. Ridgeway, who had made a very favourable impression on Hardy, came with his producer and 'the three chief characters' to rehearse some scenes at Max Gate. The producer, Mr Filmer, had found the script more narrative than theatrical, and wished to make changes for curtains and better cues; Hardy gave him freedom to do as he thought fit, and the result was a re-arrangement without cuts. So successful was the play that, after being performed at the Barnes theatre from 7 September, it was transferred to the Garrick, where it continued from 2 November, running more than 100 nights in all. Much to Florence's pleasure, Hardy accepted medical advice, and did not trouble to see the London production. Instead, the players came down on 6 December, and performed the play in the Max Gate drawing-room. One of the company thought that the playing of the Stonehenge scene in the shadows by the firelight quite beautiful. She noticed that Hardy spoke of Tess 'as if she was someone real whom he had known and liked tremendously'.

28

The Coming of the End

Hardy regretted that, as a result of not visiting London, he had not met some of his surviving friends as often as he wished, among them Edmund Gosse, who, after his retirement from the librarianship of the House of Lords in September 1914, had visited the western front, met Gide twice in Paris, and become acquainted with several of the younger poets. After writing regularly for the *Daily Mail* and being suddenly dismissed, he was 'snapped up' by *The Sunday Times*, for which he continued reviewing to the end. He had earned both acclaim and envy; his successful cultivation of the eminent reminded Evelyn Waugh of Mr Tulkinghorn in *Bleak House*. In January 1925 he received a knighthood, but Hardy's congratulations were deferred until he received Gosse's good wishes for his eighty-fifth birthday, when he claimed the advantage over his friend of being able to read a 'brilliant article' by him every week in a Sunday paper. Hardy's reference to the 'so-called honour', and his statement that Gosse had given distinction to it, leave no doubt that he regarded it with scant approval, as he felt certain Gosse had known.

He had been alarmed to think that *The Life of Thomas Hardy* by Ernest Brennecke, a copy of which he had received from New York, might be published in England. Its cover announced it as not only 'the first biography of England's novelist-poet' but as 'a work which will probably always stand as the most authoritative and comprehensive book on the subject' and a record of 'every known fact of Hardy's life', the result of ten years' research and 'personal contact'. Only the early chapters were biographical, and Hardy diagnosed four sources for their information, which was too often incorrect: reference books and newspapers, assumptions that phases in a number of his novels reflected his life, notes made from a visit to Max Gate (where the writer appeared a student of German philosophy), and 'what he picked up' in Dorchester and the neighbourhood. It was much more pleasing to receive Charles Morgan's novel *My Name is Legion* and Amy Lowell's biography of Keats, which Florence had been reading to him because his eyes tired quickly. He thought 'pure serene' in 'the Chapman's Homer sonnet' derived from the 'purest ray serene' of Gray's 'Elegy', and remembered standing before a Grecian urn in the British Museum and concluding that it was the one which inspired Keats's ode. Florence's mother could remember the building at Enfield where Keats had gone to school, and he believed that she was related to John Taylor, the young poet's publisher. In June, Hardy was honoured when Cambridge students came with Cockerell and played pieces by Gibbons, Purcell, Arne, Mozart, and Haydn in the garden; Florence was sorry she had not been able to offer hospitality to the Hardy bibliophile and manuscript-collector Howard Bliss, as her sister from Canada was at Max Gate and Cockerell was staying overnight. Representatives of the University of Bristol arrived in July to award him an honorary D.Litt. This and the prospect of a University of Wessex, with a Thomas Hardy Chair of English Literature, must have been a source of unusual gratification.

Although Hardy needed to reserve his energies, the year 1925 was a busy one. There were many visitors to Max Gate, and outings included one in April to see the sketches Vivien Gribble (Mrs Doyle Jones) had done for *Tess*; she was staying with her father not far away, at Kingston Russell House in the Bride (or Bredy) valley. At the end of the month Florence went to Enfield; on her return journey she found time to attend the Royal Academy private view. In May she and Hardy visited the Granville-Barkers at Netherton Hall; in August they met Lady Pinney at Racedown (near Pilsdon Pen and Birdsmoorgate), where the talk was mainly on the past, including the Wordsworths, who had lived there from 1795 to 1797. Florence was anxious to leave in good time for Hardy's sake, and they were moving to the car when he turned to Lady Pinney and asked, 'Can you find out about Martha Browne?' He had just time to add: 'She used to live out there; I saw her hanged when I was sixteen.' As they had done each year, he and Florence made frequent 'pilgrimages' to Stinsford churchyard, usually in the evening in the summer and the afternoon during winter. On 9 October he visited the 'Mead of Memories' in the morning, when the sun shone across a worn inscription he had frequently tried to decipher; great was his joy when they discovered that it memorialized Robert Reason, who, although he died in 1819, had been remembered so well that Hardy had been able to portray him as Mr Penny in *Under the Greenwood Tree*.

Towards the end of July he had collected sufficient poems for another volume, to be published as usual in time for the Christmas sales. His first title was 'Poems Imaginative and Incidental'; he then suggested 'Human Shows' as less 'commonplace' and more commendable to readers and booksellers. Cockerell helped him again with the proofs, and recommended a number of word changes, about half of which were accepted. In making his acknowledgements Hardy showed those typical attitudes towards work which he was pleased to publish; he expected little from the volume, was weary of his own writing, and imagined his readers would be too; similarly, with reference to the production of *Tess* at the time, he professed to have 'drifted into a job' he quite disbelieved in, the dramatization of a novel. Anxious not to be accused of pessimism, he had categorized the poems in *Human Shows*, and found two-fifths of them sad or tragic, at least as many of a 'reflective dispassionate kind', the others being either 'of the nature of comedy' or 'love-songs and pieces, mostly for music'. The 'songs' are of general significance, whereas many other poems are personal and backward-looking. A few of these were inspired by ancestral traditions and birthplace recollections, another by a scene near Dogbury Gate in 1867. Others go back to Weymouth in 1869, Cornwall in 1870 and perhaps later, Oxford Street in 1872, Bath, Swanage, Upper Tooting and Surbiton, visiting Orme's Head on the way to Dublin in 1893, and Salisbury Cathedral at midnight in August 1897. One is based on an episode in *The Poor Man and the Lady*; another recalls Louisa Harding; another the death of Horace Moule. Two are very probably related to Mrs Henniker soon after Hardy became acquainted with her; more to Emma, several to her death. Though many, including some of these, were written earlier, most poems in the volume were comparatively recent. Two or three belong to a very early period, 'Discouragement' being the first of the surviving poems which were written at Westbourne Park Villas; 'Retty's Phases' was composed from a draft made in 1868. Altogether *Human Shows* suggests that, though the expression is sometimes forced, Hardy versified with practised ease. Passionate love-pieces are evident, and some narratives in ballad form are striking, but there is a noticeable increase in descriptive sketches, and, with rare exceptions such as 'Queen Caroline to Her Guests', subjects do not seem great enough to lift Hardy to those poetic levels he repeatedly achieved in previous volumes.

Florence's youngest sister Margaret Soundy, still on holiday from Canada, brought her son Thomas to Max Gate late in the autumn. Having heard so often that he must not be noisy during his stay, he was relieved, when his aunt took him upstairs and along a dark corridor to Hardy's study, by the kindly welcome of a white-haired old man whose gentleness he never forgot. The tranquillity of the place, broken only by the ticking of grandfather-clocks, must have been a trial for a young boy, who found company in the kitchen; as this was below the study, he had to be restrained even here, and Ellen Titterington, the parlourmaid, was pleased when she was asked to take him to Weymouth for the day. Florence and Kate accompanied him and his mother to Southampton for the return voyage on 6 November, and life at Max Gate remained tranquil; Florence had taken care to ensure that the remainder of her husband's life would not be disturbed by another Hardy play in Dorchester. At the end of the month Lady Pinney came with her husband, and Hardy returned to the subject of the Birdsmoorgate murder in 1856, on which she forwarded details in January. They found much in common between the stories of Martha Browne and Tess, and Lady Pinney was impressed by the sympathy he showed for such unhappy women. He would always brighten up when she was at Max Gate, Miss Titterington noticed; Lady Pinney would sit on the rug 'and talk and talk'; and Hardy would chuckle and laugh loudly over her local gossip. Another visitor who was always welcome was little Caroline Hanbury; she came a week before Christmas. Two days later Hardy was grieved to learn that Sir Hamo Thornycroft, a friend he always admired, had died; his nephew Siegfried Sassoon happened to arrive the same day from Weymouth; he left to attend the funeral at Oxford, taking a laurel wreath from Hardy. On New Year's Eve, instead of sitting up in old style to hear the Fordington bells, Florence and Hardy turned on the 'wireless' and listened to London celebrations until Big Ben announced the end of a year which, whatever he thought of his work at times, had indicated no decline in his prestige. Whereas the first edition of *Wessex Poems* had been limited to 500, 5000 copies of *Human Shows* – a larger number than for any previous volume – had been printed and almost sold out before the day of publication; since then there had been two further printings. In addition £1000 had been paid for the serialization of *Tess* in *John o' London's Weekly* from the previous October until July, two-thirds of the sum being assigned by Macmillan's to the author.

Hardy retired from his last public office, the governorship of Dorchester Grammar School, in January 1926; he needed to conserve his physical energy, and he preferred to be at home, where he found plenty to do. Soon he was signing sheets for a large-paper edition of the illustrated *Tess*, limited to 325 copies, for which he received £300; for the publication of a small-paper edition of this, limited to 1500, he agreed to a down-payment of £250. By June he had received signature sheets for a special three-volume edition of *The Dynasts*, limited to 525 copies, which appeared in 1927 with an etched portrait of him by Francis Dodd and an additional title-page epigraph, *Desine fata Deûm flecti sperare precando*; for these his fee was £1 per copy. In anticipation of his death, his publishers also wished to set up in type the early part of his *Life*, but Hardy could not agree to this proposal; it prompted him to look again at the whole, and temporize over a number of modifications. A copy had been sent to Lawrence, who read it while on duty at Cranwell and thought the early, formative period 'beautifully done'. Warned by the work of Brennecke, Hardy early in June asked John Acland, curator of the Dorset County Museum, to ensure that the doorkeeper no longer imparted information about him to strangers, and requested his solicitor H. O. Lock to insist on the withdrawal of misleading statements on himself and Max Gate staffing by the journalist R. T. Hopkins, who sent an apology, and explained that his information had been drawn from an article in the *New York Times Magazine*.

In February Hardy had written to advise the vicar Mr Cowley on the repair of Stinsford church bells, and furnished details of the 'Mellstock' associations which could be used, as the vicar had suggested, in support of an appeal in English and American papers. Two months later, in answer to an Oxford correspondent, subsequently head of religious broadcasting at the BBC, he expressed his long-held view that the reduction of the creeds and 'other primitive parts of the Liturgy' to essentials would receive such support from 'the thoughtful laity' that 'the retrogressive section of the Clergy' might be overcome. The fear that the Church would lose its hold on the public by failing to accept the universal truth of science was one of the reasons for the depression that often afflicted Hardy in his later years whenever he thought of the future of western civilization. In the meantime he had agreed to support the application for a memorial, to mark the centenary of the poet William Blake's death, in St Paul's, the cathedral of his rhythmically evocative 'Holy Thursday'.

Hardy had continued to receive royalties from Mr Ridgeway for *Tess*, which had been on tour with Christine Silver in the principal role. When receipts fell while it was played in Sheffield and Manchester during the general strike of May, he informed his agent Golding Bright that he was prepared to accept half the rate. The Balliol Players performed the *Hippolytus* of Euripides on the lawn at Max Gate on 29 June. By this time it had been agreed that Ridgeway should produce the stage-version of *The Mayor of Casterbridge* which John Drinkwater had produced by agreement with Hardy, who was to receive half the latter's fees. (Newman Flower had acquired permission to begin his serialization of the novel in *T. P.'s Weekly*, in the hope that its dramatization would increase interest in his paper.) The play was produced at the Barnes theatre, and Florence Hardy took Mrs Bugler to see it on 14 September. Six days later a 'flying matinée' was given at Weymouth specially for Hardy. Drinkwater and Ridgeway called at Max Gate before he and Florence left. The applause he received within the pier theatre, and outside when they departed, was tremendous, and he must have savoured the irony of tardy local recognition for a version of his work which in its grander original was more than forty years old. Though he was the last person to attribute great importance to his novel at the time, this was a satire of circumstance which must have given him fleeting amusement. Virginia Woolf, who had travelled with her husband by train from London to see him on 25 July, concluded that he could be 'naturally swept into imagining and creating without a thought of its being difficult or remarkable'; he could live obsessively in his imagination, but literature 'seemed to him an amusement, far away too, scarcely to be taken seriously'. They had talked of her father Leslie Stephen, and she had noticed Florence's concern for her wheezing dog Wessex, the brightness of Hardy's eyes as he talked, his mental alertness, 'his freedom, ease, and vitality', and his liking to discuss people, facts, and incidents rather than abstract matters. He gave the impression of having made up his mind, and spoke without doubt or hesitation; no trace of 'the simple peasant' seemed to be left in him.

Literature still held interest and excitement. He had looked forward to Gosse's radio broadcast of Wordsworth's 'Intimations of Immortality' ode, and had not been disappointed. In Proust he discovered a reaffirmation of the subjective view of love which had been a creative inspiration to him in *The Well-Beloved* and in early and later verse. One brief passage he noted, *'Le désir s'élève, se satisfait, disparaît – et c'est tout. Ainsi, la jeune fille qu'on épouse n'est pas celle dont on est tombé amoureux'*, summed up what he had known of falling in love, with or without marriage. In the evenings Florence read to him from books he had received, which included J. B. Priestley's *George Meredith*, Galsworthy's *The Silver Spoon*, and Wells's *The World of William Clissold*. He thought Meredith a direct descendant of Congreve and Restoration comedy, but regretted that, while brilliantly carried away by the Comic Spirit, he had failed to reveal the tragedy beneath the surface of things. He had rather tired of Napoleon, and was quite content to leave Philip Guedalla's *The Second Empire*, a history of later Bonapartism which reminded him of Louis Napoleon at Came House, until the long dark evenings. *The World of William Clissold* was not finished until past the middle of November, and, though he was less interested in the story than in the ideas it excited, he wished it had been a volume longer. Florence had found it tedious, and was pleased to find that Hardy enjoyed Aldous Huxley's *Jesting Pilate* essays when she read them to him.

It was a happy occasion when they were taken in September to see Mrs Bankes at Kingston Lacy, where once again he had the opportunity to feast his eyes on a 'priceless collection' of pictures. Some later outings and events brought sadness. A visit to his birthplace with Cecil Hanbury, the owner, to consider how it could be made tidy and secluded, filled him with regret at the state of neglect in which he found it, and he did not wish to see it again. Then Colonel Lawrence came to bid farewell, before leaving for India; Hardy, who thought very highly of his friend, was much moved by this departure. Lawrence had difficulty in starting his motor-cycle, and Hardy went back for a shawl to protect him from the cold wind; when he returned he was grieved to find that Lawrence had gone. Equally concerned that Hardy should not be kept waiting in the cold, Lawrence had run his machine into the road before starting up the engine. Shortly afterwards, in the first week of December, Hardy walked with Florence by the railway below Max Gate and saw truckloads of cattle, with animals' heads at every opening 'looking out at the green countryside they were leaving for scenes of horror in a far-off city'; it was a sight that haunted him so much that he left money to two societies for the promotion of more humane methods of transport to slaughter-houses. The Christmas season, which had been heralded outside Max Gate by carol-singers from St Peter's, was spoilt when Wessex, who, endowed, it seemed, with almost human intelligence, had been the most faithful and spoilt companion of the Hardys indoors and out, had to be put out of his misery on the evening of 27 December 1926 with a 'kind breath of chloroform' administered by two doctors while he was sleeping. After his burial in the pets' cemetery next day, Hardy wrote 'Night. Wessex sleeps outside the house the first time for thirteen years.' On hearing of his death, Barrie wrote, 'One of the best advertisements for wireless, – "Wessex liked it."' So passed away the Max Gate guardian who had been a terror to many callers. Some of the hyperbole that characterized most of Florence's emotional epistolary utterances may be suspected in the statement she wrote to Cockerell that, but for Wessex, she would have been alone for '*thousands* (actually thousands) of afternoons and evenings'. At Melbury House the following May, she and Hardy declined the offer of a puppy; Wessex had been replaced in Hardy's affection by a blue Persian cat named Cobweb.

Apart from the dating of one or two poems such as 'Seeing the Moon Rise' (August 1927), and the subjects of a few – 'Dead "Wessex" the Dog to the Household', 'The Aged Newspaper Soliloquizes' (*The Observer* on reaching its 135th anniversary in March 1926), and 'Concerning Agnes' (written after hearing of the death of Lady Grove in December 1926) – the evidence on what poems Hardy wrote in the last year or two of his life is rare. 'Christmas in the Elgin Room' and 'A Philosophical Fantasy' were revised in 1926, the latter being another effort to define the Unknowable. Although it is developed in a light conversational manner, its effectiveness is weakened by prolongation, with repetition of stale views leading to the conclusion that the course of universal things is no more than a *purposeless propension*. It appeared at the beginning of the January *Fortnightly Review*, Hardy liking to open the New Year with this kind of poem, in the belief perhaps that its provocativeness during the period of post-Christmas euphoria might play a part, however small, in the enlightenment of the Christian world. Consistency is not to be expected in one 'so various', and there is more wisdom in 'Drinking Song', which makes no effort to define the Unknown. 'Unkept Good Fridays', written on Good Friday, 1927, harks back to the Positivist recognition that many 'Christs of unwrit names' have sacrificed their lives for the welfare of a world which by and large has never been worthy of them. Hardy was finding it difficult to write verse that satisfied his critical standards; at the end of October 1926 Florence informed a friend that he had burned 'practically all' he wrote, which she thought 'the wiser plan'.

One of Hardy's first acts in 1927 was the signing of an agreement for a Czech translation of *Jude the Obscure*. Writing to Edna St Vincent Millay in the spring, on her gift of *The King's Henchman*, he told her that her play carried him back to 'those old times' it 'outshadowed', as if he were almost spontaneously inclined to use one of those arbitrary neologisms which he had added to his poetic resources, with some unfortunate consequences such as 'inbe' and 'unbe', the ambiguous – if not entirely misleading – 'outshrill', and other oddities. A question from another correspondent led him to observe that excessive attention to sport in England distracted the minds of youth from more important matters. Once again he found reading one of Granville-Barker's plays like reading a novel; this was the revised version of *Waste*, and he could not help wishing it had been one. Ten days later he and Florence spent part of his eighty-seventh birthday at Netherton Hall; afterwards he told her that it might be their last visit to the Granville-Barkers. It was a cold day, and a fire was lit for him in the library, where he sat stroking a cat on his knees as he rested. Then came visits from the Gosses, who were staying at Swanage; Sir Edmund, recalling how much they talked on past generations, was amazed at Hardy's vitality. 'Very tiny and fragile, but full of spirit and a gaiety not quite consistent in the most pessimistic of poets', he wrote. Early in July the Balliol Players performed *Iphigenia in Aulis* on the lawn at Max Gate. This was followed by visits from Cockerell, Sassoon, and the Masefields. On 21 July, in very cold windy weather, Hardy laid the foundation-stone for the new Dorchester Grammar School on a muddied site which could be seen across the fields from the front gate of his house; he used the occasion to speak of his collateral ancestor who had endowed the old school sufficiently before his death for its rebuilding early in the seventeenth century. The ceremony and inclement weather proved to be very tiring, but Hardy soon recovered, and on 9 August accompanied Gustav Holst, who had dedicated his orchestral tone poem on the subject to him, to 'Egdon Heath', then purple with heather; afterwards they visited Puddletown church, and climbed about the wide

Jacobean gallery, where Hardy must have thought of his grandfather who played there and of other ancestors who may have sat
among the choir.

One of his main literary occupations during the year was the
preparation of an updated version of his *Selected Poems*. His additional selections were ready by September; at the proof stage in
November he suggested 'Chosen Poems' for the new title, and this
was adopted. Eight of the original poems were withdrawn, and
'Hap', 'The Fiddler', 'A Trampwoman's Tragedy', and 'Albuera'
(from *The Dynasts*) were added, together with 45 poems from the
volumes published after 1916. (*Chosen Poems* did not appear until
August 1929.) By October Hardy had finished the short article
'G.M.: A Reminiscence' for publication in February 1928 on the
centenary of Meredith's birth, when it appeared in *The Nineteenth
Century and After*. He received copies of his signed edition of *The
Dynasts* at the end of November.

Outings by car with Florence included a day excursion to Bath in
August, when they both found they had lost their taste for lunching in the open air; in the city he felt like a ghost revisiting 'scenes
of a long-dead past', thinking particularly of the time when he and
Emma were there before their marriage. After a rest in the Pump
Room they returned, Florence feeling more tired than he. Some
weeks later they travelled to Ilminster in Somerset, which he had
long wished to see, chiefly for the church and its tomb to the
founder of Wadham College, Oxford; at his request they returned
past the Ham Hill quarries from which the stone for many mansions in the region had been hewn; at Yeovil he listened with great
enjoyment to the playing of three musicians during tea-time. On
21 September, after a visit from Mr and Mrs Weld, they were their
guests at lunch in Lulworth Castle; here and in the neighbouring
church Hardy found much that interested him. But for Florence's
severe cold and his fear of 'influenza', they would have visited
Gosse, who was recuperating at Bournemouth after typhoid. During October they lunched at Charborough Park; it was the first
time he had entered the house which he imagined as the heroine's
in *Two on a Tower*.

On 6 September John Galsworthy and his wife called on their
way from Devon to London. Hardy's recollection of a murder
eighty years earlier made Galsworthy ask whether his memories
of childhood had always been as vivid, or only lately. Hardy
replied that he had always remembered clearly; he could recall his

puzzlement at the age of six when his mother commented on the Rush murder, 'The governess hanged him.' During this visit the novelist and playwright Clemence Dane (Miss Winifred Ashton) called, after motoring in heavy rain from Axminster. The next day was invitingly fine, and the Hardys walked across the fields to see what progress was being made with the grammar school buildings. On 8 October a letter arrived from a Chinese man who had already been refused an appointment. It indicated that he had a tragic story to tell, and would be at the door at three o'clock. Arriving punctually, this small, melancholy-looking man with an appealing round face wished to have Hardy's advice on whether to write his tragic memories as an autobiography or a novel. He was overcome with emotion when he told the story, and sobbed aloud. He had killed his sister when it was found that she was in 'the same condition as Tess'; after reading Hardy's novel he realized he ought to have reverenced her. Hardy was moved, but Florence's scepticism was roused when their visitor asked for an autograph and suggested Hardy should help him to write his tragic history. He spoke English so badly that it was difficult to follow what he said. When she saw a volume of Hardy's poetry by the visitor's coat and hat in the hall she was more sceptical than ever. She had learned to distrust autograph-hunters.

Middleton Murry lunched with the Hardys on 30 October, when the conversation turned to Keats, whose work he had studied intensively, Hardy expressing high admiration of Severn's devotion to his friend, which must have been disinterested, he thought. (Murry, who was desperately short of money, was spending the winter at Abbotsbury for the sake of his second wife, who suffered acutely from tuberculosis. Hardy asked Gosse to inquire whether assistance could be provided from the Royal Literary Fund. This would have taken so long that Gosse appealed to Stanley Baldwin, the Prime Minister, emphasizing Hardy's support, with the result that a grant of £250 was made to Murry shortly afterwards.) The next day Henry Williamson, author of *Tarka the Otter*, called, followed by Lady Ilchester, who brought Captain Cazalet, a friend of Kipling, conversation on whom led Hardy to observe that he had 'given to party what was meant for mankind', a statement which seemed to impress the captain, who did not recognize the quotation from Dryden.

Late in October Hardy had attended a meeting in the Dorset County Museum to discuss what action should be taken to pre-

serve the Roman tessellated pavement which had been discovered
at Lott & Walne's iron foundry, near Noah's Ark in lower Fordington.
On 4 November he and Florence visited Stinsford churchyard to lay
flowers on the family tombs, and continue his work of removing
the moss which grew on them under the spreading yew, with a
small wooden scraper he had carved for the purpose; he remembered that when he was there with him, Walter de la Mare had said
he preferred them to remain green. As they drove up 'Dark Hill' on
the way to Bockhampton Cross and Talbothays, he pointed out the
spot in the hedge where he had left the umbrella which remained
forgotten until his mother had asked where it was when he
returned from school. On Armistice Day he came down from his
study and joined Florence in listening to a broadcast service from
Canterbury Cathedral; as they stood observing the two minutes'
silence he remembered his cousin Frank George, who had fallen at
Gallipoli. In the afternoon they walked by the railway, where, as
he had done so often with her, he contentedly watched a train
pass, carrying huge blocks of stone from Portland. In the evening
he talked about poaching families he had known in his boyhood,
and remembered how a pair of swingels (implements often used
by poachers in self-defence) was found under the thatch of a home
at Bockhampton. One evening he reminisced on Henry Bastow in
such a way that Florence felt he would like to meet him again more
than anyone else in the world; he knew that his old friend had
moved to Australia, but did not know that he had died in 1920.
Later, when the anniversaries of his sister's death and his wife's
fell, he wore a black hat and went about with a black walking-stick
once used by Emma. About this time he revised poems for his last
volume, which he thought fit to preface with remarks on the
charge that *Human Shows* was 'gloomy and pessimistic' and with a
denial that he had ever attempted to put forward a consistent or
'harmonious' philosophy. Next day, 28 November, he said he had
achieved all he meant to do, and wondered whether it was worth
doing.

29

His Death and After

Although Hardy's work of revising and arranging poems for *Winter Words* was not complete, there can be little doubt from his preface that he was preparing for publication on his eighty-eighth birthday. Nearly half the poems were published posthumously in the *Daily Telegraph* before the volume appeared on 2 October 1928. In drawing poems from a period of more than 60 years, one from 1866, another from 1868, every decade onwards but one being represented, the collection is remarkable. The chronological range of subjects provides one aspect of its variety, from 'Childhood among the Ferns', 'To Louisa in the Lane', and 'Standing by the Mantelpiece' (Horace Moule) to Swanage, Emma by the mill at Sturminster ('The Second Visit'), and the recent loss of Lady Grove. Another is to be found in the style and subject, from 'Drinking Song' to 'He Never Expected Much' or from the highly wrought 'Family Portraits' to 'I am the one', a quiet poem of epitaph status quite worthy to be linked with the more ambitious 'Afterwards'. Though much shorter, this volume probably contains more poems of outstanding merit than *Human Shows*. It is rather more gloomy in outlook, with an unprecedented emphasis on man's 'unreason' in 'Thoughts at Midnight', begun in 1906, and on a 'demonic force' threatening the peace of Europe in ways foreshadowed in 'Christmas: 1924', 'We are getting to the end', and 'He Resolves to Say No More'. Hardy had feared for some time that the Treaty of Versailles would prove fatal. Disillusionment combines with a grey philosophical outlook to outweigh poems in lighter mode. There were no Shelleyan implications of 'If Winter comes, can Spring be far behind?' in the title of Hardy's eighth and final volume of poetry.

His reading was slowing down. At the end of November 1927 he had completed the essay on *King Lear* in the copy of Granville-Barker's first series of *Prefaces to Shakespeare* sent by the author 'in affectionate homage' to Florence and him; he was still inclined to maintain the view adopted by Lamb and supported by A. C. Bradley that certain scenes of the play were beyond stage-presentation, though Barker's practical exposition had made him less certain. Next day Florence reported that he was very busy and cheerful. On 4 December he enjoyed a visit from Dorothy Allhusen, who talked of the pranks she played when she was a child and he was staying with her mother. Sassoon was expected the next day. Thereafter he tired quickly. On 11 December, after exerting himself too long during the previous day's visits of Mr Wells (Harper & Brothers' representative) and his wife, and Mr and Mrs H. M. Tomlinson, he went upstairs to his study in the morning, and found for the first time in his life that he was quite unable to work. The doctor expected he would recover after a rest, but his strength steadily declined; his heart weakened. Middleton Murry called and appeared more confident about his wife's recovery, but he was not allowed to see Hardy, who became greatly concerned in the next day or two that his poem 'Christmas in the Elgin Room' should be copied and sent off for publication in *The Times* on Saturday, 24 December. Gosse wrote his last letter to Hardy on Christmas Eve, after reading the poem to his family at Hanover Terrace while the 'dark rain' fell in 'the pea-soup-coloured fog'. On Christmas Day Hardy was able to scribble a note in pencil to his old friend, thanking him for his appreciation of the poem; he informed him that he was in bed, 'living on butter-broth and beef tea', and causing concern in the kitchen, though he was rather relieved, because he was unable to eat any Christmas pudding.

He had been allowed to sit a few hours daily by the fire in the drawing-room, but after Christmas he remained upstairs. On 26 December he thought about the Nativity and Herod's massacre of the Innocents; Florence read him the gospel accounts and relevant articles in the *Encyclopaedia Biblica*, and he asserted that there was no evidence to prove either story true in any detail. At the end of the year the window in the adjoining dressing-room was opened in order that he might hear the Fordington bells; he could not, and did not seem to mind. As the weather turned bitterly cold and snow fell his condition worsened, and Sir Henry Head, who lived in the neighbourhood, was called in to advise; Dr Mann also summoned a specialist from Bournemouth for consultation. Fluid at the base of the lungs was diagnosed, and pneumonia was feared. On 6 January Florence conveyed Hardy's love and best thanks to Lady Hoare for the 'delicious little bird' which she had sent and he had 'certainly enjoyed'. He was pitifully weak, she reported, and could not raise himself in bed; no visitors were allowed to see him, not even his sister Kate. Hardy could no longer listen to prose, but requested a poem now and then; one night as Florence sat by his bed he asked her to read de la Mare's 'The Listeners'. Her sister Eva came to relieve her, and Cockerell, Hardy's literary executor, was summoned by telegram on 9 January. The next day Hardy rallied, and insisted on writing a cheque for his subscription to the pension fund of the Society of Authors. It amused him to hear that Barrie, who had come to Dorchester to assist in any way he could, had called at the kitchen door to avoid disturbing him by ringing the front door bell. That evening he asked his wife to read Browning's 'Rabbi Ben Ezra'; he listened intently, and wished to hear this long poèm to the end, rather to her surprise.

After a more restful night he seemed so much better that hopes of a recovery were entertained, though they were not shared by Kate when she called later in the day. The arrival of a large bunch of grapes from Newman Flower brought pleasure to Hardy, who held them up for the admiration of Dr Mann and others, and occasionally ate one or two. Though he fancied a rasher of bacon, grilled in front of the fire as he had seen it done by the hearth in his boyhood, he was unable to eat it. Hoping that he would find time to improve them, he dictated some lines which he had composed for satirical epitaphs on his two unforgivable critics, George Moore and G. K. Chesterton, the second of whom had described him years earlier, in *The Victorian Age in Literature*, as 'a sort of village atheist brooding and blaspheming over the village idiot'. As it grew darker he requested Florence to read the verse from Omar Khayyám's *Rubáiyát* beginning 'Oh, Thou, who Man of baser Earth didst make' and ending 'Man's forgiveness give – and take!' He required no more; this kind of Promethean defiance seemed to satisfy him. In the evening he had a sharp heart attack, and an urgent call was made to Dr Mann, who came quickly; Hardy told him he had been reading J. B. S. Haldane's *Possible Worlds*, but found it too difficult. Soon afterwards his mind began to wander, and Eve Dugdale heard him talking about her. As she was taking his pulse, he cried out, 'Eva, what is this?' She took his hand, but when his hold weakened called to Ellen Titterington, who was on emergency duty in the dressing-room, telling her to bring hot-water bottles and eiderdowns from the other bedrooms as fast as she could. After doing this, Ellen was sitting on the high fender by the kitchen fire when Cockerell entered to tell the staff that Hardy was dead. Soon afterwards they heard Hardy's death announced by the BBC at the end of the nine o'clock news. Florence, from all accounts, was not present when he spoke his last words, and may have recalled a regret she had heard earlier, or imagined it for the sake of effect, when she indicated their substance at the end of Hardy's *Life*. Significantly she decided to withdraw what she had written about his last minutes: 'when a few broken sentences, one of these heartrending in its poignancy, showed that his mind had reverted to a sorrow of the past'.

When Dr Mann was recalled he could do no more than make a post mortem examination. An attempt was made to inform Henry and Kate at Talbothays, but there was no reply to the telephone call. After the body had been prepared and laid out by Eva, Florence was called in; it was the eve of her forty-ninth birthday. Never had she seen 'on any being, or indeed on any presentment of the human countenance' an expression such as she saw on the death-face: 'it was a look of radiant triumph such as imagination could never have conceived'. The radiance passed, but the dignity and peace remained, she wrote. The look of triumph was confirmed by Kate Hardy, who had come with Henry as soon as Ellen Titterington cycled over with the news early next morning; the radiance was noticed by a friend of May O'Rourke, a Catholic priest who saw him the day after Cockerell and Eva had draped him more splendidly in his scarlet doctoral robes. (He had travelled all night from Ireland, hoping for permission to see 'the great Thomas Hardy', and arrived in the dark, not long before the body was due to be taken away at eight in the morning.)

Although Cockerell had examined Hardy's will, and knew from the opening that he wished to be buried at Stinsford, he and Sir James Barrie must have agreed that Hardy deserved a higher honour in the eyes of the public. Barrie had left for London to enlist the support of the Prime Minister (Stanley Baldwin) for the burial in Westminster Abbey. Events moved too rapidly for Florence Hardy to give the question full consideration; by the afternoon of the 12th, less than a day after her husband's death, she knew that the Dean of Westminster had given his consent. Henry and Kate were united in opposition, but at length a compromise was reached; whether the suggestion came from Mr Cowley and his wife, or from Barrie, or from both parties, is uncertain. Hardy's heart was to be buried at Stinsford, his ashes at Westminster. Symbolically the idea was commendable; in execution it seems ghastly. That evening Dr Mann brought a surgeon who removed the heart; it was wrapped in a small towel and placed in a biscuit tin, which was then sealed and taken away by Dr Mann; after its return the next day, it was placed in the burial casket, which was then promptly sealed. That same morning Hardy's body was taken to the Woking crematorium, Cockerell and Barrie in attendance; it was they who took charge of the urn containing the ashes and handed it over at Westminster.

Three services in Hardy's memory began at two o'clock on Monday, 16 January. At Westminster Abbey his ashes were buried in Poets' Corner. The pall-bearers, who had met in the chapter house, were the Prime Minister and Ramsay MacDonald, Leader of the Opposition; Sir James Barrie, John Galsworthy, Sir Edmund Gosse, A. E. Housman, Rudyard Kipling, and George Bernard Shaw, representing literature; and A. S. Ramsay and Dr Walker, heads of Magdalene, Cambridge, and Queen's, Oxford, the two colleges of which Hardy had been an honorary fellow. Florence, escorted by Sydney Cockerell, and Kate Hardy were the chief mourners, with Dr Mann in attendance. Representatives of George V and the Prince of Wales were present, and seats were reserved for many distinguished people, including literary friends of Hardy, Gwen Ffrangcon-Davies, and members of Macmillan's, through whom attendance as a whole had been organized. The Dead March in *Saul* was played at the end, and Mrs Shaw, not knowing how much it had meant to Hardy in his early years, thought it 'the last word' and one of 'the most splendid things' of her life. It raised expectations in the crowds who had waited outside in the cold and rain that at long last they would soon be able to enter and file past the grave. Complaints that a notoriously heterodox writer should receive such high honour from the Church inevitably followed, and T. E. Lawrence suspected that, because he was 'too great to be suffered as an enemy of their faith', a trick had been played to make him appear as one of the redeemed. At Stinsford, where Henry Hardy was the chief mourner, the sun shone, the church was crowded, and a large number of people lined the path and stood by the gateway to see the burial of Hardy's heart in Emma's grave. At the same time another service took place in St Peter's, Dorchester, where the Mayor, with other civic dignitaries, society representatives, townspeople, and admirers from the neighbourhood, remembered one who had brought lasting renown to their midst;

simultaneously all business in the town was suspended for one hour as a token of respect.

Hardy's will ensured that Florence was well provided for. She inherited Max Gate, almost all of its contents, and all his royalties, in addition to other incomes, including £600 a year to be paid in quarterly instalments throughout her widowhood, and a portion of the remaining estate, which was to be shared equally with Henry and Kate Hardy. A further annuity was bequeathed to Lilian Gifford, and a gift of £250 to her brother Gordon. Bequests were made to the RSPCA and to the Council of Justice to Animals. Lloyds Bank were appointed trustees and executors, and Florence and Sydney Cockerell literary executors (Gosse, who outlived Hardy by only four months, being made Cockerell's deputy).

One of Florence's first tasks when she was recovering from the stress of the previous weeks was to supervise the removal of all the useless papers and clothes that encumbered certain rooms, Hardy's study particularly. There were some well-fed bonfires in the garden, Florence attending to one on which private papers and letters were burnt, and taking scrupulous care to turn the burning fragments over and ensure that all was turned to ashes. It was 'a devil of a clear-out' in the eyes of the gardener, who superintended the burning of newspapers and Hardy's old clothes. When all the garments and boxes of papers that had been kept hoarded in Emma's attics were disposed of is not so certain.

Before the end of January Florence had forwarded to Daniel Macmillan a typescript of the *Life* which Hardy had been revising until his final illness. After the publisher had read it, it was passed on to one of his readers, Charles Whibley, whose main criticism was that it contained too much detail from diaries, particularly of people met at London social engagements. Barrie was also reading a copy; soon afterwards he was considering to what extent Hardy's letters to Mrs Henniker should be used. On 26 March he sent Florence a long list of suggestions to make it 'one or two per cent' better, among them the inclusion of anecdotes and interesting details he had heard from her, such as 'the gate in the field' where Hardy was 'sad about his prospects' and 'how just before he set off to London the parson preached against upstarts, with mother and him in the church'. One very obvious result was the addition of four letters to Mary Hardy during the 1862–5 period. E. M. Forster gave some assistance. Cockerell, who had read the work during visits to Max Gate, and recommended omissions, offended Florence at the proof stage by acting as if he were in charge. *The Early Life of Thomas Hardy* (1840–91) appeared on 2 November 1928.

Meanwhile Florence had corresponded on the second volume with Barrie, who wondered whether she would ask Forster to take it in hand, and reported Cockerell's sadness at displeasing her. Though overblunt, he was doing his best to help her, Barrie wrote, wishing she were not 'so highly strung'. He had realized that the 'superlative' part of the whole book was to be found in Hardy's notebook comments on life and letters. Unfortunately, Lawrence was not at hand to give Florence confidence. After hearing of Hardy's death he had written from Karachi, telling her that she had kept Hardy alive all those years when he was 'transparent with frailty'. Three months later, after she had expressed the view that she had failed her husband, he replied, telling her that, after meeting 'so many thousands of what are estimated great men', he believed Thomas Hardy was 'above and beyond all men living, as a person'. Ordinary people could not expect ever to have been enough for him, but she had done more than most people could. The 'biography' would create trouble, but she must not let that worry her too much:

He will defend himself, very very completely, when people listen to him again. As you know, there will be a wave of detraction, and none of the highbrows will defend him, for quite a long time: and then the bright young critics will rediscover him, and it will be lawful for a person in the know to speak well of him: and all the nonsense will enrage me, because I'm small enough to care. Whereas all that's needful is to forget the fuss for fifty years, and then wake up and see him no longer a battle-field, but part of the ordinary man's heritage.

Florence had other worries besides the 'biography', but she meant to live her own life as far as she could. In June 1928, when heart-warming letters from Barrie had encouraged her to think he would marry her, she bought a car and engaged a chauffeur. She looked forward to winter months in London, and rented a flat in Adelphi Terrace, partly because Hardy had worked below in the same building, more because it was near where Barrie lived. She persuaded Ellen Titterington to accompany her as maid and cook, and they had many enjoyable outings together. At some periods she had her driver Shipton and the car to take her to see friends. Barrie would come for dinner, but was so breathless after climbing all the stairs that he preferred to meet Florence for tea or dinner at his flat, which had a lift. She was very happy in those days, Ellen recalled; 'I knew it would please her very much if she could become Lady Barrie', she wrote. Then, seeing 'the Max Gate look' return to her face, she knew that something was wrong. Florence had probably realized that Barrie's epistolary affection had misled her. They remained friendly none the less. She volunteered to help him when his secretary was on leave, and accepted his invitation to Stanway in August 1929, where the same secretary, Lady Cynthia Asquith, noticed a 'slight social strain' caused by the visit of Mrs Hardy, 'with whom I fear Barrie in the first emotion of her husband's death, pitched his relationship – a vicarious relationship – too high'. Florence had done something, in consultation with Philip Ridgeway, to atone for an episode she wished to forget, by persuading Mrs Bugler to play the part of Tess with a professional company to London audiences at the Duke of York's Theatre; she attended one of the rehearsals, and urged her not to be put off by the critics. The result was a great success; Mrs Bugler was billed as 'Thomas Hardy's Own Tess', and earned great applause, but nothing delighted her more than the arrival in her dressing-room, after the performance on 22 August, of a group of Hardy Players bearing a Dorset tribute 'to our Tess'.

The question of Hardy memorials caused Florence much vexation. Overzealously precipitate, Cockerell had organized a meeting at Barrie's flat almost immediately after the Westminster burial service, and written a letter to *The Times*, with her consent, suggesting a column on Rainbarrow like that to Hardy's namesake on Blackdown. The idea appealed to Henry Hardy, who wished to design and build it. (His death on 9 December 1928 deprived Florence of one of her dearest friends; he was the 'kindest soul imaginable' and 'I loved him', she wrote.) The more she thought of it the more she realized how alien such a memorial would have been to her husband, who had always sought to avoid personal publicity. Proof of his opposition to such a monument came from Lawrence, who had discussed the question of a memorial with him. Eventually, after differences over its siting and over the sculptor, it was agreed by the end of October 1929 that a life-size seated figure by Eric Kennington should be erected at 'Top o' Town', Dorchester. The following October she declined to unveil a

window to Hardy's memory in Stinsford church, knowing that
Somerset Maugham in *Cakes and Ale* (a fictional satire on the
cultural worship of authors by one who envied their success) had
ridiculed a second wife who 'exploits her husband's fame before
and after his death', and that some reviewers had assumed he had
Hardy in mind, though he had strongly denied such specific
intent. The unveiling of an American memorial near Hardy's
birthplace took place in March 1931; that of Kennington's statue,
on 2 September, after a very wet morning. Barrie was dissatisfied
with his speech, but Llewelyn Powys, who stood among the
onlookers, thought the ceremony testified to 'a civilized appreciation of human genius which alone can bring liberation to our
selfish emotion-ridden abject thoughts'. The statue disappointed
him; it showed a realistic likeness, but did not express the soul; it
lacked nobility, the 'deep dug-in countryman's look' so characteristic of Hardy, the 'elusive look of wisdom' referred to by the
Mayor, and that individual 'mixture of delicacy and strength'
which was loved so much by those who knew him.

Florence's completion of *The Later Years of Thomas Hardy* took
longer than she expected. For the last four chapters (the period
after 1918), almost wholly for the first two of them, she relied
considerably on memoranda left by Hardy. Accounts of their visits
to Oxford in 1920 and 1923 were written for inclusion at her request
by Charles Morgan and Godfrey Elton respectively. Another addition consisted of two appendices of letters, one to Dr Caleb
Saleeby on the 1914–18 war and philosophical questions, the other
to Edward Clodd on *The Dynasts*. A letter in each group had been
either largely or wholly included in the main text; subsequently
some justification for the first was added in a footnote, and the
other was omitted. Barrie had given invaluable advice on excisions, the chief of which were diary entries with lists of distinguished people met at London engagements, and passages, often
lengthy, of self-defence against critics. As in the first volume,
Florence deleted a number of references to Emma, but these were
relatively insignificant. Undoubtedly the publication of a work
which purported to be her biography of Hardy was a source of
apprehension to her: Hardy's authorship of the greater part of it
was not altogether a secret; his detailed preparation of the earlier
chapters must have been obvious; and critical readers would not be
slow to detect Hardy tones in most of it. She had not recovered
from the trauma of his 'compromise' interment. On 9 May 1930,

shortly after the publication of *The Later Years*, she thanked R. A. Scott-James for his favourable review, and said she would like to talk to him about 'the Abbey burial', which filled her with 'sick horror' and was 'forever' on her mind. Her relations with Cockerell were at a low ebb, and she had made things worse in 1929 by publishing 'Old Mrs Chundle' twice in America without consulting him, her co-executor; she annoyed him further in 1934, when she ignored him again, and had 100 copies of *An Indiscretion in the Life of an Heiress* published in London. The death of T. E. Lawrence as a result of injuries sustained in braking his motor-cycle to avoid cyclists after passing a rise in the road near Clouds Hill, to which he had very recently retired, was her greatest sorrow in 1935. By this time she was dedicated to welfare work in Dorchester, helping financially to improve hospital services, serving as a magistrate in the juvenile court, and organizing the amelioration of home conditions in what had been the 'Mixen Lane' slum area of Fordington. In devoted service, especially to Hardy in his latest years, Florence was one of those people who are greater than they know.

After a long illness, and a London operation which disclosed terminal symptoms, she died of cancer at Max Gate and was buried at Stinsford in October 1937. Florence's end must have been near when, according to her executor, Irene Cooper Willis, she instructed her sister Mrs Soundy to destroy a mass of papers which had remained in Emma's attics since her death. In the will she made in June she left large legacies to her four sisters and her nephew Thomas, but specially empowered Miss Willis, co-executor with Lloyds Bank, to select every Hardy article, book, manuscript, or letter she considered appropriate for preservation or exhibition in a special room (work for which was already in hand) to be provided in the Dorset County Museum. (Most of Hardy's remaining books were auctioned in London on 26 May 1938.) Max Gate was to be sold, and from the proceeds were to be drawn an initial sum for constructing, decorating, and equipping the exhibition room, and a capital sum adequate to provide income for its maintenance, insurance, and custodianship. This memorial, simulating Hardy's study, was opened by John Masefield on 10 May 1939. Max Gate was bought by Katharine Hardy, who died very wealthy from Henry's estate in October 1940, not long after the centenary of her famous brother's birth, which could not be fittingly celebrated when England was at war again, partly in consequence, as Hardy had feared, of the Treaty of Versailles.

Among Kate Hardy's generous legacies were the gift of £3000 to Dorchester Grammar School for the endowment of a Thomas Hardy scholarship to be held at Queen's College, Oxford, and the presentation of Max Gate to the National Trust, 'to retain the same in its present condition so far as possible', and to use income therefrom for the preservation and protection of Hardy's birthplace. She must have had assurance that the cottage, which was sold by Lady Hanbury to a Bockhampton farmer in 1938, would be purchased by the Trust, but it was not until after the war that, in May 1948, her expectations were fulfilled.

30

In Retrospect

> Man, like a glass ball with a spark a-top,
> Out of the magic fire that lurks inside,
> Shows one tint at a time to take the eye:
> Which, let a finger touch the silent sleep,
> Shifted a hair's-breadth shoots you dark for bright,
> Suffuses bright with dark, and baffles so
> Your sentence absolute for shine or shade.

'Others abide our question.' So, without the appropriate qualification, Matthew Arnold introduces his sonnet on Shakespeare, marvelling at the vision of a poet whose lasting greatness was beyond the perception of his contemporaries. By comparison, our knowledge of Hardy is enormous, and yet the more we know, the more we realize that experiences which were most central to much in his life and writings, including the best of his personal poems, raise questions which are finally unanswerable; too much of the crucial evidence is wanting to warrant biographical assertion, and we are left to conjecture. The issue is complicated by the heterogeneity of Hardy's reactions to people and circumstances at critical junctures; so inconsistent do they appear at times that they may seem almost contradictory.

Looking back over a long life which had brought much happiness and tribulation, Hardy himself came to this conclusion, as his poem 'So Various' illustrates in consecutive analyses. He contrasts the excitement and activating aims of his youth with a stony impassivity suggestive of old age; the staunch and tender lover with one who was also fickle of fancy; his seemingly transparent simplicity with the learning and vision of an intellect which could be read only superficially; the man of sadness with one whose cheerfulness made him a good companion; and one so slow and unadventurous that he seemed likely to produce little of any value compared with another so enterprising, shrewd, and swift in dealing with his affairs that he was expected to succeed; finally he sees himself as one who appeared not to notice or remember slights but who never forgot, with the result that the offender had cause long afterwards to make amends at the first opportunity (if he prized their friendship).

These differences and others less readily confronted or discernible must have been the product of circumstance and heredity. Mary Hardy's portraits of his parents led A. L. Rowse to hazard the guess that he derived his intelligence and tenacity from his mother; his temperament, his quiet reflective nature, and his love of music from his father; and his genius 'out of some incalculable magic in the combination of the two'. Evangeline Smith thought Hardy's father a gentleman, refined by nature; Mrs Hardy was 'hospitality itself'; her yoke was mild, for she had a mother's 'warm faithful heart'. This suggests that she was a woman with ideas which her husband readily accepted . She had seen enough of the world before her marriage to realize the value of education for her children. Home was a happy place for them, and nothing suggests that she had an unduly aggressive or provocative disposition. Emma Hardy, who was on good terms with the family for several years, was inclined to say what came to her mind, however inconsequential, but what led to bickering between her and Jemima is unknown; it may have been some unflattering comment on Jemima's household or on her eldest son, her 'boy'. (The Hardys were not 'County' enough, J. M. Barrie deduced.) Disdainfully, it seems, she refused to continue her weekly visits with Hardy to the cottage at Higher Bockhampton, as he recalled in 'The Coming of the End'; soon after his father's death, when he spent so much time visiting his lonely mother (who now felt she was 'a stranger' in her own home), Emma was so incensed that she would not allow any of her husband's family to enter Max Gate. So it continued until her death twenty years later. Hardy was naturally embittered, and found some satisfaction in continuing the attack on the sanctity of marriage ties for incompatible couples, which he had already had cause to launch in *The Pursuit of the Well-Beloved*, in *Jude the Obscure*. An interesting sidelight on Emma's implacable resentment is revealed in one of the diaries of Evangeline Smith's sister Alice; they were friendly with Hardy's sisters, who had tea with them at West Stafford rectory in August 1910. 'They were so amusing about Mrs. T. H. and her hatred of them and of Thomas's Order of Merit', Alice wrote.

Emma's judgement and self-control began to decline very noticeably soon after she moved into Max Gate. Even before this her oddities, her vanity, and her social pretentiousness had been obvious in Dorchester. She made few lasting friendships. In the course of time her self-absorption, her eagerness to draw attention to herself in company, sometimes at Hardy's expense, and her occasional but growing relish in arrogating a degree of responsibility for his literary achievement out of all proportion to whatever assistance she had given in copying or suggestion, lost her the sympathy of two of her most faithful friends, Mary Sheridan and Teresa Fetherstonhaugh. Christine Wood Homer, daughter of a third, had many opportunities at Bardolf Manor, Max Gate, and elsewhere, of observing her indomitable urge to show how superior she was to Hardy 'in birth, education, talents, and manners', and concluded that 'much of the unhappiness in her married life' arose from her wishing to be *'the great one'*. The view that Emma suffered from mental derangement at times is not restricted to Hardy and his second wife; no testimony on this question is more valid than that of some of her closest friends. Nor was her vilification of Hardy in her worst moods of revulsion, which was often inflamed by jealousy of the sympathetic attention he received from ladies in London, particularly after the publication of *Tess*, confined to her diaries; even Henry J. Moule, a staunch Christian, spoke scathingly of her treatment of his friend.

Perhaps Emma remains more enigmatical than Hardy. It comes as a shock to learn that in the census of 1871 her age is given as 25. Could this have been a clerical error, or was she guilty of deliberate misinformation? The entry may harden suspicion that she was not only vain but designing. It may lend colour to the belief which Hardy shared with his wife Florence and the latter imparted to Rebekah Owen on 24 October 1915, when she wrote on the Gifford family: the father's drunken ravings, and how once at Plymouth he chased his wife into the street in her nightgown; Helen's marriage to the 'old clergyman' Caddell Holder 'to escape the life of companion to an exacting old lady', and her attempts to marry her sister to 'any man who would have her'; 'they had nearly secured a farmer when T.H. appeared'. Whatever truth there is in this, there is no doubt that Hardy fell passionately in love with Emma, that she returned his love, and that their mutual affection endured with no very serious crises for a long period. Despite having no income of her own, she encouraged him more than anyone else along the road to literary success, though more than four years had to pass before marriage with reasonable security for the future was deemed assured. However much is revealed in *Some Recollections* and several of Hardy's poems, far more on how their courtship fared must have perished when Emma, late in life, destroyed all the love-letters they had treasured. Hardy prized them highly; with them much was lost that might have supplied pointers to their future, in traits of temperament and in expectations destined to be fulfilled or compromised or annulled. By 1895 the woman who was an agnostic when he first knew her, and who attended Positivist lectures with him in the early 1880s, had become 'an old-fashioned Evangelical like her mother'; in her last years she dwelt rapturously on the 'high delights of heaven' for those who were truly saved. Hardy had no such solace; in her eyes he was an unbeliever who had fallen a victim to Satan's guile, and no happy marriage was possible without a shared belief in the tenets of the Christian Church. The couple who had read poetry together at Sturminster Newton were now intellectually and spiritually divorced.

How much each suffered from this division, and to what extent Emma found escape and delight in the company of cats and birds, in gardening and various forms of creative writing, must remain very conjectural. Unlike her, Hardy was sufficiently professional and experienced to find relief, except at the worst crises, in work which was stimulated by the prospect of publication. Yet continually and inevitably his mind reverted to their happiness years earlier, and he felt with keen bitterness, especially after her sudden death, how the views he had held on 'Crass Casualty' had been confirmed; instead of gladness, 'dicing Time' had cast a moan. Emma and he had been 'predestined sorrowers' fated to 'drink the wormwood cup'. As he remembered her, tiredly resting her arms on those of the handpost near Lanivet, he could see her crucifixion foretold. Most of all was he haunted, when it was too late to make amends, by a sense of his neglect of her, although he had spent an enormous amount of time in accompanying her season after season to London, and on numerous cycling excursions and other outings in Dorset. In 'Surview', at the end of *Late Lyrics and Earlier*, he confesses his failure to live up to his greatest ideal and hope for mankind, Charity 'that suffereth long and is kind withal'.

Each of Hardy's wives complained of loneliness at Max Gate. Emma's querulousness was usually the expression of her warped self, when a complex of simmering resentments and animosities led to an irresponsible outburst of hostility so envenomed that it was unjustifiable whatever provocation she had received; her normal self, which was very apparent in her earlier years, was happy and generous. Florence, whose dedication to Hardy's comfort, and readiness to assist him in every way she could, was unswerving, suffered from fits of melancholy. When she sought relief in writing to her friends, her feeling often outstripped her judgement. Some of her letters to Rebekah Owen were so indiscreet that she subsequently asked her to destroy them; several 'that seemed positively libellous' – on whom but Emma and the Giffords, one wonders – were burned by Rebekah's Lake District friend Mrs Heelis ('Beatrix Potter') after her death. Such outpourings were probably prompted by fatigue, but, like Emma's invectives, they presented Hardy in a false light. Both wives must have known that he was the kind of self-exacting author who, under the compulsive pressure of composition, in large works or in the complex artistries of a poem, required hours of solitude. It could be argued that he was too devoted to his work. Hardy was not a Trollope who could write regularly day after day; when he was sure of his subject, and the mood or a publication commitment motivated him, he had to press on.

If nothing appears to underline the duality of Hardy's life more than his retirement as a writer at Max Gate and his association with upper-class coteries in London, it is worth remembering that many of his best friends and Emma's lived there, and that 'crushes', concerts, and Royal Academy viewings brought increasing relief as discontent and tensions made the restrictions of home more dull, or depressing, and unendurable. Often, in Emma's later years, Hardy made business a pretext for brief visits to the capital. About the time when he sought membership of the Athenaeum Club, he pursued a policy of consorting with the great in order to enhance his prestige. This was a passing phase; he soon perceived that intelligence and liveliness of mind were not always concomitants of high rank and office, and that he could be neglected at parties by careerist acquaintances who thought it more advantageous to cultivate the friendship of people in higher positions than themselves. At the end of a long London season he was always glad to return to his work and study at Max Gate. The metropolis, however tiring, renewed friendships and the stimulation of mind, but he wished above all for a life of independence, reading, contemplation, and creativity. The 'science of climbing' in the outer world had no appeal, and 'Childhood among the Ferns' may be regarded as an early indicator of what was to be his habitual preference.

When he wrote the early part of his *Life*, he described himself as 'a born bookworm', adding significantly, after much contemplation of his past, 'that and that alone was unchanging in him'.

Ambivalence has already been noticed in Hardy's attitude to war, and a strange disparity may be seen in the writer who fearlessly challenged orthodox custom and belief, yet could be still so overwrought by adverse criticism at the height of his fame that he flinched at the thought of meeting hostile reviewers. Another Hardy contrast is to be found between the man who developed such business acumen that he had little difficulty when he was famous in tactfully persuading his publisher to accept his advice, and the author who had chosen to live his life 'only as an emotion'. His work provides further antitheses, most evidently in the voices of the Years and the Pities, representing the detached scientific or historical vision of the intellectual and the imaginative empathy which finds expression when suffering is contemplated. At times the philosopher or poet in him made him feel with Sophocles that it would be better not to be born, or with Shelley and Ethelberta that he could 'weep away' a 'life of care' until death stole like sleep upon him; yet, given the right company or activity, he could enjoy life almost to the last breath. He was happy, his wife Florence discovered, when engaged upon the most dismal poetry, and he could not have written 'Poems of 1912–13' until he had recovered his composure. As an Elizabethan wrote, 'it is a peece of joy' when a poet is able 'to poure forth' the 'inward sorrows and the greefs wherewith his minde is surcharged'.

Hardy's mood-dictated poetry does not always reflect the truth; life at Sturminster Newton was far from being 'a preface without any book', and, however deep his depression could have been at Max Gate in November 1910 when 'The Roman Gravemounds' was written, it was most misleading and ungrateful, as Florence Dugdale protested when the poem was sent a year later for publication, to persist in publicizing the view that his 'little white cat' was his 'only friend'. She knew how the expression of a passing mood in 'Wessex Heights' misrepresented his friendship with Mrs Henniker in 1896. Another type of discrepancy may be found in 'To Louisa in the Lane', illustrating how Hardy the poet could accept a belief in haunted places and ghosts which his normal self could not have entertained.

As if in contradiction of Longinus, Edward Clodd wrote to a friend on hearing of Hardy's death, 'He was a great author; he was not a great man; there was no largeness of soul.' He asserted that Hardy was ungenerous when he spoke about his contemporaries, and described him as 'a poor hesitating talker', with tenderness but 'no charm'; he never warmed to him as he did to Meredith. In assessing this judgement, one must remember Hardy's natural reserve; 'only in poetry could he give direct expression to his inmost feelings, and not until he was wound up to poetic pitch could his heart speak', Irene Cooper Willis wrote. At Aldeburgh he would be usually content to relax and listen to other distinguished guests. He was the last man to talk about himself and his achievements. Gosse, who probably knew him and his works better than any other of his friends, regretted that he gave no hint of his 'magnificent genius' in company. One of the great London hostesses, Lady St Helier (Mary Jeune), with whom he often stayed, thought he was 'the most modest person' she had ever known; 'he hated the publicity which necessarily surrounded him, and shrank from it as much as the most timid woman'. Clodd's impression was secondhand; ironically it came from Florence Dugdale in June 1910, when she told him that Hardy was 'a great writer, but not a great man', soon after Emma had imparted her husband's shortcomings (mainly the product of her own mind) and won her sympathies. Clodd was an unqualified rationalist, who probably thought Hardy a timid thinker in his later years, when, after repeatedly trying to promote his rationalist explanation of the universe, nature, and human ills, particularly in his poems and *The Dynasts*, he concluded that 'the Scheme of Things is, indeed, incomprehensible'.

Further illustration of the fortuitousness of personal indictment is provided by the lot of Florence, whose views on Hardy and Emma swung almost from one extrme to the other. A similar reversal is found in her relations with Sydney Cockerell, who, after incurring suspicion and dislike, won her warm approval, especially when he suggested she was capable of writing her husband's biography; when she annoyed him after Hardy's death, he dismissed her as 'second-rate'.

There is no evidence in his *Life* and letters to suggest that Hardy's judgement of his contemporaries was mean, though he was not given to flattery, and took his standards of measurement from those achieved by the greatest artists of the western world throughout the ages. He has frequently been criticized for material meannesses, usually without regard for his thrifty upbringing, the economies imposed by shortages during war, and the value of money in modern terms. These are petty matters in the assessment of his greatness; a fool is just as capable of largesse as a person endowed with largeness of mind or soul. In the novel, the composite art of *The Dynasts*, and in poetry, Hardy frequently reveals the vision to which Keats aspired when he wrote:

> 'None can usurp this height', returned that shade,
> 'But those to whom the miseries of the world
> Are misery, and will not let them rest.'

Those who consider he is too pessimistic should compare him with the Somerset Maugham who wrote:

> Men are mean, petty, muddle-headed, ignoble, bestial from their cradles to their death-beds; ignorant slaves now of one superstition, now of another, and illiberal; selfish and cruel. . . . Everything in life is meaningless, the pain and the suffering are fruitless and futile. There is no object in life. . . .

At the gloomiest of times Hardy never lost his trust that the Christian ethic supplied the key to human amelioration. His belief that the prevalence of truth would free mankind may have been inherited from Shelley's youthful idealism; he did not allow despair to destroy it. One must continue to wonder how such a humanitarian faith can grow in the face of material self-seeking, media-manipulation for factional ends, and legacies of unreason and superstition. Hardy could feel, as he informed H. G. Wells after receiving from him a three-volume set of his new novel *The World of William Clissold* in September 1926, that a writer may be read or listened to, and find twenty years later that he might 'just as well not have written a line'; yet his views had not changed fundamentally from those of 'To Sincerity', a poem he wrote in February 1899.

The most reliable testimony in the evaluation of Hardy must come from those who knew both the man and his works. None is more telling than that of younger intellectuals who, in the disillusionment and desolation created by unparalleled catastrophes of war, sought vision and leadership for the renewal of civilized values and faith. The view of J. C. Powys that Hardy was 'an original poet of first-rate philosophic weight and power' came to be shared by J. M. Murry, who like many of his contemporaries found most support and hope for the future in the moral principles which animated the more significant of Hardy's works. Although Hardy's wife Florence regretted his decline from what he was when she first knew him (when, at the time of writing *The Dynasts*, his mind was 'luminous'), T. E. Lawrence, after a career which had brought him into contact with 'thousands of what are estimated great men', had no doubt that he was incomparably superior, and described him soon after his death as 'the most honourable stopping place' [*sic*] he had ever found. As late as 1955 his friend E. M. Forster informed Lionel Trilling that Keats was 'almost the only great man' he had ever wanted to 'be with' as opposed to 'meet'; the other one, he added, was Thomas Hardy, 'with whom I was a little and still miss'. Siegfried Sassoon during his first stay at Max Gate thought he was 'the nearest thing to Shakespeare' he would ever walk with, and never left without 'an impressive awareness' of 'the simplicity of true greatness'.

Bibliography and References

The Collected Letters of Thomas Hardy, ed. R. L. Purdy and M. Millgate, 7 vols (Oxford: Oxford University Press, 1978–88).

Emma Hardy Diaries, ed. R. H. Taylor (Ashington, Northumberland: Mid Northumberland Arts Group and Carcanet New Press, 1985.)

Friends of a Lifetime: Letters to Sydney Cockerell, ed. Viola Meynell (London: Jonathan Cape, 1940) pp. 274–316.

R. Gittings, *The Older Hardy* (London: Heinemann, 1978).

R. Gittings, *Young Thomas Hardy* (London: Heinemann, 1975).

F. E. Hardy, *The Life of Thomas Hardy* (London: Macmillan, 1962).

The Life and Works of Thomas Hardy, ed. M. Millgate (London: Macmillan, 1984).

M. Millgate, *Thomas Hardy: A Biography* (Oxford: Oxford University Press, 1982).

The Personal Notebooks of Thomas Hardy, ed. R. H. Taylor (London: Macmillan, 1978).

R. L. Purdy, *Thomas Hardy: A Bibliographical Study* (Oxford: Oxford University Press, 1954).

Thomas Hardy's Personal Writings, ed. H. Orel (Lawrence, Kan: University of Kansas, 1966; London: Macmillan, 1967).

The Variorum Edition of the Complete Poems of Thomas Hardy, ed. J. Gibson (London: Macmillan, 1978).

Additional chapter-by-chapter notes follow, chiefly bibliographical, giving sources for some of the more interesting items not obtained from the above or indicated in the text. Two abbreviations are used:

monograph, followed by the number, refers to the two volumes of *Thomas Hardy: Material for a Study of his Life, Times and Works*, ed. J. Stevens Cox (St Peter Port, Guernsey: Toucan Press, 1968 and 1971);

THYB, followed by the year, refers to *The Thomas Hardy Year Book*, ed. J. Stevens Cox and G. Stevens Cox (St Peter Port, Guernsey: Toucan Press).

Chapter 1

Presentation of *The Book of Common Prayer*: Evelyn Hardy, *Thomas Hardy: A Critical Biography* (New York: Russell & Russell, 1970; first published London: Hogarth Press, 1954), pp. 21–2.

James Hardy and the 1851 census: *monograph*, 51.

Chapter 2

Conversing with Lawrence: *The Letters of T. E. Lawrence*, ed. David Garnett (London: Jonathan Cape, 1938) p. 474.

Chapter 3
Keats and Drane: *monograph*, 51.
The maypole garland: William Archer, *Real Conversations* (London: Heinemann, 1904).
Glow-worm story: from the account Hardy wrote for Alfred Pope; cf. *Letters*, vol. IV, pp. 183–4.
Isaac Last and the 'British' school: *monograph*, 44.
The High Street on market days: *The Mayor of Casterbridge*, ch. 9.

Chapter 4
Drowned boy, Shadwater Weir: *monograph*, 1.
John Hicks: C. J. P. Beatty, *Thomas Hardy's Career in Architecture* (Dorchester: Dorset Natural History and Archaeological Society, 1978).
Barnes: Giles Dugdale, *William Barnes of Dorset* (London: Cassell, 1953).

Chapter 5
See Handley C. G. Moule, *Memories of a Vicarage* (London: Religious Tract Society, 1913); *monograph*, 27; Ted Ward, *Henry Moule of Fordington* Poole: Ted Ward [1983]).
Chaplain at the execution of Martha Browne: Charlotte Lindgren, *Thomas Hardy Journal*, October 1985, p. 23.
'The eternity of Hell': Irene Cooper Willis's essay on Hardy (The Thomas Hardy Society Ltd, 1981) p. 13.

Chapter 6
Letters of Mrs Martin to Hardy: Evelyn Hardy, *Thomas Hardy's Notebooks* (London: Hogarth Press, 1955) pp. 123–9.
Horace Moule's advice on composition: Lois Deacon and Terry Coleman, *Providence and Mr. Hardy* (London: Hutchinson, 1966) pp. 88–91.
Charles Fourier: Lennart A. Björk, *The Literary Notes of Thomas Hardy*, vol. I (Göteborg: University of Göteborg, 1974) pp. 2–3.
All Saints', New Windsor: Hardy gives the wrong date; see Ellen Dollery, *Thomas Hardy Journal*, January 1987, pp. 37–8.
Hardy's sketch of the old church at Fawley: Princeton University Library.
Findon and *The Hand of Ethelberta*: R. Gittings, *The Thomas Hardy Society Review 1984*, pp. 306–7.
Hardy on the stage at Covent Garden: Desmond Hawkins, *Hardy: Novelist and Poet* (Newton Abbot: David & Charles, 1976) pp. 13–15.

Chapter 7
Tryphena Sparks: cf. *The Dorset Year Book*, 1971–2, pp. 75–80; *Notes and Queries*, November 1972, pp. 430–1; Michael Rabiger, 'The Hoffman Papers', *THYB*, 1981 (which significantly give no support to the view that Hardy and Tryphena were ever engaged); and John Doheney, 'Thomas Hardy's Relatives and Their Times', *THYB*, 1989.
Macmillan's reply of 10 August: Charles Morgan, *The House of Macmillan* (London: Macmillan, 1944) pp. 87ff.
'The Poor Man and the Lady' story, as told by Hardy to Gosse: *The Sunday*

410   *Bibliography and References*

Times, 22 January 1928, reprinted in *The Thomas Hardy Society Review 1981,* pp. 207–10.
Catherine Pole: See Rabiger, 'The Hoffman Papers', op. cit.
Turnworth: Beatty, *Thomas Hardy's Career* . . ., op. cit.

Chapter 8
Services in the National School: K. Phelps, *The Wormwood Cup* (Padstow, Cornwall: Lodenek Press, 1975) pp. 12–13.
Emma's reminiscences: *Some Recollections,* ed. Evelyn Hardy and R. Gittings (Oxford: Oxford University Press, 1961).
John Morley and *Desperate Remedies*: Morgan, *House of Macmillan,* op. cit. pp. 93–4.
Horace Moule and Tryphena: Rabiger, 'The Hoffman Papers', op. cit.
Slape House: C. J. P. Beatty, Introduction to *The Architectural Notebook of Thomas Hardy* (Dorchester: Dorset Natural History and Archaeological Society, 1966) p. 8.
Macmillan, Morley, and *Under the Greenwood Tree*: Morgan, *House of Macmillan,* op. cit., pp. 94–9.

Chapter 9
Violent storm (and *Far from the Madding Crowd*): F. A. Hedgcock, 'Reminiscences of Thomas Hardy', *National and English Review,* October 1951.
Leslie Stephen: F. W. Maitland, *The Life and Letters of Leslie Stephen* (London: Duckworth, 1906); Noel G. Annan, *Leslie Stephen: His Thought and Character in Relation to his Time* (London: MacGibbon & Kee, 1951).
Waited on by James Pole: Rabiger, 'The Hoffman Papers', op. cit.
Mrs Smith: Lady Grogan, *Reginald Bosworth Smith: A Memoir* (London: James Nisbet, 1909).

Chapter 10
Leslie Stephen: see notes to Chapter 9 above.
Hardy's notes on Comte's *Social Dynamics*: Björk, *Literary Notes* . . ., op. cit., p. 65.
Editors of *The Shotover Papers*: *The Thomas Hardy Society Review 1975,* pp. 15–16.

Chapter 11
Hardy's notebooks: Björk, *Literary Notes* . . ., op. cit., pp. xxix, xxxi–11, 173ff, and 1–33 *passim.*
Piano: letter to Howard Bliss, Princeton University Library.
Elizabeth, Empress of Austria: Joan Haslip, *The Lady Empress* (London: Weidenfeld & Nicolson, 1965).
The Return of the Native, choice of title: Carl J. Weber, *Hardy of Wessex* (London: Routledge & Kegan Paul, 1965) pp. 105–6 and note.

Chapter 12
Knapdale: Morgan, *House of Macmillan,* op. cit., pp. 66–7.
Hardy's reading: Björk, *Literary Notes* . . ., op. cit. , pp. 92ff. and notes in vol. II; also pp. 65, 92, 63, 68.

Chapter 13
Reading in 1879: Björk, *Literary Notes . . .*, op. cit., pp. 122, 124–5, 126.
Bosworth Smith: Lady Grogan, *Reginald Bosworth Smith*, op. cit.
Hardy's visit to Harrow School is recorded in his *Life* (F. E. Hardy in the Bibliography above).
Fee increased proportionately: Edmund Blunden, *Thomas Hardy* (London: Macmillan, 1958) p. 48.

Chapter 14
No evidence for visit to Greenwich Observatory: *The Observatory*, December 1990, pp. 185–7.
Concert organized by the Smiths: M. E. Bath, *THYB*, 1973–4, pp. 41–2.
(Sir) George Douglas: Oliver Hilson, *Gleanings in Prose and Verse* from Sir George's writings (Galashiels: A Walker, 1938).
Douglas and Hardy: *Hibbert Journal*, April 1928, pp. 385–98.
Plagiarism in *The Trumpet-Major* and *A Laodicean*: Weber, *Hardy of Wessex*, op. cit., pp. 119–22, 126–8.

Chapter 15
Gosse: Evan Charteris, *The Life and Letters of Sir Edmund Gosse* (London: Heinemann, 1931; Ann Thwaite, *Edmund Gosse: A Literary Landscape* (London: Secker & Warburg, 1984).
Bosworth Smith called . . . Alice: Bath, op. cit., p. 42.
Giles Symonds: *THYB*, 1972–3, pp. 24–6.

Chapter 16
Evangeline and Alice Smith: Bath, op. cit.
Villa Trollope and *Doctor Thorne*: Anthony Trollope, *An Autobiography* (London: Williams & Norgate, 1946) p. 114.

Chapter 17
Munby at the Lushingtons': Derek Hudson, *Munby, Man of Two Worlds* (London: John Murray, 1972) p. 412.
Alice Read: letter from her to Howard Bliss, 10 April 1928, Miriam Lutcher Stark Library, Austin, Texas.
Apparent change of setting for *The Woodlanders*: *THYB*, 1971, pp. 46–52.
Tess steadily ennobled: J. T. Laird, *The Shaping of 'Tess of the d'Urbervilles'* (London: Oxford University Press, 1975).
Hardy's sketches (and notes on them) at Wool Manor: at the Dorset County Museum, Dorchester.
The Hardys in Scotland with Sir George Douglas: *Hibbert Journal*, op. cit.

Chapter 18
Raymond Blathwayt: *Black and White*, 27 August 1892.
Rebekah Owen: For this and subsequent references to her, see Carl Weber, *Hardy and the Lady from Madison Square* (Waterville, Maine: Colby College Press, 1952).
Florence Henniker: See prefaces and appendices in *One Rare Fair Woman*, ed. Evelyn Hardy and F. B. Pinion (London: Macmillan, 1972).

Chapter 19
Dinner in honour of Meredith at Burford Bridge: Siegfried Sassoon, *Meredith* (London: Constable, 1948) pp. 227–30.
Gissing at Max Gate: John Halperin, *Gissing: A Life in Books* (London: Oxford University Press, 1982) pp. 227–8.
Jude's early reading and Hardy's: W. R. Rutland, *Thomas Hardy: A Study of his Writings and their Background* (Oxford: Basil Blackwell , 1938) pp. 21–2.
Story publicized by Ford Madox Ford: see his *Mightier than the Sword* (London: George Allen & Unwin, 1938) pp. 128–30.
Lady Grove: Desmond Hawkins, *Concerning Agnes* (Gloucester: Alan Sutton, 1982).

Chapter 20
Austrian empress: Haslip, *The Lady Empress,* op. cit.
Visit to Montacute: John Cowper Powys, *Autobiography* (London: Macdonald, 1967) pp. 227–30.
Rudyard Kipling: H. Orel, *The Unknown Thomas Hardy* (Brighton, Sussex: Harvester Press, 1987) pp. 93–4.
Journey to Tryphena's home and grave at Topsham: Deacon and Coleman, *Providence and Mr. Hardy,* op. cit., p. 64.
Emma's objections to *Pioneers of Evolution*: letter to Edward Clodd, 29 March 1897, Brotherton Collection, Leeds University Library.
Emma to Rebekah Owen, 24 April 1899: Colby College Library.
Emma to Mrs Grahame: Bodleian Library, Oxford.
Bertha Newcombe: Brotherton Collection, Leeds University Library.
Hardy and Emma cycling: *monographs,* 20, 5, 17.

Chapter 21
Lengthy discussion with William Archer: Archer, *Real Conversations,* op. cit.
Letter to Rebekah Owen: Colby College Library.
Llewelyn Powys's visit to Max Gate: *monograph,* 64.

Chapter 22
Years later . . . distant relative: Rutland, *Thomas Hardy,* op. cit., p. 13.
Florence Dugdale: R. Gittings and Jo Manton, *The Second Mrs Hardy* (London: Heinemann, 1979).
How the staging of Hardy began in Dorchester: *monographs,* 17, 71.
Whymper and the Matterhorn route: Edward Clodd, *Memories* (London: Chapman & Hall, 1916) p. 85.
Emma to Lady Hoare: Wiltshire Record Office, Trowbridge.
Florence won over to Emma: Marguerite Roberts, *THYB,* 1980, pp. 14ff.

Chapter 23
Florence's attempts to secure publication for Emma: Roberts, (op. cit.).
Florence to Clodd (Crippen and Hardy): Brotherton Collection, Leeds University Library.
'Non-acceptors': *monograph,* 29.
The Hardy love-letters and Browning: Florence Hardy to Howard Bliss, 10

January 1931, Princeton University Library.
Newbolt's letter of thanks: Miriam Lutcher Stark Library, Austin, Texas.
Journey with Kate Hardy (Mary was ill) and Florence Dugdale to Bath, Bristol, and Gloucester; Mrs Henniker on Hardy; and Florence on 'The Roman Gravemounds': Brotherton Collection, Leeds University Library.
Newbolt's account of the gold medal presentation: *The Later Life and Letters of Sir Henry Newbolt*, ed. M. Newbolt (London: Faber & Faber, 1942) pp. 166–8.
Poems in the attics: *monograph*, 20, p. 48.
Emma started a prayer: Roberts *THYB*, op. cit., p. 13.
Visit of A. C. Benson and Gosse: Ann Thwaite, *Edmund Gosse*, op. cit., end of chapter 16.
Oh! would I were a dancing child: New York Public Library.
Miss Wood Homer: *monograph*, 18.
Emma's maid: *THYB*, 1973–4, p. 9.
Amos Barton: George Eliot, *Scenes of Clerical Life*.

Chapter 24
The happy laugh he had when he was young, and the diaries: 16 January 1913, Brotherton Collection, Leeds Univerity Library.
Revolver in her bedroom: Florence to Clodd, Brotherton Collection.
Obvious to Mabel Robinson that Hardy and Florence were engaged: Roberts, *THYB*, op. cit., p. 29.
A mistress named Florence Dugdale: *THYB*, 1973–4, p. 8.
Ellen Titterington: *monograph*, 59.
Colvin, Hardy, and Elgar: J. N. Moore, *Edward Elgar: A Creative Life* (Oxford: Oxford University Press, 1984) p. 649.
The question to be settled in a week: Brotherton Collection, Leeds University Library.
Teresa Fetherstonhaugh: Weber, *Hardy and the Lady from Madison Square*, op. cit., p. 171.
One of the Max Gate servants and books on birds: *monograph*, 65.
Only a *little* affection: Florence to Lady Hoare, 22 July 1914, Wiltshire Record Office, Trowbridge.
Outings by car with Hermann Lea: *monograph*, 20.
'utterly weary of life'; 6 December 1914, Wiltshire Record Office, Trowbridge.

Chapter 25
Introduced to H. G. Wells: Florence to Wells, 8 August 1915, University of Illinois Library.
'mischief-making tactics': Wiltshire Record Office, Trowbridge.
Too many local calls: Colby College Library.
Hardy's will: *monograph*, 36.
Florence to Rebekah Owen on Mary Hardy, after the funeral, Hardy's will, Emma's diaries, Wessex, and the shawl: Colby College Library.
Tea-party at West Stafford rectory: *THYB*, 1973–4, p. 46.
Mr. Britling Sees It Through: University of Illinois Library.
Florence retracts all she has written against Cockerell, and begs Rebekah

Owen to burn her injudicious letters: Colby College Library.
Mrs Sheridan: Weber, *Hardy and the Lady from Madison Square*, op. cit.,
    p. 192.
Rehearsal of *The Mellstock Quire*: *monograph*, 15.
Sassoon at Max Gate: Siegfried Sassoon, *Siegfried's Journey, 1916–20*
    (London: Faber & Faber, 1945) pp. 88–93.

Chapter 26

Llewelyn Powys, 24 January 1920: *The Letters of Llewelyn Powys*, ed. Louis
    Wilkinson (London: John Lane, 1943).
Sassoon: Sassoon, *Siegfried's Journey*, op. cit., pp. 147–50.
Florence to Paul Lemperley: Colby College Library.
Barrie: *Letters of J. M. Barrie*, ed. Viola Meynell (London: Peter Davies,
    1942).
Robert Graves, *Goodbye to All That* (London: Jonathan Cape, 1929).
The mummers' play at Max Gate: *The Thomas Hardy Society Review 1982*,
    pp. 235–7.
Vere H. Collins: See his *Talks with Thomas Hardy at Max Gate, 1920–1922*
    (London: Duckworth, 1928).
Lady Cynthia Asquith at Max Gate: *monograph*, 63.
Sleep in the room where he wrote *The Return of the Native*: *The Thomas
    Hardy Society Review 1980*, pp. 187–8.
Barthélémon, three versions of a story on: *Old Mrs Chundle and Other
    Stories* (London: Macmillan, 1977) pp. 119–21.

Chapter 27

Mrs Stanley: *monograph*, 14, where the dating is unreliable; see p. 55 of *The
    Personal Notebooks of Thomas Hardy* (bibliography above).
'Memento Mori': in *Fortnightly Review*, February 1920; see Frederic Harri-
    son, *Novissima Verba* (London: Fisher Unwin, 1921) pp. 27–34.
John Buchan on *Late Lyrics and Earlier*: 2 June 1922, Dorset County Museum.
E. M. Forster at Max Gate: *Selected Letters of E. M. Forster*, Vol. 2, ed. Mary
    Lago and P. N. Furbank (London: Collins, 1985) p. 31.
Brigadier-General J. H. Morgan: Blunden, *Thomas Hardy*, op. cit., pp.
    164–5.
May O'Rourke: *monograph*, 8.
T. E. Lawrence: H. Montgomery Hyde, *Solitary in the Ranks* (London:
    Constable, 1977); *The Letters*, ed. Garnett, op. cit.
The Prince of Wales at Max Gate: *monographs*, 59, 12, 15, 66.
Marie Stopes: Blunden, *Thomas Hardy*, op. cit., p. 169.
'O Jan! O Jan! O Jan!': *monograph*, 15.
Glastonbury Festival: Berta Lawrence, *Thomas Hardy Journal*, May 1987,
    pp. 62–5.
Florence receives *Saint Joan*: *monograph*, 52, item 149.
Rehearsal of two scenes at Wool Manor: *monograph*, 2.
Cockerell at Max Gate in January 1925: Wilfrid Blunt, *Cockerell*, (London:
    Hamish Hamilton, 1964) pp. 214–16.
Florence and Mrs Bugler: *monograph*, 1.

Reported to Charlotte Mew: New York Public Library.
Filmer's arrangement without cuts: Blunden, *Thomas Hardy*, op. cit., pp. 170–1.

Chapter 28
Hospitality to Howard Bliss: Princeton University Library.
Lady Pinney: *monograph*, 25.
Thomas Soundy: *The Thomas Hardy Society Review 1977*, p. 75.
Ellen Titterington: *monograph*, 59.
Jesting Pilate: Miriam Lutcher Stark Library, Austin, Texas.

Chapter 29
Mr Wells and his wife: Brotherton Collection, Leeds University Library.
Lady Hoare: Wiltshire Record Office, Trowbridge.
Death of Hardy: Ellen Titterington, *monographs*, 4 and 59.
A friend of May O' Rourke: *monograph*, 8 and Roberts, *THYB*, op. cit., p. 63.
Barrie had left for London: cf. Florence to Howard Bliss, 11 March 1930, Princeton University Library.
Mrs Shaw and the Dead March in *Saul*: Roberts, *THYB*, op. cit., p. 64.
Hardy's will: *monograph*, 36.
Bonfires in the garden: *monograph*, 6.
Barrie and Hardy's *Life*: Roberts, *THYB*, op. cit., pp. 74–9.
Ellen recalled: *monograph*, 59.
Florence at Stanway: Lady Cynthia Asquith, *Portrait of Barrie* (London: James Barrie, 1954) p. 171.
Mrs Bugler's London success: *monograph*, 1.
Hardy memorials: Blunt, *Cockerell*, op. cit., pp. 218–22, and Roberts, *THYB*, op. cit., pp. 67ff.
Llewelyn Powys and Kennington's statue of Hardy: *monograph*, 70.
R. A. Scott-James and the Abbey burial: Miriam Lutcher Stark Library, Austin, Texas.
Florence's will: *monograph*, 36.
Hardy's remaining books: *monograph*, 52.

Chapter 30
Epigraph: Browning, *The Ring and the Book*, I, 1367–73.
A. L. Rowse, *The English Past* (London: Macmillan, 1951) pp. 171–2.
Evangeline Smith: Rabiger, 'Hoffman Papers', op. cit., pp. 48–9.
Twenty years later: Florence Hardy to Rebekah Owen, 5 May 1914, Colby College Library.
Alice Smith's diary: Bath, op. cit., p. 46.
Florence to Rebekah Owen on the Giffords: Colby College Library.
'Beatrix Potter': Colby College Library.
Clodd on Hardy: 14 January 1928, Miriam Lutcher Stark Library, Austin, Texas.
Hardy's reserve and the expression of his innermost feelings in poetry: Irene Cooper Willis's essay on T.H. at Colby College Library, published

as 'Monograph No. 1' by the Thomas Hardy Society, 1981, p. 6.

Lady St Helier on Hardy: See her *Memories of Fifty Years* (London: Edward Arnold, 1909) pp. 240–1.

Forster on Keats and Hardy: *Selected Letters*, ed. Lago and Furbank, op. cit., p. 259.

General Index

420 General Index

Index to Hardy's Prose and Poetry